IN THE SHADOW OF THE WHITE HOUSE

IN THE SHADOW OF THE WHITE HOUSE

A Memoir of the Washington and Watergate Years
1968–1978

JO HALDEMAN

Set in Minion
Printed in the United States

Book design by STARLING

Interior photographs by Joanne H. Haldeman

10 9 8 7 6 5 4 3 2 1

Publisher's Cataloging-in-Publication data
Names: Haldeman, Joanne H., author.
Title: In the Shadow of the White House : a memoir of Washington and Watergate years 1968–1978 /
Jo Haldeman.|
Description: First Hardcover Edition | A Genuine Vireo Book | New York, NY ; Los Angeles, CA:
Rare Bird Books, 2017.
Identifiers: ISBN 9781945572081
Subjects: LCSH Haldeman, Jo. | Haldeman, H. R. (Harry R.), 1926-1993. | Nixon, Richard M.
(Richard Milhous), 1913-1994. | Watergate Affair, 1972-1974—Personal narratives. | United States—
Politics and government—1968-1978. | BISAC BIOGRAPHY & AUTOBIOGRAPHY / Political
Classification: LCC E860 .H35 2017 | DDC 364.1/32/0973—dc23

To our grandchildren
Allan, Hilary, Joseph, Christopher, Katherine, and TMO

Contents

PART THREE: WATERGATE

PART FOUR: THE TRIAL

PART FIVE: PRISON

Introduction

By Evan Thomas

IN THE SUMMER OF 2013, I went to visit Joanne "Jo" Haldeman to talk about her late husband, H. R. "Bob" Haldeman. I was writing a biography of Richard Nixon, and I wanted to know more about his famously tough chief of staff. With his piercing eyes and flat-top crewcut, Haldeman was an intriguing mystery to me.

Haldeman was arguably the most powerful White House chief of staff ever. He virtually created the command structure of the modern White House. Paul O'Neill, who served as a high-ranking official in the Johnson, Nixon, and Ford administrations and then as George W. Bush's secretary of the treasury, told me that Haldeman ran the tightest ship of any presidential staff. The quality of analysis and thinking was as high as that of any other modern White House, according to O'Neill.

Haldeman made sure that decisions were reached and carried out, and that the president's orders were followed up on. He seemed to relish his role as the enforcer. "Every president needs an SOB," he once told a fellow aide. "And I'm Nixon's."

The press began referring to Haldeman and his colleague John Ehrlichman as "the Berlin Wall," and it's true that Haldeman saw it as his job to protect and even wall off the secretive and lonely chief executive. Haldeman wanted to shield Nixon from the world and the world from Nixon. And yet Haldeman had great empathy for his boss. In his daily diary, he wrote with a kind of affectionate bemusement about the yearnings and quirks of the president he once described as the "strangest man I ever met."

I hoped that Jo Haldeman would help me better understand Nixon's fall—
and the failure of his otherwise brilliant top aide. She was in her mid-eighties
when I visited her, but still very alert and alive with memories of her years in
Washington. I had heard that she was writing her own memoir.

Jo graciously received me at the Newport Beach house where she was
staying with her kids, as she has every summer for many years. My wife, Oscie
(who went to high school with one of Jo's daughters), and I found a handsome,
elegant woman who has borne a great deal of suffering with dignity, strength,
and good humor. Jo was open and warm with us, but she did not disguise a
degree of sadness. She gave me a copy of her draft memoir, which I agreed not
to quote from for my own book, but which helped inform my judgments, not
just about H. R. Haldeman, but about his tortured boss.

Jo was, throughout her marriage, devoted to her husband. She loved him
and cared for him, stood by him, and tried to comfort him. But, for a time,
her husband took her for granted and neglected her. So great was his duty
to the president, so all-consumed was he by Nixon's demanding and difficult
personality, that Haldeman submerged his own humanity—and with it, his
good judgment. Jo could only watch and suffer as her family was engulfed
by tragedy.

Jo's memoir is a moving, gripping—indeed, at times, harrowing—story
of the climb to power and the swift and terrible fall that awaits men who
overreach and fail to heed their more human, softer sides (or their wiser and
gentler wives). There are some comic moments—Nixon's awkwardness is not
to be believed. Like a Greek tragedy, the story is one of hubris, of overweening
pride. But it is equally a story of love and redemption, a fascinating morality
tale of a great marriage that almost dies, and then is reborn. It absorbed me,
and it will keep you turning the pages as the Haldemans rise and fall—before
finding truer meaning and even a measure of peace and forgiveness.

IN THE SHADOW OF
THE WHITE HOUSE

This book is a personal account of my experience as the wife of H. R. "Bob" Haldeman, assistant to the president and chief of staff for President Richard Nixon. Spanning ten years, from 1968 through 1978, my memoir progresses from our early Washington days through Watergate and its aftermath.

Jo Haldeman at #11 Bay Island, August 2013.

Prologue

"**G**RANDMOTHER, WE'RE STUDYING WATERGATE in school." This offhand comment, made by my oldest grandchild over Memorial Day weekend, 1995, was the seed that eventually grew into this book.

My grandson's remark and the casualness of it affected me deeply. It made me sad to think that a new generation of Haldemans was growing up with only a textbook explanation of Watergate, which would be portrayed as the defining event of the Nixon administration. As difficult and public as that time had been for us, our life in Washington had included so much more.

I realized that it was important to me that our six grandchildren have a greater perspective on Bob's and my extraordinary experience. Bob would have loved to talk to them about his role in the White House and the accomplishments and ideals of the Nixon presidency. He also would have openly shared his thoughts on the evolution of Watergate. But he had passed away eighteen months earlier, and that opportunity was gone. If our story was going to be told, I would have to be the one to do it. I made a commitment to myself to provide that legacy.

My first attempt to reconstruct those years was to make a scrapbook for each grandchild, but I soon discovered that photographs and articles could not convey the whole story. I then took a memoir writing class. Although writing was new to me and did not come naturally, my commitment far outweighed my self-doubts.

I always knew exactly where my story would begin—the sail with Bob in Newport, when I first became aware of what the future might hold for us after the 1968 Republican Convention. I worked to select the appropriate vignettes to carry the narrative along. Some were humorous, others were informative.

I did my best to ensure that the content was factually correct and that the dialogue captured the essence of the individuals and the conversations. Eventually, I felt at ease expressing myself, and a book began to emerge.

Most of my information came from weekly letters that I wrote to our families in California. I transferred the pertinent material onto index cards, which I categorized by subject and date. Two other invaluable resources were the many photographs I took and the scrapbooks I made to document our life in Washington. I referred to personal calendars, memorabilia, notes that I made on special occasions, and the journal I kept during the trial. To confirm dates and current events, I consulted Bob's monthly White House calendar, magazine articles, newspaper stories, and the Internet. In addition, my reference materials included several books written about both the presidency in general and the Nixon administration specifically.

When I experienced periods of doubt over my ability or authority to proceed, I was bolstered by a conversation I had with Bob in 1987. As he was preparing his keynote address on "Surviving Challenge and Trauma" for the Young Presidents' Organization University in Venice, Italy, Bob raised that I, too, should participate in the program. I was stunned. What did I have to contribute?

"Jo, *you* have a story to tell," Bob insisted.

Bob stressed how difficult it must have been to live with him as chief of staff, a driven man under great pressure, single-mindedly serving the president. He talked about how I dealt with the trauma of the Watergate trial and the ordeal of his imprisonment. He said that it was important for me to be forthright and honest, including my frustrations and our differences of opinion. Bob was steadfast in his conviction that I had a story to tell.

Writing solely from my own perspective, I have tried to be as truthful and accurate as possible. I recognize that the recollections of others, including my own children, may differ from mine. In no way does this book cover everything our family experienced during this time period. This is not a story of our family. Neither is it Bob's story, nor an explanation of Watergate.

What follows is my story.

Preface

BOB AND I HAD been married twenty years when we moved to Washington in 1969. It was a turbulent time in our country's history. The generation gap was widening, and counterculture values were replacing past social and moral codes. Growing frustrations over the Vietnam War and racial and gender inequalities divided our nation.

Technology was in its infancy and had not yet evolved from analog to digital. We lived in a world without personal computers or the Internet. We listened to music on vinyl records. We recorded events on film without sound. We watched twelve VHF channels on television sets with antennas and no recording devices. We went to a theater to see a movie. There were no CDs, DVDs, DVRs, iPods, iPads, Kindles, digital cameras, or videos.

Telephones had rotary dials and had to be connected to the wall by a cord. We did not have answering machines, caller ID, or cordless phones—let alone smartphones with voice mail and texting. It was expensive to call long-distance to another area code, and the most common way of communicating from afar was through letters.

Terrorism was not an issue. There were no security checks at the airport, and friends and family members could accompany passengers to the boarding gate. A luxury Lincoln Continental sold for $6,046, and a gallon of gas was thirty-five cents. A domestic postage stamp cost six cents, and a double cheeseburger, forty-nine cents.

The Haldeman family in Los Angeles, 1965.

PART ONE

CALIFORNIA

Jo, We Need to Talk

July 1968

"**J**O, WE NEED TO talk."

Bob's five words send out a red flag. Something's up, but I know him too well to ask what it is. He'll tell me when he's ready.

The two of us are about to go for a sail on his twelve-foot Sunfish, and we're standing in water up to our waists. With beads of sweat glistening on his forehead, Bob tries to get the tiller connected. He forces a stubborn cotter key into place, while I steady the boat.

We are at my parents' summer home with our four children. For years, we have spent Bob's month-long vacations here on Bay Island in Newport Beach, California. Ordinarily, Bob would be out sailing every afternoon, but not this year. He has been on the campaign trail with Richard Nixon, who is expected to become the Republicans' presidential candidate at their convention next month. This is nothing new for Bob. Over the past twelve years, he has taken periodic leaves of absence from his job in advertising to work on five Nixon campaigns.

Mother and Dad, Adele and Joe Horton, wave from under a blue umbrella on the porch, as a gust of wind carries our little boat out into the bay. Our four children, Susan, Hank, Peter, and Ann, are swimming off the dock with other children from the island. For a while, I can hear their shouts, but soon, it's just the rhythmic sound of the water slapping against the hull. Bob and I are alone, and it's a good time to talk. I wait for him to begin.

At last, he breaks the silence. "I need your input, Jo. But you have to promise not to repeat anything I tell you."

I nod.

"As everyone knows, Nixon's got the nomination in the bag," Bob says. "And this time, I think he's going the whole nine yards."

My grip on the side of the boat tightens. *President Nixon. Is this possible?* Two years after John F. Kennedy narrowly defeated Richard Nixon in 1960, Bob managed his unsuccessful campaign for governor of California. *Will he really win this time?*

The wind is brisk in the turning basin as we tack back and forth. A gull screeches above us and dives for a fish.

Bob continues, "If Nixon does get elected, I think there's a good chance he'd offer me a job." A pleased smile spreads across his face. "*If* I get the opportunity to work in the White House, I don't see how I could pass it up."

I can't believe it. What an incredible opportunity for him, as well as for the children and me. Up until this minute, the two of us have never talked about how a Nixon presidency might affect our lives. Suddenly, I see my husband in a different light. I swing around to get a good look at the tan, six-foot man bent over the tiller. With a closely cropped crew cut and piercing gray-green eyes, he looks confident and in control.

Sailing on a reach, Bob heads for the leeward side of Harbor Island. It's less windy, and we will be able to talk better. Being a pragmatist, he immediately begins discussing the logistics of a move to Washington. Through the years, he has been transferred several times as he climbed the corporate ladder. We have lived in New York, San Francisco, Connecticut, and Los Angeles. I tell him that I can handle another move and that the thought of living in our nation's capital is thrilling.

Bob explains that most incoming administration families move in January, at the time of the inauguration. However, we decide that it would be better if the children and I wait until the following summer. This delay would avoid disrupting their school year and allow Susan to graduate with her high school class. Hank would be entering a new school as a junior. Peter would go into the seventh grade, and Ann, the fifth grade.

"A delay works for me, too," Bob says, as we glide along the glassy water. "It'd give me more time to familiarize myself with my job. I could put in as much time as I need at the office and not feel guilty." He pauses. "One thing's for sure, though. If I do get a job in the White House, my salary will take a big cut. And I won't be getting any month-long summer vacations either."

Advertising has been Bob's sole career. He started work in New York as a twenty-two-year-old research assistant at J. Walter Thompson Company. Now, at age forty-one, he is vice president and manager of the Los Angeles office.

In the lee of Harbor Island, the sail remains limp, and the sun beats down. Reaching into the pocket of his madras trunks, Bob pulls out a ChapStick and liberally applies the lip balm. Feeling stiff, I shift positions. The Sunfish rocks with my movement, and the boom swings across, grazing Bob's head. Annoyed, he frowns at me—furrowed brow, steely eyes, and tight lips. I call it the "Haldeman look." It's intimidating but fleeting.

We drift in silence, and my thoughts wander. The only involvement Bob has ever had in politics has been with one man, Richard Nixon. It started when Bob was at UCLA in the 1940s and Nixon took an uncompromising stand against communism in the Alger Hiss case. This made a deep impression on Bob, whose grandfather had strong anticommunist beliefs.

Bob didn't meet Nixon until after we were married. On a trip to Washington in 1951, he was introduced to Senator Nixon by a friend who was a secretary in his office. Five years later, J. Walter Thompson gave Bob a leave of absence to volunteer as an advance man for Nixon in the Eisenhower/Nixon reelection campaign. Since then, he has followed Nixon's career, gladly giving his time and energy to get him elected. Describing Richard Nixon as brilliant, Bob believes that there is no other world leader living today who has his unique vision and grasp of international affairs.

A light breeze fills the sail, and the boat gathers speed. "How long do you think we'd be living in Washington?" I ask.

"Eight years max," Bob says. "That is, if Nixon's reelected."

Eight years sounds like a long time to be gone from Los Angeles. This is our home. Both Bob and I were born here. Our children are fifth generation "Angelenos," and all of our relatives live in the area. The two of us are active in the community, the children's schools, and our church. Bob would have to give up serving on the boards of the California Institute of the Arts, Coro Foundation, and Junior Achievement, as well as the UCLA Alumni Association and the University of California's Board of Regents.

"Don't worry, Jo," Bob says, guessing my thoughts. "I promise that we'll pack up as soon as the second term's over. I'll want to get back to LA as much as you."

Heading for Bay Island, we reenter the main channel. The wind picks up, and Bob leans back to stabilize the heeling boat. I get doused with water. "One more thing," he says, raising his voice. "Although I have no intention of taking on a high profile job, it might be hard to remain anonymous. To the press, public figures are public property. You should be aware of that."

I can tell that Bob is studying me for my reaction, but his concern about publicity seems pretty far-fetched. I don't bother to respond.

"Just want you to know that in DC, no one's immune from the press," he adds.

"Interesting," I say absent-mindedly. My mind is already racing ahead to the election and what it might mean for our family.

Nixon's the One

A s MUCH AS I want to share everything Bob has told me, I keep it to myself. At night, I lie in bed, imagining what our lives will be like if we move to Washington. I get goose bumps when I think about the possibility of Bob's working in the White House. On the other hand, it's a daunting time to be in our nation's capital. This has been a year of great social unrest and terrible violence. The Vietnam War divides our country, and race riots endanger our cities. In March, President Johnson announced that he wasn't going to seek a second term because of the war. In April, Martin Luther King Jr. was assassinated in Memphis, Tennessee. Last month, Sirhan Sirhan shot and killed Bobby Kennedy in the Ambassador Hotel here in Los Angeles.

Our next president will be facing monumental challenges.

August 1968

WHEN BOB ASKS IF I would like to attend the Republican convention, I am thrilled. He also arranges for Susan and Hank to go, as well as Susan's boyfriend.

The air is hot and humid in Miami, but the delegates hardly notice. They live in an air-conditioned world from sunup to sundown. Wearing a red, white, and blue paper dress and a plastic "straw" hat, Susan works as a "Nixonette," distributing campaign buttons. Hank is a "runner" and is given a press badge for clearance on the convention floor. Susan's boyfriend monitors convention events on a battery of television sets in a trailer.

At 2:00 a.m. on the third night, the delegates elect Richard Milhous Nixon. An avalanche of colored balloons cascades from the ceiling, and the band plays "California, Here I Come." With Nixon buttons carefully pinned onto the lapel of my white knit suit, I wave a "Nixon's the One" pennant and cheer until I'm hoarse. I'm surprised to see how caught up I am in all of the hoopla. Next to me, Bob's seat in our reserved box is empty. He is watching the convention on television with Nixon in a penthouse suite at the Hilton.

The next afternoon, Bob and I, along with the three children, attend a small party honoring the new Republican presidential nominee. The mood is jubilant as Mr. and Mrs. Nixon welcome family members, friends, and top staff. Hank, Susan, and her boyfriend chat with the Nixon daughters, Tricia and Julie, and Julie's fiancé, David Eisenhower. After pounding out "Home on the Range" and a few show tunes on the piano, Nixon circulates among the guests to work the room. He tries to be personable, but his awkwardness shows. He approaches me and extends a hand.

"Well, how's the drinking member of the family?" Mr. Nixon asks, knowing full well that I don't drink and never have. Ill at ease, he relies on this joke, and I laugh politely.

That night, the convention comes to a climax, and this time, Bob is seated next to me in the box. At exactly 11:00 p.m., Richard Nixon steps up to the podium. Glancing at his watch, Bob nudges me and points to the hour.

"Take note, Jo," he says, with a smug grin. "Prime time television."

"America is in trouble today," Nixon warns, "not because her people have failed but because her leaders have failed. When the strongest nation in the world can be tied down for four years in a war in Vietnam with no end in sight… When the nation with the greatest tradition of the rule of law is plagued by unprecedented lawlessness… My fellow Americans, tonight I accept the challenge and the commitment to provide new leadership for America."

Once again, I am on my feet, cheering and waving my pennant. I am convinced that there is only one man who can do the job. The United States needs Richard Nixon. *And Richard Nixon needs my husband.* My heart bursts with pride to be Bob Haldeman's wife.

◆

AFTER FOUR EXHAUSTING DAYS in Miami, everyone is ready to head home. Susan's Nixonette dress is torn, and the band on her hat is missing. Hank has blisters on his feet from wearing his dress loafers every day, and Susan's boyfriend's eyes are bloodshot from monitoring so many hours of television. When Bob asks me to join him on Nixon's chartered jet for the flight back to

California, I eagerly accept, and the children return on a commercial flight without me.

I'm excited to be included with the top staff of the Nixon/Agnew campaign, but it's unnerving to be in the presence of these two men who might become the future president and vice president of our country. When they come down the aisle, I find it difficult to engage in light conversation. It's easier to chat with Pat Nixon and Judy Agnew, who follow their husbands through the cabin.

Halfway across the country, we make a brief stop in Austin, Texas, where the Nixons and Agnews plan to make a courtesy call on President Johnson. Watching Bob board the helicopter to fly to the LBJ ranch, I try to remember each detail so I can describe the scene to his parents later. They love hearing about his involvement in the campaign.

As we step off the plane in Los Angeles, I spot Bob's mother, Betty Haldeman, waving wildly in a sea of enthusiastic supporters. A little over five feet tall, "Non" generally gets lost in a crowd, but today she's easy to find. Bedecked with Republican jewelry and campaign buttons, she's wearing a "Nixon's the One" straw hat and waving a pennant. There's no question which candidate she favors, but I know that the stars in her eyes are for her son, Bob.

Let's Win this One for Harry

THREE WEEKS AFTER THE Republicans convene in Miami, it's the Democrats' turn to hold their convention in Chicago. The chaotic scene that unfolds is in sharp contrast to the well-organized, united Republican event. The Democratic Party is split over the war, and there are violent confrontations both inside and outside of the International Amphitheatre. Comfortably seated in our den, I watch the events live on television. I wince when I see the New Left protestors being beaten by the police, who are accused of using "Gestapo tactics." It's hard to accept that this scene is taking place in the United States.

On August 29, Vice President Hubert Humphrey and Senator Edmund Muskie of Maine are eventually chosen as the Democratic presidential and vice presidential candidates.

Nixon sees the chaos at the Democratic Convention as a good opportunity to jump in and make a strong stand for law and order. When I hear that he intends to kick off his campaign with a motorcade through Chicago's Loop, it seems to me that it's a risky move. I worry that it will incite the "peaceniks" and there will be more riots. I'd give anything to talk to Bob about it, but I don't. Even if I knew how to track him down, I wouldn't pursue it. Bob has always kept his professional life separate from his home life, and I don't interfere.

September 1968

AT NOON ON SEPTEMBER 4, half a million people turn out to greet Nixon in Chicago. In contrast to last week's violence at the Democratic Convention, the crowd showers his motorcade with confetti. The press writes glowing reviews of the event, and I realize how wrong I was to worry.

Nixon takes a substantial early lead over Humphrey, but when Governor George Wallace of Alabama declares his candidacy for a third party, it cuts into the conservative vote. Wallace has the Deep South wrapped up, and the race tightens. The overriding issues are the war in Vietnam, law and order, and the loss of respect for America. Campaigning is tough, and none of the candidates is exempt from heckling. Angry demonstrators frequently interrupt their speeches and shout obscenities.

As chief of staff of the campaign, Bob lives out of a suitcase, often working eighteen to twenty hours a day. He gets home infrequently, and we communicate by phone. Most of our conversations start with his asking, "What's up with the kids?" No matter how tired, he always wants to know what's going on with the children and me.

October 1968

EARLY FRIDAY MORNING, OCTOBER 25, my world turns upside down. Bob's father undergoes emergency heart surgery and doesn't pull through the operation. I desperately need to reach Bob. All I know is that he's somewhere on the East Coast.

Harry Francis "Bud" Haldeman led an active life, and his passing will shock his oldest son terribly. Standing in a cold hospital hallway, I place call after call from a pay phone. With a pile of quarters dwindling in front of me, I finally get Bob on the line. I try to break the news as gently as possible, but there are long silences between my words. On the other end, I hear his voice grow husky. He falters and breaks down. In my mind, I visualize his tear-stained face.

Three days later, Bob takes time off from the campaign to join family and friends in Los Angeles for his father's memorial service. He brings with him a handwritten letter of condolence from Nixon to his mother. "Let's win this one for Harry" is scrawled across the bottom of the page. Non is deeply touched. She frames the letter and hangs it in the living room of the Haldeman vacation home in Palm Springs.

Mr. President-elect

I T'S ELECTION DAY, NOVEMBER 5, and the race is a toss-up. A Harris poll shows Humphrey winning by three points, but the Gallup Poll shows Nixon leading by two. I wake up feeling both apprehensive and excited. This is going to be one of the longest days of my life. Immediately after the children leave for school, I walk around the block to my polling place.

The sight of the American flag hanging over the entrance to my neighbor's garage gives me a rush of patriotism. As I proudly mark my ballot for Richard Milhous Nixon and Spiro Theodore Agnew, I feel my palms getting clammy. Today, my future rests in the hands of seventy-three million Americans.

After voting, I meet up with Bob, who voted by absentee ballot. Leaving the children at home with Non and a housekeeper, he and I will fly to New York on Nixon's chartered jet. As part of a group of only five top advisors and their wives accompanying the possible future president of the United States and his family, I am humbled and overwhelmed.

As soon as we step inside the plane, red, white, and blue balloons and streamers engulf us. A victory cake, decorated with the White House and inscribed with "Richard Nixon 1968," makes me feel uneasy. Bob keeps saying that this election is up for grabs, and I hope the cake and decorations aren't premature.

Uncertainty creates tension, and I don't hear anyone predicting victory. Bob Finch, the former lieutenant governor of California, nervously paces the aisle. A long-time personal friend and advisor of Nixon, he broods about the outcome of Nixon's last presidential election.

"The Boss lost to Kennedy by less than one hundred twenty thousand votes," Finch mumbles, attributing the narrow defeat to the "flagrant voting fraud in Texas and Illinois."

As always, Bob appears to have his emotions well under control. While I work on my needlepoint, he fills in a *Los Angeles Times* vote-tally sheet. The way he quickly writes down his projected numbers reminds me of how he does crossword puzzles. Using a pen rather than a pencil, he's fast and decisive.

"If my addition's correct, Nixon has two hundred fifteen electoral votes in the bag," Bob says, handing me the tally sheet. "It takes two seventy to get elected, so it's still too close to call."

Later, Mr. and Mrs. Nixon invite the five wives to come up front to their private cabin for a brief visit. I know they want to be gracious, but the conversation is stilted. As much as I would like to say something pertinent and meaningful, I end up simply wishing them good luck and commenting on the decorations and the cake. I feel more comfortable talking with Tricia, Julie, and David, who are seated in the rear of the main cabin. The three of them are outgoing and relaxed, and Julie and David talk about the plans for their wedding in New York next month.

When we land in New Jersey, it's dark. Most of the country has voted, but in the West the polls are still open. I am physically and mentally exhausted, and yet we still have a long night ahead of us. As soon as he gets off the plane, Bob climbs into a limousine at the head of an extended motorcade. I am directed to take a seat on a chartered bus at the end. With a police escort running interference, we careen through the empty streets of Newark and New York City. For those of us bringing up the rear, it's a wild ride. I feel like I'm at the tail end of a game of mobile "Crack the Whip."

I'm grateful when the bus finally arrives at the Waldorf Astoria Hotel. Bob is already with the Nixons in the penthouse on the thirty-fifth floor of the Waldorf Towers. I push the elevator button for the eighteenth floor, where three other staff wives and I have been assigned a suite. Jeanne Ehrlichman is the wife of John Ehrlichman, an advance man. Nancy Ziegler's husband, Ron, handles the press, and Dolores Higby's husband, Larry, is Bob's assistant.

Anxious to see the latest election returns, we head straight for the TV. Still wearing the suit that I traveled in, I sprawl on the floor in front of the screen. Two phones are beside me. The black one is for hotel calls. The pristine white one is a direct line to Bob.

11:00 p.m. The white phone rings. Bob sounds upbeat. "Hi. How are things going with you and the ladies?"

"Great," I answer. "But what about Humphrey's lead?"

"Don't worry. It's too early to tell anything." Bob pauses. "Pat and the girls have gone back to their suite, and I'm here alone with Nixon. He's superstitious about watching television or listening to the radio, so he's been relying on me to keep him posted. For the last three hours, I've been giving him the latest count."

3:00 a.m. The white phone rings. Bob sounds frustrated. "Nixon wants to make a victory statement. He believes that it's 'historically significant' to do it at the exact moment that he had to concede to Kennedy. I'm trying to talk him out of it."

4:00 a.m. The white phone rings. Bob's voice is energized. "Watch Illinois. This is it. If the rest go as projected, we're going over the top."

8:36 a.m. The white phone rings. Bob is ecstatic. "It's over! We did it! ABC just signed off. We won, Jo! We won. Nixon's going to the White House!"

"Oh, Bob, I'm so thrilled. Congratulations!"

I return the receiver to its cradle and remain motionless on the floor. *The White House. President Nixon. President Richard Nixon in the White House.* My eyes feel scratchy, and my body is stiff. Standing up, I look at myself in dismay. My pleated skirt is a mass of wrinkles, and I can't find one shoe.

I glance at my watch. It's 6:00 a.m. in Los Angeles, and I'm anxious to talk to Non and the children. Everyone is jazzed up. They each get on a different extension and talk at the same time. First, we discuss the returns, and then come the questions. "What happens now? Will we get to go to the inauguration? Will Dad be working in the White House? Will we have to sell this house? What about schools?"

"I have no idea what happens right now," I tell them. "Dad *hopes* to be a part of the Nixon White House, and if that's the case, yes, we would move to Washington after you complete this school year. We could be there up to eight years." I'm glad Bob and I have already discussed these logistics. It gives me confidence in reassuring the children.

9:25 a.m. The white phone rings. Bob's voice is hoarse. "We're having a small victory celebration. Bring the other ladies with you and come on up."

At the penthouse, Jeanne, Nancy, Dee, and I face a crush of bodies looking every bit as bedraggled as we do. The one exception is Bob, who appears remarkably fresh. His suit is unwrinkled, his tie is straight, and he has even shaved. With an exuberant hug, he lifts me off my feet. In our excitement, we talk in shorthand.

"We won." "Congratulations." "Long night." "Exhausted." "Children?" "Excited." "Mom?" "Thrilled!"

Out of the corner of my eye, I spot the newly elected president of the United States heading toward us. I freeze. As the prospective leader of the free world, he suddenly looks different. He's taller and more formidable. There's an aura about him.

I frantically grab Bob's hand. "What do I call Mr. Nixon now?"

"Mr. President-elect," he says without faltering.

"I have to say all of that? It's so awkward."

"All of that," Bob repeats firmly.

Flustered, I give a partial curtsy as Nixon pats Bob on the back and smiles at me. I wait for him to say something presidential.

"Well, how's the drinking member of the family?"

"Congratulations, *Mr. President-elect*," I say, looking him right in the eye.

The words come out perfectly.

Alone in the Crowd

ON WEDNESDAY MORNING, NOVEMBER 6, *The New York Post's* six-inch headline screams, "NIXON IS THE ONE." Hubert Humphrey concedes at 11:30 a.m., and within half an hour, Richard Nixon is on his way downstairs to make his first public appearance as the president-elect.

In the Grand Ballroom of the Waldorf Astoria, I am swallowed up in a sea of jubilant campaign workers waiting to cheer their hero. A wild roar surges across the room as the Nixon family walks onto the stage. Forming a line, the president-elect, Mrs. Nixon, Tricia, Julie, and David hold hands. They seem to be saying, "Here we are, the all-American family who made it into the White House."

I search for Bob. Straining to see past the victory balloons and Nixon signs, I finally spot him standing in the wings on the left side. With his arms folded across his chest and a slight smile on his face, he reminds me of a proud football coach. His expression is serene. Down on the ballroom floor, surrounded by bedlam, I feel out of sync. I know I'm tired, but this is different. I'm all by myself, an outsider looking in.

The president-elect addresses the throng. His words pass in and out of my consciousness. Something about "winning being more fun than losing" and "a great philosophy is never one without defeat, but always one without fear." The crowd cheers at every pause. "I saw many signs in this campaign," Nixon continues, "but the one that touched me the most was the one I saw in Deshler, Ohio. Standing in a crowd, a teenager held up a sign saying, 'Bring Us Together.'"

Bring us together. I latch onto the words. Looking up at Bob, I feel as if the two of us were standing on opposite shores. An impassioned mob of people separates us. *Bring us together...*

Julie presents her father with a piece of crewelwork that she made during the campaign. It's the Great Seal of the United States. I smile. The gesture adds a sense of poignancy to the scene. President-elect Nixon raises both arms high above his head and gives his victory wave. The crowd roars its approval as he and his family walk off the stage.

It's over. People start to leave, and I'm surrounded by chaos. A woman with a Nixon sash across her ample bosom steps on my foot. A balloon pops behind me. I look around for Bob. He's gone. I'm alone in the crowd.

Historically Significant

THE NEWLY ELECTED PRESIDENT and his top staff plan to leave immediately for Key Biscayne, Florida, where the Nixons have vacationed for the past seventeen years. Wives are included, and Bob explains that the trip will be part celebration, part vacation, and part work. I'm excited, and I'm glad that Bob alerted me to this possibility earlier. I packed for the occasion, and Non agreed to stay on with our children.

For security reasons, the president-elect cannot travel commercially. The government has assigned him an Air Force 707 jet, but as soon as I step on board I can see that something's different. We have been given a converted cargo plane, and it has no windows. Someone speculates that this must be a political "dirty trick," but Bob thinks that it's just an oversight. He tells me that if President Johnson had been aware of the situation, he never would have allowed it to happen.

At this point, I don't care. I've been without sleep for thirty hours, and I'm still wearing the same clothes I had on when we left Los Angeles. We can't get to Florida fast enough. The engines roar, we buckle our seat belts, and our seats vibrate. Bob becomes absorbed in a *New York Times* crossword puzzle, and I pull out my needlepoint. The steward comes down the aisle and, much to my amazement, informs us that we will be taking off shortly. With no windows, I was convinced we were already airborne.

Before heading to Florida, we put down at Andrews Air Force Base in Maryland so Nixon can pay his respects to former president Dwight Eisenhower. "Ike" is in Walter Reed Hospital with a heart condition, and the visit is historically significant to the president-elect.

The flight to Miami seems endless and claustrophobic. Playing bridge with Bob and Carol Finch helps to pass the time. When we finally arrive, I can hardly wait to get outside. The door opens, and warm air floods the cabin. In the soft glow of the moonlight, I can see gently swaying palm trees in the distance. At the side of the tarmac, a small group of enthusiastic supporters cheers and waves "Nixon's the One" pennants. I make an effort to smile and wave back.

The next morning, the sun beats down on our villa at the Key Biscayne Hotel. Normally early risers, Bob and I are still asleep when the phone rings at 10:00 a.m. Before Bob finishes shaving, his twenty-three-year-old assistant, Larry Higby, knocks on our door. As the two of them confer over room service breakfast, the phone rings. Soon, people are coming and going. Nixon has much to accomplish over the next seventy-five days. His administration must be in place by the inauguration on January 20.

When Bob tells me that there are a zillion appointments to make on every level—including the cabinet, White House staff, ambassadors, and all the government agencies and departments—I'm more than curious to know what role he will play. He doesn't seem to be concerned and hasn't mentioned it.

A lovely morning turns into an intense work session, and I slip outside to join the other wives on the beach in front of our villa. Jeanne Ehrlichman, Nancy Ziegler, Dolores Higby, and I don't have political backgrounds. None of us has ever lived in Washington, so we turn to the "old pros" in our group to explain government protocol, as well as the ins and outs of life in Washington. Carol Finch and Betty Harlow give us tips on real estate, schools, churches, and the weather. They don't mention the one thing that's uppermost in our thoughts. No one dares to speculate on what part her husband might play in the new administration.

Later, Jeanne tells me that her family is happy in Seattle, and she doesn't think that they are interested in moving to DC. She's involved in community projects, John's law practice is thriving, and their five children love their home on the water at Hunt's Point. I'm surprised. If Bob is given the opportunity to become part of the White House staff, I don't see how he could pass it up. Like Jeanne, I love our life in LA, but I wouldn't let that hold us back.

On our first full night in Key Biscayne, the president-elect plans another historically significant event—a "victory dinner." He wants it to be in symbolic contrast to the gathering that he and his staff had eight years ago, following his loss to John Kennedy.

"I sense an impending disaster," Bob grumbles, as soon as he hears about the dinner. "I haven't the foggiest notion who's supposed to be organizing this."

There will be seventeen guests, and Bob wants to get to the restaurant and check on the arrangements before the others arrive. He is anxious to leave as soon as he's dressed, but I discover a run in one of my stockings and have to replace it. When I reappear, I get the steely-eyed Haldeman look.

At the Jamaica Inn, we are escorted to the English Pub. My heart sinks. Instead of being seated outside, where we can enjoy the sunset on this balmy evening, we are in a dark private dining room with a depressing red and black décor. A solitary round table, slightly off-center, is set for us. There are no flowers, place cards, or wine glasses.

Bob turns to the *maître d'* and asks if he has something that could be used for place cards. When the *maître d'* obligingly gives him a reservation pad, Bob hands it to me along with his felt tip pen.

"I'll tell you the names, and you print them as fast as you can." As Bob dictates, I write. Each name appears on the back side of a slip of paper labeled: "date, server, table, persons, check no." As soon as I complete a "place card," Bob folds the paper in half and sets it on the table. He decides who sits next to whom.

The guests start arriving before I'm finished, but Bob calmly keeps things moving. There is no cocktail hour. Nixon wants everyone to be seated immediately. The Ehrlichmans are late, because they took naps and overslept. Carol Finch's teapot leaks, dripping hot water on the president-elect's left knee. We use water glasses to make our toasts. Nixon repeatedly tells us that he wants the theme song from *Victory at Sea* to be played as loudly and as often as possible at the various inaugural events.

The evening is awkward, but it isn't the "disaster" that Bob feared it might be.

When Bob and I return to our villa, we place a call to the children. Instead of going right to bed, the two of us decide to take a walk on the beach. Bob removes his shoes and socks and throws his suit jacket and tie on the bed. I take off my shoes and stockings, and we step outside. Moonlight reflects off the ocean, and the air is warm. Bob pauses to search the sky for his favorite constellation and has no trouble finding the three stars in Orion's belt. We hold hands and walk slowly, leaving a trail of footprints in the damp sand.

Tonight, we have each other. There's no reason to hurry.

Seashells

THE NEXT FOUR DAYS fly by. Bob works, and I play. I live in shorts and bathing suits, while he wears a sport coat and tie whenever he meets with Nixon, and a dark suit on more formal occasions. This attire seems out of place in such a tropical setting, but the respect it shows is important to the president-elect.

The Nixons are staying in a bungalow not far from the Key Biscayne Hotel, and Bob is there much of the time. He and the president-elect have an extremely close working relationship and spend hours together daily. Socially, however, their relationship is surprisingly formal and impersonal. I am amused to observe this on Sunday morning as Bob and I eat breakfast by the pool.

"Good morning, Bob," the president-elect says, nodding as he strolls by with his family on the way home from church.

Returning the nod, Bob replies, "Good morning, Mr. President-elect."

The Nixons continue on their way, and Bob and I resume our breakfast.

In contrast, my renewed relationship with Jeanne Ehrlichman flourishes. Bob and I met John and Jeanne when the four of us were undergraduates at UCLA. Several years later, our paths crossed again, when John attended Stanford Law School and Bob worked at J. Walter Thompson in San Francisco. Jeanne and I have not seen each other since then. On a two-hour walk to the lighthouse, we reminisce and speculate. Along the shoreline, we search for seashells, saving the prettiest.

"Let's keep these," Jeanne says. "Years from now, it'll be fun to have them as reminders of this special time together."

"They'll *always* be with me," I promise.

◆

THE FIRST APPOINTMENT OF the Nixon administration is announced on our final day in Florida. Rose Mary Woods, Nixon's secretary for the past seventeen years, will serve as personal secretary to the president of the United States. When I congratulate her, I can't help but wonder what Bob's role will be and when his appointment will be announced.

Before leaving, I pull open the sliding door of our villa and step out onto the lanai. I will miss this beautiful setting with its white sand beach and sparkly ocean. But I will miss being with Bob even more. We are going our separate ways. Over the next three months, he will be living in New York City, where he will work full-time on the transition. I will be headed home.

As Bob meticulously packs his suitcase, he pauses and looks up. Our eyes lock, and I sense a deep inner confidence in him. We both know that a new chapter in our lives is about to begin.

Transition

I RETURN TO CALIFORNIA by myself, and Bob accompanies the Nixons on their flight to Washington. Tomorrow, while the incoming and outgoing presidents and their wives get together, Bob will be meeting in the White House with Johnson's acting chief of staff. *Chief of staff. Could that be Bob's role? A top managerial job in the White House would be a perfect fit for him.*

On Wednesday, November 13, Bob calls from Nixon's transition headquarters at the Hotel Pierre. He tells me that the president-elect's second appointment is going to be announced soon and I should listen to the news.

When the newscaster says that my husband, Harry Robbins Haldeman, has been appointed assistant to the president, White House chief of staff, I'm overjoyed. Although I had considered this possibility, now that I hear it, I have trouble believing it. I'm so proud of Bob and excited for our family. When I ask him what exactly this entails, he unhesitatingly recites his new job description.

"My primary responsibility will be to enable the president to function more effectively. With no independent schedule of my own, I'll oversee the administration of the White House. That includes the president's schedule, as well as the flow of both paperwork and people in and out of the Oval Office."

True to form, Bob is concise and to the point. When he adds that he will be available to the president at all times, operating at his beck and call, I know him well enough to take him literally. He's saying that his work will take priority over the children and me, and momentarily, I'm concerned. Then I remind myself how much of a family man Bob is. *Certainly, being part of the White House won't change our routine at home that much.*

◆

BOB AND I HAVE always worked as a team in raising our children. Now that he is living in New York, I miss his hands-on help in parenting. Communicating once again by long-distance phone calls, I try to be upbeat. But often that's not easy.

Today in particular has been filled with frustration, and for the last twelve hours, I've done nothing but nag the children. Thanksgiving and Christmas are almost here, and I have to sell our home, purchase a new house in Washington, find schools for Hank, Peter, and Ann, follow up on college choices for Susan, and pack for the move.

I'm tired of handling things on my own. Needing reassurance, I reread a letter Bob wrote to me when he left on the campaign. His words of support encourage me once again.

> *Hi Jo,*
>
> *After a tearful farewell, I'm sitting on the plane... I know that you'll be doing double duty as both parents, and that in many ways this period is going to be tougher for you at home than it is for me.*
>
> *In spite of my constant flow of comments and suggestions on the subject of dealing with our four characters, I have absolute and complete confidence in your handling of anything that may arise. Just don't take it too seriously...*
>
> *I'm very proud and grateful for your marvelous willing acceptance of this one more disruption of our lives. It would be impossible to do without your attitude. See you in a couple of weeks.*
>
> *All my love, always,*
>
> *Bob*

◆

ON THANKSGIVING NIGHT, BOB calls from his apartment at the Wyndam Hotel. His voice sounds wistful as he tells me how much he misses the family, but he adds that he had a surprise visit. The president-elect called him at eight this morning and asked if he could come by. "He stayed for *two hours,*" Bob says in amazement.

"Nixon came over to *your* little apartment?" I question. "On *Thanksgiving*?"

"Yeah, I think he just needed to get away for a while." Bob chuckles. "Word got out that the president-elect was here, and the entire hotel staff lined up outside to greet him. The poor manager was so excited he was shaking. He couldn't even hold his camera still enough to take a picture. It was pretty funny."

December 1968

ON A FOGGY AFTERNOON in early December, the children and I head for the airport to pick up Bob. The president-elect plans to spend a few days in Los Angeles, and we are given VIP passes onto the tarmac to greet his plane. Shivering in the fog, we unfurl a ten-foot homemade banner, saying "Welcome Home—Bob Haldeman!" Bob smiles and waves as soon as he sees us.

With Bob behind the wheel of our green Ford station wagon heading for home, I can relax. For a brief period, I have someone else to pay the parking attendant, battle the traffic, and settle the children's arguments. It's heaven.

After dinner, the children go upstairs to do their homework, and Bob and I settle in the den. "Just like old times," he says, collapsing onto the oversized chair in the corner. Giving a yawn, he stretches and puts his feet up on the ottoman.

The phone rings. Answering it, Bob straightens up. As soon as he says, "Yes, sir," and reaches for his yellow pad, my heart falls. *Why does Nixon have to call now?* It's exciting to receive a call at home from the president-elect of the United States, but tonight I want Bob to myself.

At least the conversation is short, and when Bob hangs up, he turns to me with a grin. "Well, you and the kids sure 'one-upped' the president-elect."

"What do you mean?" I ask.

"He's feeling pretty sorry for himself. His last words were, 'Nobody had a welcome home sign for *me* today.'"

The Inauguration

January 1969

ALL TOO SOON, IT's the New Year. In twenty days, Richard Nixon will be inaugurated, and Bob will take over as chief of staff of the White House. To prepare for the job, he has been reading every book he can find on the subject and interviewing top staff members from previous administrations.

Although Bob shuns publicity, I occasionally spot his name in the newspaper. It's usually imbedded in an article which I eagerly cut out and paste into my scrapbook. I save everything I can to document this extraordinary time.

Over the last month, each member of our family has been receiving beautifully hand-addressed invitations to various inaugural events. The countdown is on, and I throw myself into working out the logistics for our trip to Washington. Plane tickets have to be purchased, and hotel reservations made. Between Bob's mother, my parents, our children, and Susan's boyfriend, we have sixteen suitcases, containing three inaugural ball gowns, two sets of white tie and tails, three tuxedos, two fancy dresses, three fur wraps, and enough long underwear and clothes for four days.

Once in Washington, our family checks into a large suite on the eleventh floor of the Statler Hilton Hotel. The cold weather and leaden skies can't begin to dampen our enthusiasm, but the sight of armed soldiers posted on the surrounding rooftops is sobering. Because of a growing concern that antiwar demonstrators might try to disrupt the inauguration, the District police, the US Army, and the National Guard have all been deployed to maintain security.

During the next few days we don't see much of Bob. He is totally focused on the president-elect, as well as the last minute details for the turnover in the

White House. The rest of us participate in every event we can. While Mother, Non, and I slowly move through long receiving lines at teas and receptions, the children tour Washington with their grandfather.

On Sunday afternoon, Bob and I take advantage of a break to do some house hunting. A White House driver takes us to look at residential areas in the District, as well as Maryland and Virginia. It's discouraging to find that nothing compares to our home in LA and prices are high.

As we head back to the hotel, the army communications radio in the car crackles with an odd message: "Searchlight One to Welcome." The garbled words make no sense to me, but Bob and our driver respond immediately. Sergeant Grill screeches to a stop at the corner of Foxhall and Reservoir Roads, and Bob scrambles out of the car. Darting across the street, he heads for the bright red public phone booth.

"Sorry, Jo," he apologizes, as he climbs back into the car. "That was the president-elect. He has no idea where I am, and I had to get back to him right away."

"What's this thing about a searchlight and welcome?" I ask, confused.

"They're our White House code names," Bob explains. "The Signal Corps assigned them. The president-elect is Searchlight, and the senior staff all have code names that start with 'W.' John Ehrlichman is Wisdom. Henry Kissinger's Woodcutter. Ron Ziegler's Whaleboat. And I'm Welcome."

"Welcome?" I exclaim. "It sounds silly."

"Don't laugh. You've got a code name, too."

"*Me?* What is it?"

"Welcome Two."

◆

TODAY, JANUARY 20, AT exactly noon, Richard Nixon will be sworn in as the thirty-seventh president of the United States. At that moment, the dream Bob confided in me six months ago in the middle of Newport Harbor will become a reality.

It's bitter cold. Icy wind whips at the ends of my red wool scarf as I stand in front of the Statler Hilton. A large chartered bus pulls up, and our children and their grandparents join others on board. They will be taken to a reserved section of seats to watch the inauguration.

Sergeant Grill drives Bob and me directly to the East Front of the Capitol, where thousands of people are already assembled. Along with other special guests, we climb the stairs and enter the Rotunda. When we step out onto the inaugural platform, the scene is striking. It's a patriotic moment right out of the history books. The band is playing, flags are waving, and people are enthusiastically greeting each other. I pause and blink in wonder. Bob reaches for my hand. I can only imagine what this must mean to him.

We follow the red-carpeted steps down to our seats, where I am between Bob and Dr. Henry Kissinger. Six rows in front of us are four empty chairs reserved for the incoming and outgoing presidents and vice presidents. Somewhere in the distance, our family is lost in a sea of American flags. Trying to spot them is hopeless, and a pang of guilt hits me. I trust they can see everything and are keeping warm.

Shortly before noon, the band plays a fanfare, and everyone turns to look at the top of the steps. Flanked by an escort of three senators and three representatives, Richard Milhous Nixon stands erect. With a look of pride and dignity, he slowly proceeds down the steps. When he passes our row, Bob straightens up. It's as if he were standing at attention. I, too, throw back my shoulders.

Wearing a bright pink coat and a fur pillbox hat, Pat Nixon takes her place between Chief Justice Earl Warren and the president-elect for the swearing-in. In her hands are two family Bibles, both opened to Isaiah 2:4. A tight smile is frozen on her face, and I wonder what she is thinking. The chief justice administers the single-sentence oath of office: "I do solemnly swear that I will faithfully execute the office of president of the United States, and will to the best of my ability, preserve, protect, and defend the Constitution of the United States."

We have a new president and first lady. A twenty-one-gun salute erupts, and the United States Marine Band plays ruffles and flourishes, followed by "Hail to the Chief." *President Nixon* stands at the podium ready to give his inaugural address. His words and ideas hold such promise. Bob appears to be completely absorbed and moves only once, to give me a nudge when he hears a line he especially likes.

"Until he has been part of a cause larger than himself, no man is truly whole."

I sense that this will become Bob's creed, and I make a mental note to get a handwritten copy of it for him.

With the speech ringing in my ears, I watch as President and Mrs. Nixon turn and lead the way back up the steps. Along with the other dignitaries who have been seated on the platform, Bob and I find our way back to the Rotunda. In front of us, the Nixons are abruptly ushered into a side room, and Bob cranes his neck to see where they are going. In his rush to catch up, he brushes against me.

"Wait for me," he calls over his shoulder. "I'll be right back."

A heavy wood door, with the number 206 on it, closes after him. I press myself against the wall to avoid the crowd of people streaming past me. Five minutes pass before Bob emerges. I know he's upset as soon as I see the Haldeman look.

"Somebody sure goofed," he says. "There's the president seated at a table, and he's handed his first set of presidential documents to sign…and guess what? No one has a pen."

"You're kidding." I say. "So what happened?"

Giving a broad smile, Bob reaches into his breast pocket and pulls out his ever-present felt tip pen.

Taking my arm, Bob navigates me through the crowd to the room where lunch is being served. We take our seats along with congressional leaders, members of the new Nixon cabinet, and presidential advisors and assistants. As we eat, Bob keeps checking his watch. At noon today, he became responsible for the management of the White House, and he's anxious to get over there. We leave before dessert. Racing down the Capitol's 165 steps, we arrive at the car where Sergeant Grill is patiently waiting with the engine running and the heater set on high.

Pennsylvania Avenue has been roped off for the parade, but that doesn't deter Sergeant Grill. He cruises along the empty road, passing enthusiastic spectators who have staked out their locations early. They cheer and wave small American flags. However, the atmosphere changes at Twelfth Street, where a group of antiwar protestors is gathered. Raising their fists, they shout, "Four more years of death." Their anger is real, and it's scary. I lean away from the window, closer to Bob.

Sergeant Grill drops us off at the west gate of the White House, where a guard checks our credentials. Opening an unobtrusive side door, Bob ushers me into the ground floor of the West Wing. He knows exactly where he's going, and all I have to do is tag along behind him. On our way to the back stairs, he points out Henry Kissinger's office and the Navy Mess. As we climb the steps to the main floor, I have to convince myself that I'm actually in the inner sanctum of the White House.

This Place is a Zoo

THE WHITE HOUSE HAS 132 rooms, and many of these are offices in the East and West Wings. At this moment, crews are hard at work converting them to meet the needs of the incoming administration. As Bob and I make our way down a hall in the West Wing, we are surrounded by organized bedlam. Painters are touching up scratch marks and repainting damaged walls. Housekeepers are polishing brass and dusting furniture. Old desks are being carted off as new ones are being delivered. New directories are being installed on the phones. Fires are being laid in the fireplaces, and fresh arrangements of colorful spring flowers are being placed in each room.

Heading for the Oval Office, Bob and I step aside to avoid two movers carrying the last of President Johnson's three television sets. Other movers are disassembling his two wire-service ticker tapes.

"Johnson's got a ton of electronic stuff in here," Bob says. "President Nixon wants all of it to go. He's adamant about getting rid of the taping system, too. He doesn't see any reason to record conversations like Kennedy and LBJ did."

The small office adjacent to the Oval Office is Bob's. The room is cozy with its bookshelves and crackling fire. Weak, winter sunlight filters in through a large window, and an oil portrait of Nixon hangs above the mantle. I try to visualize Bob working at the dark wood desk. *Bob wants this with all his heart, and whatever lies ahead in the next four or eight years, I am confident that he can handle it. I'm so proud of him.*

Before moving on, Bob shows me a tiny closet next to the Oval Office. He explains that a navy steward was assigned to sit there during Johnson's meetings to take drink orders for the president and his guests. Four colored lights in a box on the wall would light up, indicating what each person requested: red, white, green, or yellow—coffee, tea, Coke, or Fresca.

As we check out the other offices, I note the hodgepodge of furniture. There are a variety of desks—metal, traditional, contemporary, and Swedish. Vending machines, teletypes, coffee machines, and water coolers fill the hallway. So many electrical cords run along the ugly linoleum floor, I have to be careful where I step. Above me, an egg crate ceiling diffuses the florescent lighting.

Band music in the distance signals the start of the inaugural parade. Grabbing my hand, Bob leads the way along a temporary boardwalk to Pennsylvania Avenue. The White House lawn is frozen, and my breath forms in cloudy puffs. Entering the presidential review tent, we are hit by a blast of warm air, and once again, I worry about our family standing on a sidewalk in the cold. We slip into our reserved seats next to Reverend Billy Graham and Bebe Rebozo. The tall, fair, charismatic evangelist and the short, dark, unassuming Floridian banker have little in common, but both are close friends of the president.

Pointing to the Nixon family seated directly in front of us, Bob whispers, "Watch the president. He's like a little kid at Christmas. He loves a parade."

I enjoy watching Bob. He, too, loves a parade.

◆

TONIGHT, BOB JOINS THE family for a room service dinner in the dining room of our suite. There are ten of us, each formally dressed for the inaugural ball. Bob rises to give a toast. He taps his water glass with his knife.

"To the president of the United States, Richard Milhous Nixon."

"To the president," the rest of us respond.

My father stands next. "To a special son-in-law, who brings us together tonight in our nation's capital through his loyalty and dedication to a cause."

"To Bob." "To Dad." We clink glasses and sing two songs that are a Horton family tradition, "*Hoch Sollst Du Leben*" ("Here's To Your Health") and "For He's a Jolly Good Fellow."

Now it's Non's turn. She's been itching to get to her feet. After proposing toasts to her son and the family, she toasts her late husband. "To my dear Bud, who is here in spirit, looking down on his son with great pride."

Poignant in their sincerity and simplicity, the toasts exemplify the love we feel for each other and for our country.

◆

THERE ARE SIX INAUGURAL balls in different locations around DC. With rain coming down in torrents, we're lucky to have one of them right here in the Statler Hilton Hotel. Our expectations are high, and I feel like royalty in my white *moiré* silk gown, with its jeweled yolk and mandarin collar. Bob proudly dons his father's white tie and tails.

Unfortunately, the ballroom is not the regal scene we envisioned. Jammed with people, the noise level is unbearable, making it impossible to talk, let alone hear. We wander around, trying to find someone we know. Our large gold tickets, with "Presidential Box" printed on them, are useless. I jam mine back into my evening bag to keep as a souvenir.

"Let's get out of here," Bob shouts in my ear. "This place is a zoo."

"We can't leave," I yell back. "We just got here, and we have to dance."

"What?" Bob shouts.

I raise my voice. "We have to dance. The inaugural ball is one thing my friends will ask me about when I get home."

"You're kidding!"

Taking my hand, Bob pushes his way to the dance floor. With hardly enough space to move, we shuffle in place to the beat of the music. In the crush of people, I soon realize that no one can see my fancy new dress. It makes absolutely no difference what I'm wearing.

After two dances, we give up and head back to our suite. Trying not to disturb our parents, who came up earlier, we quietly slip into our room. Bob changes into his pajamas and disappears into the bathroom. I take off my ball gown and hang it on the back of the closet door next to his tails. Feeling whimsical, I impulsively drape the sleeve of his jacket around the shoulder of my dress. I take a step back. *You look good together,* I muse. *All set for that next chapter in your lives.*

Chief of Staff

"THAT NEXT CHAPTER" BEGINS the following morning when Harry Robbins Haldeman—husband, father, son, and son-in-law—is sworn in as White House chief of staff. Before leaving the hotel for the ceremony, however, the rest of us have to have our sixteen suitcases packed and in the lobby. We are on a countdown, and by tonight we will be back in California. Only Bob will remain in Washington.

Today's event is a White House family affair, and the East Room is crowded. Excited chatter wafts through the room, and some of the younger children work off their excess energy by running and sliding across the parquet floor. Others climb on the satin upholstered chairs that line the walls.

In the main hall, three marines in dress uniform take their position at the foot of the Grand Staircase. As they raise their trumpets to play ruffles and flourishes, followed by "Hail to the Chief," the room falls silent. A feeling of profound respect engulfs me.

All eyes are on the president and the first lady, who stand motionless on the upper landing of the red-carpeted stairway. Together, they slowly descend and walk to the middle of the East Room, where the president delivers a short pep talk to his incoming staff and their families. When he tells us that we will each play an important part in his administration, it makes me feel special and needed.

Chief Justice Earl Warren takes his place at a podium on a riser placed against the wall. A gold damask curtain hangs behind it, and the American flag stands on the left. Looking distinguished in his long black robe, the chief justice instructs the men and women in front of him to raise their right hands. My eyes never leave Bob as he solemnly repeats his oath of office. With his tucked-in chin and rigid posture, he resembles a Boy Scout, earnestly giving his pledge to God and country.

Bob looks so trusting. He actually appears vulnerable. And yet, I have always considered him to be in*vulnerable.*

Bob knows what he wants and goes after it with resolve. He has done everything he can to prepare himself for this job, and he doesn't doubt his ability. Bob firmly believes that the president of the United States deserves to have a White House that functions *perfectly*, and he's convinced that he can provide that. Being chief of staff of the White House means more to him than anything he's ever done…or ever will do.

As soon as the brief ceremony ends, the family and I rush over to congratulate Bob. Non's eyes tear up as she embraces her son. We are all so proud of him, and I wish I could hang on to this moment forever. Standing in this grand room, with its three gigantic, Bohemian cut-glass chandeliers, I have a sense of stepping into history. This is now Bob's world, and soon it will be mine as well. I'm excited and a little scared of what lies ahead for me. But for now, the children and I will be finishing up the school year in Los Angeles, leaving Bob to settle into his new job here in DC.

◆

OUR RETURN HOME JOLTS me back to reality. The flight is rough, and the airline loses our sixteen suitcases. A seven-inch rainfall yesterday left our house with no heat, no phone, a leaky roof, and a flooded basement. Southern California is declared a federal disaster area.

February 1969

WITH BOB AT THE White House, I take a greater interest in the international and national news. In the month of February, Yasser Arafat is acknowledged as leader of the Palestine Liberation Organization, and Golda Meir is sworn in as Israel's first female prime minister. Tear gas is used to quell riots at the University of Wisconsin.

Bob plans to be home for our twentieth wedding anniversary on February 19, and I know exactly what I want to give him. To obtain that segment of the inaugural address that means so much to him, I enlist the help of Appointments Secretary Dwight Chapin.

At a black tie dinner party in our home, I give Bob the framed quote. Underneath a gold embossed presidential seal, Nixon's uneven scrawl spreads across the White House stationery. With a pleased look, Bob stands and reads the memorable words out loud. "Until he has been part of a cause larger than himself, no man is truly whole…"

◆

PRESIDENT NIXON LEAVES ON his first presidential trip abroad on February 23. During the two-week tour, he will meet with world dignitaries in Brussels, London, Paris, Bonn, Berlin, and Rome. Bob is responsible for the logistics. When he calls from London the night after arriving, I'm anxious to get his report on how everything is going.

"I blew it, Jo," he says.

These are not words I ever expected to hear from Bob. He doesn't often make a mistake and has never admitted to "blowing" anything.

"My alarm never went off yesterday, and I overslept."

"Oh, Bob…"

"I missed the helicopter from the White House to Andrews Air Force Base, and they had to send a second chopper just for me. I boarded *Air Force One* with only two minutes to spare."

"Did the president know you were late?"

"Yes. And, unfortunately, I had to walk right past him to get to my seat."

"And…?"

"He gave me an icy stare and said, 'Good morning.' That was it."

"That was it?"

I feel for Bob. He strives for perfection and is proud of his reputation as a manager. A recent newspaper article reported, "Haldeman's mind goes lickety-split… [He is] a coordinator and technician, rather than a policy man…a highly efficient organizer."

The Women Behind the Men

As SOON AS THE president returns from his whirlwind tour of Europe, he flies to Florida for the weekend, and Bob goes with him. I'm glad that I haven't moved to Washington yet, since Bob doesn't seem to be spending much time there. Eager to see him, I accept invitations to two White House parties in March. While I'm in DC, Bob and I will look at houses, and I will research schools for Hank, Peter, and Ann.

March 1969

ON FRIDAY, MARCH 14, I check into the Jefferson Hotel, where Bob is temporarily residing. In the living room of his suite, I'm greeted by a huge arrangement of spring flowers with a handwritten card from him. Although the hotel is only four blocks from the White House, a driver takes me to the West Wing to meet Bob for dinner. He greets me at the side door, and we continue down the hall of the ground floor to the White House Mess. The simple, cheerful dining room has no windows but is well lit. Fresh flowers are on the tables, which are covered with white tablecloths. The waiters are navy stewards. Bob seems very much at home, speaking to people and calling the stewards by name. I don't recognize anyone, but I know everyone is important. I feel special.

The next day, I join Bob at the White House again. As I follow him up the back stairs to his office, he tells me that the Nixons plan to redecorate. Working with architects, decorators, and interior designers from Williamsburg, Mrs. Nixon is in charge of the Oval Office, and Bob is responsible for the rest of the West Wing.

"It's going to be terrific," he says, pointing to piles of paint chips and fabric samples spread out on his desk. "Antiques in the Oval Office, and quality reproductions for the staff."

In the evening, Bob and I attend two different functions. While he dresses for the Gridiron dinner, where members of the administration are traditionally roasted by the press, I dress for Mrs. Nixon's dinner honoring the White House wives. This is new to me, and the protocol is intimidating. I wish Bob were going to be at the White House with me. I ask him for advice.

"Just follow the other ladies," he says. "Do what they do. I'm sure you won't be the only one there for the first time."

Dressed in white tie and tails, Bob leaves first. When the zipper in the back of my dress gets stuck, I have to ask the doorman to zip me up. A White House car takes me to the south entrance of the White House, where we wait in a long line of government "limos" that look exactly like our black Mercury sedan. We inch ahead. Then suddenly my door is opened by a uniformed White House social aide. Stepping out of the car, I silently repeat Bob's words like a mantra.

"Follow the ladies. Do what they do. Just follow the ladies. Do what they do."

Swept up in a steady stream of elegantly dressed women, I enter the Diplomatic Reception Room. Expecting to see others who are obviously here for the first time, I'm disappointed. No one looks lost. For a brief moment, I feel terribly alone. I check my fur stole, and as I start to climb the stairs to the Entrance Hall, a woman breezes past me.

"Isn't it fun to be here without your husband for a change?" she asks in a bubbly, enthusiastic voice.

"Sure is," I reply, attempting to sound blasé.

Halfway up the red-carpeted stairs, an attractive woman with reddish hair taps me on the shoulder. "Would you mind zipping me up?" she asks, pointing to the back of her dress. "Gerry had to leave before I finished dressing this evening."

I smile. I'm happy to help her. When I discover that the woman is Betty Ford, wife of Representative Gerald Ford, I realize that sometimes it makes no difference who you are or where you are—certain situations are universal.

On the upper landing, I'm given a card with my dinner table number on it. I'm delighted to find that I am seated next to Julie Eisenhower. Effervescent and gregarious, Julie is a good hostess at our table for eight. As she talks, she gestures a lot, and her dark hair bounces on the shoulders of her white lace dress. When the army's Strolling Strings pause at our table to play "Lara's Theme" from *Doctor Zhivago,* I get goose bumps. The feeling of being surrounded by twenty violinists playing my favorite song in the State Dining Room of the White House is surreal. The only thing missing is Bob.

After dinner, coffee is served in the main hall, where I notice a stately, older woman standing alone. Sensing that I've finally discovered someone else who might be here for the first time, I introduce myself.

"I know who you are, my dear," the woman says, extending her right hand. "I'm Mrs. Warren."

"It's nice to meet you," I say. "Is your husband part of the Nixon White House?"

"No, dear, he's the chief justice of the Supreme Court." Mrs. Warren smiles pleasantly and drifts away.

◆

IN ORDER TO GIVE more people access to the White House, President and Mrs. Nixon have introduced "White House Church," a nondenominational Sunday service, and "Evenings at the White House," occasional celebrity performances, which are held in the East Room.

On Sunday morning, Bob and I attend White House Church. A raised platform and rows of gold-backed chairs have been set up in the East Room. The service today will be conducted by the minister of a Presbyterian church in California, and the Washington Cathedral Boys Choir will be performing.

Guiding me to the last row of seats, Bob explains that he wants to keep a low profile and plans to remain in the background at White House events. I understand this but am confused when he immediately leaves me to socialize with other guests.

This evening, we return to the White House for a surprise fifty-seventh birthday party for Mrs. Nixon, who thinks that the president is giving a stag dinner. As soon as we enter the main hall, Bob and I are separated. He is told to mingle with the men, and I am directed to hide in the East Room with the wives. I huddle in a corner with a group of women I have never met. Across from us a large portrait of Martha Washington hangs on the wall. My heart is beating excitedly, and I can't believe where I am and what I'm doing. As soon as the US Marine Band strikes up the first notes of "Happy Birthday," it's our cue, and we rush out and shout, "Surprise!"

While waiting to go down the receiving line, Bob and I chat with Henry Kissinger. According to protocol, the White House chief of staff outranks the national security advisor, so we precede Henry. When Bob greets the president, once again I'm fascinated by their brief, impersonal exchange. Now it's my turn.

Extending his hand, the president asks, "Got a handle on that drinking problem yet?" He looks pleased with himself for making such a clever remark.

"I'm working on it," I reply. Giving a lighthearted laugh, I move on to greet Pat and the girls.

The State Dining Room is set up for an informal dinner with ten round tables of eight. Bob is at one, and I'm at another. We are again serenaded by the army's Strolling Strings, who are playing Mrs. Nixon's favorite show tunes. When a green and white St. Patrick's Day ice cream cake is brought in for dessert, the violinists switch to a round of "Happy Birthday," and everyone sings.

The president stands to give a toast, but Pat stops him. She asks him to wait until she blows out the single candle on top of the cake. She blows, we clap, and Nixon stands again. He raises his wine glass.

"I would like to ask Mamie to give the toast to Pat," the president says and sits down.

There's a frozen smile on Pat's face, and from what I can tell, Mamie Eisenhower is caught off guard. I feel for both women.

"To a great friend and girl," Mamie says and sits down.

Two old friends of Nixon each toast the president, but neither one mentions Pat. The president beams and stands once again. "A toast to everyone with March birthdays, and to St. Patrick," he says.

The situation is awkward, and I'm embarrassed. This is the perfect opportunity for the president to acknowledge his wife's love and support through the years. Now that the two of them are at the summit of his career, she deserves to be recognized in her role as first lady.

When Rose Mary Woods stands, I'm afraid to look. Instead, I study a tiny piece of braised celery clinging to the edge of the tablecloth. She raises her glass.

In a strong, clear voice, Rose gives her toast. "To the woman behind the man."

◆

AFTER SPENDING HOURS LOOKING at houses, Bob and I find one we like in Kenwood, a residential section of Chevy Chase, Maryland. The pretty colonial home has six bedrooms, and with its tall, white columns and long front porch, it reminds us of our home in Hancock Park. Although the lawn is brown and the dogwood trees and azaleas are bare, our real estate agent assures us that soon the garden will look like a fairyland.

Air Force One

T HE WEEK IS OVER, and it's time for me to return to California. I have a ticket on a United flight, but I gladly forfeit it when Bob invites me to join him on *Air Force One*. We will be traveling with the president and first lady on their trip to the West Coast, which I can hardly believe. *What an extraordinary way to wrap up my visit to Washington.*

First thing on Friday morning, March 21, a White House driver takes me from the Jefferson Hotel to the ground floor entrance of the West Wing. Showing my new, laminated photo ID card to the White House guard, I enter the building. This time, Bob is not here to greet me, and I'm on my own. Climbing up the back stairs, I methodically count each of the seventeen steps to the first floor. A secretary gives me a friendly nod as we pass in the hall, and it's reassuring. Although I'm no longer intimidated by these surroundings, I know that I will never cease to be in awe of actually being here.

When Pat McKee, Bob's secretary, tells me that he's with the president in the Oval Office, it sounds unreal. I still find it hard to comprehend that Bob is chief of staff of the White House. *I wonder if I ever will.*

I hear the choppy rumble of a helicopter as it lowers itself onto the South Lawn, and forty-five minutes later, I'm escorted out to it. From my assigned seat in the rear, I watch as the others climb aboard. The last two people to appear are the president and Bob, who are deep in conversation and seem oblivious to the cold. The minute the president takes his seat, the door is closed, and *Marine One* noisily lumbers skyward. Banking to the right, we pass directly over the National Mall. Not far below us, sunlight glints off the Washington Monument and the Capitol. A full Fourth-of-July view. Gripping Bob's arm, I puff up with pride.

Six minutes after taking off, the chopper sets down at Andrews Air Force Base next to *Air Force One*. Actually, the Boeing 707 is technically "*Air Force*

One" only when the president is on board. President and Mrs. Nixon enter through a door in the front, which opens into the presidential lounge area. Bob and I climb the stairs in the rear with the rest of the traveling party. Nudging me along the aisle, he tells me that the rear section is reserved for the Secret Service and a rotating group of eight members of the press.

The twelve seats in the next compartment are for the cabinet, senior White House staff, government officials, and visiting dignitaries. The first two seats on the right have cards with our names on them. I'm excited, but I try to act calm and collected as a steward in a wine-colored blazer welcomes us aboard. The flight information card he hands me shows that we will be making a stop in Missouri in two and a half hours. Across the aisle, Secretary of State Bill Rogers greets us. His wife, Adele, holds up a needlepoint she is working on and explains that her goal is to make a seat pad for every chair in the Reception Room at the State Department.

Not long after takeoff, Bob excuses himself to go up front to a staff work area, which is next to the president's lounge. When he returns, John Ehrlichman and Henry Kissinger are with him. The three of them are wearing personalized *Air Force One* flight jackets. There is a lot of teasing and joking between them, and soon Henry is regaling us with stories about his experiences as a foreign policy consultant during the Kennedy administration. In a low, gravelly voice and thick German accent, he describes one of his lunches in the White House Mess.

"My knife slipped when I was cutting my lamb chop," he says. "The chop sailed across the table and landed on Dean Rusk's plate." Everyone laughs.

"But," Henry adds, with perfect timing, "there's more. The secretary of state proceeded to eat it."

We make a brief stop in Kansas City, Missouri, for the president to deliver to Harry Truman the Steinway piano that was in the White House during his presidency. An admirer of Truman, Bob is excited to be part of the small group accompanying the president. Clutching his movie camera, he boards the helicopter while the rest of us wait on the plane. When he returns, Bob is beaming.

"That was an amazing experience," he exclaims. "And I was even able to film the president playing a few bars of the 'Missouri Waltz' while Truman looked on."

Say "Cheese"

L ATE IN THE AFTERNOON, we approach Point Mugu Air Weapons Station, fifty-five miles south of Santa Barbara. Looking down on the rolling surf and the sage green hillsides, I can almost smell the salty beach air mixed with the pungent aroma of eucalyptus. The scene is a familiar one. For Bob and me, this is home.

After landing, Bob points to a cluster of soldiers in battle fatigues standing off to the side of the runway. He explains that they are Seabees who have just returned from active duty in Vietnam. The president looks proud as he shakes the hand of each man, and I wonder what his thoughts are as their commander in chief. I'm honored to be here with them, and at the same time, I'm upset that the country isn't more united in giving them the support that they deserve. This war is tearing us apart, and our soldiers have become the biggest losers.

When Nixon took office two months ago, there were 550,000 US troops in Vietnam, and 300 men were being killed each week. He stated that his first priority as president was to obtain a lasting peace with honor. I hope he can accomplish this.

After reviewing the troops, President and Mrs. Nixon board a helicopter to view a potentially disastrous oil slick in the Santa Barbara Channel and then continue down the coast to San Clemente. They will spend the night at the Cotton estate, which they are considering buying. The one-story, Spanish-style house is on twenty-six acres with a lot of privacy. Located next door to a Coast Guard station, it would make an ideal Western White House.

Bob and I remain on *Air Force One* with a few other members of the White House staff. Our final destination is El Toro Marine Base near San Clemente, and I can hardly wait to get off the plane. I'm exhausted and would love to head straight for Bay Island, but Bob wants to check out the Cotton house before the

Nixons arrive. As soon as our bags are transferred, Bob and I take off in a car from the motor pool.

Heavy black clouds hang over the hills in the distance, and by the time we reach San Clemente, it's raining hard. Turning off the main road, Bob proceeds up a long, gravel driveway. We park in the turnaround area near a grove of towering eucalyptus and palm trees. Sharing an umbrella, the two of us scurry over to the entrance. We are so close to the ocean that I can hear the waves breaking.

Nixon's valet, Manolo Sanchez, lets us in. As the heavy, wood front door closes behind us, we cross an inner patio with a tiled fish pond in the center. When we enter the living room on the far side, Bob gives a nod of approval. He likes what he sees, and so do I. Next, we check out the four bedrooms. Each has its own fireplace, and Manolo plans to have the fires lit when the Nixons arrive.

Manolo's wife beams when we walk into the kitchen. The Cuban couple has worked for the Nixon family for years, and they know Bob well through past campaigns. Wiping her hands on her rumpled apron, Fina gives him an enthusiastic hug. Manolo points to two steaks sitting on the counter and says that he will be barbecuing them for the Nixons' dinner.

The phone rings, and Manolo reports that the president's helicopter has just landed at the Coast Guard station next door. The Secret Service will drive them over to the house in a golf cart. Manolo grabs a freshly pressed white jacket, and Fina changes aprons. Taking my arm, Bob walks briskly over to the front door.

"We're outta here!" he calls over his shoulder, as we step outside.

With the windshield wipers set on high, Bob drives slowly down the long driveway and heads toward the freeway. In an hour we'll be at Bay Island, where our children are staying with my parents.

Dinner tonight at #11 is drawn out longer than usual. Knowing that Bob has to leave for Washington the next day, no one wants to break up the gathering. With Mother and Dad seated at either end of the rectangular table, three generations of Hortons jabber away. Empty dessert plates remain in front of us, and a half eaten homemade Bundt cake sits on the sideboard. The leftover leg of lamb and green beans have been put in the refrigerator, and the dirty dishes are in the dishwasher. We talk until 11:00 p.m.

What an extraordinary day.

◆

WHEN I WAKE UP this morning, although I am sad that this special time with Bob is coming to a close, I am excited about our day today. I will be accompanying Bob right up to the time that he boards *Air Force One*.

Everyone is still asleep when the two of us quietly open the kitchen door and slip outside. It's high tide, and I can hear the water lapping against the seawall at the end of the island. The lawn in the middle green is damp with dew.

There is nothing comparable to Bay Island with its twenty-three houses, caretaker's cottage, tennis court, and large flower garden. Separated from the rest of the world by a footbridge, the tiny island is charming, but difficult to access. The residents have to use push carts or golf carts to transport their luggage and groceries. Located at the far end of the island, my parents' house has unobstructed views of the bay. From the front porch, we see up the channel, including the Fun Zone and Balboa Pavilion. From the dining room in the back, we look out on the turning basin, where the afternoon sailboat races take place. Seated at the dinner table, we are treated to fantastic sunsets.

Walking along the cement path, Bob's hard-soled shoes grate against grains of sand. In his business suit, carrying a briefcase in one hand and a garment bag in the other, he looks out of place. Once we reach the motor pool car, Bob throws his bag on the back seat, and we opt to take the ferry to the mainland. The captain is a gangly teenager in torn jeans and a beat-up straw hat. He gives two quick toots on the whistle and closes the gate after the third car. The engines grind as we push away from the dock. When we reach the middle of the channel, I look to my left to catch a final glimpse of Bay Island. At #11, Daddy is raising the American flag. A breeze catches it, and the stars and stripes slowly unfurl.

The morning sun breaks through the clouds as we drive thirty-five miles down the coast to San Clemente. When Manolo welcomes us at the house, he gives an enthusiastic thumbs-up, and Bob responds with a thumbs-up of his own. He's relieved to see that the March weather has warmed up enough for the president to work in the patio, where an open briefcase and some papers have been left scattered on an empty chaise.

"The Boss is up there," Manolo says, pointing to a small turret at one end of the house. "He's on the phone."

Bob excuses himself and heads for an outside staircase, leading up to the hideaway office. Manolo ushers me into the living room, where Pat Nixon, John Ehrlichman, and Adele Rogers are discussing campus unrest.

"I've been meeting with the student body presidents from USC, Stanford, and Cal Tech, among others," John is saying as I walk in. "These guys are bright, capable young men, and I actually think we can ride out this rebellion stuff. The secret here is not to overreact."

When Bob and the president join us, they are both looking at me. "Got your camera, Jo?" Bob asks. He knows that I always have my Kodak Instamatic with me. I enjoy taking photos as much as he enjoys taking home movies.

"Mrs. Cotton would like a picture of the president and the first lady in her home," Bob explains. "We're counting on you."

Counting on me? I rush out to the car to get my camera, but when I see that there are only two pictures left on the roll of film, I panic. *What if they don't turn out?* I return to the living room, where the Nixons are patiently waiting. For the next few minutes, I'm the one issuing orders, suggesting that the president of the United States and the first lady pose by the fish pond in the patio.

"Face the sun," I tell them. "Stand closer together... Now say 'cheese.'"

I concentrate on the lighting and the composition. I like the contrast between his dark blue suit and her three-piece, brown plaid dress. I click twice, and when it's over, I hope that I've done everything right to capture that "Kodak presidential moment."

At 9:30 a.m., two helicopters noisily approach the Coast Guard station next door. While Fina and Manolo wave goodbye from the front door, the president and his entourage cross the driveway and walk over to the waiting choppers. Following Bob, I climb aboard the first one. As soon as the Nixons take their seats, the blades start to rotate, and we slowly rise from the pad. Suddenly, the helicopter starts to vibrate wildly. Banking to the right, it hovers only a few feet above the ocean. Like everyone else, I instinctively lean to the left, desperately trying to compensate for the severe tilt. The shaking continues for about thirty seconds, which seems like an eternity.

"If it weren't for the honor of riding in this presidential helicopter, I would be making the trip by car," Henry Kissinger mumbles when we return to the pad.

The second attempt to take off goes smoothly, and twenty minutes later, there's an audible sigh of relief when we put down at El Toro Marine Base. Next to us, *Air Force One* looks big and *safe*.

Pat Nixon joins Bob and me as we walk over to a crowd of supporters, who are standing behind a wire fence at the far end of the field. Pat wants to speak to my parents, who are here to drive me back to Bay Island. When it's time for Bob to board, it's hard to say goodbye. Facing another indefinite separation, we exchange a hug and kiss. Then he's gone.

It's Called the Watergate

O N MARCH 28, FIVE days after Bob returns to Washington, he calls late at night from Camp David. Dwight Eisenhower died today, and I'm anxious to hear what Bob has to report.

He speaks hesitatingly. "It's been a tough day for the president...I was with him in the Oval Office when he got the news...about Ike's death... He was pretty choked up."

"That's got to be rough on you, too," I say, moved by Bob's description.

"It has been hard," Bob agrees. "The president's sentimental, you know. He even broke down and cried. It was pretty awkward, but he feels better now that he's at Camp David. Mamie says it was Ike's favorite place."

April–May 1969

TIME DRAGS OVER THE next couple of months. The war continues to be the biggest issue in the news, and the North Vietnamese army launches a small but savage attack into South Vietnam. In Santa Barbara, the oil slick starts to cause major problems, and drilling is suspended. Governor Ronald Reagan dispatches the National Guard to Berkeley after students clash with the police over "People's Park." Convicted of assassinating Senator Robert F. Kennedy, Sirhan Sirhan is sentenced to death.

I miss Bob. Normally, he's a great help around the house, and there's a lot to do to get ready for our move. Relying on long-distance phone calls, we do our best to make decisions together. In order to keep track of all that I need to accomplish, I make a large chart on a roll of shelf paper and tape it to the kitchen wall. At the top, I write, "JO'S JOBS" in capital letters. Under it are several categories: List Home, Buy Home, Schools, College, Moving

Company, Utilities, and Dogs. Some of these I can quickly check off; others will take longer.

June 1969

SUSAN'S GRADUATION FROM MARLBOROUGH School is a happy diversion. Bob makes a point of being home for the event, and we host the Father-Daughter Tea Dance that follows. All thoughts of Washington fade as I watch our seventeen-year-old daughter and her father dance an old-fashioned fox trot. It's a poignant moment.

No sooner do I start catching up on things here at home than there are problems with the contractor in Chevy Chase. We keep hitting snags, and I'm anxious to have everything completed in three months when the children make the move. Mother is a big help. Not only does she have a decorator's license, but she agrees to come to Washington with Hank and me at the end of the month.

As a summer boarder at St. Albans, his new school, Hank will undergo a rigorous six-week course in English grammar. In the meantime, Mother and I plan to spend one week with Bob in his new two-bedroom apartment. The recently completed complex overlooks the Potomac and is a convenient commute to the White House. Several members of the Nixon cabinet live here, as well as Rose Mary Woods.

It's called the Watergate.

When Bob leaves for work each morning, a White House driver takes Mother and me out to Chevy Chase, where we spend our days looking at paint chips, swatches of fabric, carpet samples, and wallpaper books. The residential area of Kenwood is picturesque with its meandering stream and lush cherry trees lining the streets. The lawn in front of our home on Chamberlin Avenue has been freshly mowed, and the dogwood trees and azalea bushes are in full bloom.

Before we return to California, Bob invites Hank, Mother, and me for dinner on his new patio. When we arrive at his office, Bob's secretary informs us that he's in with the president. It's a balmy evening, and we wait outside on the small terrace, which is completely enclosed by bushes and the canopy of a large walnut tree. A garden table has been set for four; opposite it, birds flutter down to drink from a birdbath. The setting is serene, with the exception of the cicadas. Their buzzing is so loud it makes it hard to carry on a conversation.

As soon as Bob joins us, a navy steward from the White House Mess appears. Taking our dinner orders, the young man is so formal, he appears to be standing at attention the entire time. The food is simple and somewhat bland, but eating al fresco in this hidden patio at the White House is beyond anything I ever imagined.

As we are scraping up the last crumbs of our mocha angel food cake, a movement inside Bob's office catches our attention. "Good grief, it's the president," Bob says. "But what's he wearing?" Leaning forward to get a closer look through the window, he exclaims, "It's a smoking jacket! I didn't even recognize him."

"Does the president often work late?" Mother asks.

"No," Bob replies, looking concerned. "Actually, I have no idea what he's doing in my office at this time of night." Pushing back his chair, he stands. "I'd better go and check. Be right back."

Mother, Hank, and I watch in fascination as the shadowy forms of the president and Bob move into the Oval Office. When we can't see them anymore, we continue our conversation in low tones.

Half an hour later, Bob returns and apologizes. "I'm sorry. The president was in one of his pensive moods and wouldn't stop talking." He pauses. "Of course, he had no idea that all of you were out here. He just assumed that I was working late."

Why didn't Bob just tell the president that he was having dinner with his family? Mother looks over at me but doesn't say anything. She doesn't have to, I know what's going through her mind. She has the same question I do.

◆

PRESIDENT NIXON ANNOUNCES THAT the US will withdraw twenty-five thousand soldiers from Vietnam as part of his program of "Vietnamization." Georges Pompidou is elected president of France, succeeding Charles de Gaulle. In an apartment in London, Judy Garland is found dead.

When I return to California, my life feels fragmented. I have a husband, a son, and a home in Washington, as well as three children, four dogs, and a home in Los Angeles. In Kenwood, the painter is delaying my tight schedule, and in Hancock Park, I'm dealing with termites.

The Nixons have bought the Cotton estate, where they plan to spend most of the summer. This is good news for the children and me. It means that Bob will be able to stay with us when our family is at Bay Island.

July 1969

THE FOURTH OF JULY provides us with a wonderful opportunity to be with the extended family at Bay Island. Each year, Hortons and Haldemans gather at #11 to celebrate the occasion. While everyone helps with the decorations and the food, Bob's contribution is homemade peach ice cream.

Two blockbuster news events take place this month. On July 19, Senator Ted Kennedy drives his car off a bridge into the water on the island of Chappaquiddick. He leaves the scene, and his female companion drowns. The next day, *Apollo 11* astronaut Neil Armstrong becomes the first man to set foot on the moon. Reaction to the first is shock and morbid fascination; to the second, wonder and pride.

Susan, Peter, Ann, and I watch the moon landing on live TV. We are spellbound as Armstrong steps out of the lunar module and declares, "That's one small step for man, one giant leap for mankind." Bob watches in the Oval Office with the president and *Apollo 8* astronaut Frank Borman.

When the astronauts return to Earth four days later, Bob is with the president on the USS *Hornet*, witnessing the splashdown somewhere in the middle of the Pacific Ocean. From there, they continue on an around-the-world tour, visiting Guam, Djakarta, Bangkok, South Vietnam, New Delhi, Lahore, and Romania. President Nixon is the first American president ever to visit a Communist country, and the tour is proclaimed a great success. Bob's first words on his return are, "I'm pooped."

H. R. H. His Royal Highness

August 1969

OUR HOME IN Los Angeles has sold and is in escrow. Susan is getting ready to attend Stanford; Hank completes summer school at St. Albans; Peter returns from camp in Colorado; and Ann is mad at me. In packing for the move, I gave away the stuffed elephant collection that her father gave her when he was on the campaign trail in 1960. All four children are anxious to get out of this cluttered house and move to #11 Bay Island for the month.

From the outside, my parents' blue and white Cape Cod summer home looks deceptively small for having six bedrooms and six baths. The cozy L-shaped living room is decorated in bright blues and yellows. Sliding glass doors open onto a large front porch. It's a place where nothing ever seems to change. Other than a coat of paint every ten years, #11 and its furnishings remain the same. Even the summer routine is totally predictable.

Every Friday around noon, my mother and father arrive from Los Angeles and park in the garage on the peninsula. Loading up the family's tomato-red golf cart with their suitcases and groceries, they drive across the bridge onto the island. After getting settled, my parents spend much of their time sitting on the front porch. Daddy also enjoys tinkering with his thirty-one-foot power boat, while Mom gets out her canvasses and oils to paint scenes around the island. On Monday mornings, the two of them return to their home in West Los Angeles, where my father goes into his law office three days a week.

On Saturday, August 9, President and Mrs. Nixon arrive in California for what is being billed as a "working vacation." While they are transported by helicopter to the new Western White House, Bob joins us at #11, which has been thoroughly checked out by the Army Signal Corps and Secret Service. The island and the footbridge have been declared "secure," and three phones with direct lines to the White House switchboard have been installed.

The American flag waves from the flagpole at the side of the house. Bob's suitcase lies open on the bed in our downstairs bedroom, and in the living room a long white cord snakes its way out to the White House phone on the front porch. The chief of staff is in residence, and we all feel the excitement.

Monday is Bob's first day of commuting to the Western White House. Wearing a blue-and-white-striped seersucker suit, he joins me for breakfast on the porch. The morning sunlight reflects off his small American flag lapel pin.

The air is still, and the bay is glassy smooth. Seagulls screech and dive, as they follow a live bait boat out the channel. An eighteen-foot US Coast Guard boat cruises toward the island, slowly passing a sleepy-eyed pelican perched on a buoy.

"Here's my ride," Bob says, watching as two young men in immaculate white uniforms expertly dock the boat. After wrapping the bow line around a cleat, one stands at attention while the other remains seated at the wheel.

Grabbing his suit jacket and briefcase, Bob gives me a kiss and strides out to the dock. The gold monogram on the briefcase glints in the bright sunshine. "H. R. H." Harry Robbins Haldeman. *Or, perhaps, His Royal Highness…* I smile. Both Coast Guard men salute as Bob steps on board. They cast off, and the boat slowly moves away from the dock. From his seat in the stern, Bob turns to wave to me, as well as neighbors who have come out from their houses to see what's going on.

A few feet from the dock, the driver suddenly accelerates, and Bob is thrown off balance. With its siren wailing, the boat flies across the bay, breaking the strictly enforced five-mile-an-hour speed limit. A rough wake creates havoc for other boats. The sleepy-eyed pelican spreads his wings and takes flight.

This evening, after the Coast Guard delivers Bob home again, he quickly changes into faded blue shorts and a madras shirt. With a bowl of Fritos and a beer, he pauses at the round table in the living room where Hank and Peter are playing a game of Risk.

"That was some commute this morning, Dad," Hank comments, as Peter moves his armies on the board and captures Kamchatka.

"Well, that was the first and the last of it," Bob says. "I told the Coast Guard they're to stick to the speed limit." He takes a swallow of beer. "And no sirens!"

The boys and I exchange glances. *Might there be a slight chance that their father actually enjoyed being "His Royal Highness" for a few minutes this morning?*

The Presidents' Men

A HEAVY FOG CREEPS across the bay on Saturday morning, August 16. As I lie in bed, I hear the low, deep calls of the foghorn in the distance. The president is golfing this weekend, and Bob has both today and tomorrow off. Although this trip has been billed as a "working vacation," he hasn't had much time off. Even when he's here with us, the White House switchboard is always able to reach him. The fog lifts after breakfast, and I find Bob reading on the front porch. A long cord stretches from the living room to a white phone under his chaise.

He looks up. "Jo, we need to talk."

We need to talk. These are the same words that Bob used when we went for that unforgettable sail last summer. Dragging a chaise over to him, I'm curious to hear what he has to say.

Bob puts down his book. "It's been seven months since I started working at the White House, and by now, you have a pretty good idea what my job's all about. You've also been exposed to some of the hardships that go along with it."

I nod in agreement, thinking of the president's demands on him and Bob's long working hours, lack of a vacation, cut in salary, and separation from the family. On the other hand, this is a once-in-a-lifetime experience, which far outweighs any of the negatives.

Bob shifts positions and continues, "When you and the kids are living in Washington, I want Sundays to be family time. I've asked Larry to set those days aside on my calendar so we can—"

The white phone rings, catching Bob in mid-sentence. His left hand drops down, and he fumbles for the receiver. While he listens, his right fingers drum on the arm of the chaise. Looking annoyed, he issues a slew of directives in an irritated tone.

"Jeez, Larry, how many times do I have to tell you? All you've gotta do is to come up with a sandy beach, and it's gotta have privacy. There must be *someone* around who can take care of this for the president. It doesn't take a whole lot of brains to get this staffed out, you know."

I don't like hearing Bob talk like this to his young assistant. Bob prides himself on the efficient way he manages things, but his manner can be harsh and demeaning. In advertising, his secretary described him as an "exacting but fair taskmaster." I assume he runs the White House that same precise way, but from what I'm seeing, he's becoming more demanding and less sensitive. Larry worked for Bob at J. Walter Thompson; consequently, he's used to Bob's way of operating. Fortunately, Larry seems to take the criticism in stride and appears to remain devoted to him.

Bob hangs up and pushes the phone back under the chaise. His annoyed expression vanishes, and his tone changes. He continues our conversation exactly where he left off. "We can have family dinner on Sunday nights. I'll barbecue steaks or chicken and make a Caesar salad. I've been—"

The phone rings again. For a second time, Bob's arm goes down, and the white receiver comes up. "Look, Ron," he says, using the same belittling tone with the press secretary. "The president needs his privacy. That means no media when he goes swimming. Got it? *No* media. Handling the press is your job, remember? Larry's job is to staff out a beach with no rocks. It can't be any clearer than that."

I'm uncomfortable listening to Bob berate Ron, and I resent the white phone with its long cord running along the porch. It connects Bob to this other world; it's his "umbilical cord."

The conversation ends, and once again, Bob returns to me. "As you know, Jo, I've been putting in ridiculously long hours at the White House. But when you and the kids move, I don't want work to interfere with my time with the family. That time together is important. And I've made it clear to my staff that they should get home at a reasonable hour each night."

"I'm sure their wives appreciate that," I say.

"Also, I wanted to talk to you about our routine at home. Unless you need me to take part in the usual social events, I'd prefer to avoid them. I don't want to feel pressured to attend school functions, neighborhood parties, and church every Sunday." Bob pauses to apply ChapStick to his lips. "I hope that's okay with you."

"Don't worry," I assure him. "I can handle all of that on my own."

When I ask about entertaining, Bob surprises me by saying that he's interested in having occasional, small dinner parties, which would include other members of the White House staff. He tells me that we will have many opportunities to attend various White House functions.

Reaching under his chaise, Bob pulls out a book, *The Presidents' Men*. "Patrick Anderson has written about the careers of White House assistants since FDR," he says. "After reading about how their commitment took such a toll on their families, I realize how much is going to fall on your shoulders."

"Look, Bob, you don't have to worry about me," I interject. "The children and I are really lucky to have a father and a husband who has such an incredible job. I mean it. You're the one who deserves our full support." Our eyes meet. "You don't have to tell me how hard your job is. But it's for the highest cause, and the whole thing will be over in eight years at the most."

"It's just that I think we should go into this with our eyes wide open," Bob says, putting the book back under the chaise.

"We are. You've thought of everything, and I'm not worried. If something should come up, the two of us can handle it. We've got our wonderful family... and, more importantly, we have our faith." I pause. "Would it help if I read Anderson's book?"

"No!" he answers emphatically. "It's pretty dry...not your sort of thing."

The following morning, everyone is up and out early. It's quiet, with the exception of the steady clink of a halyard hitting against the metal mast of the neighbor's sailboat. With a twinge of guilt, I take *The Presidents' Men* from the nightstand and curl up in one of the wing chairs in the living room. Scanning the pages, I make a note of every reference to a presidential aide that I can find.

> The aide must be willing to be used as a political lightning rod to draw criticism away from the president...

> The aide will almost certainly develop an enemy or two among his fellow staff members, his rivals in the harem...

> The aide must be willing to subject himself to another man's interests, to accept another man's decisions, to run another man's errands, to be permanently number-two...

> The president, when he leaves office, has at least been president; the assistant, when he leaves, has been—what? A man who stood in the shadows of power, who played

a mysterious role in a complicated process, a man who got little credit for his successes and ample blame for his mistakes, a man who will seem a braggart if he seeks credit, but whose good works will soon be forgotten if he does not…

A president's trusted aide can attain power and glory, but the power is precarious, and the glory may become tinged with notoriety, for there are many dangers inherent in his position. The scrutiny of the press will magnify both the aide's virtues and his faults…

As the aide departs from the White House, bloody but not quite bowed, he must watch with envy as the new president's team marches in—crisp, confident, eager to clean up the mess in Washington, to get the country moving again…

Patrick Anderson doesn't paint a very pretty picture, and I can understand why Bob doesn't want me to read the book. As I look at the list of pitfalls, however, I don't see how most of them would apply to him. I can't imagine his ever being "scrutinized" by the press or striving for power and glory. I'm sure if there were even a hint of a scandal or any misconduct, he would deal with it openly and impersonally.

Stretching, I close the book and return it to the nightstand.

◆

AT LONG LAST, THAT time has come. It's the last week in August, and I'm standing alone in our empty house on Muirfield Road. A hazy sun casts elongated shadows on an enormous Allied moving van as it negotiates the turn at the bottom of the driveway. Its cavernous interior holds everything we own.

Groping for a handkerchief wadded up in the pocket of my grubby Levi's, I wipe away a tear. This forty-two-year-old house, with its weathered shingles and six large white columns, is an odd combination of elegance and funkiness, but for four and a half years, it has been our home. I'm sad that we had to sell it. Living here has been a wonderful period in our lives, and I linger just long enough to say goodbye.

Jo and Bob Haldeman at a White House state dinner, April 10, 1970.
Photo by Ollie Atkins, White House Photographer

PART TWO

THE WHITE HOUSE

Super Non

September 1969

THE EARLY MORNING AIR on Thursday, September 4, is hot and oppressive. The pungent scent of boxwood surrounds me, and I take deep breaths. I associate the fragrance with having lived in the East many years ago, and I love it. Standing at my post at the front door of 5330 Chamberlin Avenue in Chevy Chase, Maryland, I watch a large black and orange moving van pull up and park at the curb. As furniture pours out, I call out where each item goes. The sun rises higher, and the humidity becomes almost unbearable. Sweating, I worry about Non, who insists on making up all ten of the beds.

At noon, a station wagon stops in front of the house, and Jeanne Ehrlichman climbs out. Carrying a large picnic basket, she surprises us with lunch.

"Since moving to Washington, I feel like Cinderella," she tells us as she unpacks fried chicken and homemade brownies. "I spend half my days in grubby work clothes—concentrating on the children, the house, and the garden. Then at night, I live like royalty. A White House car picks me up and whisks me off to join John at a black tie dinner at some embassy. When I get there, I'm still trying to get the dirt out from under my fingernails."

The Ehrlichmans bought a home in Great Falls, Virginia, at the time of the inauguration. Jeannie has been living here for eight months, and I hang on her every word. It's hard to believe that I, too, will soon be attending functions at embassies and the White House.

In the meantime, Non and I work to get the house in order. Bob's mother is a tiger. She works nonstop each day until I tell her it's time to quit. On Sunday night, when it's time to leave for a celebratory dinner, I can't find her anywhere.

After calling her name and knocking on her door, I step inside her room. A yellow linen dress is carefully laid out on the bed, tan Ferragamo shoes are placed side by side on the floor, and a gold charm bracelet is spread out on the dresser. The only place left is the bathroom, where at last I find her. Super Non has fallen sound asleep in the bathtub.

Monday, September 8, is move-in day for the Haldeman family, and the first to arrive are our four dogs. After boarding at the White House kennel for the past week, our Dalmatian and three pugs excitedly explore their new home. Each has a bed in the kitchen, and a new doggy door opens into the backyard.

In the late afternoon, I eagerly await the children's arrival. A meatloaf is in the oven, and tapioca is cooling on the kitchen counter. Non bustles in and out of the rooms, making a final inspection. Finally, a sleek black Mercury sedan turns the corner and stops at our front walk. Without waiting for the White House driver to open the doors, Susan, Hank, Peter, and Ann spill out. Dropping their bags in the entry, the children start to look around. Before I know it, Ann has let the dogs out of the kitchen, and bedlam ensues. With four dogs and four children going in every direction, it's as if we have always lived here.

Camp David

NON RETURNS TO CALIFORNIA, and life with Bob settles into a routine. Every weekday morning, a White House car arrives at exactly 7:15 a.m. to get him. Larry Higby and Dwight Chapin are already in the car, and the three of them use the twenty-minute commute to the White House to review their daily schedules. At night, Bob returns home about 7:30 p.m.

At forty-two, Bob is managing the largest White House staff in history. He has three aides in his personal office, as well as three secretaries. Eight other White House aides report directly to him. Bob has already established a reputation for running a tight ship. At 8:15 a.m., he has a White House staff meeting, followed by a one-on-one meeting with the president in the Oval Office. The two meet again at the end of the day.

Meanwhile, my focus is on the children and their schools. Susan doesn't leave for Stanford until September 22, but the other children start this week with a combination of orientation programs and classes. Hank is a junior at St. Albans, Peter is in the seventh grade at Sidwell Friends, and Ann is a fifth grader at National Cathedral School. Filling out the many registration forms, I am self-conscious about writing "The President" as Bob's employer and "The White House" as his place of employment.

◆

ON THURSDAY, SEPTEMBER 18, Bob spends the day in New York with the president. When he returns home, it's late, and I'm in bed, reading. His footsteps are heavy as he comes up the stairs. Putting down my book, I watch as he wearily removes his tie and pulls off his shoes and socks.

"The president's going to Camp David this weekend," he says. "Do you and the children wanna go?"

"My gosh," I say, trying to grasp what Bob just said. "Are you kidding? We'd love to go."

"This will be a good time for you to see the place. I'll be going by chopper with the Nixons. Are you okay driving with the kids?"

"Of course. That won't be a problem."

I try to read my book, but my mind is spinning. *We are going to Camp David. Just the president, the first lady...and us...*

The next afternoon, we are on our way. After driving through the Maryland countryside for about an hour, we come to Catoctin Mountain Park. As the road starts to twist and turn, we are sure that Camp David can't be much further.

Susan spots the simple wood sign, which is virtually camouflaged by trees. Making a right turn, I follow a paved road through the woods for about a mile. Arriving at an unpretentious guardhouse, we find two marines splendidly attired in full dress uniform. They snap to attention the minute our dirty station wagon comes to a stop. Rolling down the window, I'm embarrassed to have them see how scruffy I look in my jeans and sneakers.

A marine steps forward and salutes. "Welcome to Camp David, ma'am." His words are as crisp as his appearance. "Mr. Haldeman is with the president right now. He will be joining you later for dinner."

Bending slightly, to prevent creasing his pressed jacket, the young man hands each of us a map. Pointing to a cluster of small, dark rectangles with his white-gloved finger, he says, "You and your family will be berthed in Sycamore, Linden, and Walnut. All meals will be served at Laurel."

A jeep appears in front of us, and I'm told to follow it to our cabins. Deep shade makes it impossible to see past the trees on either side of the road. Patches of sunlight, breaking through the heavy fall foliage, provide glimpses of the staff barracks, a playing field, a volleyball net, and a tennis court. Eventually, the jeep stops in front of three plain wood cabins, whose sizes vary from small to tiny.

There are fifteen cabins at Camp David, each named after a tree. Bob and I are assigned to Sycamore, which is slightly larger than the others. Stepping inside, I find myself in a living room, engulfed in red birds. The curtains, upholstered furniture, and wallpaper are all covered in a print featuring exotic red birds with long tails. The pattern seems too sophisticated for the simple room with its window air conditioner, gurgling radiator, and open bottle of Airwick.

In the bedroom, two navy blue windbreakers are spread out on the twin beds, and I can't resist trying on the smaller one. Looking at myself in the mirror above the dresser, I instinctively straighten up to better show off the round Camp David patch on the right side.

A note from Bob propped up in the corner of the mirror suggests that I select a movie. Thumbing through a black three-ring notebook, I find that the movie choices are limited and cater to Camp David's all-male staff. The movie I choose is an innocuous comedy, starring Bob Hope.

The screen door slams, and Susan, Hank, Peter, and Ann burst into the room. "Let's get going," Hank says. "I want to check out the rest of this place."

Looking around, I have to laugh. All five of us are wearing "our" Camp David jackets.

At Laurel, we are greeted in the living room by Commander Dettbarn of the US Navy. After welcoming us "aboard," he points to a collection of red Schwinn bicycles and suggests that we go for a ride before dinner. The fall colors are vibrant as we pedal along an asphalt road through the woods. At the perimeter of the camp, the road ends abruptly and the scene changes. A barbed wire fence runs along the property line, and soldiers in battle fatigues peer down at us from a raised sentry station. Without saying anything, the children and I turn around.

Back at Laurel, two stewards in red Camp David blazers take drink orders and pass *hors d'oeuvres*. Larry and his wife, Dolores, are here, and they recommend the toasted tortilla chips with melted cheese and green chili, which were a favorite of President Johnson.

Bob joins us at 7:00 p.m., just as dinner is announced. He has changed out of his coat and tie into khaki pants and a sweater. The wood-paneled dining room with its royal blue carpet and stone fireplace is inviting. China is displayed on a hutch against the wall, and the large oval table in the center of the room is covered with a bright red tablecloth. At each of the eight place settings, there's a blue menu with a gold tassel and a white linen napkin, folded to look like a chrysanthemum blossom. Ann doesn't want to unfold hers and asks if she can take it home.

Our choice of entrée is lobster, steak, or chicken, followed by a dessert of big, gooey pieces of chocolate cake. The instant we finish, the stewards begin rearranging the captains' chairs from the table. They pull back shutters to expose a movie projector recessed in the wall, and in front of the opposite wall, they set up a screen. Large bowls of hot, buttered popcorn are brought in, and the lights are dimmed. The children groan when I tell them what movie I selected, but we stick with it to the bitter end.

The next morning, Bob and I are awakened by our porch door banging closed as a steward delivers our newspapers. On our way to Laurel, I collect some of the brightly colored leaves that carpet the ground. Bob walks beside me, clutching *The Washington Evening Star*, *The New York Times*, and *The Washington Post*.

At breakfast, the steward tries to hide a smile when I order banana pancakes, bacon, hash browns, fried eggs, and coffee. While eating, Bob and I read the papers. The war dominates the news. An article on the upcoming lottery for the draft causes my stomach to churn. Hank turns sixteen next month, which means that he could be called up in two years. I dread the thought of it. *What if he is sent to Vietnam? I don't know what I would do.*

With perfect fall weather, the children and I have a wonderful weekend. We swim in the large staff pool, ride bikes, bowl, and play tennis and croquet. Bob joins us when he can. When we're packing to leave on Sunday, I ask if he wants me to drive him in one of the golf carts to the helicopter for the flight back to the White House. His answer is an emphatic "no."

"The president and first lady should never be aware of staff or their families when they're at Camp David," he tells me. "It's the one place where they can be completely on their own. You've got to understand this, Jo…and respect it."

Things Are Never Going to Be the Same

WHEN WE RETURN HOME Sunday evening, Susan packs for Stanford. Sitting on the guest bed in Susan's room, Ann watches every move her big sister makes. As I enter the room with a mound of clean laundry, Ann wistfully remarks, "Things are never going to be the same." Although the two girls are eight years apart, I know this separation will be a real adjustment for our younger daughter.

Later when I go upstairs to say Ann's prayers, I find her talking to Bob in his office.

"Things are never going to be the same, Dad," she says.

Bob puts down his pen. Looking her straight in the eye, he replies, "You're absolutely right." The words aren't cold or cruel. He speaks the truth, and there's strength in his honesty. Ann appears satisfied.

◆

THE NEXT MORNING—AT exactly 7:15 a.m.—a White House car pulls up to the front walk. Carrying his briefcase, Bob strides out. Twenty-five minutes later, a green Mustang convertible stops at the same spot. Our neighbor Harry C. has offered to drive Hank, Peter, and Ann, along with his own son, to school on his way to work. He has assured Bob and me that taking our children won't be an imposition.

A couple hours later, Susan loads her suitcase into the car, and we depart for Dulles. After putting her on a flight to California, I return home to an empty house. *Ann was right. "Things are never going to be the same."*

◆

AS CHIEF OF STAFF of the White House, Bob is required to have a "secure" home, and Mr. Sherman of the Secret Service insists on installing a full-fledged security system. Arriving promptly at 9:30 a.m., on September 26, he has an army of men with him. Dressed in dark suits and ties, they immediately fan out and begin testing locks, raising windows, opening doors, and taking Polaroid pictures.

Close to noon, the men gather around the kitchen table to compare their research. Following a lengthy discussion, Mr. Sherman tells me that our house has too many outside doors for them to provide us with complete security.

"Your best protection, ma'am, is your dogs."

"Our dogs!" I exclaim, glancing at the three pugs snoring in their beds. Pokie, our Dalmatian, is stretched out under the kitchen table. "You can't be serious."

Mr. Sherman looks helpless and shrugs.

Over the next few days, the Secret Service installs the best security system they can under the circumstances. The following week, the Army Signal Corps installs seven phones with multiple lines. One line connects directly to the White House switchboard, and one to the Signal Corps. The third is our personal line, and the fourth is an intercom. The fifth button is for "hold." Additionally, a heavy "portable" phone is bolted to the floor of our station wagon between the driver and front passenger seats. It's green, and it looks like something that the army would use in war. I don't dare touch it.

◆

LATE THIS MONTH, I get an unexpected phone call from the Greyhound bus station in the District. A former housekeeper of ours has traveled across the country, hoping to work for us again. I'm surprised and delighted. As part housekeeper, cook, laundress, and babysitter, Bertha is just what I need.

Our family loves Bertha. She's devoted to us, but she has one major drawback: Bertha is a "bull in a china shop." In her first week, not only does she accidentally ram the handle of the vacuum cleaner through our most valuable painting, but in her zest for cleanliness, she also uses a solvent that removes the finish on our kitchen floor.

On the other hand, Bertha is a good cook and we love her Mexican dinners. As soon as I hear the rhythmic cadence of her hands patting mounds of *masa* into homemade tortillas, I can easily overlook her faults.

Shades of Gray

October 1969

ALTHOUGH AN OPINION POLL indicates that well over half the country approves of President Nixon's Vietnam policy, the antiwar organizers make plans for a "Moratorium to End the War on Vietnam," with events to be held around the country on the fifteenth of every month. The first rally is scheduled for October 15. In Washington, a huge demonstration is expected on the National Mall, which stretches from the Lincoln Memorial to the Capitol. Vice President Agnew lambastes the demonstrators as Communist "dupes" and calls opponents of the war "an effete corps of impudent snobs who characterize themselves as intellectuals." North Vietnam's prime minister encourages the protestors in a letter: "...may your offensive succeed splendidly."

The National Mall isn't far from the White House, and it's only a few miles from the children's schools. Hank, Peter, and Ann haven't been exposed to anything like this before, and I worry that they might get swept up in all of the excitement and rhetoric. I envision lots of disrespectful hippies who smoke pot and use drugs.

Because she is younger, Ann will probably be minimally affected; however, I am concerned about the boys. At twelve and almost sixteen, Peter and Hank are at impressionable ages. I also worry about Susan. Stanford has been referred to as a "hotbed of liberals," and I'm not sure what effect the Moratorium will have on her.

I'd like to get Bob's advice on the situation; he is invariably levelheaded. The only problem is I never know if he's going to have the time to talk, and even when he does, he often only half-listens. I devise a system. I write a note telling him what I want to discuss and put it in with his mail. This way, he can tell me when he's available, and I can have his full attention.

Tonight, Bob glances at my note but doesn't acknowledge it. I try to keep myself occupied while he goes through the mail and places several phone calls. First, it's the president. Then, Attorney General John Mitchell. The last call to Larry is the longest. When he hangs up and turns to me, I comment that I'm probably the only wife who has to make an appointment to speak to her husband.

He laughs, but I'm serious. When I have Bob's full attention, I express my concerns about the children and the upcoming Moratorium. He says he's not worried, as long as they don't show signs of rebelling or taking drugs.

"There's always going to be something going on that we don't like," he explains. "That's life, Jo. We have to trust our kids. We've prepared them to make good decisions. They might make a few mistakes, but in the end, they'll be fine."

Bob is right. Although the Moratorium is the largest protest in the history of the antiwar movement, it doesn't appear to have any negative impact on Susan, Hank, Peter, or Ann. Throughout the United States, diverse groups of people come together and peacefully demonstrate their opposition to the war.

◆

ON WEDNESDAY EVENING, OCTOBER 22, President and Mrs. Nixon entertain members of the White House staff and their families at an all-American picnic on the South Lawn. Despite the freezing cold and biting wind, the 2,500 guests are in a festive mood. They patiently wait in long lines to help themselves to hot dogs and hamburgers served inside two huge tents.

After dinner, we huddle on bleachers to keep warm as the US Marine Corps drill team entertains us. Wearing dress blues, one hundred Vietnam veterans present the colors and go through their precise drills and marches. I'm bursting with pride and patriotism. *Our soldiers deserve our respect. If only the antiwar demonstrators understood this. Everyone wants peace. It's just that we don't agree on how to get it. The protestors want the United States to walk away from all that we have fought for in the past. The president wants to phase out our troops and achieve a peace with honor.*

Suddenly the lights dim, and everything is quiet. We sit in darkness. A single marine emerges from the shadows into the penetrating beam of a spotlight. He walks to the center of the lawn. He wears camouflage fatigues and his battle helmet. With the lighted Washington Monument behind him, the young man slowly raises a bugle to his lips and plays "Taps." The twenty-four soulful notes hang suspended in the night air, as if they were mourning those who have given their lives to preserve our freedom.

The bugle cries, and so do I.

November 1969

TONIGHT, NOVEMBER 3, THE president will address the nation on Vietnam. Sixty million Americans wait to hear what he has to say. The atmosphere is tense, and our country is divided. The doves hope that the Moratorium has pressured Nixon into announcing troop withdrawals. The hawks insist on an "honorable" peace. I can only imagine the anxiety Bob must be experiencing in the West Wing right now.

Hank turns on the TV in the den, and I settle on the couch with a pad and a pencil to take notes. At exactly 9:30 p.m., Nixon appears on the screen. Seated at his desk in the Oval Office, he's wearing a dark blue suit with a small American flag in the lapel. In a firm, steady voice, he states that the US will keep its commitment. Our troops will remain in Vietnam until the Communists negotiate an honorable peace or until the South Vietnamese are able to defend themselves. The president reaches out to the young people and tells them that he respects their idealism and shares their desire for peace. He appears confident, and his tone is presidential.

"So tonight," Nixon concludes, "to you, the great silent majority of my fellow Americans, I ask for your support.... Let us be united for peace. Let us also be united against defeat. Because let us understand: North Vietnam cannot defeat or humiliate the United States. Only Americans can do that."

When it's over, I realize that I'm gripping the arm of the couch. Hank doesn't move. It was a strong speech. Both he and I are moved by its clarity and impact. The phone rings, and the White House button lights up. The operator tells me that Mr. Haldeman is on the line.

"Wasn't the president terrific?" Bob sounds ecstatic. "What'd you think?"

I'm amazed that Bob wants to hear my reaction, and I read my notes to him. He listens attentively and agrees with most of my comments. He tells me that he plans to make follow-up calls to get feedback on the general reaction around the country. He won't be home until after midnight.

Fired up by Bob's interest in my opinion, I impulsively crush my notes into a tight ball and aim for the wastebasket across the room. The wad of paper arcs high in the air and drops in.

"Two points," I say under my breath. "Tonight, I score!"

The next day, thirty thousand letters and fifty thousand telegrams pour into the White House. They are overwhelmingly favorable, and Nixon's approval rating rises to 68 percent in the Gallup Poll. To quote the press, "The great 'silent majority' has spoken."

◆

ON THURSDAY, NOVEMBER 13, the children and I join Jeanne Ehrlichman and her children on a NASA flight to Florida. Our two families have been invited to witness the *Apollo 12* moon launch the next day at Cape Canaveral.

Bob and John will meet us there at the last minute. With thousands of antiwar protestors pouring into the nation's capital for the second Moratorium on Saturday, they think they should remain in Washington as long as possible. A massive crowd is expected, topping last month's turnout. Emotions are running high, and there is fear of violence. Concerned, Bob decides to spend the night at the White House.

"Where?" I ask. "Your office is so small."

"I can sleep in the bomb shelter in the basement," he explains. "It's not bad. It has a bed and a bathroom...but no windows."

When the children, Jeanne, and I arrive in Cocoa Beach, Florida, our flight is met by a sleek NASA limousine, which transports our families to a seedy motel on the beach. Although ominous, black clouds are closing in above us, the seven children insist on taking a quick swim in the ocean. By evening, a full-fledged thunderstorm engulfs us.

At midnight, following a dinner at NASA where Jeanne and I were seated at the head table, Dr. Thomas Paine, the director of NASA, drives our two families directly onto the *Apollo 12* launchpad. In the darkness, the Saturn V rocket resembles a throbbing monster being held in check as it hisses and lets off steam. In just a few hours, three astronauts will be strapped in their seats in the space capsule, and for the second time in history, man will be on his way to the moon.

On Friday, a thick cloud layer obscures the morning sun, posing a threat to the launch. Adding to the gloominess of the weather is the deep disappointment of our children. For security reasons, they will be watching the liftoff from an office in the Space Center more than a mile away.

Jeanne and I have reserved seats on a small grandstand on the tarmac. When a single, heavy raindrop plops onto the ground, I immediately wonder how this will affect the launch. By the time Bob and John join us, the rain is coming down in torrents. The four of us huddle together under two umbrellas and wait.

Half an hour passes. Then, a man's voice comes over the loudspeaker. The countdown begins. "Five, four, three…" Before he can say "two," a jagged bolt of lightning cuts across the sky directly above the rocket.

"Two," the voice calmly continues. "One. Zero… We have liftoff."

The rocket moves slowly, struggling to gain the tremendous force it needs to break free. When the sound catches up with us, the powerful roar causes the grandstand to tremble. Little puddles of rainwater dance and jiggle on the asphalt below. On the launchpad, the scaffolding collapses, and *Apollo 12* climbs steadily upward. Its mighty roar turns into a deep rumble when it is swallowed up by the low-lying storm clouds. Soon, only a dull glow is left in the leaden sky.

As soon as the launch is over, Bob and John leave to join the president on *Air Force One* for the return flight to Washington. They are concerned about the march that will take place tonight, as well as the demonstration tomorrow. A second car takes Jeanne and me to Patrick Air Force Base, where we board *NASA One* with Dr. and Mrs. Paine and our children. Having seen very little of the rocket liftoff, the children are upset. Shortly after takeoff, their complaints go quiet when a violent thunderstorm surrounds our Gulfstream turbo-prop. There is silence as wild gusts of wind, rain, and hail buffet us on all sides. When one of the children asks for a throw-up bag, Jeanne and I try to reassure everyone by reciting The Lord's Prayer out loud. Unfortunately, this has the opposite effect and only conveys a greater sense of doom.

The skies clear on our approach to Washington. Looking down, I can easily identify the Capitol and many government buildings. It's a beautiful sight, made even more spectacular by a long procession of twinkling lights.

Jo and Bob in Hawaii. 1945.

Jo and Bob's wedding. Los Angeles, February 19, 1949.

Jo and Bob at Bay Island. July 1969.

Ann, Hank, Susan, and Peter at Bay Island. July 1968.

Betty Haldeman (Bob's mother) at the White House. November 1971.

Joe and Adele Horton (Jo's parents) at #11 Bay Island. Summer 1981.

#11 Bay Island, Newport Beach, California.

Susan and Hank at the Republican Convention.
Miami, August 1968.

Richard Nixon, the Republican nominee for president,
with Hank, Hank Mitchel, and Susan. August 1968.

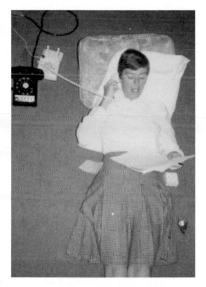

Jo on election night at the Waldorf Astoria. New York, November 5, 1968.

Jo and Bob playing bridge with Carol and Bob Finch on windowless government plane. November 6, 1968.

Bryce Harlow, John Ehrlichman, Bob Finch, and Bob dressed in dark suits for official business in Key Biscayne, Florida. November 1968.

President Nixon's handwritten quote from his first Inaugural Address. Jo's anniversary gift to Bob. February 19, 1969.

Bob being sworn in as Chief of Staff by Chief Justice Earl Warren in the East Room of the White House. January 21, 1969.

Bob with Dwight Chapin and Rose Mary Woods. Key Biscayne, Florida, May 1970.

Ron and Nancy Ziegler on the inaugural flight of the new Air Force One. January 2, 1973.

John Ehrlichman, Henry Kissinger, and Bob wearing their personalized flight jackets aboard Air Force One. March 1969.

Bob and Larry Higby at #11 Bay Island. August 1969.

Bob sailing his Sunfish at Newport Beach.

Jo's photograph of President and Mrs. Nixon.
The patio of the Western White House. San Clemente, March 1969.

Bob's departure from Bay Island via Coast Guard boat on the first leg of his
commute to the Western White House. August 1969.

*Susan, Hank, Peter, and Ann wearing
Camp David jackets at the bowling alley.
Camp David, September 1969.*

*Susan being served hors
d'oeuvres by a Navy steward.
Camp David, June 1970.*

*Non, Ann, and Peter eating lunch on the terrace of the President's cabin, Aspen.
Camp David, May 1970.*

*Ann in Sycamore cabin
with its red bird décor.
Camp David,
September 1969.*

*Jo and Bob enjoying hors d'oeuvres with
Larry and Dolores Higby in Laurel cabin.
Camp David, May 1972.*

*John Ehrlichman surrounded by "his harem," Jeanne Ehrlichman,
Nancy Ziegler, and Jo. Camp David, May 1972.*

Peter at the President's desk on the new Air Force One. *1970.*

Susan, Peter, and Ann play cards on windowless back-up plane during cross-country flight. June 1972.

Hank before boarding Jet Star for flight to California. September 1971.

The presidential yacht Sequoia.

Jo and Jeanne Ehrlichman
aboard the Sequoia. *June 1971.*

A White House car delivers the family to a waiting helicopter for the flight to
Williamsburg. March 1971.

Jo at Bob's new custom-built desk.
The West Wing of the White House, February 1970.

Jo, Bob, and Ann at the dress rehearsal of 1776.
The East Room of the White House. February 1970.

Following a rain delay, Jo helps set up chairs for Tricia's wedding in the Rose Garden. The White House, June 12, 1971.

President Nixon dancing with his daughter, the new Mrs. Edward Cox. The White House, June 12, 1971.

The three pugs: Amy, Dottie, and Patsy.

The totaled station wagon. December 1971.

Bertha and Little Oscar. September 1972.

The serpentine line stretches all the way from Arlington Cemetery to the White House.

"It's the march," Tom Ehrlichman says, with his head glued to the window. "They're carrying candles."

NASA One lands at Andrews Air Force Base, where two White House cars wait for the Haldeman and Ehrlichman families. Our driver asks if the children and I would like to drive past the Arlington Memorial Bridge on the way home.

"You'll be able to see the peace march up close, ma'am," he says. "It's quite a sight."

Thinking of Bob in the bomb shelter last night, I ask if we will be safe. Our driver assures us that there won't be a problem.

As we draw near the single-file procession coming across the bridge, our car slows down to keep pace with the demonstrators. I expect to see angry hippies with clenched fists, shouting obscenities. Instead, I observe a great variety of people. There are peace symbols and crosses, colored beads and gold jewelry, tie-dyed T-shirts and button-down oxford cloth shirts, beards and shaved faces, long hair and clipped haircuts. Each face is lit by a flickering candle representing the loss of an American life in Vietnam. The line moves in silence, and all I hear is the muffled sound of shuffling feet.

The impact of the scene is overwhelming. Up until this moment, I have generally viewed life in terms of black and white. I considered the antiwar demonstrators a bunch of hippies whose cause and tactics I did not support. To me, the march was unpatriotic and disruptive; therefore, it must be bad. In contrast, the moon launch was patriotic and unifying; therefore, it must be good. Tonight, however, I see "the hippies" as individual people expressing great sensitivity and compassion. I can no longer define life so simply, and my thinking changes.

Violence is predicted for the Moratorium the following day. Hundreds of paratroopers stand at alert with their rifles loaded, as a crowd of five hundred thousand assembles on the National Mall. Bob reports that when he surveyed the scene from a helicopter, it was "weird" looking down on a barricade of buses cordoning off a two-block area around the White House. The Department of Justice is mobbed. The American flag is torn down and burned. The protestors replace it with the Viet Cong flag—the flag of our enemy.

These acts are despicable, and ordinarily I would have passed harsh judgment on the Moratorium. However, when I read that splinter groups performed the more irreverent acts and that there were fewer arrests than predicted, I have a more reasoned outlook. I recognize that the greater mass of demonstrators was relatively orderly and peaceful.

I now view the protestors in shades of gray.

Antisocial and Nonsocial

December 1969

OB AND I WERE raised as Christian Scientists, and our faith has always been an important part of who we are. I am a new member of the Christian Science Church in Chevy Chase, and the three children are enrolled in the Sunday School. Unless Bob is traveling or working, he goes to church with us.

On Sunday, December 14, Bob suggests that we all attend White House Church, followed by a tour of the redecorated Oval Office. I'm excited about the invitation, but the children prefer to stay home. This isn't the first time this has happened, and I'm annoyed at them for passing up another special opportunity. Today, I fight a losing battle with the two boys and make an enemy of Ann. On a freezing cold morning, I force her to get dressed up and accompany her mother and father to the White House.

As we enter the main hall, the three of us are engulfed in the spirit of Christmas. The six marble columns are decorated with garlands of fresh greens, and the two cut-glass chandeliers give off a warm glow. The red carpet extends the length of the room, where a giant Christmas tree stands at the far end.

Rows of gilded chairs and a raised platform fill the East Room, which will be used for both the church service this morning and the entertainment tonight. Ann and I follow Bob to the last row of chairs, where he points to three seats. Looking at all of the adult heads in front of her, Ann worries that she won't be able to see.

"This is where Dad wants to sit," I tell her. "He likes to remain as inconspicuous as possible."

I don't think our ten-year-old understands the logic in this, but today it doesn't matter anyway. There's not much to see. The highlight of the service is The New York Avenue Presbyterian Church Choir singing Handel's *Messiah*. At the end, everyone stands and joins in a rousing last round of the "Hallelujah Chorus."

After enjoying cookies and punch in the State Dining Room, Ann and I follow Bob along the West Colonnade to the Oval Office. As soon as we step inside, Bob asks what we think of Mrs. Nixon's decorating.

"It's interesting," I say, struck by the intensity of color. The blue rug features a large gold presidential seal, which intensifies the strong gold fabric in the drapes, chairs, and couches. Realizing that I should say more, I quickly add, "The room certainly looks presidential."

The president's massive dark wood desk was once Woodrow Wilson's and was used by Nixon when he served as vice president. A portrait of George Washington by Charles Willson Peale hangs above the fireplace mantle, and Pat Nixon's collection of porcelain Boehm birds is on display in the built-in cabinet by the door.

"The Oval Office should command your respect," Bob says. "And that's what President Nixon wants to achieve."

"Respect," he repeats.

◆

HAVING LIVED IN WASHINGTON for three months, I continue to be amazed at the number and variety of social events that we are asked to attend. Each invitation is hand-addressed in fancy calligraphy to *The Honorable and Mrs. Harry Robbins Haldeman.* I am invited to receptions, teas, weddings, breakfasts, luncheons, and dinners. These are held in private homes, embassies, clubs, churches, various government buildings, and the White House. Tickets are available for symphonies, plays, horse shows, and private movie screenings.

Using Carolyn Shaw's *The Social List of Washington, D.C.,* commonly referred to as *The Green Book,* as my guide to protocol, I bone up on the rules of Washington society. Miss Shaw writes that these rules are of "momentous importance… They are not a social affectation, as many would have you believe… Protocol is, in part, a code prescribing deference to rank, and from this evolves the order of 'who outranks whom' among officials." I discover that I take on Bob's rank when he's not present at an official function.

Many of our friends assume that Bob and I see the Nixons socially, but this simply is not the case. We are not "friends." Although the president and Bob spend long hours together, it's on a purely professional basis. Nixon knows very little about our family. This is not to say that he's uninterested. His handwritten note to Bob's mother at the time of his father's death was deeply moving, and he generally calls Bob on his birthday and our anniversary.

When the Nixon family was living in California after he served as vice president, Bob and I would occasionally see them at receptions and large dinner parties. Julie babysat for our children a couple of times, and once Bob and I had dinner at their home. It was just the four of us, but even then the conversation was stilted. Nixon is uncomfortable socially and has an aversion to small talk. He's content to rely on little private jokes when he's at parties, and it's obvious that his reference to "my drinking problem" falls into that category.

Bob claims that he, too, is uncomfortable with small talk. He describes himself as "antisocial," because he doesn't like parties, and me as "nonsocial," because I'm ambivalent about them. When he tells me that he dreads the thought of being seated between "two babbling women" at dinner, I don't take him too seriously. On most social occasions, Bob thoroughly enjoys himself, preferring small parties where he knows everyone. Always well-informed, he converses easily on a variety of subjects.

Looking for a way to save Bob from "suffering through" another dinner in the State Dining Room, and yet still enjoy the entertainment afterward, Larry comes up with a plan. He suggests that Bob and I eat in the Housekeeper's Office. Bob is delighted with the idea and decides to try it out at an informal White House dinner honoring Bob Hope.

Bob is working late on Sunday, December 14, so I drive into the White House alone. The guard at the west gate knows me and only glances at my ID. White House drivers give me a wave in the parking lot, and secretaries and staff greet me by name as I walk down the hall. I feel at home.

I meet Bob in his office, and we walk over to the East Room together. Waiting for the Nixons to make their appearance, we mingle with the other guests. When several people gather around Bob, it's obvious that he enjoys being the center of attention. He is charming. Standing off to the side, I observe the group. *How can my husband possibly describe himself as being antisocial?*

When President and Mrs. Nixon arrive with Dolores and Bob Hope, a receiving line is formed in the Blue Room. According to protocol, Bob precedes me in going down the line.

Nixon extends his hand. "Good evening, Bob."

Bob shakes hands. "Good evening, Mr. President."

"Hope you enjoy yourself tonight."

"Yes, sir. I plan to. I'm a big fan of Bob Hope."

A casual observer would never know that these two men spend hours together every day. When it's my turn to greet the president, I know what's coming.

"Good evening, Mr. President."

"Well, well, well. Do you like Bob Hope, too? Just remember to stay sober tonight so you can enjoy his show."

"I'll try, Mr. President." I smile. "I'll try."

When the military social aides announce that dinner is being served, everyone files into the State Dining Room. Instead of following them, Bob and I discreetly head for the stairs. It feels like the two of us are playing hooky.

"Hi, y'all." White House Social Secretary Lucy Winchester greets us as we step into the small Housekeeper's Office on the ground floor.

With a shy grin, the president's good friend Bebe Rebozo stands and shakes hands with both Bob and me. The desktop in front of him has been cleared to accommodate a formal place setting. Bob, Lucy, and I have similar set-ups on three small tables. A formally dressed waiter serves us the same five-course dinner that's being served in the State Dining Room.

As soon as Bebe takes a bite of the Grande Marnier soufflé, he declares that he makes a better one. His secret ingredient is a topping of melted vanilla ice cream, and he promises to send me the recipe.

When dinner is over, Bob and I rejoin the other guests in the East Room for the entertainment. We sit in the back row.

◆

MONDAY, DECEMBER 15, BRINGS another round of antiwar protestors to the nation's capital for the third Moratorium. Although it's miserably cold the following night, a group of about two hundred demonstrators is determined to disrupt the National Christmas Tree Lighting Ceremony on the Ellipse. At

5:30 p.m., Bob, Ann, and I huddle together with other families at the base
of a towering Norway Spruce tree. From a spot nearby, the protestors shout
obscenities as a blustery wind whips at their Viet Cong flags. Interrupted by
jeers, the president tries to speak before lighting the tree.

"All we want for this nation is not only peace now, but peace in the years
to come..."

"*One, two, three, four. We won't fight your f***ing war.*"

"...Peace for all people in the years to come...the kind of peace...that
gives a chance for our children also to live in peace."

"*Ho, Ho, Ho Chi Minh. NLF is gonna win.*"

The president manages to complete his remarks. A pleased smile spreads
across his face as he pulls a lever and nine thousand small red and white lights
illuminate the seventy-five-foot tree.

◆

THE PRESIDENT ANNOUNCES A further reduction of troops, bringing the total
to 115,500 men brought home since he took office. At the same time, he
promotes SALT, the Strategic Arms Limitation Talks, with the Russians. Cult
killer Charles Manson and his followers are arraigned in a Los Angeles court.
And at the movies, the box office favorites are: *Midnight Cowboy*, *Easy Rider*,
and *Butch Cassidy and the Sundance Kid*.

The Nixons plan to celebrate Christmas at the Western White House,
and I'm delighted. This means we get to spend the holidays in California with
our families.

On Saturday, December 20, Bob travels with the president on *Air Force
One*, while the children and I fly on a government backup plane. It's eighty
degrees when we arrive at my parents' home in Bel-Air. Sunshine streams into
the living room through the sliding glass doors, casting a hazy light on their
artificial tree with its large silver balls. Home for the holidays, Susan joins
Hank, Peter, and Ann in the pool.

On Monday night, Susan is presented at the annual Las Madrinas
Debutante Ball, an event that raises money for Children's Hospital. Exchanging
her ragged jeans for a white formal and long white gloves, she looks radiant as
her father proudly escorts her around the dance floor.

We spend New Year's week in Palm Springs at Smoke Tree Ranch, where both the Hortons and the Haldemans have vacation homes. My parents' hacienda-style house is within walking distance of Non's one-story contemporary house at Rock 12, where we always stay, along with Bob's sister and brother and their families. An American flag hangs from a brand new flagpole at the end of the front walk, and the Army Signal Corps has installed two pristine white phones.

"The phones have pictures of the White House on them," Non exclaims. "Look, Bob, the one in the family room even has a long cord so you can take it out to your chaise by the pool."

I don't share Non's enthusiasm. I'm starting to view the White House phone as an intruder.

Non is in her element. With the Nixons vacationing at Bob and Dolores Hope's hillside home, she is thrilled that the president can look down on Smoke Tree. Taking our evening walks on the desert, we always pause and say a daily prayer. Recently, Non has added to our ritual a little wave to the Nixons.

January 1970

WHEN OUR WEEK AT Smoke Tree is over, everyone takes off in different directions. My father drives Hank, Peter, Ann, and me to the airport, where we board a helicopter for the short flight over the mountains to El Toro Marine Base. From there we fly to Washington on a small government Jet Star. Throughout the trip, a bag of groceries never leaves my side. It's filled with food that I can't buy in Washington: corn tortillas, Knudsen's cottage cheese, Thomas' English muffins, Pioneer sourdough French bread, and Van de Kamp's cinnamon-crumb "dunkettes."

Dignity in the White House

I T SNOWS ON TUESDAY, January 20, the first anniversary of Nixon's
inauguration. Watching the white flakes silently swirl through the air,
I become pensive and think back on the highlights of this past year. In
particular, I'm reminded of the inaugural address and Bob's reaction to
it. He immediately identified with the words, "Until he has been part of a cause
larger than himself, no man is truly whole." The quote has had a continuing
presence in our lives. In Nixon's handwriting, it hangs in our den in an antique
gold frame. A burgundy leather scrapbook with the words "Truly Whole"
embossed in gold on its cover sits on the coffee table in our living room.

Since moving to Washington, the White House has become an integral
part of my life. During the week, I usually attend several social events there,
and when we entertain at home, most of our guests are members of the senior
White House staff. I serve Bebe Rebozo's Grand Marnier soufflé for dessert,
and Bob shows his White House movies for entertainment.

In Bob's films, we see Henry Kissinger with Charles de Gaulle on the steps
of Le Grand Trianon and Nixon playing the piano for Harry Truman. Bob even
has pictures of Pope Paul VI at the Vatican. Holding his Bolex Super 8 camera
at his side, he surreptitiously filmed the president's private papal audience. As
a result, depending on whether Bob was sitting or standing, the Pope appears
either sideways or upside down.

Bob and I also accept a variety of invitations. In the last ten days, we have
attended a dinner party at the home of columnist Joseph Alsop, a play at Ford's
Theater, the ballet at the Kennedy Center, and the wedding of the son of the
secretary of state to the daughter of the secretary of agriculture.

Though exciting, there's also a downside to being married to the chief
of staff. Bob's work consumes most of his time and attention, even when he's

at home. Other than making an appearance at the dinner table, he's usually working in his office upstairs. Although it's becoming increasingly difficult for the two of us to have a spontaneous discussion, my system of leaving notes in his mail is a workable solution. We talk eventually, always at his convenience.

Another downside to Bob's job is the White House phone. Although I was initially intrigued to have seven government phones in our home, each with direct lines to both the White House and the Signal Corps, they are becoming my nemeses. They can interrupt, delay, or change my entire routine.

Sometimes, even being at White House events can be a challenge. When people fawn over Bob, they often look right through me. There are times when he forgets to introduce me or leaves me standing alone while he socializes with others. An irritated frown or impatient word from him can easily cut through the exhilaration of the moment. Despite the perception of my being the confident and gracious wife of H. R. Haldeman, I often feel insecure and alone.

A lighter side to our Washington life comes at our family dinner on a rainy Sunday evening in January. Bob is making a Caesar salad while Hank, Peter, Ann, and I watch. Wearing a dark blue apron with gray vertical stripes, he mashes anchovy and garlic in a wooden bowl. Next, he adds lemon juice and olive oil and mixes them with a fork.

Looking up, Bob tells us that he finally got his Fedco card. He explains that Fedco is a discount store available to federal employees. It is something new, and he is delighted to be a member.

"The application process was pretty funny," Bob says, breaking up two heads of romaine. "On the form, it asked who my employer was, and when I wrote, 'The President,' the clerk wanted to know the president of *what*. I had to add 'of the United States.'"

Bob cracks a coddled egg on top of the greens and continues. "Then, the clerk thought I was kidding when I wrote, 'The White House' as my place of employment, and she refused to process my application."

"So how did you get the card?" The children ask. All four of us are caught up in Bob's narrative.

Adding homemade croutons and Parmesan cheese, Bob replies, "Larry reminded me that I have a White House ID card, so I showed it to her."

"Oh, Dad," the children groan.

Unperturbed, their father tosses the salad with a flourish. "Voila!" he says, bowing.

The children and I applaud.

Bob's Caesar salad is delicious, but I wonder if he will ever use his prized Fedco card. With the exception of shopping for me at Christmas, our anniversary, and my birthday, he hasn't set foot in a store for over a year.

◆

THE PRESS GIVES HIGH praise to the president's efforts to increase the dignity of the White House and to allow more public access to events. The West Wing has been handsomely redecorated, and both White House Church and Evenings at the White House are acknowledged as successful ways to entertain more guests.

On January 27, however, the pursuit of respect and dignity goes a little too far. The air is chilly, and the sun plays hide-and-seek with dark, foreboding rain clouds. The decision to hold the state arrival ceremony of Harold Wilson, the prime minister of Great Britain, on the South Lawn is delayed until the last minute. One of Bob's young assistants escorts me to the stairs of the South Portico, where I find a spot on the fourth step to watch the ceremony.

Buttoning up my navy blue wool coat and winding a cashmere scarf twice around my neck, I try to keep warm. My legs are cold, and I wish I could wear my new red plaid pantsuit. But I can't. Women don't wear pants at the White House. As drummers and trumpeters assemble on the balcony above me, Bob comes out a side door and scurries over to join me. Ruffles and flourishes are played, followed by "Hail to the Chief." With the flags of the United States and Great Britain waving behind them, the president and the prime minister walk across the lawn to a temporary platform. Seemingly unaffected by the cold, Nixon is not wearing a coat. He speaks first, followed by Wilson. The pageantry of the ceremony creates a feeling of great respect.

Then, I spot the White House Police. Standing at attention in their new uniforms, they look out of place. Their double-breasted white tunics, loops of twisted gold braid, and shiny black Napoleonic hats, trimmed with gold filigree, are like costumes from a Sigmund Romberg operetta.

"The police look like the men's chorus in *The Student Prince*," I say, nudging Bob.

"Someone sure goofed," Bob replies, with a scowl spreading across his face.

The press has a field day with the spectacle, but it is soon remedied. Three days later, when I return to the White House to observe a press conference, the police are back in their old uniforms.

Mr. Haldeman, It's the President

THE PRESIDENTIAL PRESS CONFERENCE is another White House "institution" that the president is attempting to dignify. In the past, this occasion has been chaotic. Reporters would jockey for position and shout out their questions all at once. Tonight, they are seated and raise their hands to be recognized. The reporters are orderly and respectful, and the new system appears to work well. I observe from a seat in the back of the room, where Bob has told me to sit.

Afterward, Bob and I meet up, and the two of us go downstairs for dinner in the Executive Mess. Located on the ground floor near Henry Kissinger's National Security Council office, the wood-paneled dining room is available only to the president's top aides. The navy oversees both the Mess and the Executive Mess, and the food is simple, but good.

Tucked away in a booth, I almost forget about the outside world. It's not often that Bob and I get to have time together like this. But it doesn't last long. Shortly after we're served our entrée, a steward appears with a phone on a long cord.

"Mr. Haldeman, it's the president."

"Yes, sir," Bob answers, quickly swallowing a mouthful of carrots. "You did a monumental job tonight." Pause. "No, sir, not at all. You hit hard on the questions, and what's more, you aced those guys with your new system. There was a lot more respect than in the past."

Clearly, the president is unhappy with the quality of the reporters' questions. Patiently encouraging and reassuring him, Bob compares Nixon's press conferences to those of Charles de Gaulle. When he hangs up, he continues our conversation right where we left off.

After dinner, Bob and I join six other members of the White House staff and their wives in a room on the ground floor. Rows of chairs face a large portable screen, converting the room into a theater. We have been meeting here once a week to watch a special showing of the popular BBC TV series, *Civilisation*, an introduction to art history narrated by Sir Kenneth Clark.

Tonight's subject is Early Christian and Byzantine Art, and we quickly become absorbed in the world of Constantine and Justinian. A phone rings somewhere behind us, and a steward whispers in Bob's ear that the president would like to talk to him. Bob takes the call in the back of the room, and from what I overhear, it's about the press conference again.

During the break, Irish coffee and cookies are served. No sooner does Bob fill his plate than he is called to the phone once more. It's the same subject, the press conference. Responding to the president's questions, he agrees with him and compliments him. I'm fascinated to hear how solicitous he is of Nixon. Bob would never be this tolerant with anyone else.

We return to our seats, and a powerful scene of the resurrection appears on the screen. Just as Byzantium springs to life, the phone rings. For the fourth time tonight, Bob and the president discuss his press conference. Nixon never asks where Bob is or what he's doing.

February 1970

PETER TURNS THIRTEEN ON Wednesday, February 11, and our family plans to celebrate at dinner. Shortly after arriving home, Bob receives a call from the president, who has decided on the spur of the moment to go to Florida. This means that we have only an hour to be together before Bob has to take off again.

Peter has requested apple crisp instead of a birthday cake. In order to keep things moving, I have to serve it right out of the oven. It's so hot, it melts the candles, which droop and sag as he tries to blow them out.

As Peter is opening his first present, a piercing call comes from the kitchen. "Mr. Haldeman, your car is here." Standing at the kitchen window, Bertha has a good view of the road. She loves being the first to spot the arrival of the White House car and relishes the drama of shouting the news from the kitchen.

Bob leaps up from the dining room table. "Happy Birthday, Peter," he says, giving his son a clap on the back. "See you in four days. I'll be home Sunday night."

Suddenly, Bob is no longer with us. A half-eaten dish of apple crisp is left at his place, and a crumpled paper birthday napkin lies on the floor under his chair. This is not the way things were supposed to go.

◆

THURSDAY, FEBRUARY 19, IS our wedding anniversary, which we celebrate at the White House. The president and Mrs. Nixon are giving an informal dinner party in honor of Andrew Wyeth, the American realist artist.

Wyeth's paintings are on display in the main hall, where they can be viewed both before and after dinner. A tempera painting titled *Distant Thunder* appears to attract most of the attention. It shows a young woman lying asleep in a meadow, unaware of an approaching storm. As Bob and I wait our turn to study it up close, he grips my waist with both hands and gently steers me through the crowd.

"The girl reminds me of Susan," he remarks.

Leaning back against Bob, I momentarily close my eyes. I feel his closeness. My mind goes back to the night we were married. The church was large, and there were many guests. Bob was twenty-two, and I was twenty. We had met five years earlier, when his sister Betsy introduced us. She was my best friend in high school. *How could we have ever known that someday her brother would become my husband and that he and I would be celebrating our twenty-first wedding anniversary at the White House?*

◆

THREE DAYS AFTER THE Wyeth dinner, I return to the White House. With the Nixons at Camp David and Hank and Peter skiing at Blue Knob, Bob, Ann, and I plan to attend the afternoon dress rehearsal of the Broadway hit musical *1776* in the East Room. Based on the signing of the Declaration of Independence, the show will be the entertainment for tomorrow's Evening at the White House. Bob has offered to give Ann and me a special tour of the recently refurbished West Wing and his new office before the show.

Instead of entering the West Wing by the side door on the ground floor and climbing up the back stairs to get to Bob's office, Ann and I use the newly remodeled entrance on the North Front. A marine in full dress uniform steps forward and holds open one of the double doors.

"Wow," I hear Ann say under her breath.

The press corps lounge is gone. Instead, an elegant reception room greets us. High quality Williamsburg reproductions have replaced the worn, over-sized leather chairs and sofas. No more discarded newspapers and ashtrays overflowing with cigarette butts. With a rich blue carpet on the floor and historical paintings lining the walls, the conversion is remarkable.

The receptionist recognizes me and buzzes for Bob, who appears at a side door. He asks what we think of the décor and explains that the press has been relocated. The White House swimming pool has been covered over, and a new Press Briefing Room has been constructed on top of it.

On our way back to his office, Bob shows Ann and me the newly decorated offices and conference rooms. Even the hall has had a makeover. Plush carpeting and indirect lighting have replaced the linoleum floors and fluorescent lights of the Johnson years.

Bob has moved from his former cubbyhole adjoining the Oval Office into the large, southwest corner office at the other end of the hall. It was originally assigned to Vice President Agnew, who has moved to the Executive Office Building (EOB), across a private street within the White House compound. Sunlight floods in through six tall windows. A fire is burning in the fireplace, and an arrangement of fresh flowers is on the coffee table. The oil portrait of Richard Nixon from Bob's old office hangs on the wall next to an American flag in a brass stand.

Ann plops down in her father's desk chair and swivels around. "Your desk is humungous," she says.

"Yep," Bob replies. "Nine feet long. I designed it myself." The desk is immaculate. There are only a few personal items, including a couple of framed family photographs.

Pointing to a panel of three lights, Ann asks, "What are those for?"

"They show me where the president is—the Oval Office, the family quarters, or on the grounds."

On the way out, we stop at his secretary's desk, and Bob points to another panel of lights. "Green tells Pat that I'm available; yellow, I'm with the president; and red, I'm not to be disturbed." *The way Bob operates, I'm sure she takes the lights very seriously.*

Before walking over to the East Wing for the rehearsal, Bob asks us to wait while he strides down the hall to the door of the Oval Office. Turning around, he retraces his steps, carefully placing one foot in front of the other. His shoes are size twelve, and he uses them as rulers.

"…twenty-nine, thirty, thirty-one, thirty-two," he says. "Only thirty-two feet separating me from the president."

With only members of the White House staff present for the dress rehearsal of *1776*, it doesn't matter where we sit. Ann is relieved when her father suggests that she and I take seats in the front row, and he sits directly behind us. The show is captivating, particularly in this historical setting. When it's over, Ann has found a new hero, John Adams. The American statesman was driven and demanded a lot of himself, as well as others. Traits that remind me of Bob.

Flaps

March 1970

SUBJECTED TO AN ENDLESS series of cold, wet days in early March, I jump at the chance to be in a warmer climate when Bob suggests a trip to Florida. The president plans to spend a long weekend in Key Biscayne, and there's room for the children and me to fly down on a support plane.

Hank chooses to stay home. Peter, Ann, and I are driven to Andrews Air Force Base, where we board a prop-driven Convair. Most of the thirty-six seats are filled with Secret Service and army communications personnel. Nixon's doctor and his wife are also on board, as well as Manolo, who is in charge of the president's new Irish setter. King Timahoe was a gift from the White House staff. Due to stormy weather and strong headwinds, the trip takes four hours, twice as long as usual.

It's pouring rain when we land at Homestead Air Force Base. Carrying umbrellas, two aides in dark suits and ties scurry out on the tarmac to escort the children and me across the runway to a small helicopter. Twenty minutes later, our Huey puts down in a parking lot in the Key Biscayne marina. A driver is waiting to take us to the Key Biscayne Hotel.

Our villa has two bedrooms upstairs and one downstairs. Phones are everywhere, and each of them has eight lines. When the one marked "White House" rings, I answer it, and a White House operator informs me that Bob and the president are still in the Oval Office.

Bob doesn't arrive until 2:30 a.m. Climbing into bed, he describes the trip down as "a disaster." The president vacillated on leaving Washington due to the bad weather, and when he finally decided to go, starter problems on *Air Force One* caused more delays.

The four of us sleep late the next morning and awaken to bright sunshine and warmer temperatures. While eating breakfast at a poolside table next to Henry Kissinger, Bob tells us that the president and Bebe have left for Grand Cay and don't expect to return until tomorrow.

"Bebe's the perfect companion for the president," Bob says. "He never talks. Bill Safire says that the president likes solitude, and being with Bebe is just like being alone." Bob chuckles gleefully, and it sounds like, "Hee, hee, hee."

When Bob adds that there is no phone connection on the island, I smile. Now we may finally have some uninterrupted time with him.

Although Bob spends time with the children and me on the beach both Friday and Saturday, he's also on the phone a lot. He tells me that he's dealing with "flaps." When a press boat gets too close to Bebe's yacht, the *Julie*, it creates a flap. When the White House mistakenly releases inaccurate information about the number of men killed in Laos, it creates another flap. Bob is particularly frustrated when the White House press corps makes no attempt to correct the report. I hear Bob using the term "flap" more and more these days. Ordinarily, addressing a flap is a two-part effort: first, resolve the issue, and second, put the best light on it.

Following a partial eclipse Saturday morning, Bob and I walk to the lighthouse. When we return to the villa, we are surprised by the delivery of three huge platters of cold cuts. They were given to the Nixons, but the Secret Service won't allow the first family to accept any gifts of food. Bebe had the trays sent over to us. Feeling like the "king's tasters," we ask friends to join us in sampling the array of meats, cheeses, dips, salads, fruits, and breads.

Sunday, the heavy rumble of thunder, followed by torrents of rain, wakes us up. From the porch, I watch as the surf angrily lashes at the beach, leaving scads of jellyfish stranded on the sand. Bob is on edge all morning. Larry looks haggard.

The phone rings, and after a brief conversation, Bob calls out, "Get packed, Jo. We're leaving in half an hour. You and the kids are coming with us."

The president has had enough of Florida's stormy weather. By 2:30 p.m., we are standing on a rain-soaked helipad, adjacent to the Nixons' house. Bob boards *Marine One.* Peter, Ann, and I follow Tim, the Irish Setter, aboard a second helicopter.

At Homestead, we meet up with Bob on *Air Force One* for the flight back to Washington. We take our assigned seats in the first two rows, on the right side of the VIP section. As soon as we are airborne, Bob starts working on *The New York Times* crossword puzzle, and I work on my needlepoint. Behind us, Peter and Ann put on large, padded headsets to listen to music in stereo.

◆

Two weeks later, on Sunday, Bob is at the White House, dealing with a major flap. The postal workers' walkout in New York City threatens to turn into a national strike. If the Air Traffic Controllers and the Teamsters also strike, it could cripple the country. The president has cancelled his plans to go to Camp David and is holed up in his office at the Executive Office Building.

Bob is extremely busy, and I'm surprised when he asks if the children and I would like to join him at his office. Home for spring break, Susan is the only one interested in going. She and I meet Bob in the deserted lobby of the West Wing. The offices are dark, and the halls are empty, with the exception of a few people with tense expressions who scurry by.

Trying to stay out of the way, Susan and I settle by the fire in Bob's office. We keep our voices down and quietly observe all that goes on. One minute Bob is on the phone, and the next, he's conferring with the secretary of labor, the postmaster general, the domestic affairs advisor, and the press secretary. He dashes off a few memos and makes more calls. In between, he meets with the president in his EOB office.

Lunch is put off until Bob is able to take a break. Being a Sunday, the Mess isn't open, so the three of us do the next best thing. We get hot dogs, hamburgers, and ice cream bars from the vending machine on the ground floor and eat in Bob's office.

"This is amazing, Dad," Susan comments. "I can't believe that I'm having a picnic in the White House in the middle of a national crisis."

The afternoon is memorable. Watching Bob on the job is fascinating. I'm impressed by his clarity of thought and ability to make quick decisions. By the time Susan and I leave, we have a much greater understanding of what Bob's work entails.

The next afternoon, the president declares a state of national emergency. In a seven-minute statement, he calls on the US Armed Forces and National Guard to distribute the mail in New York City.

April 1970

ON SUNDAY, APRIL 5, the postal strike is finally over. Lasting two weeks, it was one of the largest wildcat strikes in our nation's history. The following Wednesday, I'm in the Senate gallery witnessing another one of the president's battles. This time it's his second attempt to fill a vacancy on the Supreme Court.

When the appointment of G. Harrold Carswell goes down in defeat, I worry about Bob's having to bear the brunt of Nixon's disappointment and frustration. I want to do something special for him tonight and decide to fix a nice dinner.

The children eat early in the kitchen, while I set the table in the dining room for Bob and me. I use the good china and silver. With prune soufflé cooling on the counter, I prepare fried chicken, green beans, and a tossed salad. Popovers are in the oven when the White House phone rings.

"Good evening, Mrs. Haldeman." It's Pat, and I expect her to tell me in her usual cheery voice that Bob is about to leave the office. The timing is perfect.

"Hi, Pat."

"Mr. Haldeman asked me to call and tell you that he will be delayed this evening."

"Oh…"

"He's on the *Sequoia* with the president and the attorney general."

"Do you know when he'll be home?"

"The president wants to eat dinner as they cruise down the Potomac to Mount Vernon. After that, they will chopper back to the White House. Mr. Haldeman should be home around nine thirty or ten."

"Oh…nine thirty or ten… Thank you, Pat."

I struggle to keep my tone light, but Bertha overhears the conversation. She knows how disappointed I am. Giving me a reassuring smile, she helps me clear the table and store the food in the refrigerator. I pour myself a bowl of cereal and eat alone at the kitchen table.

Parental Concerns

WE LIVE WITH VIOLENCE on a daily basis. We see it in the news every night as we watch the fighting in Vietnam. In addition, this month there are bombings in New York City and a deadly earthquake in Turkey. On several major US campuses, antiwar students set buildings on fire and battle the police. Threats of violence force the Nixons to cancel their plans to attend both Julie's graduation from Smith and David's from Amherst.

Ann's school has to be evacuated due to a bomb scare. The girls are sent across the street to the shelter in the basement of the National Cathedral. When I pick her up after school, Ann is eager to share what she experienced.

Over a period of several nights, student radicals at Stanford set fires, break windows, and throw rocks. In Susan's weekly collect call home, she tells Bob and me that she skipped classes in order to attend protest rallies. The Haldeman name is becoming more widely known, and she tries not to be recognized. At one rally, she hid behind an antiwar banner in an attempt to avoid being filmed by a camera crew.

Hank has his driver's license and is quite independent. I don't see much of our sixteen-year-old, except at mealtimes. His main communication with me is over the use of the car and the phone. Although he looks like a liberal with his shoulder-length hair, wire rim glasses, and heavy boots, he's an outspoken conservative on national issues and the war. I'm concerned when he attends a huge "Earth Day" rally at the Washington Monument. He tells me that it will be peaceful and has nothing to do with the antiwar demonstrations. Still, I worry about the widespread use of marijuana and other drugs at all large gatherings.

At Sidwell Friends, a Quaker school, Peter, thirteen, is exposed to a liberal environment. I'm relieved that he doesn't appear to be unduly affected by the peace demonstrations. However, I'm not happy when he paints his bedroom door black and moves most of his furniture out in the hall. He's now sleeping on his mattress on the floor.

At ten, Ann is more concerned about having to participate in mandatory piano recitals and school plays. Appearing as Toto in *The Wizard of Oz,* she gratefully disappears under her costume, Peter's brown shag bathroom rug. In *The Sorcerer's Apprentice,* she plays the role of a chair.

When Bob and I discuss the children, he assures me that as parents we've given them a good moral foundation, as well as the tools to work through their problems. I hope he's right. The young people today face much greater challenges than we ever did.

Perks

O N APRIL 10, I attend a state dinner at the White House in honor of the chancellor of West Germany. I wear my inaugural ball gown, and Bob is in white tie and tails. In the Entrance Hall, the US Marine Band plays ruffles and flourishes, followed by "Hail to the Chief." Every head turns to watch as President and Mrs. Nixon, along with Chancellor Willy Brandt, slowly descend the red carpeted Grand Staircase.

Throughout the evening, we are immersed in protocol and pomp. Social aides in their dress uniforms are posted at every door along the main hall, and an honor guard stands at the entrance to the State Dining Room. At dinner, Nixon is at his best when he gives his toast. Combining the serious side of the chancellor's visit with some humorous remarks, he has everyone laughing at his reference to the "infiltration of Germans" on his White House staff. When he names Kissinger, Ehrlichman, and Haldeman, I get goose bumps. I can hardly wait to tell Non that the president of the United States referred to her son in a toast at a formal state dinner. I can already hear her embellishing the story as she shares it with friends.

◆

AT MIDNIGHT ON MONDAY, April 13, Bob and I are awakened by the jarring ring of the White House phone. He jerks up and fumbles for the light. From the caller's deep voice, I can tell that it is Henry Kissinger. Something has gone terribly wrong with *Apollo 13*. The space flight was launched three days ago, and the astronauts should be preparing to land on the moon. Bob tells Henry that at this point, there is nothing Nixon can do, and it's better to let him sleep.

He reminds Henry that the president doesn't function well when he's tired. *I'm glad I don't have to make that decision.*

Within minutes of Henry's call, the phone rings again. It's Dwight Chapin, who gives Bob an update from NASA. After that, Henry calls two more times. Instead of going back to sleep, Bob remains sitting up in bed with the light on.

"There's been an explosion in the *Apollo* command ship," he tells me. "The mission has to be aborted. The only way for the three astronauts to get back to Earth is in the lunar landing module. It wasn't built for that purpose, and no one's sure if they can make it back."

Lying on my side, I stare out the window. As I think of those men in space, a feeling of helplessness surges through me. Then, I remember that I can pray. Searching the sky for the moon, I silently repeat a hymn.

> *O gentle presence, peace and joy and power.*
> *O Life divine, that owns each waiting hour.*
> *Thou Love that guards the nestling's faltering flight,*
> *Keep Thou my child on upward wing tonight.*

The next day, NASA reports that the lunar module's supply of oxygen, water, and power is critically low. The astronauts' families remain in seclusion, and the nation is kept in suspense for three days. When the module finally splashes down in the Pacific, everyone breathes a collective sigh of relief. I hear the news on my car radio, while I'm driving in Georgetown to attend a garden tour. Simultaneously, people start cheering. Drivers wave and honk their horns, and I enthusiastically join them.

The near-tragedy has weighed heavily on the president, and I can only imagine how relieved he is. Tonight's Evening at the White House with Johnny Cash gives him the perfect opportunity to share his elation.

"I'm honored to be here, Mr. President," I say as I greet him in the receiving line. "What a special occasion."

"It sure is! What a great day!" Nixon says, pumping my hand enthusiastically. "Our whole country was united in prayer for those brave men. And they pulled through."

As I move on to greet Pat, it occurs to me that the president is so euphoric, he forgot to mention my "drinking problem."

Then, I hear his voice call, "Don't go overboard on your toasting tonight."

◆

THE NEXT DAY, THE Nixons fly to Hawaii to welcome the astronauts. While they are there, the president announces a troop withdrawal of 150,000 men from Vietnam over the next year. They will be replaced by trained South Vietnamese soldiers. The withdrawal is evidence that "Vietnamization" works. Pleased with the surprise element of the announcement, Bob calls it a "real bombshell." Both he and Henry have been frustrated by a recent increase in security leaks to the press.

"The only way to prevent a leak is not to tell anyone," Bob states.

◆

ONE OF THE PERKS of Bob's position is the use of the presidential yacht. In order to maintain the *Sequoia,* the crew takes it out on a regular basis. When it is not being used officially, the yacht is available to top White House staff. On the night of April 21, Bob suggests that we take a cruise with the Ehrlichmans and my parents, who are visiting us.

The six of us board the 104-foot classic yacht at exactly 7:30 p.m., or seven bells. Its creamy white exterior and varnished wood interior, combined with the formality of the crew, are reminiscent of the old-world elegance of 1925, when the *Sequoia* was built.

Tonight, the rectangular table in the teak-paneled dining room is set for six. Napkins are intricately folded in the shape of a swan. On a white tablecloth, a centerpiece of fresh orange and yellow marigolds sits between two silver candlesticks. As we eat, we cruise down the Potomac to Mount Vernon. After dinner, a traditional ceremony to honor our first president takes place on the deck. The yacht stops at George Washington's grave, and the crew lines up on deck, according to height. They salute and stand at attention while "The Star Spangled Banner" is played over loudspeakers. The six of us place our hands over our hearts. There are tears in my eyes as I sing our national anthem. I'm keenly aware of where I am—and who I am. I'm living a part of American history. The events that I experience through Bob will be written about in the history books someday. The feeling is indescribable.

In addition to the cruise on the *Sequoia*, my parents spend the weekend at Camp David and attend an Evening at the White House. Bob provides them with a memorable week, and I'm sure their heads are spinning as they pack to go home. But when they say goodbye, I'm the one who is at a loss. I miss them more than ever and don't understand why. On the surface, I have everything. Bob gives me so much, and because of him, I lead a charmed life. And yet, on this visit, Mom and Dad have given me something, too. Not until I return home from the airport do I figure it out. Through their deep interest and support, my parents made me feel important. To them, I am special, and I desperately need to know that.

◆

SPRING IS HERE IN all its glory. Kenwood is captivating with its cherry trees in full bloom. The top is down on our neighbor's little green Mustang as Harry C. drives through a tunnel of pink flowers and stops to pick up our children for school. I take deep breaths of the perfumed air as I walk out with Hank, Peter, and Ann. The fifty-year-old giant trees are spectacular, and every year at this time, spectators flock to our neighborhood. On Sundays, the traffic is controlled by a policeman. Lemonade stands pop up on many of the streets as the children in the area take advantage of the opportunity to make money.

This year, Martha Mitchell, the wife of the attorney general, is part of the annual Kenwood House and Garden Tour and decides to use the occasion to provoke Bob. Martha is a character, and her personality grates on Bob. Constantly seeking publicity, she has been described as a misfit in the staid Nixon White House.

Accompanied by an entourage of press, Martha tells her driver to stop at Ann Haldeman's juice stand. With her encouragement, a large photo of the two of them appears in *The Evening Star*. The columnist writes, "The exaggerated blonde with a beehive hair-do, minx-like grin, and spiky high heels said 'be sure and send this picture of Ann and me to Bob. He'll die.'"

Bob doesn't die, but he's not happy. The main reason he puts up with Martha is out of respect for her husband. John Mitchell has told Bob that he truly loves his wife and wants to please her.

Weird

MARTHA'S ANTICS ARE A diversion from a growing concern over the Vietnam War. After South Vietnamese troops cross the border in pursuit of the Cambodian Communists, there is a fear that the president might expand the war into Cambodia. On several campuses, antiwar students clash with police, and the National Guard is called out at Ohio State and Stanford.

On April 29, the situation is tense, and the White House announces that the president will address the nation tomorrow night. Bob calls to say that he will be working late, and I should cancel our plans to attend a reception at the Japanese Embassy. Non is visiting us for the week, but instead of being disappointed, she is consumed with the news and appears to thrive on the excitement.

At 9:00 p.m. on Thursday evening, April 30, the president appears on television. Non, Hank, and I watch his speech in the den. Bob is at the White House. Seated at his desk in the Oval Office, Nixon points to the map of Cambodia behind him and states that the Communists now control a quarter of that country. From hidden Communist sanctuaries, North Vietnamese forces have been attacking the South Vietnamese army, as well as American troops. Nixon tells us that it's time to act, and the United States, in cooperation with South Vietnam, will be launching attacks in Cambodia.

"This is not an invasion," Nixon states with assurance. Rather than expanding the war, he stresses that this will help to end the fighting and win a just peace. On the other hand, he warns that if the United States "acts like a pitiful, helpless giant, the forces of totalitarianism and anarchy will threaten free nations and free institutions throughout the world."

"Way to go!" Hank says when the speech is over.

Non jumps up and claps her hands. Her charm bracelets jangle annoyingly as we struggle to hear the commentators. "Wasn't the president marvelous?" she exclaims.

I lean my head back against the couch and momentarily close my eyes. This is a bold move by the president, and I wonder how the country will react.

The White House phone rings. It's Bob, asking for my reaction to the speech. I read him my notes, concluding that it was "decisive, clear, and to the point."

"I'll be staying late to monitor some of the follow-up calls," he says. "Tell Mom that I'm sorry. Say goodnight to her for me."

Flicking off the lights in the den, I pause before going upstairs. This is the second time Bob has sought my opinion after one of Nixon's speeches, and I'm flattered. His interest is in marked contrast to the times he treats me with indifference.

May 1970

THE NEXT DAY, THE president makes it clear that his action in Cambodia is an "incursion," not an invasion. The hawks back his decision, while the doves oppose it. Speaking with a friendly crowd at the Pentagon, the president refers to our soldiers as "the greatest." He contrasts them with the "bums" who are "blowing up the campuses" and "burning up the books."

Nixon's comments generate a tidal wave of protests from antiwar politicians, journalists, students, professors, clergy members, and business leaders. Susan calls to tell us how upset she and her friends are. At Kent State, student protestors burn down an army ROTC building. Eleven eastern colleges promote a nationwide academic strike, and the National Student Association calls for the president's impeachment.

The Nixons retreat to Camp David for the weekend, but Bob remains in DC. He works at the White House both days. We don't get together as a family until Sunday night, when Non voices what we all are thinking.

"I don't understand why the president called those students 'bums.'"

"These have been rough days, Mom," Bob explains. "The president has been really cranked up over the reaction to Cambodia, and whenever he thinks about how deserving our soldiers are, he gets emotional. He wasn't calling every student a bum, just the destructive ones." Bob pauses. "Plus, he's bone tired, and that's not good."

From my end of the table, I study Bob and think that he's the one who looks "bone tired." *How can he face another day like this? When will it all end?*

Three days later, on Monday, May 4, our country hits a new low. Along with everyone else, I'm sickened when I hear that members of the National Guard have shot students on the Kent State campus. I sit in disbelief, watching replays of the scene on TV. I'm numbed by the sight of blood and the sounds of gunshots and screams. When it's over, four students are dead, and nine others are wounded. This could be happening on any campus in these troubled times, and once again I worry about Susan at Stanford. Although the Kent State shooting incites more demonstrations, she assures Bob and me that she's okay.

"My child was not a bum," a father of one of the dead students states.

My heart goes out to him, as well as the other parents. I can't imagine what it would be like to lose a child. No pain could be any greater. I also feel for the president, who has to carry the burden of responsibility.

Mammoth antiwar demonstrations break out across the country. Students march through the streets, chanting and throwing rocks. Strikes close 450 colleges and universities, and the National Guard is called out on 21 campuses. So much is happening so fast, it's impossible to take it all in.

Over the next couple of days, Bob spends long hours at the White House. The children, Non, and I don't see much of him. When he arrives home late at night, it's obvious that he's driving himself and his staff hard. Throughout it all, however, he remains positive. He believes that every negative circumstance can be turned around.

"There's an opportunity in all of this," he says, climbing into bed. "But I sure wish I could figure out what it is."

For someone so sure of himself, Bob seems to be at a loss. It's hard to see him struggle, but I admire his expectancy of good. It's typical, and I love him for it.

◆

A NATIONAL DAY OF protest has been called for Saturday, May 9, and thousands of demonstrators are expected to flood Washington. Out of concern, schools in the area are closed the day before, and Bob thinks that the children, Non, and I should get out of DC. He insists that we spend the next couple of days at Camp David.

"The media's building this up really big," he says. "There's a darn good chance there could be some violence."

Hank stays home, but the rest of us leave on Friday morning. Driving through the rural Maryland countryside, I find it hard to believe that I'm seeking refuge at the presidential retreat. Once we get there, I'm amazed at how removed I feel. No matter what goes on in the rest of the world, nothing ever seems to change at Camp David. It's as if we were in a cocoon, and it's comforting to be cared for by the overly solicitous staff. All we have to do is answer their questions: "What time would you like dinner served, ma'am? How would you like your steaks cooked tonight? What movie have you selected?"

While eating dinner, I look over at our favorite steward, Pair. He stands erect, off to the side, waiting to serve the next course. I wonder what he thinks about the Vietnam War and the killings at Kent State. I would love to ask, but I don't. An invisible line separates us, and my questions would only put him in an awkward position.

Tonight, at 10:00 p.m., the president holds a televised press conference in the East Room of the White House. He has a lot riding on his performance, and Non, Peter, Ann, and I are glued to the television in Laurel's tiny living room. The reporters ask about the incursion into Cambodia, the air strikes against North Vietnam, the "bums" remark, and the tragic killings at Kent State. Nixon's answers are strong. He looks presidential and acts confident. His chin is slightly raised, but not enough to appear combative. His smile is relaxed, not forced.

"This country is not headed for revolution," the president states in a firm voice. "Students are trying to say they want peace, and they want to stop the killing. They say we ought to get out of Vietnam. I agree with everything that they are trying to accomplish."

When Bob calls later, he describes the performance as "masterful" and adds, "The president really zinged the press tonight." He pauses. "You should see what's going on in DC. The Mall's covered with sleeping bags, and kids are swarming all over the place. The army has barricaded the White House with buses, and soldiers are sleeping in the halls at the EOB. It's like a battle zone."

"You'd never know it here at Camp David," I reply.

The next morning, sunshine filters through the budding dogwood trees as I walk over to Laurel for breakfast. When Pair reports that everything is calm in Washington, Non, Peter, Ann, and I decide to return home. Once we are on the road, I turn on the radio to get the latest news report. What we hear is surreal. At 4:30 a.m., the president visited the Lincoln Memorial.

"He did *what?*" Ann calls out from the back seat.

"Shh," Non says, turning up the volume.

The report is sketchy. We learn that while the president was at the Memorial, he talked informally with some of the student demonstrators. A sophomore from Syracuse describes Nixon's conversation as rambling and disjointed.

I don't hear from Bob all day and have to rely on news accounts to keep me informed. This evening, when I make a brief appearance at a neighborhood cocktail party, I'm sure the other guests think I have inside information on the president's strange visit. I appreciate that no one mentions it. When Bob finally arrives home, he looks drained. I can hardly wait to hear what he has to say, but I know better than to push him. I hold back. But Non doesn't. At the dinner table, she hits him head on.

"Why'd the president visit the Lincoln Memorial this morning?" she asks immediately after our moment of silence.

"All I can tell you is that he's exhausted," Bob says. "He couldn't sleep and became sentimental looking out at the lighted monuments. Apparently he felt compelled to show Manolo the Lincoln Memorial at night, so he got a White House driver to take them there. No one else knew anything about it."

"How weird," Peter comments.

"It was weird," Bob agrees. "But he's done this type of thing before. Sometimes during the campaign, when he got overtired, he'd take off late at night. To make matters worse, when he's run-down, his speech slurs, and it sounds like he's been drinking."

I'm sure Bob wants to give a logical explanation for the president's actions, but I'm surprised to hear him talk so candidly. He never reveals anything personal about Nixon.

Bob tells us that John Ehrlichman called about 5.00 a.m. to inform him that the president was at the Memorial with Manolo. Bob took off as soon as he could, and by the time he caught up with the two of them, they were at the Capitol. Other staff members joined them, and everyone went to breakfast at the Mayflower. It was special for Nixon, who hadn't eaten in a local restaurant since he and Pat had moved into the White House. When he left, the waitresses walked out with him and waved goodbye. Bob tried to talk him into taking a nap when they got back to the White House, but the president insisted on going over to the EOB to meet the soldiers, who had spent the night there.

As he talks, Bob plays with his spoon. Slowly turning it over and over between his fingers, he says, "The president's beat. Pooped. He's got to get some rest. I think we've finally convinced him to go to Florida for a long weekend."

Our plates are empty, but we linger at the table. It's been an unsettling day, but Bob stresses the fact that the president had reached out to the student demonstrators and wanted them to know they share the same goal, ending the war.

Poor Nixon. He tries, but he can be so awkward at times. I'm beginning to think that he's his own worst enemy.

◆

THROUGHOUT THESE HECTIC DAYS, Susan continues to stay in touch. She says she feels torn between empathizing with her fellow students and being respectful of her father and supportive of the Nixon administration.

Hank remains solid in his support of the president. He attends a debate on Cambodia in the House of Representatives, interviews John Ehrlichman, and writes an article for the National Cathedral School paper. In the St. Albans Government Club, his argument in favor of the Cambodian incursion is so compelling six liberals walk out. The final vote is fourteen to eleven in favor of the *conservatives*.

Nixon finally gets away for four days of rest and relaxation. But he's too keyed up to take advantage of them. While Peter, Ann, and I enjoy the beach in front of Villa 74 at the Key Biscayne Hotel, Bob works. If he is not on the phone, he is meeting with the president. After selling their apartment in New York, the Nixons bought a house next door to Bebe Rebozo on the bay side of the key. Bob spends much of his time in this compound, screened from the road by a large hibiscus hedge.

On our return flight to Washington, the president invites Henry, John, and Bob to come up to the front cabin, where he awards them "The Presidential Order of the Blue Heart." In recognition of their "valor in times of stress," Nixon gives each of them a small, blue fabric heart, which was handmade by Bebe's girlfriend at Nixon's request.

On the surface, it's a light moment, but it's also symbolic of the deep allegiance these three men have to their president. They stood by him throughout the "bums" remark, the shootings at Kent State, the protests, and finally, the strange visit to the Lincoln Memorial.

All the King's Krauts

I N A SPECIAL MESSAGE to Congress on May 21, the president proposes the Emergency School Aid Act to assist in the desegregation of public schools. Public opinion is finally starting to rally behind the president. In New York City, construction workers break up an antiwar rally on Wall Street, and one hundred thousand people march in support of the US policy in Vietnam. The Senate finally confirms Nixon's third nominee for the Supreme Court, Harry A. Blackmun.

Six blacks die in race riots in Georgia, and police kill two students in Mississippi. Society in general remains unsettled. The Gallup Poll reports that 75 percent of those questioned feel the influence of religion is declining. Coed dorms have taken over on the campuses. Both sexes dress in ragged jeans, pierce their ears, wear heavy jewelry, and wear their hair well below their shoulders. Pantsuits are "in" for women.

When Bob is selected to receive UCLA's Edward A. Dickson Alumnus of the Year Award, I'm proud of him. As a past president of the Alumni Association and former member of the Board of Regents, he has strong ties to the University. Five years ago, he headed the campaign to raise the first million dollars for the construction of Pauley Pavilion. On Saturday, May 23, he will be honored for having "demonstrated his devotion and interest in the University in a most distinguished way."

In working on his speech, Bob tries to find a subject that will be timely and have an impact. On our flight to California, he discusses a couple of ideas with me. Thumbing through *Time, Newsweek,* and *U.S. News and World Report,* I comment that all three magazines are featuring stories on the isolation of the president.

"That's it, Jo," Bob exclaims. "I've got my talk."

The black tie dinner is held at the Century Plaza Hotel in Los Angeles. Walking up to the podium, Bob looks confident and at ease. He nods to a few people in the audience, thrusts his hands into his pockets, and begins.

"I would like to depart from the traditional speech that is given on an occasion such as this, to share with you some thoughts I have on a subject about which I feel deeply and believe that you do too—the presidency of the United States."

Bob quickly gets down to the nitty-gritty of his subject. Comparing the "elusive secret command headquarters" of the Communists in Cambodia to the "Eastern Establishment media," he explains that "the secret nerve center in the jungle labyrinth of Manhattan Island" is where an "enormously powerful group of men" gather every Sunday to decide what the media line will be for the coming week.

Flashing a toothy smile, Bob is enjoying his tongue-in-cheek presentation. "Who could have known two months ago when this evening was planned, that this week—the week I make the only public speech I'll probably make all year—would be 'isolation of the president week' and that the major media would be blaming me for that isolation?"

Explaining the president's decision-making process, Bob cites the polls showing that there is a two-to-one favorable margin of support for the incursion into Cambodia. He concludes, "Fortunately, both for him and for the world, the president is in far closer touch than that little group who selected 'isolation of the president as this week's password."

The applause is enthusiastic, and Bob eats it up. He looks pleased with himself, and I'm amazed. I can hardly believe that this is the same person who told me that he wanted to remain anonymous. It's a touchy thing to make fun of the media, and I'm worried that he might have gone too far.

It doesn't take long for Bob's name and face to appear in newsprint. *The Washington Post* features a cartoon on its editorial page with a smiling Haldeman, standing in front of a padlocked door to the Oval Office. To a group of discouraged-looking reporters, Bob is saying, "He's not isolated—he just doesn't want to see anybody!"

June 1970

THE FIRST WEEK IN June, *Time* magazine has Bob on its cover, along with Henry Kissinger, John Ehrlichman, and John Mitchell. A banner across the top identifies them as "Nixon's Palace Guard." In explaining how the White House staff operates, the article features the isolation of the president.

> Suddenly it is fashionable in Washington to fret and fulminate that a palace guard has separated Nixon from realities. In the White House, the key figures around the president are Staff Chief H. R. (Bob) Haldeman, Domestic Affairs Aide John Ehrlichman, and National Security Advisor Henry Kissinger. Because of…their closemouthed habits—the Teutonic trio is now known as "the Berlin Wall"… One administration official calls them "all the king's Krauts"; another speaks of "the throne nursers"… Bob and John are widely called "Von Haldeman" and "Von Ehrlichman."

The article states that instead of having a sixty-button telephone console on his desk like Lyndon Johnson, Nixon has only three direct lines. These connect him to Bob, John, and Henry. According to *Time,* Bob and John "screen nearly every person admitted to the president's lair," as well as every piece of paper and every briefcase. I'm not surprised when I read, "Haldeman mocked the critics last week by announcing that the 'new password' among the eastern media was 'isolation of the president.'"

As I continue reading, I learn more specifics about Bob's workday. Acting as the "city manager of the White House," he "sees that things get done." Bob starts each morning with a tightly run senior staff meeting. Later, he emerges from a meeting with the president with two to ten pages of notes. "He's the only Nixon man who has no schedule of his own. His is shaped entirely by Nixon's."

Bob takes the article in stride and laughs at the description of himself as "Von Haldeman," a "throne nurser," and one of the "king's Krauts." In general, he's indifferent to references to his "glower, militaristic crew cut, and abrupt way of issuing orders." However, I can see why some members of the White House staff are troubled by these references and would like him to soften his image.

In an Associated Press article, Bob is given high marks for his "zero-defect philosophy of management." He is described as a boss who demands as much of himself as he does of his dedicated team of workers. His "young and eager-to-please" office staff, most of whom are in their twenties, "is referred to as the 'Beaver Patrol.'"

An associate is quoted, "Haldeman is in the Oval Office so often he's usually trying to get out while everyone else is trying to get in." A columnist writes, "Proximity to the president is power."

There's no way that Bob can remain anonymous now. With so much press coverage, he has become a public figure overnight. He no longer bothers to duck out of sight at news conferences, stand hidden in the wings at rallies, or sit in the back row at White House functions.

I remember Patrick Anderson's observation: "The scrutiny of the press will magnify both the aide's virtues and his faults." I wish they would provide a more balanced picture of Bob. I'm uncomfortable with the way his pragmatism, proximity, and power are being described. To me, his "zero-defect philosophy of management" results from his demand for perfection, rather than any attempt to gain power. I regret that his character, integrity, and sense of humor are rarely mentioned.

May I?

J UNE IS A TRANSITIONAL month in Washington, when the freshness of spring surrenders to the humidity of summer—or as Ann puts it, a time when "the air is thick." In Kenwood, the cherry trees and azaleas have lost their blossoms, and the garden is a mass of green. Inside our home, the air conditioner automatically kicks in when the thermostat reaches eighty degrees.

On Tuesday evening, June 9, Bob and I attend a small dinner party at the White House, honoring the *Apollo 13* astronauts and their wives. Two months ago, the near-tragedy of their mission united our country. Tonight, just seventeen of us are seated at a single table in the State Dining Room, and the conversation is relaxed and chatty. No one mentions the aborted flight to the moon.

Following coffee in the Blue Room, everyone walks out to the South Lawn, where the presidential helicopter waits to take the astronauts and their wives to Camp David. A marine in dress uniform stands at attention beside the steps leading up to the open door of the chopper. With Bob on one side of me and the president of the United States on the other, I have my back to the magnificent lighted façade of the White House. The night air is balmy, and a light breeze ruffles my hair as I look up at a sky blanketed with stars. Somewhere up there is the moon that these three men tried to reach. As they and their wives board the helicopter, I can sense Nixon straightening up. He solemnly raises his right hand and gives a crisp salute as the chopper slowly rises from the ground. It veers to the right and disappears.

Our small group is left standing in a black void. No one breaks ranks until the low, guttural sounds of the whirling blades can no longer be heard.

◆

FOUR DAYS LATER, SIX top staff members and their families spend the weekend at Camp David for a "White House mixer." Bob is supposed to be with us, but after much vacillation, the president decides to go to Florida. Bob accompanies him.

Although this is the seventh time that I've driven to Camp David, I miss the turnoff and end up in Pennsylvania. We arrive an hour later than planned. With so many of us here, every cabin is occupied, including Aspen, the president's cabin. Susan and I are assigned to Tricia's bedroom, and John and Jeanne Ehrlichman stay across the hall in the Nixons' room. A large presidential seal hanging on the wall above the bed is disconcerting.

While I'm unpacking, Bob calls from Key Biscayne. He sounds miserable. The weather is unbearably hot and humid, and he complains that last night he got "stuck" having to watch *Patton* for the second time with the president. Nixon is fascinated by the hard-driving World War II general and loves George C. Scott's portrayal of him.

I miss Bob. It's hard not to have him here with me among all these families. I think the formal and disciplined Camp David staff is mortified to have seventeen children, ranging in age from four to twenty-three years, racing around. While the younger children play in the president's kidney-shaped pool, the five college students—barefoot and dressed in hippie attire—strum guitars, cruise around in golf carts, and lounge on the porch of the presidential cottage. No one wants to go home on Monday morning, which dawns cold and rainy. The "White House mixer" is considered a great success.

Bob returns home shortly after I do, and I'm eager to tell him about the weekend.

"Want to hear about Camp David?" I ask, as he sorts through the mail in the kitchen.

Preoccupied with an official-looking letter, Bob mumbles a barely audible, "Sure."

I give an overview of the past two days. When I describe how recklessly some of the teenagers drove the golf carts, Bob frowns. I'm not sure if he's reacting to what I'm telling him or something he's reading. When he picks up the White House phone and asks the operator to get Larry on the line, I realize he hasn't heard a word I've said. I quietly retreat to the front porch. A warm rain is beating down, and water gushes off the roof. Standing with my back to the kitchen, I fixate on a single late-blooming pink tulip. Folded over on itself, it succumbs to the downpour. From the kitchen, Bob's hearty laugh filters through the closed French doors.

All I want is to have Bob listen to me. Larry was with him all this weekend, and I don't see how the two of them can still have so much to discuss. It's the same old story. The president, Henry, John, Larry, and a few others all take precedence.

A memory of yesterday's volleyball game at Camp David flashes through my mind. After Jeanne Ehrlichman served an ace, John ran over and gave her a congratulatory hug. The image contrasts vividly with Bob's indifference tonight. Catching myself, I know that it's not fair to compare Bob and John. They have such different temperaments. *But what's happening to Bob and me?* I'm sure we give the appearance of being a devoted couple. We have never had any real differences of opinion, and our commitment to each other is very deep. *And yet, there are times when I feel so left out. I attribute it to Bob's growing insensitivity, but could it be that I'm the problem? Am I overreacting and becoming overly sensitive?*

By the following evening, my questions and doubts are forgotten. In the warm, fragrant night air, Bob and I stand arm-in-arm on our front lawn. Ann and Emilie, her best friend who is visiting from California, are running around trying to capture fireflies in empty mayonnaise jars. They plan to read by their light. The scene is enchanting, and soon Bob and I are catching fireflies, too.

◆

SUSAN TELLS BOB AND me that a friend from Stanford is hitchhiking to Washington, and she has invited him to stay with us. While he's here, she hopes that he will have an opportunity to visit the White House.

When Mark arrives, he's barefoot, reeks of cigarettes, has shoulder-length, uncombed hair, and gives the appearance of having slept in his clothes all week. My immediate concern is how Bob will react. He has a negative view of hippies and never hesitates to make his opinion known.

Much to my amazement, he is unfazed by Mark's appearance and suggests a tour of the West Wing. His one requirement is that Mark must wear shoes and a blazer. Bob agrees to supply the jacket, and Hank will donate shoelaces for Mark's shoes, which he digs out of his backpack.

Three days later, I lead the way to Bob's office with four children in tow. Ann and Emilie are dressed in simple party dresses, white socks, and Mary Jane shoes. Ann's hair is neatly braided, and both the girls have perky hair bows. On the other hand, Susan has the current teenage "earthy" look. With her long hair parted in the middle and limply hanging down on either side of her face, she is wearing a brown print dress, dark brown tights, and thick-heeled brown shoes.

With clean, shiny hair slicked back into a ponytail, Mark shuffles along next to us. Bob's blue blazer hangs loosely from Mark's narrow, stooped shoulders. His shoes are laced, but he has no socks. Although I notice several raised eyebrows as we pass Bob's straight-arrow Beaver Patrol in the hall, Mark appears to pass inspection.

Pat McKee buzzes, and the chief of staff comes bounding out of his office. With his hand extended, Bob enthusiastically welcomes our spruced-up hippie. Our tour of the West Wing goes without a hitch. Bob and I look beyond our stereotypical concept of a hippie, and Mark and Susan give us credit for genuinely accepting him.

◆

IN REBUKE TO NIXON'S incursion into Cambodia, the Senate repeals the 1964 Gulf of Tonkin Resolution, which authorized the president to use military force in Southeast Asia. By the end of the month, the last American soldiers are withdrawn from Cambodia, where over 350 of them lost their lives. President Nixon signs an extension of the Voting Rights Act, allowing eighteen-year-olds to vote. In London, Edward Heath becomes prime minister, as the Conservatives win a majority in Parliament.

Our family is packed and ready to leave for another summer in California. On June 25, Bob takes off from Andrews Air Force Base on *Air Force One*, while the children and I follow in a windowless cargo plane. The Nixons' two dogs, Tim and Pasha, are with us on their way to the Western White House. After landing at El Toro Marine Air Base, Bob and the rest of the presidential party travel by helicopter down the coast to San Clemente. Mom and Dad meet the children and me and drive us to Newport.

This evening, a Coast Guard boat slowly crosses the bay and delivers Bob to Bay Island. Gripping his briefcase, he crosses the lawn to #11. After changing into striped seersucker shorts, a short-sleeved shirt, and a pair of beat-up espadrilles, he heads for the porch. Across the bay, houses and boats are tinted pink in the glow of the setting sun. Here at #11, Bob softly strums a classical tune on his guitar. A long white cord snakes its way across the weathered gray planks of the deck and disappears under his chaise.

July 1970

THE FAMILY GOES ALL out with its decorating this Fourth of July. In no time, #11 looks appropriately patriotic with red, white, and blue crepe paper streamers, balloons, and flags.

Susan and Hank are not with us. With their father's help, they were able to get summer internships in Washington. Susan has a job at the White House Conference for Children and Youth, while Hank works at the Senate Republican Policy Committee.

After spending twenty-two days at the Western White House, President and Mrs. Nixon return to DC. Bob goes with them. In his absence, I spend more time with my parents, who follow their summer routine of arriving every Friday for a four-day weekend. Mom enjoys cooking and painting, while my father works on his boat and tinkers with his telescope. Both do a lot of reading. Mom's eclectic collection of books is crammed into shelves above the mantle and includes mysteries, philosophies, and novels, as well as books on cooking, art, and metaphysics. Daddy reads thick biographies of statesmen and explorers. Occasionally, he focuses on home repairs. Today, it's an extension cord.

My father's flip flops slap against his feet as he shuffles across the porch and steps into the living room. "I don't think I can fix this, Adele," he says, planting himself in front of the red wing chair, where my mother sits reading a Dick Francis mystery. Dad holds up a cord that looks as if a rat had been chewing on it.

As the discussion continues, I'm fascinated to see how involved my parents become in trying to resolve such a mundane issue. Trying to picture Bob and me having a similar conversation, I realize that the two of us haven't discussed ordinary household problems for two years. Instead of being relieved, I suddenly yearn to have a dialogue with Bob over an extension cord, a leaky faucet, or a clogged vacuum cleaner. I'm tired of communicating with him by notes and working around his schedule. I know that I agreed to be a supportive wife, but I miss our partnership in sharing the little things that crop up every day.

August 1970

WHEN THE NIXONS RETURN to the Western White House in August, they stop overnight in Puerto Vallarta, Mexico, for a meeting with President and Mrs. Diaz Ordaz. Carol Finch, Jeanne Ehrlichman, Nancy Ziegler, and I fly down on a government Jet Star the day before our husbands arrive on *Air Force One.*

As part of the presidential party, we stay in the Camino Real, a glitzy new hotel that towers over one of the beautiful white sand beaches of Puerto Vallarta. After enjoying an afternoon swim in the ocean and a late dinner, Carol, Jeanne, Nancy, and I take a midnight dip in the Finches' penthouse swimming pool. The warm night air is the same temperature as the water. Floating on my back, I look up and see the rising moon. Below us lies a town of tin shanties. I'm struck by the stark contrast between the "haves" and the "have-nots."

The next morning, colorfully decorated burros and flag-waving children line the presidential route as the motorcade passes from the airport into town. The heat is intense, but confetti falls like snow. Tiny pink, orange, and turquoise paper "snowflakes" float down on the long line of black limousines. Bob is probably filming the scene on his movie camera.

President Ordaz hosts today's lunch, and the guests are seated at long tables with translators sitting or kneeling behind them. The entrée is half a pineapple with a whole fish standing upright on top. A red rose sprouts from its dorsal fin. Across from me, President Ordaz's brother-in-law smiles broadly and shows me the correct way to eat it.

The Nixons' reciprocal luncheon the following day features roast beef, Yorkshire pudding, strawberry mousse, and petit fours. As on all presidential trips abroad, everything is flown in from the United States. This includes not only the food and the White House china, but the president's bulletproof limousine as well.

Once again, we sit at long tables, and I have to rely on the interpreter to communicate with the animated woman next to me. When I admire her beautiful jewelry, she surprises me by taking off her beetle pin and attaching it to my dress.

When the beetle moves, I'm horrified to discover that it is alive. Covered with tiny diamonds and rubies, it pulls on its little gold chain as it walks in circles on my chest.

On our return flight to California, Jeanne, Carol, and I accompany our husbands on *Air Force One*. Because of the intense heat in Puerto Vallarta, the air-conditioning has been turned up in the cabin. I sneeze.

Caught without my hankie, I turn to Bob and tentatively ask, "Can I borrow your handkerchief?"

"You mean, '*may* I,' not '*can* I,'" he says, giving me the Haldeman look.

I know Bob is not keen about sharing his things, and I'm used to his blunt way of talking to me, but in front of others it's embarrassing. I look over at Jeanne and wonder what she thinks. Sometime, I would like to talk to her about my relationship with Bob; however, I have never discussed my feelings with anyone. Now is not the time to begin.

The Silent Majority

September 1970

SUMMER IS OVER. SATURDAY, September 5, is my final night at Bay Island. A stunning sunset lights up a layer of low-lying clouds. From the dining room window, we look out on the bay. Two sailboats silently glide by, catching the changing colors in their listless sails. Across the lawn, the giant eucalyptus tree is silhouetted against a broad expanse of flaming reds, oranges, and purples.

At dinner, my sisters, Milly and Gay, bring in a decorated sheet cake with "Farewell to Summer" written across it. My father stands and proposes a toast. Raising our water glasses, three generations of Hortons sing *"Hoch Sollst Du Leben,"* followed by a round of "For We Are Jolly Good Fellows." The scene is reminiscent of many summers in the past, but instead of returning to Los Angeles, Susan, Peter, Ann, and I will be departing for Washington.

The next day, standing on the steps of a Jet Star at El Toro, the four of us wave goodbye to my parents and Non. Four hours and 2,320 miles later, we put down in Maryland at Andrews Air Force Base. It's 1:30 a.m., and a White House car is waiting for us.

At home, I face two months of accumulated mail and a calendar full of appointments. We spend the weekend at Camp David, and the children start school the next day. After getting Susan off to Stanford, I have to deal with an infestation of ticks. They are in every nook and cranny of the kitchen, as well as embedded in our Dalmatian's fur.

October 1970

IN OCTOBER, THE PRESIDENT proposes a "standstill" cease-fire in Vietnam, pending a formal peace agreement. Hanoi doesn't respond. Anwar Sadat is elected president of Egypt, and in the Philippines, a typhoon kills almost eight hundred people. In the world of rock music, singer/songwriter Janis Joplin dies from drug-related causes, only sixteen days after the death of guitarist Jimi Hendrix. They were both twenty-seven years old.

An off-year election is coming up in November, and it looks as if the Republicans might lose thirty seats in the House, as well as all but one in the Senate. Although Nixon didn't want to get involved, he reverses himself and campaigns for Republican candidates in twenty-two states. While he's on the road, a grand jury clears the National Guard of any wrongdoing at Kent State and indicts twenty-five students. This incites the antiwar protestors, and demonstrations flare up again.

In response, the president increases his rhetoric and calls for those who oppose the vocal minority of liberal activists to stand up and be counted. Capitalizing on the "silent majority" catchphrase that he used in a speech last year, he appeals to the huge, quiet constituency of the political center. To counter the obscenities that are shouted at nearly every rally, Nixon adds a new line: "The four-letter word that is the most powerful of any in the world is 'vote.'"

Bob is noticeably upset after a campaign rally in San Jose, California. In a late night phone call, he angrily describes the hecklers who shouted obscenities at the motorcade. They threw garbage at his car, and when a rock hit it, the driver slammed on the brakes so hard it caused the car behind them to ram into them. Another rock shattered a window in the bus carrying the White House staff.

"The press should clobber those guys," Bob tells me. "They should show the American public what those 'peaceniks' really stand for. This is the first time a president of the United States has ever been subjected to anything like this, and it's a *major* news story. We've got to keep things cranked up."

◆

ON HALLOWEEN, I CELEBRATE my forty-second birthday with Susan on the Stanford campus. Flying out to Los Angeles with Bob on *Air Force One*, I hitch a ride to Northern California on a Jet Star with Al Haig and John Ehrlichman.

As much as I love spending three days with our daughter, I'm appalled at the condition of the Stanford campus. The students look grungy and act as if they have no pride. Trash is everywhere. Stray dogs wander wherever they want, and I discover a cat licking up spilled milk on the kitchen table in Susan's coed fraternity house, where I am staying. In answer to my question about the mold on the tiles in the girls' bathroom, I'm told the bathroom is "cleaned" once a week by one of the boys. He climbs through the window with the garden hose and washes everything down.

Susan loves Stanford, but I regret that she is on the campus at such a troubled time. Although highly intelligent, most of the students today are rabidly antiestablishment. They show little respect for anything traditional, which includes the professors and the campus. Dressed like hippies, they trash the grounds, skip classes, protest the draft, and hold mass rallies for peace.

On my return flight to Washington, the atmosphere on *Air Force One* is tense. When Bob hears that the media is predicting an overall Republican defeat in the upcoming election, he calls it a "conspiracy of the press."

Newsmakers

November 1970

IN NOVEMBER, THE ELECTION results aren't as dire as the press had predicted. The "silent majority" comes through, and the Republicans lose only twelve House seats. This means a slight increase in the Democrats' majority. Ted Kennedy wins reelection following his first campaign since Chappaquiddick.

With the election over, I thought Bob would be around more, but that's not the case. He is home only four days between November 1 and November 22. His travels take him to San Clemente, Key Biscayne, Camp David, and even Paris, for the funeral of Charles de Gaulle.

When he's out of town, Bob's crew cut suffers. As a teenager, he was told that a buzz cut was the only way to keep his hair manageable; however, his fine hair grows fast, and he worries about keeping his weekly appointment with the White House barber. Milton Pitts, who also cuts the president's hair, has a barber shop on the ground floor in the West Wing. Next door, Henry Kissinger and his National Security staff hold their briefings in the Situation Room.

The press is intrigued by Bob's crew cut, and before long a reference to it appears in print. "Is it true that H. R. Haldeman will permit no long-hairs to visit President Nixon?" a columnist writes. "Has the president banned his aides from having long hair?"

At home, Bob and Hank joke about their hair. It's the crew cut versus the hippie look. Bob promises he will let his hair grow whenever his oldest son gets a haircut. Hank reciprocates. They both know they're safe. Neither one will ever concede.

◆

HENRY KISSINGER, VICE PRESIDENT Agnew, and Martha Mitchell are the newsmakers in the Nixon administration. Their larger-than-life personalities consistently attract the media's attention. Journalists love to write about Henry's good-natured jokes and womanizing. Ted Agnew, who describes himself as "an attack dog," is famous for giving inflammatory speeches. And Martha's flamboyant antics fill the gossip pages almost daily.

It's obvious that John Mitchell adores his wife, but her unpredictability is often embarrassing. Her obsession for attention drives Bob nuts, and at social events, both he and I try to avoid her. At a small Washington dinner, however, Bob finds himself trapped. His indifference to Martha only encourages her, and after dinner, she makes a determined effort to sit on his lap. Perching herself on his knee, she appears to have him right where she wants him. For someone always in control, Bob appears helpless. The other guests and I try to overlook the scene Martha is creating.

Like Martha, Ted Agnew is often referred to as a "loose cannon," and I don't know why Nixon chose him as a running mate. His remarks are clever, but they are often offensive. When he calls the antiwar demonstrators, "an effete corps of impudent snobs" and "nattering nabobs of negativism," he incites the opposition. I don't think it helps Nixon's image when the vice president classifies critics of the administration as the "4-H Club of the hopeless, hysterical hypochondriacs of history."

December 1970

AT TWENTY-FOUR, LARRY HIGBY is twenty years younger than Bob. They have an intense working relationship similar to Bob's with the president, with one major exception—Larry and Bob are personal friends. When nothing else is going on, they eat lunch together in Bob's office, using the time to get caught up. Bob's standing order from the Mess is a meat patty, cottage cheese with a slice of canned pineapple, Ry-Krisp, and a glass of Constant Comment iced tea.

Thursday, December 3, is one of those rare occasions when Bob and Larry can put aside work and enjoy a casual evening together with their wives. We are in New York City, where Bob attended an earlier meeting of the executive board of the Kennedy Center. The four of us enjoy a leisurely dinner and the theater, where we see *Applause,* starring Lauren Bacall.

The following evening, after the president addresses the National Association of Manufacturers, we assemble on the rooftop of an office building in lower Manhattan to wait for the helicopter to transport us back to *Air Force One.* The night is unseasonably warm, and a light breeze makes it feel almost tropical. A full moon looms low on the horizon. Below us, on my right, I can see the twinkling Christmas lights of midtown, and on my left, the black void of Wall Street. For a brief moment, the chopper hovers, silhouetted against the giant orange moon. The sight is breathtaking.

"Wow!" Bob exclaims.

"It's magical," I say in wonder.

Overboard

EVER SINCE THE INAUGURATION, Bob has kept a diary. Up until recently, he wrote in longhand, filling the pages of several journals with his neat, slanted handwriting. Now he uses a Dictaphone to record his daily entries onto cassettes. Generally, he dictates late at night in his upstairs study, and I can hear the soft drone of his steady, flat monotone as I read in bed.

Two years ago, Bob Rutland, a historian and former neighbor, wrote to Bob, begging him "to record carefully in a diary each day of your association in the White House... You have the opportunity to tell historians the side issues..."

Bob wrote back a letter, consisting of two sentences. "I agree with you, and I will do it. Thank you for your wise counsel."

Bob never talks about his diary. Only a handful of people know that he's keeping one, and no one has seen what he has written. Writing is a chore for him, but he's good at documentation. His written word is just as clear and straightforward as when he speaks. He always says that it's up to the communicator to get his message across. If others fail to understand, the communicator has only himself to blame.

Bob's journals and cassettes are being stored at the White House for safekeeping. Sometimes I wonder what will happen to them when Bob retires. Although he has no intention of writing a book, I'm sure Bob Rutland was right when he wrote that historians would find the diaries of the chief of staff invaluable.

◆

A WEEK BEFORE CHRISTMAS, the temperature drops and there's a light snowfall. After Bob puts the lights on our Christmas tree, the children and I join him to decorate it. Suddenly rock music comes blasting through the two living room speakers. Overpowering the Christmas carols coming from the music box in the revolving tree base, it startles everyone but Susan. Home for Christmas vacation, she has brought the newly released album *Jesus Christ Superstar*. The honky-tonk strains of "Herod's Song" replace "Silent Night." Soon, I find myself humming along, as Herod asks Jesus to "prove to me that you're no fool; walk across my swimming pool."

On Christmas Eve, we join our neighbors for carols at the base of a huge lighted tree in the center of Kenwood. We dress formally for dinner and then change again for the midnight service at Washington National Cathedral.

As we are opening our gifts on Christmas morning, the White House phone rings. When Bob leaps up to answer it, my heart falls. This is family time, and I can't imagine why anyone would be calling. Bob is smiling when he rejoins us in the living room.

"That was the president," he says, smiling. "He wanted to wish everyone a Merry Christmas. Then he told me to take five minutes off anytime I wanted to today."

January 1971

IT'S THE FIRST DAY of the New Year. Peering out the bedroom window, I'm enthralled. Bright sunlight glistens on a blanket of fresh snow. Every bush and tree is jacketed in white; there's no sign of our front walk or the road. We had planned to spend the weekend at Camp David with the Ehrlichmans, but the heavy snowfall makes the drive impossible. Fortunately, our two families are able to hitch a ride on a government helicopter leaving from the Pentagon.

Snow swirls around us as we land in two feet of powder on the playing field at the presidential retreat. Once we are "berthed," eleven Ehrlichmans and Haldemans spend most of our time outside. We drive bright yellow snowmobiles, slide down hills on saucers and toboggans, have snowball fights, and take long walks.

The Nixons are also here, but you would never know it. Bob repeats his warning about their need for privacy, and he makes it very clear that we are staff, and staff is to stay out of sight when the first family is around. After a three-hour meeting with the president, Bob reports that Nixon has remained in Aspen since he arrived and has no idea how beautiful the snow is. When Jeanne hears this, she suggests that we ask Pat, Tricia, and Julie to join us for a walk. Bob dismisses the idea with a swift Haldeman look.

♦

AFTER SPENDING A FEW days at Camp David, the first family decides to fly out to the Western White House. Of course, this means that Bob has to go, too, and I accompany him. Within forty-eight hours of leaving the snowy presidential mountain retreat, the two of us are basking in the sun in Palm Springs. We are staying with Non at Smoke Tree Ranch, while the Nixons are in San Clemente. It's a working vacation for Bob, and once again the White House phone connects the president to his chief of staff.

Late morning on January 9, Bob is stretched out on a chaise by the pool with the White House phone at his side. Beads of sweat glisten through his closely cropped crew cut. Reaching for his ever-present yellow pad and felt tip pen, he places a call.

"Happy Birthday, Mr. President. Any special plans for today?" Bob pauses to listen, and a frown creeps across his face. "I'm sorry to hear that. I agree…it was a stupid idea." Another pause. "Don't worry about it, sir. It won't do much harm. Just forget it and have a great day."

"What was that about?" Non asks as soon as Bob hangs up.

"The president was talked into taking a walk along the beach as a photo-op for his birthday," Bob explains.

"What's wrong with that?" Non questions.

"He's worried because he was wearing his dress shoes."

Envisioning the president plodding through wet sand in his black wingtips, I feel sorry for him. Undoubtedly the press will contrast this scene to photos of the charismatic Jack Kennedy, barefoot, in rolled up khakis, tossing a football on the beach with his handsome family.

♦

JANUARY 20, 1971, IS the second anniversary of the president's inauguration, and Bob steadfastly maintains that Nixon is capable of becoming one of history's greatest leaders. The president has a brilliant mind and an unbelievable grasp of global affairs. Bob believes in him and serves him with his whole heart. I respect this total dedication, even though I think that he sometimes carries his loyalty to extremes.

On January 29, I accompany Bob and a few White House staff members on *Air Force One* to the Virgin Islands, where the president will spend a long weekend at Caneel Bay, the Rockefeller resort. In the meantime, I have been invited to join our friends George and Kathleen Bell on their forty-five-foot yacht, the *Sarabande*.

During the day, the Bells and I sail from island to island, swimming and snorkeling in hidden bays. At night, we anchor in the shelter of a cove and sleep on the boat. Sunday afternoon, Bob and Larry join us. Bob is "on call," and the Army Signal Corps will contact him via shortwave radio if he's needed. He and Larry are both eager to take turns skippering, and soon the five of us are flying along on a run with billowing sails.

Suddenly, a lot of static and a garbled message come over the radio. I make out the words "Searchlight" and "Welcome." Bob tenses up. He considers a call from the president urgent, and he asks George to return to Caneel Bay immediately.

George jibes the *Sarabande* and reverses our course. The boat heels, and we're doused with saltwater. Bob's fingers drum on the deck, while Larry's right leg nervously jiggles. When we enter the protective cove of Caneel Bay, the wind dies. Drifting about a hundred yards offshore, Bob becomes frustrated and decides there's a faster way to make it to land. He thanks the Bells, walks to the bow of the boat, and dives into the water. Larry follows. Swimming as hard as they can, they finally reach the beach, where they run for their parked jeep. There is a cloud of dust as they speed away and disappear into a grove of tamarind trees. Kathleen and George are speechless.

It doesn't take long for the press to get wind of Bob's "dramatic leap overboard and heroic swim." *The Washington Post* writes, "The Bob Haldemans were on the *Sarabande*…when the Nixons were at Caneel. They had sailed for only three hours when Haldeman's squawk box began to beep. To save time, the ever-needed assistant, who's the picture of crew cut vitality, jumped overboard and swam back."

Once again, I'm reminded of one of Patrick Anderson's quotes. "The aide must be willing to subject himself to another man's interests…to be permanently number two..." As number two, Bob's time, thoughts, and actions are totally focused on number one: President Richard Nixon.

February 1971

ON OUR RETURN TO Washington, people tease Bob about his "heroic" swim and dedication to the president. As the center of attention, he joins in the camaraderie, ignoring me. His indifference hurts, and I feel insecure and alone. I wonder if any of the other White House wives experience similar feelings.

On Thursday, February 4, Governor Nelson Rockefeller is giving a dinner party for this wife, Happy. Hoping to make her feel more at home in Washington, "Rocky" invites ten guests to their thirty-acre estate on Foxhall Road.

Unfortunately, the party fails to accomplish its objective. Instead of revolving around Happy, the evening is all about her square-jawed, patrician husband. At the dinner table, Rocky and his male friends dominate the conversation, which focuses on revenue sharing, government reorganization, and how to gain nonpartisan support for the president. Seated at the other end of the table, Happy doesn't say much and looks miserable.

After dinner, the men remain seated, while cigars and brandy are served. The wives "retire" to the living room. With only the women surrounding her, Happy finally becomes talkative. At 10:00 p.m., she abruptly stands and announces that she's going to bed. With that, our hostess strides past her guests and leaves the room.

As Happy climbs the stairs, we can hear Henry Kissinger's distinctive voice coming from the dining room. "Rocky, why don't you just buy Happy that chateau in France?"

Another male voice adds, "That should make Happy happy."

The remark is followed by laughter. It's sad. Financially, politically, and socially, Happy is a woman who has it all. But Happy is clearly missing something that money can't buy.

Many women in Washington are married to prominent men. I'm beginning to see that some are able to make their marriages work, while others are not. It's a challenge.

Can You Keep a Secret?

IN FEBRUARY, RICHARD NIXON'S popularity falls to a new low. For the first time, his approval rating in the Gallup Poll has slipped to 50 percent, and a Harris Poll gives Senator Edmund Muskie of Maine the lead over Nixon in a trial run for the presidency. Bob remains unruffled as he continues to reassure the president. Always upbeat and never dwelling on the downside, he buoys Nixon up in a steady, cheerful voice. Although I have my moments of frustration, I'm proud of the job Bob is doing, and I believe that Nixon can accomplish great things in a second term.

The news in general is not good. Unemployment hits a ten-year high. The Vietnam War drags on, and many strongly believe that it is "morally wrong." Heroin use in the military is way up. In Saigon, a US Air Force officer is given a three-year sentence for smoking marijuana, and many military units are plagued with racial unrest. The SALT talks with Russia are stalemated. And to top it off, at the Bob Hope Classic Golf Tournament Vice President Agnew's first two shots go wild and hit three spectators.

Early Tuesday morning, February 9, Los Angeles is hit by a 6.6 earthquake, the biggest in thirty-eight years. I get the news while volunteering at the Junior League Thrift Shop in Georgetown. Phone lines are down in Southern California, and I can't reach anyone in the family. Out of desperation, I ask the White House operators for their help. In no time, I'm talking to my mother, followed by Bob's mother. The large, plate glass window in my father's office shattered, covering his desk with glass. The elevators stopped working in Non's high-rise condominium on Wilshire Boulevard. After carrying her canary in its cage down sixteen flights of stairs, she vows to find another place to live.

◆

FEBRUARY 19 IS OUR twenty-second wedding anniversary. I spend the morning volunteering at Juvenile Hall, where once a week I help file the casework for an overworked probation officer. In the evening, Bob and I dine on soft-shell crabs and creamed spinach at Rive Gauche in Georgetown. When dessert comes, he wishes me a Happy Anniversary and hands me a small, beautifully wrapped box. I am delighted with his gift—a gold charm of the White House. When we were first engaged, he gave me a bracelet with a single charm, a church. Since then, he has added others to commemorate the birth of each child, as well as birthdays, anniversaries, trips, and other milestones in our marriage.

After dinner, we have tickets for *John and Abigail*, which is playing at Ford's Theater. Several times during the performance, I find myself empathizing with Abigail. Although she and John have a strong relationship, his driving interest in the politics of our young country puts demands on their marriage.

Our row empties during intermission, but Bob and I remain seated. We talk about the play, which leads to a discussion of the White House. Leaning in, he asks if I can keep a secret. I nod, eager to hear what he has to say.

"A couple of days ago, the president had the Secret Service install a taping system in the Oval Office and the Cabinet Room." Bob's voice is low. "You can't tell anyone. The only people who know about it are the president, Larry, Alex Butterfield, and me."

"Why'd he do it?" I ask, looking at him in amazement. All I can think of is how adamant Nixon had been about having President Johnson's recording system removed.

"Johnson's been pushing him to do it," Bob explains. "LBJ's been working on his memoir, and he says that his recorded conversations are invaluable. They're an indisputable source."

Bob stands to let a man cross in front of him on his way to his seat. Once reseated, Bob continues. "Both Kennedy and Johnson used a hidden switch to tape conversations, but President Nixon's too mechanically inept for that." Bob laughs. "The poor Secret Service guys had to figure out something else. They finally installed a system that's voice-activated."

Others file back to their seats as I mull over all that Bob has shared with me. The houselights dim, and the play resumes.

Bob, We Need to Talk

March 1971

THE FIRST SUNDAY IN March, the weather is raw. An icy wind cuts through the naked limbs of the cherry trees, and their giant arms twist slowly back and forth. It feels good to be in the den with a fire crackling in the fireplace.

Seated at the round table in the corner, I write two letters—one to Mom and Dad and one to Non. I correspond with them every week, sharing the many interesting events that are a part of the privileged life I lead. I know they hang on every word. And yet, I don't write everything. I don't reveal the things Bob tells me in confidence, like the White House taping system. And I don't share the growing concerns I'm having about my relationship with Bob.

Although Bob can be very thoughtful on special occasions, like our anniversary, it's not easy to live with him on a day-to-day basis. He is becoming more abrupt with me and frequently treats me with indifference. I try to keep things running smoothly by remaining in the background.

I keep my feelings bottled up inside me, but I am reaching my breaking point. I have even wondered what Bob would do if I took the children and returned to California. It's a crazy thought, and I catch myself. *Don't be foolish, Jo. Bob warned you that his attention would be focused on the president. It's only for a limited time. Focus on and appreciate the extraordinary lifestyle that he's providing for you.*

◆

I save everything I see about Bob in magazines and newspapers and paste it in my scrapbooks. At first there was very little, but recently there have been more frequent references to him. Several quotes resonate with me as they describe Bob's dedication to the president.

> Bob Haldeman, at 44, is lean, un-faddishly crew cut, and tanned (a result of his thirst for sunshine). When he breaks into a hungry grin, he can charm, but more often he appears formidable and preoccupied... He hates small talk... Despite Haldeman's penchant for bluntness, the younger members of the staff approach him by first name and seem to dote on him.
>
> —Christopher S. Wren, *Look*

> Haldeman is indispensable to the president; his loyalty quotient is measureless.
>
> —Bryce Harlow, counselor to the president

> Above all else, Haldeman lets you know that his total commitment is to serve the president...not the press or the politicians or the public.
>
> —Dom Bonafede, *CPR Journal*

> "He's the perfect alter ego," an old associate said. "It's almost as if Haldeman ceased to exist when Nixon took office." Given this relationship, nothing counts except guarding the president's serenity and carrying out the president's wishes.
>
> —Peter Goldman, *Newsweek*

> Until he has been part of a cause larger than himself, no man is truly whole.
>
> —Richard Nixon, Inaugural Address 1969

> My whole existence is pointed toward carrying out another man's directives and being of service to him. That automatically changes one... I get impatient with trivia, and I get impatient with people who don't figure out their own solutions and get them done... The great leaders are

gone. The towering leaders are going. There aren't any
great leaders now, except Richard Nixon.
                                    —Bob Haldeman, in various interviews

*Bob's commitment to a cause larger than himself is so strong
and all-consuming, I sometimes think that I might be losing
him to President Nixon.*
                                    —Jo Haldeman's state of mind, March 1971

◆

ON MARCH 13, PETER, Ann, and I leave a gloomy, cold Washington to join
Bob in Florida for a weekend in the sun. Instead of staying at the Key Biscayne
Hotel, the four of us share one of Bebe Rebozo's houses with Larry and Dolores
Higby and their ten-week-old daughter. Located next door to the Nixons'
home, the contemporary one-story house is on the bay side of the key. A fried,
brown lawn runs to the edge of a seawall instead of a beach. Staying so close
to the president is convenient for Bob, but I don't like it. I prefer our villa on
the ocean side, where we are independent. I feel trapped here, and my stifled
frustrations and anxieties start to get the better of me.

Sunday morning, it's sunny and hot with very little humidity, and Bob
and I are the first ones up. Carrying our breakfast trays to the enclosed lanai,
we take seats at the wrought iron table. Neither of us says anything as we eat
and read the paper. We are practically touching one another, and yet it's as if a
huge gulf separates us. My emotions well up inside me, and before I know it,
they spill out.

"Bob, we need to talk."

The words hang above me, like a black cloud suspended in the still
morning air. We've been married for twenty-two years, and I've never spoken
out like this.

"No problem," Bob mumbles, hidden behind the first section of *The
Washington Post.* "We can talk. Can it wait until this afternoon?"

"Sure," I say, wondering what made me speak out. It's not like me.

Soon, others join us at the table, and I'm grateful for the interruption.
Larry looks as if he just stepped out of the shower, alert and eager for the day to
begin. Dee follows him, carrying baby Jennifer. Peter and Ann have that fuzzy

Sunday morning look. The chatter grows louder, food appears, spoons clink in cereal bowls, and newspapers are strewn on the table and the floor. The sun climbs higher, and someone switches on the air conditioner. Frigid air blasts, and we disperse.

Changing into trunks and polo shirts, Bob and Larry station themselves at the edge of the seawall. Arranging two chaises, they set up a place to work. A white phone sits on the lawn between them; its long cord stretches back to the house. While waiting for them to finish up, I join Peter and Ann for a swim in the bay, which is interrupted by the appearance of several giant manta rays. The two men talk until late in the afternoon. Bob finally puts down his yellow pad, and Larry gets up.

"It's your turn, Jo," Bob calls out.

My turn…

Passing Larry on my way out to the seawall, I give a weak smile. Withered blades of grass crunch under my feet as I take each step. I don't really know what I am going to say. *How do I go about conveying my insecurities to my husband, who is so put together?* When I reach him, he flops over onto his stomach to allow the last rays of the sun to beat down on his back. His right arm dangles at his side, and his fingers rest on the receiver of the phone. Spreading my towel across the plastic ribs of Larry's vacated chaise, I sit sideways, in order to face Bob's prone body.

"I hate to bother you…" I say. It's hard to start the conversation, and I regret beginning on an apologetic note.

"What's up?" Bob asks lightheartedly.

Avoiding eye contact, I try to get to the heart of the problem. Bob likes people to come right to the point, but I'm not at all sure what my point is. "I want to talk about…us. You know…about our marriage."

"What do you mean? Have I done something?"

"No, no. Not exactly," I quickly respond, realizing that I have to be more specific. "It's about your work…or rather, the effect of your work on me. You're totally preoccupied with your job, and I feel that it's driving a wedge between us."

Bob looks puzzled. "I don't understand how you can feel that way, Jo. I include you in everything I possibly can. I've got a heck of a lot of demands on me, and it's not like I have a whole lot of time to be with you and the kids." He pauses to wipe a trickle of sweat running down his neck. "I realize that this has got to be tough on you, but I don't know what more I can do."

"The children and I can deal with your not being around. It's just that… that when the two of us are together in public, you so often ignore me, and…" I lower my voice in embarrassment. "…it makes me feel left out. Also, it's demeaning to write notes when I need to talk to you. It would be nice if we could have normal conversations about the children or routine things that come up around the house."

"You write notes because it's the best way for us to communicate," Bob says. "As you well know, my job is to serve the president, and that consumes more hours than there are in the day. I have to prioritize…which should not be news to you."

As always, Bob doesn't mince words. He is businesslike, direct, and clear.

"I know, but I don't see how you can keep humoring the president the way you do. Wherever we are, or whatever we're doing, you *always* put him first. It's as if you were married to him rather than to me."

"Oh, come on, Jo. That's ridiculous, and you know it."

I do know it, and I instantly regret saying it. Bob is irritated, and I worry that I may have crossed the line. After a strained silence, he speaks. "I work my tail off trying to put things in a positive way for the president. He gets nothing but negative stuff dumped on him all the time." Bob gives a resigned sigh. "I deal with an incredible number of issues every day. When we talked in California, before moving to DC, I told you how time-consuming my job would be…I thought you understood."

"Oh, Bob…I did…I do. It's just that it was a lot easier to accept at the time than it is to deal with it now."

"I'm sorry, Jo. In the future, I'll try to be more aware of things." Bob's fingers start to drum on the White House phone. He's ready to move on. Clutching his brightly colored beach towel around his shoulders, he stands.

"I've got a suggestion," he says, looking pleased. "How about flying out to California for ten days? Larry and I were just going over the logistics for a presidential trip to the Western White House at the end of the month. You could come along with us."

"That'd be really nice," I say, making an effort to sound enthusiastic. "Thanks."

I know that Bob is trying to be helpful, but a trip to California is only a Band-Aid. He has no concept of the depth of my feelings. I blame myself for not expressing them well. He responded in character—the ever-efficient chief of staff. I love his self-assurance, and I appreciate his attempt to understand me. These qualities will help me get through the next five and a half years. In the meantime, I plan to savor being a part of history in the making.

Together, Bob and I walk back to the house. In his right hand, he carries the white phone.

Tennis Lessons

April 1971

FOUR DAYS AFTER RETURNING from the trip to California, I'm on my way to Colonial Williamsburg for Easter with Bob, Peter, and Ann. We fly down in a marine helicopter and stay in the Norton-Cole house on the main street of town. It's a historic home and has no phone connection, which means the children and I have Bob all to ourselves. The Nixons are at Camp David, and for almost two full days, Bob cannot communicate with the president. With no interruptions, we dye Easter eggs and then hunt for them in the charming garden filled with lavender, daffodils, and blooming fruit trees.

When we return to Kenwood, spring is at its height, and sightseers flock to the area to see the cherry trees. Capitalizing on all of the activity, Ann and a neighborhood friend devise a way to make more money than a lemonade stand. All they need is a dog, a bucket, and a sign. With light pink cherry blossoms collecting on the ground like snow, the two little girls drag Bea Alice's old, black Labrador retriever, Cinders, out to the curb, where they have her sit. In no time, they have cars lined up and eager customers waiting to drop their nickels into a plastic pail. Propped up in front of them, a cardboard sign reads, "PAT THE DOG. FIVE CENTS."

In late April, the antiwar protestors are back in full force. Two thousand veterans camp on the Mall. Seven hundred of them gather at the Capitol to toss away their war medals in protest. On April 24, five hundred thousand demonstrators call for an end to the war at the "Vietnam War Out Now" rally. In an attempt to shut down the government, they stop traffic. The police move in, and several thousand people are arrested.

"The right to demonstrate for peace abroad doesn't include the right to break the peace at home," the president states in an impromptu news conference.

I continue to be concerned about the impact these large, angry gatherings might have on our children—particularly Hank and Peter, who are more independent. I'm not at all sure I know what is going on, and I think Hank may be smoking marijuana. After he returns home from one of the demonstrations, I decide to ask him, hoping his answer will be no.

"Did you smoke pot this afternoon?"

"Yes."

I'm taken aback and search for the right follow-up question. "Were you experimenting?"

"No, Mom. I've done this before." Hank looks me right in the eye, which I appreciate. But it's also unnerving.

"Oh? Where?"

"At concerts."

"Oh, really?" *I'm at a loss. I know so little about this sort of thing. I hope Hank can't sense how vulnerable I feel.* "Well, be careful," I advise. "Don't do anything foolish."

"I won't."

I don't respond, and Hank walks away.

Irritated with myself, I turn to Bob later, who reminds me that Hank was honest and up-front about the incident. "He's a good student, Jo, not some wild-eyed liberal. Wait until he gets into real trouble. Then, we'll clamp down."

◆

I RARELY CALL BOB at the office, and when I ask to speak to him today, the White House operator tells me that he can't be reached. This is the first time this has happened, and it concerns me.

These operators are famous for their skill in tracking people down—anywhere, anytime. When I question the operator further, she finally concedes that Bob is at the Chevy Chase Country Club. I'm dumbfounded. It's the last place I would expect to find him. When I ask why, there's a long pause.

"Mr. Haldeman wanted to surprise you, Mrs. Haldeman," the operator explains. "He's been taking tennis lessons."

Tennis lessons? Instantly, I regret pursuing Bob's whereabouts. I ruined his surprise, and I put the White House operator in an awkward position. Bob isn't a natural athlete, and I'm touched that he would do this. I look forward to playing doubles with the Ehrlichmans and the Higbys at Camp David and the White House.

May 1971

Bob would like to show off his new tennis skills at Camp David over the weekend of May 14, but he ends up in Florida with the president instead. Non, the children, and I follow through with our plans to join the Ehrlichman family at the mountain retreat.

At breakfast on Saturday, Pair informs us that Mrs. Nixon will arrive this afternoon. My relationship with the first lady is distant and impersonal. She has her own set of friends from California, who often stay at the White House. When my friends ask if I spend much time with Pat, they are surprised when I tell them that I rarely see her.

This weekend is no exception. Following Bob's repeated instructions, we do everything in our power to stay out of sight. However, on Sunday morning the eight of us are caught off guard at the bowling alley. The phone rings in the middle of our second game, and John leaps up to answer it.

"Hold the presses, everyone," he calls out. "Mrs. Nixon's on her way over here."

We know the drill well and swing into action. In no time, the bowling balls are lined up according to size, shoes are returned to their cubbyholes, and the hand towel is neatly folded. We tear the used score sheets off the score pad and jam them into our pockets, leaving no telltale trash behind us. Whisking Non out the door, we make a mad dash through the woods to Laurel.

"This is silly," Non exclaims, once we are all safely inside. "It's not natural to run away from Pat. She's here alone. Why don't you ask her to join us?"

Jeanne nods in agreement, but I know better than to question Bob's orders. When I explain to Non that her son is the one who made the rule, she concedes. She will readily accept anything he suggests.

I wonder if Pat has any idea of what we go through to give her privacy. It must be hard to always be in the public eye, and I don't envy her. By her expression, she often gives the impression that she doesn't much care for her official role as first lady. I think she puts up with it and does what's required of her to be a good team player. In fact, I can think of only two couples who seem to thrive on a political life together: Joyce and Don Rumsfeld and Nellie and John Connally. All four of them appear to be completely at ease in public.

The day after we return from Camp David, I attend a luncheon given by the cabinet wives in honor of the first lady. When they present her with an elegant bed tray and breakfast set, she smiles weakly and thanks them.

Pointing to the gift, the woman next to me asks, "Does Mrs. Nixon often eat breakfast in bed?"

"I don't know," I reply.

"You don't know?" The woman looks puzzled. "I thought she was a friend of yours."

"No. Not really."

"Oh?" The woman's eyebrows go up.

Once again, I try to explain that although the president and Bob have a close working relationship, that closeness doesn't extend into our social lives. The woman looks dubious.

Here Comes the Bride

A T NOON ON MAY 20, Nixon announces that the United States and the USSR have agreed to a limitation on antiballistic missiles, which is a "significant development" in the SALT talks. To improve Sino-US relations, Nixon eases a twenty-year-old embargo on trade with Communist China. An American table tennis team will soon be playing ping pong in Peking. For a president who wants détente with Russia and China, things finally look promising.

June 1971

ON A HOT SATURDAY morning in early June, Hank graduates from St. Albans. The ceremony is impressive in the huge National Cathedral with its pointed arches and flying buttresses. Bob and I are proud parents as Hank walks down the aisle with fifty-five members of his class. Next fall, he will enter UCLA as a freshman.

A week later, on June 12, Bob and I attend Tricia Nixon's wedding to Edward Ridley Finch Cox in the Rose Garden of the White House. Because of a threatening storm, the ceremony is delayed. Planes circle above us, trying to get an accurate read on the weather.

Standing at the edge of the lawn, looking up at the ominous sky, Bob says, "The president's hanging tough. He and Tricia are determined to have this outside."

As a few scattered drops start to fall, he leaves to confer with Nixon, and I seek shelter under the eaves of the West Colonnade. Soon a light steady rain is coming down, and water begins to collect in puddles on the plastic runner that extends down the middle of the lawn and ends at an arbor at the far end of the garden. Hovering near a stack of gilt chairs with members of the White

House staff, I wait for a decision to be made. As soon as the rain lets up, Lucy Winchester calls out, "It's a go," and we swing into action.

Grabbing two chairs, I put them in place and go back for more. Each time I walk across the lawn, I can feel it squish beneath my green satin shoes. By the time the last chair is in place, the guests are being ushered in. They have been "on hold" in the South Hall for the last half hour. Bob and I take seats on the aisle in the last row, where he's in a good position to film the ceremony. Behind us is the tulip tree, where Susan and I hid yesterday to watch the dress rehearsal.

The air is warm and fragrant, and the black clouds above us create an iridescent lighting effect. The bright oranges, yellows, and greens in my dress are muted, and the garden has an ethereal look with its lush greenery and many arrangements of white roses.

Tricia looks like a princess on the arm of her proud father, who is beaming. Wearing a soft-pink dress, Pat appears relaxed and sparkly, with a glowing smile. Holding hands, she and the president are gracious and gregarious as they follow the bride and groom back up the aisle. I've never seen Nixon look so genuinely happy. Even his social awkwardness has left him, and for once he doesn't joke about my "drinking problem."

After a reception in the East Room, the guests wave goodbye to Mr. and Mrs. Cox from the steps of the West Portico. Back inside the main hall, the president approaches Bob and me. He's jazzed up, and his voice is loud as he greets us.

"Hey, Bob," he says, clapping him on the back. "How about coming up to the residence for a few minutes? Pat and Julie'll be there, and we can talk over the wedding."

"Yes, sir," Bob responds. Turning, he hands me his camera. "Thanks, Jo. I'll meet you in my office."

Without a backward glance, Bob is gone. A long red carpet separates us. In the midst of the dispersing crowd, I am alone. As the early evening shadows lengthen, I retrace my steps to the West Wing, slowly walking along the West Colonnade. The deserted wedding setting is serene, bringing to mind the lingering memory of the president and Pat holding hands. For one brief moment, they emerged from their protective shells and exposed a softer, more human side. Their emotions appeared genuine and uninhibited.

As I'm about to leave the Rose Garden, I spot the Ehrlichmans at the other end. Wrapping his arm around Jeanne's waist, John starts humming "Here

Comes the Bride" as they walk in step. Following the white canvas runner, they stop at the rose-covered gazebo where Tricia and Ed had been married earlier. I grab Bob's camera to film them as they feign reverence and recite their impromptu version of the marriage vows. As the three of us enter the West Wing, I notice that John still has his arm around Jeanne's waist.

Bob shows up at his office half an hour later. He is pleased with the day. The wedding went without a hitch, and even the weather did what he wanted it to do.

Pentagon Papers and Peas

THE FOLLOWING DAY, A major flap creates a big problem for John and Bob. While the Ehrlichman and Haldeman families cruise down the Potomac on board the *Sequoia*, the two men huddle together in deep discussion. A story in *The New York Times* consumes their attention. At lunch, they finally divulge what it's all about.

"Something's got to be done immediately," John growls, as he and Bob join us in the dining room. "The *Times* and whoever illegally leaked the information should be hauled into court." He rolls his eyes, and his eyebrows go way up like two dark, bushy exclamation points.

Bob explains that a seven-thousand-page classified document was stolen from the Pentagon—a study of the Vietnam War that Secretary of Defense McNamara commissioned in 1967.

Looking over the buffet table, loaded with platters of roast beef, lamb chops, peas, rice, various salads, and fresh fruit, I find it hard to get too excited over another government leak. Particularly one that predates this administration.

"These are Pentagon documents that have been turned over to the *Times* illegally," Bob states. "Classified material should never be made public. Once that happens, it threatens everything else that's classified. This is about national security."

With a full plate, Bob turns from the table and starts to walk across the room. His foot catches on the piano bench. Pitching forward, he loses his grip on his plate. Sixteen of us freeze as we watch Bob's lunch sail through the air like a Frisbee. With uncanny timing, a steward appears in the doorway. Standing ramrod straight, he extends his right arm and catches the "Frisbee" without even blinking. Calmly walking over to Bob, he hands him the plate.

"I believe this is your lunch, sir," the steward says formally.

The food is intact—with the exception of the peas. They arc all over the place, even on the piano keys. The incident breaks the tension of the *Times* story, and Bob and John relax during the rest of the cruise.

The press refers to the leaked report as the "Pentagon Papers," and for the next week, the story continues to make headlines. *The Washington Post* and two other papers also obtain copies and start publishing them. The Justice Department issues a warrant for the arrest of Daniel Ellsberg, a former Pentagon aide, who stole the report and turned it over to the *Times*.

The Pentagon Papers continue to be the main focus of attention over the weekend of June 19, when we are in Key Biscayne. The weather is unbearably hot and sticky. In a three-hour meeting with the president, Bob swelters in a coat and tie, while Nixon, smoking a cigar, is in swim trunks and a sport shirt.

When Bob is free late in the afternoon, he's eager to take a sail and rents a Sunfish. Unfortunately, the wind dies, leaving him becalmed. The eighty-degree ocean is glassy smooth, and Bob doesn't get back to the villa until after dark. Sunburned and covered with patches of dried saltwater, he's a pathetic sight.

On the return trip to Washington, *Air Force One* makes a stop in Atlantic City, New Jersey, where Nixon addresses a gathering of businessmen. I join the thousands of cheering spectators who line the sidewalk to watch as the presidential motorcade drives by. Suddenly, a slow-moving convertible sedan passes in front of me with Bob standing on the running board. Clutching his camera with both hands, he's calmly filming the scene.

What Would the President Do
Without You?

A T 7:50 A.M., ON Sunday, July 11, the White House phone rings in our bedroom at Bay Island. Bob answers it midway through brushing his teeth. Following a brief conversation, he turns to face me and announces, "Well, it's all set. The president's going to China."

I am speechless. I can hardly comprehend what he's telling me. *Nixon hates the Communists. Why would he be going to China? No one goes to China. It's been closed off from the rest of the world for at least twenty-five years.*

Bob finishes brushing his teeth and steps back into the bedroom. "Henry's been secretly meeting with the Chinese in Peking," he explains. "The trip's planned for early spring."

The whole concept of a presidential trip to China is surreal to me. "Will you be going, too?"

"Yep," he replies with a grin. "But you can't say anything. It'll be announced in four days."

When the White House phone rings again, I slip out of the room. Bursting with excitement, I can hardly contain myself when I pass my father in the living room. With the American flag bunched up under his arm, he's on his way out to the flagpole at the side of the house. Raising the flag is his daily ritual. This morning, a tremendous sense of patriotism sweeps over me as I watch Daddy. I'm proud to be an American. I have goose bumps thinking about *Air Force One* landing in China, knowing that Bob will be on it. This is one secret that's hard to keep.

Speaking from the NBC studios in Burbank on Thursday, July 15, at 7:31 p.m., Nixon tells the world that the following statement is being read simultaneously in China:

> …Premier Chou En-lai on behalf of the People's Republic of China has extended an invitation to President Nixon to visit China at an appropriate date before May 1972. President Nixon has accepted the invitation with pleasure. The meeting…is to seek normalization of relations between the two countries and also to exchange views on questions of concern to the two sides.

Reaction from the press is immediate and positive. In Warsaw, the announcement is described as a "shocking somersault." In Paris, *Le Monde* calls it "a great turning point in world politics." In the US, the media uses words like, "stunning…unbelievable…historic…groundbreaking."

Of course, Bay Island is abuzz over the news, and neighbors ask if Bob will be traveling with the president. Much to my surprise, some wonder if I, too, will be included in the presidential party.

August 1971

A MONTH LATER, I'M sitting on the beach reading the *Los Angeles Times* when a story with the headline "Haldeman Wields Real Power" catches my attention. The article raises some interesting questions about Bob's developing role as chief of staff.

> Observers say the White House power behind the throne is H. R. Haldeman… Ordinarily a behind the scenes operator, the tall, crew cut Haldeman is emerging more and more in the open as the No. 1 man…Haldeman is in charge, whether at the White House or when the president is on the road. Few people get to see the president without his go-ahead. Most documents pass over his desk before they get to Nixon.

Haldeman seems to have staked out a command post similar to that of Sherman Adams when he ran the White House show for President Eisenhower...

The hot lash of some of Haldeman's memos extends to the east side or first lady's wing of the Executive Mansion. 'He hires and fires,' said one aide explaining the Haldeman power... Most of the palace guard are aware of the power Haldeman wields and they don't dare buck him.

Spreading out his towel next to me, Bob flops down on his stomach. Looking over at him, I wonder how this can possibly be the "power behind the throne." Although people in Washington are obsessed with power, I actually think that Bob is oblivious to it. At least, it's not something for which he is consciously striving. As he has said, he uses the power that comes with his job to achieve the most good for the president.

"What would the president do without you?" I ask, putting the paper aside.

"He'd probably bumble along," Bob replies in a voice muffled by his towel.

Bob's answer is lighthearted, but something about the references to his power makes me feel uneasy. A sightseeing boat pauses offshore. When the passengers wave, I wave back, glad to have the diversion.

Washington Daze

S
EPTEMBER IS A TRANSITIONAL month. One moment, I'm enjoying summer in California, and the next, I'm experiencing fall in Washington. Peter is starting the ninth grade and faces a series of orthodontist appointments. Now a seventh grader, Ann is happy to resume her weekly English riding lessons. Susan transfers as a junior from Stanford to the University of Minnesota, where she can be closer to her boyfriend, who is starting medical school there. As she has done in the past, she checks in every Sunday with a collect call home.

Hank gets a ride on a government Jet Star to California, where he is an incoming freshman at UCLA. When the Draft Extension Bill is signed into law this month, draft deferments for this year's college freshmen are abolished. I agonize over the likelihood of Hank's being called up for the army. I am torn between fully supporting the president's policy on the war and living in fear of our son's being sent to Vietnam.

The biggest social event this fall is the long-awaited opening of The John F. Kennedy Center for the Performing Arts on September 8. Although tickets to Leonard Bernstein's production of *Mass* are at a premium, Bob and I have seats in the presidential box. Nixon refuses to go. The Kennedy/Camelot mystique irritates him, and Bob tells me that he wants to avoid "running into a batch of Kennedys" on opening night.

Standing in a crush of people in the lobby of the new $70 million Center, I'm not as impressed as I expected to be. Compared to the elegance of the Music Center in Los Angeles, the plain architecture is stark and lacks warmth. Henry

Kissinger captures the scene perfectly when he looks up at the colored flags hanging from the ceiling and asks where the TWA ticket counter is located.

The Center has five theaters, and tonight's performance is in the Opera House, where the carpet, walls, seats, and curtain are all red. The production is a spectacle, incorporating a symphony orchestra, rock band, recorded music, marching band, and chorus. At the end, as choir boys walk up the aisles singing "Peace Go with You," the audience stands and sings along with them. When everyone starts holding hands, I watch with amusement as Bob deliberately thrusts his hands into his pockets. He doesn't like participating in this sort of forced public display of sentimentality.

The press picks up on Bob's attendance at the opening. In one article, he is mentioned as a VIP whose "crew cut and erect bearing convey unmistakable celebrity status if not instant recognition. When one young lady passed by, she asked, 'Which astronaut is he?'"

Ten days later, when Bob and I are walking at Camp David, he tells me that the president asked him to describe our evening at the Kennedy Center. "He was really funny," Bob says, pausing for me to collect a handful of fall leaves. "He said that if he's assassinated, he wants Lawrence Welk to conduct the symphony orchestra playing *Dante's Inferno*."

"You're kidding."

"Sometimes the president can come up with some pretty strange stuff. The worst is, I'm not always sure if he's serious or not."

◆

ON SEPTEMBER 16, BOB gives a dinner party for his staff and their spouses on board the *Sequoia* while cruising down the Potomac. Following drinks outside on the deck, dinner is announced. The dining room table is set for twenty-two, and there are place cards. On my left, a young man with thinning, sandy-colored hair and horned-rimmed glasses slips into place and introduces himself.

"Hi, Jo. I'm John Dean."

When John Ehrlichman was appointed domestic affairs advisor, Dean became the next White House counsel. Dressed in a tan gabardine suit and Gucci shoes, the thirty-one-year-old bachelor has been described by the press as "the one swinger on the staid White House staff." He is a good conversationalist, and I enjoy talking with him. Seated on my right is Alex

Butterfield, whom I've known since college. He and his wife Charlotte attended UCLA, where they used to double date with Bob and me.

A stiff breeze cuts across the Potomac as the *Sequoia* docks. Bob and I say goodbye to our guests and thank the crew. Gripping the railing of the gangplank, I walk in front of Bob. We chat about the evening, and I tell him how much I enjoyed meeting John Dean and talking with Alex. A strong gust of wind blows my coat open, and I shiver.

October–November 1971

BOB'S MOTHER LOVES WASHINGTON, and it seems to love her back. She captivates everyone she meets, whether it's the staff at Camp David or the guests at a formal state dinner honoring President Tito of Yugoslavia. Many find it hard to believe that this small, gregarious woman is the mother of the formidable, Teutonic "Von Haldeman."

Good friends with Walt and Lillian Disney, Non is thrilled to accompany our family to the formal opening of Disney World in Florida. Bob has been invited to represent the president at the opening ceremonies. Standing in the crowded lobby of the Contemporary Hotel, Non cranes her neck to get a better view of her son as he gives a brief talk and presents an American flag to the park.

Since the February earthquake, Non has become a permanent resident of the Los Angeles Country Club. Surrounded by friends, she is in her element. Bob's mother is his best PR, in both LA and the nation's capital.

December 1971

IN DECEMBER, KENWOOD'S CHERRY trees and dogwoods are bare, and outdoor Christmas lights have replaced pumpkins and corn stalks. On the other side of the world, the situation between India and Pakistan intensifies, and the United Nations Security Council meets in an emergency session. In San Francisco, the lights go out on the Golden Gate Bridge due to a power failure. The Libertarian Party is formed. And *Jesus Christ Superstar* is the hottest show on Broadway.

Although this is a busy month for me, I continue to volunteer once a week at the District of Columbia Complaint Center, a hotline to government services. I am one of several anonymous women who answer a bank of phones. We listen to the complaints and refer them to the proper authorities to correct the problem. The list is endless—backed-up sewers, no heat, leaky roofs, abandoned cars, and decomposing rats.

When I leave the office on December 15, I drive to Georgetown to buy a plum pudding for Christmas Eve. As I continue on Wisconsin Avenue to pick up Ann's carpool, I can't get my mind off several stressful calls I received this morning.

A horn honks. There's a screech of brakes, followed by a shattering thud. My station wagon has been hit broadside and spins out of control. When it comes to a stop, I'm headed in the wrong direction. In front of me, an older man is struggling to get out of his car.

I'm physically shaken, but I'm thinking clearly. This is my fault. Distracted by my thoughts, I ran a red light at the intersection of Garfield and Wisconsin. In despair, I look over the damage. The right side of the station wagon is bashed in, and two windows are shattered. Glass is everywhere, including shards protruding from the plum pudding, which was knocked onto the floor. Using a pay phone in the lobby of a nearby apartment building, I make several calls. The police arrive, and the other driver and I exchange information. He drives away, but my car has to be towed. Bob sends a White House car to pick me up. Acting with decorum, the driver helps me into the back seat. Gingerly placing the mangled plum pudding back into its box, he hands it to me.

"Mom, you're late," Ann says the minute we pull up at National Cathedral School. "Why are you in a White House car? It's *so* embarrassing."

"Just get in," I tell her, as she and two other girls squeeze in next to me. "I had an accident, and the station wagon's been totaled."

No one dares to speak. Our drive home is in silence.

◆

TWO WEEKS BEFORE CHRISTMAS, Bertha tells us that she has to leave for Mexico to get her final immigration papers. A burly, black-haired man named Oscar will drive her. The children and I watch as he loads her things into his car.

"Merry Christmas," Peter, Ann, and I call out as the two of them drive away.

"*Feliz Navidad,*" Bertha and Oscar shout back.

Over the next ten days, Bob is also gone. When Susan and Hank arrive home for the holidays, we decorate for Christmas, but without Bob and Bertha a subdued tranquility falls on our house. Although Bob calls occasionally from Camp David, the Azores, Key Biscayne, New York, and Bermuda, I hear nothing from Bertha.

Overseeing Bob's personal affairs while he's gone, Larry calls to tell me that some of Bertha's papers have come back from the Immigration Department.

"She's had her physical, and it looks like she'll be back in the US sometime next month." Larry pauses. "Did you know that Bertha's five months pregnant?"

I'm speechless. In my mind, I start counting backward. *November, October, September, August, July. July! We were in California then, and Bertha was house-sitting. Hmmm.*

When Bob returns home, I hesitate to tell him that we're going to have a baby in the house. But he takes the news in stride.

"Not too much we can do about it now, is there?" he asks.

January 1972

WE BEGIN THE NEW Year with two arrivals: a new car and Bertha. A blue Ford Thunderbird replaces the station wagon, and Bertha moves back into her old room. She's reticent to talk about her pregnancy, but Oscar's around a lot, doting on the mother-to-be.

Nixon has been in office for three years, and another presidential race is starting to heat up. Eleven Democrats are already in the running, and it looks as if Senator Edmund Muskie of Maine will be the candidate. Nixon turns fifty-nine and declares his candidacy for a second term by entering the New Hampshire primary. Bob says that at one time the president was intrigued with the idea of having John Connally as his running mate. Not only would the former Democratic governor of Texas help bring in the Southern vote, but he would appeal to disgruntled Democrats. Nothing comes of it, however, and Agnew remains on the ticket. Attorney General John Mitchell announces that he will resign in order to take over as Nixon's campaign director, heading up the newly formed Committee to Re-Elect the President (CRP). With the slogan "Four More Years," Nixon's campaign gets off to a well-organized, well-managed start.

Things look good for the president. There's a lot of hype over his trip to China next month, and the news from Vietnam is positive. Nixon approves the withdrawal of an additional seventy thousand American troops and discloses his proposal of an eight-point peace plan, which includes provisions for the return of all prisoners of war. Henry Kissinger represents the United States in negotiations with the North Vietnamese. In recognition of Henry and the president's joint effort to end the war and establish a lasting peace, *Time* magazine features the two of them on its cover as the "Men of the Year." Bob tells me that neither one is too happy about having to share the honor.

Housewives and Treason

O N TUESDAY, JANUARY 18, Bob addresses the Upper School at National Cathedral School. His topic is, "The Role of Women in Today's World." As I take a seat in the back of the auditorium, I wish that Ann could be here with me, but the Lower School is not included in the program. I listen attentively as Bob emphasizes the importance of women in both the home and the workplace. After speaking for about twenty minutes, he calls for questions.

Responding to one of the students, Bob says, "Some women choose to have careers, but those who do not have just as important a role as housewives."

When he mentions the word "housewives," the girls bristle. A sea of hands goes up, but Bob maintains his cool and integrity. He denies the charge that he is suggesting that a wife should be subservient to her husband.

"In a marriage, it takes both the husband and the wife to complement and complete the union," he explains. "Marriage is a partnership, and one person should never be subservient to the other."

I know that Bob believes what he says, but his words bring to mind the conversation we had in Key Biscayne nine months ago. At the time, our marriage was far from being a partnership, and I had felt compelled to speak up.

The bell rings, and the students quickly disperse. As Bob and I step outside, a blast of icy wind hits us. We walk briskly across the bleak campus. At the street, a White House driver stands beside the open rear car door. As soon as Bob climbs in, he is whisked away. I retrace my steps to the Thunderbird and head off in the opposite direction.

◆

THE MOOD IS FESTIVE on January 20, the anniversary of Nixon's inauguration. Along with their spouses, the cabinet and White House staff celebrate the occasion in the State Dining Room. There are many toasts, and the president is the last to stand. He talks about his foreign accomplishments and the restoration of decency to public life.

"Because we were here these past years," he concludes, "America is a better place in which to live. The world is a safer place in which to live, and whatever happens in the election really doesn't matter. We can all be very proud. And I am very proud of everybody in this room."

Across the table from me, Martha Mitchell's fixed, dimpled smile is replaced with an expression of veneration. Watching a single tear run slowly down her cheek, I regret judging her so harshly in the past. The president compares the upcoming election to a football game and tells us that this is the fourth quarter. As a player on the Nixon team, I'm inspired to be more supportive of Bob. Realizing how self-consumed I've become, I resolve to change.

February 1972

BOB AGREES TO BE interviewed by Barbara Walters on the *Today* show. Remembering the reaction to his speech at the UCLA Alumni Dinner and his talk at Ann's school, I'm uneasy. His tongue-in-cheek remarks did not endear him to the press, and his reference to housewives upset the students. This time, Bob assures me I have nothing to worry about. He plans to use his national exposure on TV to emphasize the president's many accomplishments.

The interview is on February 7, and I watch it while eating breakfast on a tray in the den. As soon as I see Bob and Barbara, comfortably seated by the fire in his office, I feel less anxious. The scene is homey and reassuring. She begins by asking him about domestic issues, covering his management style, the president's schedule, and plans for the campaign. Bob exudes confidence, and his answers are direct and concise.

Changing subjects, Barbara talks about the Vietnam War. When she asks about Nixon's reaction to critics of his war policy, Bob shifts positions and straightens up. "Before [the president's] talk on television, you could say that his critics…were *unconsciously* echoing the line that the enemy wanted echoed."

I put down my mug of coffee and lean forward. Bob's words and change of posture send out a signal, and I sense something big is coming.

"Now that the peace plan is out there, the only conclusion you can draw is that critics are *consciously* aiding and abetting the enemy of the United States."

I'm astonished. "Consciously aiding and abetting the enemy" is the definition of treason. For Bob to use these words in the context of people critical of the war means he is effectively saying many congressmen, educators, and businessmen are committing treason.

The media immediately reacts to Bob's interview. This evening, "The Haldeman Affair" is the lead story on all three network news channels. The next morning, it is featured in Evans and Novak's "Political Report" in *The Washington Post*.

> With rare unanimity, Mr. Nixon's politicians agreed…it was folly for Haldeman…to agree to be interviewed on NBC's "Today" show: [and] it was folly compounded for him to charge Vietnam critics with "consciously aiding and abetting the enemy."

> …But it was also conceded that Haldeman's power is such that only the president himself could scold him, much less impose any discipline. And nobody in his wildest imagination expects Nixon to dress down his most trusted aide.

Pat Oliphant, a widely syndicated political cartoonist, has a cartoon of Nixon patting the head of a vicious watchdog. The drooling dog looks like Bob. A framed picture of Joe McCarthy is on the wall behind them. The infamous senator is grinning in approval. The *Los Angeles Times* wastes no time in printing an editorial that bitterly attacks Bob. Titled "Dissent Is Not the Nation's Enemy," it is brutal. This is our hometown newspaper. Bob went to school with its publisher, Otis Chandler, whose mother and father are close friends of Bob's parents.

> The latest and most indecent [attack] was H. R. Haldeman's outrageous assertion that the critics are now aiding and abetting the enemy of the United States. Which is crying "treason," as destructively, as poisonously, as the word was ever thrown about even in the worst days of the early 1950s.

When the columnist Nicholas Timmesch quotes Bob as saying, "I guess the term 'son of a bitch' fits me," Bob shrugs it off. His indifference bothers me, but I figure he has the president's approval. Nixon must have wanted Bob to say what he did. As Patrick Anderson wrote, "An aide must be willing to be used as a political lightning rod to draw criticism away from the president."

China

ORTUNATELY, THE "HALDEMAN AFFAIR" is short-lived. The negative publicity about Bob is overridden by news reports of the president's upcoming trip to China.

Ten days after the Barbara Walters interview, Bob's mother and I huddle on the steps of the South Portico of the White House. It's freezing cold, but we wouldn't think of missing this moment. In front of us, *Marine One* sits on the South Lawn, waiting for the presidential party to board. The twenty-minute helicopter ride to Andrews Air Force Base is the first leg of the trip to China.

Spotting his mother and me, Bob bounds over to give each of us a last-minute hug. There are only thirteen people in the official party, and he is one of them. The president is coatless, as he often is, as he delivers his farewell remarks to a small gathering of cabinet officers and congressmen. Waving from the top step of the helicopter, President and Mrs. Nixon turn and step inside. As soon as the door closes, the giant blades start to rotate.

Bob's gone. My husband is on his way to China. What an incredible opportunity for him to be a part of history. I continue to wave, even after the helicopter takes off. Non clutches a handkerchief and wipes her eyes.

After brief layovers in Hawaii and Guam, the Nixons will fly to China, where they will spend five days in Peking. From there, a Chinese plane will take them to Hangchow for a day of sightseeing before they depart for Alaska. Much of the trip will be televised live via satellite to a worldwide audience of an estimated six hundred million people. The occasion is historic, and the press coverage is a monumental undertaking.

On February 19, Bob calls from Oahu to wish me a happy twenty-third anniversary. Later, one of his aides braves a snowstorm to deliver a dozen yellow roses. Gordon Strachan plods through the wet, slushy flakes to get to our front door. Buried inside the bouquet is a card in Bob's handwriting. As soon as I read it, I burst into tears, embarrassing poor Gordon. I am deeply touched by Bob's caring. Responsible for the all of the logistics of this trip, he has taken the time to remember the two of us.

The next night, Non, Peter, Ann, and I are glued to the TV, mesmerized by the sight of *Air Force One* approaching the airport in Peking. The commentator explains that only a handful of foreign journalists has been allowed in the country since it was taken over by the Communists twenty years ago.

"Now," he proclaims, "the greatest anticommunist leader in the world is about to land in the People's Republic of China!"

"And Bob is with him!" Non exclaims.

A ramp is wheeled into position, and the front door on *Air Force One* opens. We catch our breath. President and Mrs. Nixon wave as they look out on this strange, unknown country. No one moves as we watch them proceed to the bottom of the stairs. It's a historic moment as Premier Chou En-lai steps forward to shake hands with the president of the United States. Non claps her hands in anticipation.

Suddenly, the TV channel changes. Everyone looks puzzled, and Peter quickly jumps up to switch it back. We catch the tail end of the handshake.

Over the next five nights, we are enthralled by the live coverage of the president and first lady attending a banquet in the Great Hall, visiting the Ming tombs, and walking along the Great Wall. When they visit the Forbidden City, it's another historic moment. As the presidential party enters the centuries-old home of the emperor and his household, we look for Bob. Ann spots him wearing a furry, black trapper hat. Non jumps up and points to her son.

For the second time, the TV channel suddenly changes, and we can't figure out why this happens at such crucial moments. Ann discovers the culprit. It's Non. Her charm bracelet works like a remote control. Whenever she excitedly waves her hands, the motion changes the channel.

Once Non removes her bracelet, there are no more interruptions. Each event is so foreign and wondrous. When it's over, the trip to China is universally acclaimed as a "remarkable diplomatic breakthrough." The president's surprise visit with a seriously ill Chairman Mao Tse-tung at his residence is considered a coup, and the highlight for Bob is meeting the charismatic Chou En-lai.

When he arrives home, Bob has sixty-five rolls of movies and many gifts for the family, each wrapped in musty Chinese newspaper.

Nixon proclaims, "This was the week that changed the world." The event is acknowledged as being "beautifully choreographed to show the president as a great leader." The news coverage is extraordinary, and, as one commentator candidly puts it, "If you're a candidate in the presidential campaign, how do you top this?"

Although I never hear Bob take any credit, a White House staff member is quoted as saying, "The China trip was Bob Haldeman's masterpiece, his Sistine Chapel."

A White House Docent Program

March 1972

I ENJOY THE WIVES of the senior White House staff, and I'd like to find a worthwhile project for all of us. As a former docent at the Los Angeles County Museum of Art, I realize that a similar program could be set up in the White House. As docents, the women would take an extensive training course to prepare them to give VIP tours. Not only would this be good PR for the Nixon administration, but it would give the wives a chance to participate in a meaningful White House activity.

Bob likes the idea and encourages me to discuss it with Lucy Winchester. The White House social secretary's approval is essential. He explains that the staffs of the first lady and the president can be territorial, and I should be aware that certain jealousies exist between them. Although the docents would come from the West Wing, their training and scheduling would be managed by the East Wing.

When I explain the docent program to Lucy, she is interested and agrees to present it to the wives at a meeting in May. However, she makes it clear that the credit for the program would go to the first lady.

◆

FOR JOHN EHRLICHMAN'S FORTY-SEVENTH birthday on March 19, Jeanne hosts a family party for him at George and Kathleen Bell's farm in Middleburg, Virginia. Nineteen of us gather for an afternoon of football and Frisbee, followed by a buffet supper on the terrace.

Seated on the low wall surrounding the Bells' eighteenth century stone terrace, I find myself comparing John and Bob. They are so similar the press gets them mixed up. One journalist recently referred to them as "Hans" and "Fritz," the *Katzenjammer Kids* in the comics. Both men were raised in Christian Science and graduated from UCLA. Bob went into advertising, and John got a law degree from Stanford. Their paths overlapped again as advance men before moving up in the hierarchy of the Nixon campaign.

They are smart, competitive, and demanding. They tease a lot, and each has a hearty, spontaneous laugh. John's wit and sarcasm have a greater cutting edge. Bob's sense of humor tends more toward slapstick. On the other hand, he seems more intense than John, whose big, teddy bear frame and easygoing personality make him appear more approachable.

Approachable. I turn the word over in my mind. *I feel comfortable with John. Might he be someone with whom I could discuss my relationship with Bob? John knows him well, both professionally and personally.* The idea is reassuring.

◆

At the end of the month, everyone's attention is focused on Vietnam, where North Vietnamese troops have launched an all-out attempt to conquer South Vietnam. In a massive attack, the Communists rely on the poor performance of the South Vietnamese army, as well as the underlying support of the antiwar movement in the United States. President Nixon doesn't yield and authorizes the Seventh Fleet to fire on enemy troops amassed around the Demilitarized Zone.

The war won't go away. Hank is closer than ever to being drafted. His lottery number is nine, which means if there is a draft next year, he will most likely be inducted. This is a terrifying thought for me. I know Hank thinks about it, too. On his desk I find a well-worn paperback edition of *Mastering the Draft.* The cover is black, and the title is written in ominous red letters.

April 1972

On April 15, the North Vietnamese offensive threatens to cut South Vietnam in half. When the president orders an extensive bombing attack on Hanoi and

Haiphong Harbor, protests erupt across the United States. On April 27, the Paris Peace Talks resume, after being halted last month.

In other news, the United States and Russia, along with seventy other countries, agree to ban biological weapons. Two giant pandas arrive in the US from China. And Bob's mother is the first woman to receive the Salvation Army's prestigious Sally Award.

A storm rages outside our home on Saturday, April 22. Thunder rumbles in the distance, and rain drips from the eaves onto already saturated flowerbeds. I sit by a warm fire in the den, pasting photos, menus, and invitations into a large black leather scrapbook.

Late in the afternoon, Bob calls from Camp David, where he and John Ehrlichman are spending the weekend with the president. He laughs when he tells me that my "Easter gumdrop tree" is still standing in front of Laurel. Easter was three weeks ago. However, the staff won't touch it unless he gives the word.

Picturing the scene, I laugh, too, but our conversation is cut short by Bertha. Awkwardly standing in the doorway, she informs me that she is having her baby. It's not easy to get her into the low, sleek Thunderbird, but we manage. Flying along rain-slicked streets, the two of us arrive at the hospital without a moment to spare.

Two days later, Little Oscar and his mother come home to the Haldeman household. With a wild shock of black hair like his father's, he has his mother's lusty voice. In no time, he settles in. Bertha finds a way to work him into her daily routine, and Bob manages to ignore an occasional misplaced diaper or baby bottle. The boys take Little Oscar in stride, and Ann loves to mother him.

May 1972

THE MONTH OF MAY arrives in all its glory. The days are warmer, and soft pinks and fresh spring greens fill the garden. Bertha gives Little Oscar sunbaths, and Ann does her homework outside. Setting up a card table under the flowering cherry trees, she has her parakeet and dog with her.

On Tuesday morning, May 2, J. Edgar Hoover, director of the FBI for forty-eight years, dies in his sleep. Bob is the one to inform the president, who in turn names L. Patrick Gray as acting director.

Two weeks later, while campaigning for the presidency, Governor George Wallace of Alabama is shot in Laurel, Maryland. One of the four bullets lodges in his spine, paralyzing him. Once again, Bob is the one to tell the president. That night, when we are attending a special screening of *The Godfather* with the Ehrlichmans, Bob and John are called back to the White House. Frustrated by the way the investigation into the shooting is being handled, Nixon wants to do something about it.

"Another flap," Bob mutters when he returns home after midnight. "The FBI and Secret Service are supposed to be getting to the bottom of the shooting, but it's impossible for those two agencies to work together. They spend more time blaming each other for their mistakes than in checking out the guy who committed the crime. The president's really fed up."

Despite the possibility of having to spend the rest of his life in a wheelchair, Wallace says that he will stay in the race. To make a point that the assassination attempt is not going to intimidate him, Nixon walks with Secretary John Connally from the White House to the Treasury Department in broad daylight.

On May 9, the US mines Haiphong Harbor and intensifies its bombing of North Vietnam. During an airstrike, South Vietnamese pilots accidentally drop napalm bombs on their own civilians, including children.

Nine days later, Lucy Winchester presents the idea of a docent program to the wives of the president's senior staff. We meet in a room next to her office in the East Wing, where several rows of gilded chairs have been set up facing a podium. On each seat there is a White House pad and a sharpened White House pencil. At exactly 10:30 a.m., Lucy walks over to the podium.

"As you may or may not know, it takes over a hundred staff members to work a White House social event," she states. "Each of them, including the military aides and ushers, receives a fact sheet, which must be memorized. As docents, you, too, will be expected to become completely familiar with the same fact sheet… Whenever you are at an event, you must always remember to remain in the background, and you are to give the credit for *everything* to the first lady."

Lucy's words sound condescending, and when she warns that the press will pick up anything negative that we might say, I look over at Nancy Ziegler. The wife of the press secretary raises her eyebrows and shrugs. Lucy's final comment is, "Don't forget…staff doesn't exist."

I'm disappointed when Lucy suggests that we meet again "sometime in the future." Hopefully, at that time, she will be more enthusiastic about the program and will express a greater confidence in these capable women.

◆

WHEN SOUTH VIETNAMESE TROOPS evacuate Hue and abandon Quang Tri to the advancing Communist army, American military commanders step up their B-52 raids on North Vietnam. In other news, the United States returns control of the island of Okinawa to Japan after twenty-six years. The Duke of Windsor dies, and *The New York Times* gets the Pulitzer Prize for its story on the Pentagon Papers.

After spending ten days at Camp David, Bob takes off again. He leaves with the Nixons on a twelve-day trip to Austria, Russia, Iran, and Poland. Peter, Ann, and I spend the next weekend at the presidential retreat with the Ehrlichman family, Nancy Ziegler, and her two little girls. Surrounded by three ladies and eight children, John is the only man here. Although he is a good sport, I'm sure he'd give anything to be on the presidential trip with Bob and Ron Ziegler.

On Sunday, May 28, Bob calls from Leningrad. Ecstatic, he gives a glowing report on the president's weeklong Russian Summit with Soviet Premier Leonid Brezhnev. Not only is Nixon the first American President to set foot in Moscow, but, as a result of the SALT talks, he and Brezhnev sign the Anti-Ballistic Missile Treaty, effectively halting the nuclear arms race.

Immediately after their return to the United States, the Nixons leave for a week at Camp David. In order to be with Bob, the two children and I head back to the mountain retreat. The weather is unbearably hot and humid, and we spend most of our time in and around the large staff swimming pool. Poor Bob has to wear a coat and tie whenever he meets with Nixon. On one occasion, he reports that the president had both the air conditioner and a fire going at the same time.

A week is a long time for us to be here. After four days, Peter and Ann are bickering, our laundry has piled up, and we've exhausted the supply of appropriate grade-B movies. As we're sitting down for dinner on Friday night, the president calls to tell Bob that he and Pat would like to leave as soon as possible. Bob passes the information along, and within forty-five minutes the Nixons are boarding *Marine One*.

Rather than taking the helicopter, Bob drives home with the children and me. It's special to be together as a family on this beautiful, warm evening, and I love having my husband sitting beside me. Only one thing separates us—the oversized, portable phone. *The ever-present umbilical cord.*

A Third-Rate Burglary

June 1972

OLLOWING AN ATTACK ON his wife by the Manchester *Union Leader* newspaper, Senator Edmund Muskie withdraws from the presidential race. Senator George McGovern of South Dakota becomes the Democratic nominee through grassroots support in the primaries. As a left-wing dove, he favors unconditional amnesty for the draft dodgers and calls for unilateral withdrawal from South Vietnam without any assurances concerning the return of our POWs. His approach to welfare is for the federal government to give $1,000 to every man, woman, and child in America.

On June 16, the first lady leaves for a three-day campaign swing through Texas, California, and South Dakota. While she's out of town, the president will spend the weekend in Florida. It's his last chance to be in Key Biscayne before the weather gets too hot and humid.

Hank is in California, and Peter is with Susan in Minnesota, but Ann and her friend Bea Alice fly down with Bob and me on *Air Force One*. When we check into the Key Biscayne Hotel, we find that "our" villa has been repainted a bright yellow. In its new, overdone, red, white, and blue living room, a faux marble replica of the Washington Monument sits on the coffee table.

"Some Republican decorator really got cranked up over this," Bob remarks as soon as we step inside.

Sunday, June 18, dawns warm and windy. After celebrating Father's Day at breakfast by the pool, the four of us return to the villa. Although the president is at Walker's Cay with Bebe, Bob explains that something has come up and he needs to spend time on the phone. Armed with the Sunday papers, I settle on the terrace, while Ann and Bea Alice swim in the ocean. Buffeted by the strong wind, I cram the papers I'm not reading under my chaise to keep them from blowing away. The lead story in *The Miami Herald* is about the withdrawal of troops from Vietnam, and there's a feature article on McGovern's campaign. When I see that the Watergate complex is mentioned in a small story in the middle of the front page, I'm interested. *The Watergate.* That's where Mother and I stayed with Bob while decorating our new home.

Under the headline "Miamians Held in D.C. Try to Bug Demo Headquarters," the article describes a burglary that took place after midnight yesterday. On June 17, five men were arrested for breaking into the Democratic National Committee Headquarters in the Watergate. Dressed in business suits, they wore rubber surgical gloves and carried burglary tools, surveillance equipment, walkie-talkies, and cameras. Four of the men are from Miami, but the fifth is a former employee of the CIA presently working as a security consultant in Washington.

The story is weird. I'm curious to hear what Bob has to say about it, but I don't want to interrupt him while he's working. Peering through the glass doors, I can see him seated on the red, white, and blue striped couch in the living room. In front of him, the White House phone and Washington Monument sit side-by-side on a white glass-top coffee table. I wave to the girls and go back to my reading.

Two hours later, Bob steps outside. Blinking in the bright sunlight, he sits down on the chaise next to me. "What's the deal on this crazy break-in at the Watergate?" I ask, without wasting any time.

"The whole thing's ridiculous," Bob says. "I can't imagine why anyone would want to bug the Democratic headquarters. It's the last place in the world to get inside information."

"Have you talked to the president?" I ask.

"Yeah. He and Bebe just got back. I don't think he knows about the break-in yet, unless he read about it in the paper."

Bob stands and stretches, and I suggest that we eat lunch by the pool. On the way out, I toss this morning's papers into the kitchen wastebasket. Frequently I find an article that I want to save, but today there's nothing special.

Over the weekend, Key Biscayne is hit by the tail end of a hurricane. On Monday, our flight back to Washington is delayed, and *Air Force One* doesn't take off until after dinner. Bob spends much of the time with the president in the forward cabin.

I give no further thought to the break-in until the next morning at breakfast. *The Washington Post* has an article titled, "White House Consultant Tied to Bugging Figure." It states that the name of Howard Hunt was found in the address books of two of the burglars. Hunt supposedly has connections to the CIA, as well as to the White House, where he was a consultant for Charles Colson. One of the burglars has been identified as James McCord, a security consultant at the Committee to Re-Elect the President. I've never heard these names before, and when I ask Bob, he says that he doesn't know either Howard Hunt or James McCord.

As with other flaps, Bob talks about containing this one. However, as much as he would like to prevent the break-in caper from becoming an issue in the campaign, the Democrats are determined to keep it going. Lawrence O'Brien, Democratic National Committee chairman, files a million-dollar lawsuit against the CRP for damages, and the FBI announces that it's starting an investigation. Press Secretary Ron Ziegler minimizes the break-in and refers to it as "a third-rate burglary." In a press conference on June 22, the president states that no one in the White House was involved.

On Wednesday, June 28, the president announces that no new draftees will be sent to Vietnam. A wave of relief sweeps over me, and I couldn't be happier. Hank must be on cloud nine.

Georgetown, Here We Come

July 1972

THE PRESIDENT AND FIRST lady plan to spend two weeks at the Western White House, and Bob flies out with them on *Air Force One*. Susan, Peter, Ann, and I travel on a windowless government backup plane. Hank has a summer job at the CRP in Washington and will not be coming out to California.

While my sister and her four children spend the month at my parents' house on Bay Island, our family will stay across the bay on Harbor Island. Friends have lent us their two-story, waterfront home, and by the time the children and I arrive, the Army Signal Corps has already installed three White House phones. Bob's Sunfish is waiting for him on the dock.

Our first weekend here, Bob is free on Sunday, and the president calls only once. Enjoying lunch outside on the patio, Bob, Peter, and I have a rambling conversation about life in Washington. This turns into a discussion about Georgetown, and much to my surprise, both Bob and Peter are soon rhapsodizing over the benefits of living there.

"Let's move, Mom," Peter exclaims.

Although I have no desire to pack up and move again, I find myself quietly mulling over the idea. *Georgetown is charming, and it's convenient. It would be an easy commute to the White House, as well as to the children's schools. We don't need our big house in Kenwood. Maybe we could find a townhouse…*

Before I know it, I tell Bob and Peter that I'm willing to go along with the idea and will call a real estate broker as soon as we return to Washington. I don't do things impulsively, and my commitment startles me as much as it does my husband and my son.

•

ON THE FOURTH OF July, Haldemans and Hortons assemble at #11 for dinner and fireworks on the beach. Addressing the nation, President Nixon talks about plans for the bicentennial celebration four years from now. Dressed in a red blazer, white shirt, and blue tie, he announces that he has named the presidential jet the *Spirit of '76* to commemorate the occasion.

Just as things are heating up for the Republican Convention next month, Martha Mitchell is back in the news. Issuing her husband a public ultimatum, she says that if their marriage is to survive, John must choose between her and politics. He responds by resigning from his job as campaign director at the CRP and making it clear that "the happiness and welfare" of his wife and daughter come first. Clark MacGregor, a former Minnesota congressman, replaces him.

Both political parties plan to hold their conventions in Miami this year, and the Democrats meet first on July 10. From an eclipse of the sun on opening day to the final moments of the convention, things do not go well for them. The Democratic Party is in shambles. Taken over by George McGovern and the radical activists of the New Left, it is being run by amateurs in the name of "open politics." Without the backing of the traditional organizers, there's no control or discipline on the convention floor. Long debates on abortion and gay rights cause the sessions to run throughout the night into the next morning. Hubert Humphrey is booed, and one commentator refers to the scene as the "Mad Hatter's tea party." Senator McGovern is finally selected as the Democratic presidential candidate.

Along with the rest of the nation, Bob and I follow the wild proceedings on television. On the final night, he drives to San Clemente to watch the convention with the president and John Connally. The night is chaotic. The vice presidential nominating process gets bogged down in trivia, and there's a three-hour debate over the nominee. During the free-for-all, the delegates nominate thirty-nine people, including Martha Mitchell and Mao Tse-tung. At last, Senator Thomas Eagleton of Missouri is selected as McGovern's running mate. By the time McGovern gives his acceptance speech at 2:48 a.m. Miami time, Bob has returned home. The minute it's over, the White House phone rings.

"Yes, Mr. President," Bob answers. He listens and then laughs. "You're absolutely right. The Democrats blew it this time. I feel kinda sorry for poor old George. The only voters awake for his speech live in Guam." Pause. "Teddy Kennedy should be their candidate. His speech was brilliant."

Over the next two weeks, the Democrats continue to have problems. Senator Eagleton admits on TV that he has undergone electric shock therapy for depression, but McGovern states that he's still behind him "a thousand percent." By the end of the month, however, McGovern changes his mind. The former director of the Peace Corps and President Kennedy's brother-in-law, Sargent Shriver, replaces Eagleton as the vice presidential candidate.

In the news, Jane Fonda visits North Vietnam, where she uses Radio Hanoi to urge American soldiers to defect to the enemy. She is photographed on a North Vietnamese tank, laughing with the gun crew. It's disturbing, and some people call her a traitor.

Four More Years

August 1972

O N THE FIRST OF **August**, our family moves across the channel to Bay Island, and the Watergate caper flares up again. In a campaign speech in Ohio, McGovern charges that the president is at least indirectly responsible for the Watergate break-in. A check earmarked for Nixon's reelection campaign is found on one of the burglars, and Senator William Proxmire proposes the creation of a commission to investigate the bugging. As with all flaps, Bob says that his overriding objective is to "contain and minimize any potential political damage."

American B-52s deliver the heaviest raids so far against North Vietnam. The president's plan for Vietnamization moves forward, and the last US ground combat unit is deactivated. A Harris Poll shows that 74 percent of the people polled think that South Vietnam should not be allowed to fall into the Communists' hands, and the first lady speaks out against Jane Fonda in a rare press conference at the White House. Governor George Wallace withdraws his third-party candidacy. And the World Congress of Nudists meets in Yugoslavia. Rain and cool weather force the thirty thousand participants to wear clothes.

◆

WITH THE REPUBLICAN CONVENTION coming up, Bob flies back to Washington, where he spends much of his time holed up at Camp David with the president. By the middle of August, Miami is teeming with Republican delegates who are determined to show the nation how a convention should be run. Like the Democrats, however, they have their share of demonstrators.

The air-conditioned Miami Beach Convention Complex, with its patriotic red, white, and blue décor, contrasts sharply with the heat and angry crowds outside. Police sirens wail, and a residue of tear gas lingers in the oppressive humidity. In Flamingo Park, thousands of antiwar protestors congregate in a tent city. In the "People's Pot Park," hippies give out free nausea bags at a "vomitorium." A sign over a box with Nixon's picture on it says, "Throw up here." At Nautilus Junior High School two miles away, the Young Voters for the President has set up headquarters. Hank is one of the three thousand young volunteers busy organizing Nixon rallies.

Arriving in Miami, the president gives his familiar "V for victory" wave from the steps of the *Spirit of '76*. Watching the arrival on large television screens inside the convention complex, Non and I cheer and wave our pennants along with the delegates. Everyone chants, "Four more years. Four more years."

On the night of the president's acceptance speech, there are three empty seats next to Non and me in Box D. Hank and Ann are working at Young Voters for the President headquarters, and who knows where Bob is. The children should be here by now, and I can't imagine what's delaying them. When Bob arrives, he's preoccupied with the final arrangements and wants to check things out.

"Wanna come with me?" he asks.

I'm thrilled. Tagging along behind him, I watch as aides scurry around in back of the podium. When they report to Bob, they call him "sir," and I can feel the tension each time he issues an order. Tonight, as always, Bob expects nothing short of perfection.

When we return to the box, Hank and Ann finally arrive. Ann appears to be crying, and Hank has his arm around her. He explains that they were delayed by a confrontation. Outside, the protestors are slashing tires and throwing rocks in an attempt to block the entrances to the convention complex. The police used tear gas, and Hank and Ann were caught in the crossfire. Ann's eyes are burning, but both she and her brother are exhilarated.

The minute the president steps up to the podium to give his acceptance speech, Bob looks at his watch. Giving a nod of approval to a young man on the floor with a walkie-talkie, he nudges me and smiles. "Check it out... Ten thirty... Prime time."

In his speech, Nixon talks about federal revenue sharing, reorganization of the executive branch, and an all-volunteer army. The cheers are especially loud when he invites disgruntled Democrats to join with the Republicans in a "new American majority," where the voters of both parties are bound together by common ideals.

With a Nixon/Agnew ticket, the Republicans are on a roll. By the time we arrive back in California, there's even talk of an election landslide. The Gallup Poll gives the president the largest post-convention point spread in favor of a Republican candidate in history: Nixon, 64 percent—McGovern, 30 percent. In Los Angeles, Non is so charged up she volunteers full time at the Nixon Campaign Headquarters on Wilshire Boulevard. And my mother is elected president of the Bel-Air Republican Women's Club.

Sunday evening, the Nixons give a celebrity reception at the Western White House in San Clemente. There's a feeling of confidence and anticipation as Bob and I mingle among the movie stars and political bigwigs. A mariachi band plays by the pool, and the hot pink and orange decorations are enhanced by a fiery sunset over the ocean.

The president's press conference the following week reflects the upbeat mood of the Republicans. Most of the questions focus on the campaign or Vietnam. "Jugular diplomacy" has paid off, and North Vietnam has returned to Paris for the Peace Talks. When asked if he thinks a special prosecutor ought to be appointed for the Watergate caper, Nixon states that there is hardly a need for one. Investigations are being conducted by the FBI, Senate Banking and Currency Committee, Justice Department, and General Accounting Office. In addition, Counsel to the President John Dean has conducted a complete investigation, concluding that no one in the White House is involved.

Bob considers the break-in an ill-advised political prank, and in California local newspapers give it very little coverage. I'm used to reading *The Washington Post*, where practically every page has a Watergate-related story. It's reported that Howard Hunt has been identified as one of two men who were monitoring the break-in from a Howard Johnson's hotel room. The other man is a former FBI agent named G. Gordon Liddy, currently the general counsel for the Finance Committee of the CRP.

September 1972

DRAGGING SUMMER OUT AS long as we can, the children and I don't head back to Washington until the day before school starts. Peter is going into the tenth grade at Sidwell Friends, and Ann will be in the eighth grade at National Cathedral. As a senior at the University of Minnesota, Susan is considering going to law school next year. Hank is taking the quarter off from UCLA to work for the Young Voters for the President at CRP headquarters. Rather than live at home, he's renting a house in Chevy Chase, Maryland, with five other boys.

Little Oscar is four months old and is growing by leaps and bounds. Bertha stuffs him with jars of baby food and dresses him "to the nines." He's a happy baby, and neither Bob nor I have any complaints.

Once we're back in our normal routine, I'm actually anticipating looking at houses in Georgetown. In early September, I contact a real estate broker, who immediately takes me in tow. On two occasions, Bob joins us. Peter and Ann are eager to make the move. Susan is ambivalent, but Hank is opposed.

"We're a suburban family, Mom," he says. "We've always had space…a lawn…trees. I can't picture us living in a townhouse on a busy street. Georgetown's 'grungy.' You won't be happy there."

Along with my weekly commitment at the City Hall Complaint Center, I now volunteer on Tuesday mornings at the CRP, instead of Juvenile Hall. My task of collating and stapling state campaign notebooks is menial work, but it gives me a chance to see Hank, who works in the same building. With hair more than halfway down to his waist, he joins me for an occasional lunch at Chez Françoise.

On Tuesday, September 5, Arab terrorists attack the Israeli team at the summer Olympics in Munich, West Germany. Live television coverage of the tragedy brings the event into everyone's living room, and I'm sickened as I watch it unfold. Eleven Israeli hostages are killed, and Israel retaliates by bombing Palestinian guerrilla bases in Lebanon and Syria. Senator Mike Mansfield calls for the Olympics to be abolished for good.

The American swimmer Mark Spitz wins a record seven Olympic gold medals, and the World Chess Championship is won by Bobby Fischer in Iceland. Pope Paul VI abolishes the tonsure, which has symbolized "renunciation of the world" for seminarians since the end of the fifth century. In the United States, the Watergate flap flares up again when the Democrats claim that the

Republican finance chairman paid for the break-in and established a political espionage squad. Maurice Stans defends himself by filing a five-million-dollar libel suit against the Democratic campaign chairman, Larry O'Brien.

On September 15, the federal grand jury indicts seven men (the five burglars, plus Howard Hunt and Gordon Liddy, who were monitoring the break-in) on charges of conspiring, breaking and entering, theft, and installing eavesdropping devices at the Democratic National Headquarters. A week later, a district court judge says the Democrats' damage suit and the Republicans' counter-suit cannot be tried before the election. All depositions are halted so as not to prejudice the criminal trial of the seven men.

As the campaign heats up, almost everyone is predicting a landslide victory for Nixon. The Republicans have raised an all-time record of $60 million.

"The president's in the perfect position to avoid actively campaigning," Bob says. "By using surrogate speakers, he won't have to respond personally to the political rhetoric that's being hurled at him by the Democrats. That way, he can remain presidential."

Sargent Shriver calls Richard Nixon "Tricky Dicky" and claims that he's a "psychiatric case" and "power mad." Sounding desperate, George McGovern compares the president to Hitler. Described in the press as the "candidate of amnesty, abortion, and acid," McGovern states that Nixon's "jugular diplomacy" in Vietnam descends to a "new level in barbarism." He ignores the fact that for the first time in almost eight years, a full week has passed in which no American soldier died in battle.

With the polls overwhelmingly in his favor, the president decides to join his surrogates on the campaign trail. By the end of September, Bob has accompanied Nixon on swings through New York City, San Francisco, Los Angeles, and Laredo, Texas.

After a three-year stalemate in the negotiations to end the war, there is a breakthrough in the Paris Peace Talks. Hopefully, this divisive war will be coming to an end soon.

The Post Finally Does It

October 1972

ON TUESDAY MORNING, OCTOBER 10, *The Washington Post*'s headline reads, "FBI finds Nixon Aides Sabotaged Democrats." Bob is puzzled. Before eating breakfast, he spreads out the paper on the dining room table and reads the first sentence to me. "'FBI agents have established that the Watergate bugging incident stemmed from a massive campaign of political spying and sabotage conducted on behalf of President Nixon's reelection and directed by officials of the White House and the Committee for the Re-Election of the President.'"

Bob frowns. "What a lot of baloney! 'Spying and sabotage' are nothing more than dirty tricks, and they've always been a part of political campaigns. The master of dirty tricks is Dick Tuck, a Democrat. He wrote the book on them. But when the Republicans are involved, *The Post* calls it 'spying and sabotage.'"

Taking a bite of toast, Bob washes it down with a swallow of orange juice. "It says here that a thirty-one-year-old guy named Donald Segretti worked as an 'operative of the Nixon reelection organization.' Supposedly, he hired 'fifty other operatives to conduct an undercover campaign against the Democrats.'"

"Segretti?" I question.

"I wouldn't know the guy from Adam," Bob replies.

For some reason, I feel a strange sense of relief.

◆

Representative Wright Patman, chairman of the House Committee on Banking and Currency, announces that he wants to establish another probe into Watergate. *Watergate.* The flap over the break-in finally has a name of its own.

Watergate…

◆

FOR THE LAST FOUR months, Bob has been gone almost every weekend. Calling from the presidential retreat on Saturday afternoon, October 14, he tells me that he's been with the president most of the day and expects to be free tonight and tomorrow. Would I like to come up? Leaving Peter and Ann at home with Bertha, I take off after dinner and arrive at Camp David by 9:00 p.m.

When Nixon calls early the next morning and asks Bob to come over to Aspen, I'm annoyed. This was supposed to be my time with my husband, and I don't see why the president can't wait until at least after breakfast.

Bob shaves and dresses quickly in slacks, button-down shirt, tie, and navy blazer. At the last moment, he layers on a heavy jacket, scarf, and leather gloves. A blast of cold air sweeps into our cabin as soon as he steps out onto the screen porch. The door slams shut, and the radiator in the corner sizzles and clanks in an attempt to keep our tiny living room warm. Standing at the window, I watch as Bob walks down the road. Bracing himself against the wind, he tucks the ends of his scarf into his jacket and quickens his pace.

This is not how I had imagined our day beginning. Pulling a heavy sweater over my head, I brush my hair back into place and collect the Sunday papers from the porch. Bare branches bend and sway with each powerful gust of wind, and clusters of dry, crinkled dogwood leaves swirl around my feet as I walk to breakfast. I hurry. It's cold, and I'm anxious to see the "new Laurel," which has replaced the old building.

My favorite steward, Pair, greets me and shows me around. The décor is much nicer than the worn, homey look of the old Laurel. Comfortable chairs and couches, upholstered in a tasteful tan and blue plaid fabric, are grouped around a large brick fireplace, above which the presidential seal is prominently displayed. Stairs lead down to the dining room, which features a wall of windows overlooking the woods.

I'm the only one seated at the long table. Spreading the papers out in front of me, I order my "usual": banana pancakes, bacon, fried eggs, and hash browns. An article in *The Washington Post* catches my eye, and I now understand why the president had to see Bob right away.

> ...President Nixon's appointments secretary and an ex-White House aide, indicted in the Watergate bugging case, both served as 'contacts' in a spying and sabotage operation against the Democrats...

I can't believe it. *The Post* has linked Dwight Chapin to Howard Hunt, claiming that the two of them directed Segretti's campaign of "spying and sabotage." Dwight has been a close personal friend of Bob's ever since they both worked at J. Walter Thompson Company. Up until this moment, Watergate has been a jumble of unfamiliar names. The mention of Dwight's name brings it close to home.

As much as I want to talk to Bob, I have to wait. When he finally joins me at Laurel, he spends his time on the phone talking to Henry Kissinger. Apparently, the peace negotiations have hit a snag, and President Thieu of South Vietnam isn't going along with the concessions that were agreed upon by the United States and North Vietnam.

In between calls, Bob gives me a weak smile. "Sorry, Jo. I thought we'd have more time together, but things keep popping up."

At last, it's just the two of us. In a golf cart headed for the tennis court, I ask Bob about Dwight. His answer is quick and to the point. "As I've said before, *The Washington Post* and *The New York Times* have double standards. Those two papers will go after the president in any way they can. Tying Dwight to Howard Hunt through Segretti is a cheap shot, and *The Post* knows it."

◆

ON THURSDAY, OCTOBER 19, *The Post* features another story on Dwight, which appears in the "Style" section. Bob and I are eating breakfast at home when he spots the article. Holding up the paper for me to see, he points to a full page spread by Myra MacPherson. He's amused. Next to the headline, "Dwight Chapin: Mr. Nice Guy," there's a large photo of Dwight. On the opposite page, there's a smaller picture of Bob, who I assume is being portrayed as "Mr. Bad Guy." I don't see the humor in it that Bob does.

"It's not a big deal, Jo," Bob says when he sees me frown. "It's a good story. It's complimentary to Dwight."

When he's through reading, Bob gives the paper a shove in my direction. It slides along the polished surface of the dining room table and stops in front of my mat at the other end.

"Mr. Haldeman, your car's here," Bertha shouts from the kitchen. Bob jumps up. On his way out, he pauses at my chair, and we exchange a light kiss.

Picking up the paper, I start to read. "It is impossible to tell the story of Dwight Lee Chapin without talking about Harry Robbins Haldeman." As soon as I read this first sentence, it confirms my earlier feeling about Bob's being "the bad guy." He is quoted as saying, "Every president needs an SOB—and I'm Nixon's."

The next paragraph begins, "On the other hand, Haldeman's 'Mr. Nice Guy' is Chapin...who has taken orders from Haldeman for ten years... As one acquaintance said of Chapin—now linked to reports of GOP espionage and sabotage against the Democrats—'He's not the guy who sees that Nixon's coat never touches the floor, but the guy who sees that Haldeman's coat never touches the floor.'"

There are so many flattering terms used to describe Dwight, I actually start to count them. Fourteen. "Personable, virtuous, pleasant, courteous, thoughtful, bright, self-effacing, charming, good-natured, friendly, loyal... sweet...a gentleman...dedicated. A thirty-one-year-old somebody who's got to work his heart out for somebody else."

Bob is the "somebody else" with a "tight crewcut, mechanical smile, and brusque manner." The "somebody else" who "looks the part he plays—absolute disciplinarian of the movement of people and paper between the president's office and the rest of government."

The story doesn't sit well with me. I sense that Myra MacPherson is making an end run around Dwight to get at Bob. When Bob warned me about the press before we moved to Washington, I scoffed at the idea of his ever being in the public eye. Now I see how naïve I was.

◆

OUR REALTOR TELLS ME that representatives of the Australian Embassy have looked at our house several times and are interested in buying it. They took photos recently, which they sent to their home office in Canberra. The pressure is on for me to find something in Georgetown.

This morning, October 25, Bob is so absorbed in reading *The Washington Post* that he remains standing, hardly noticing when I bring him his breakfast. Peering over his shoulder, I'm taken aback by the headline. A knot forms in my stomach when I see Bob's picture and read "Testimony Ties Top Nixon Aide to Secret Fund."

"Well, *The Post* has finally done it," he says, slowly sitting down. "At long last, they've looped me into the Watergate flap."

"How?" I ask, pulling out my chair. Ordinarily, I love breakfast, but suddenly I have no appetite.

"Supposedly, money was transferred from a secret White House cash fund to the CRP, where it was used for a 'spying and sabotage campaign.' Those guys Woodward and Bernstein say that I'm one of five people who are authorized to approve payments." Bob shakes his head in disbelief. "They even report that the FBI questioned me about it."

"The FBI? You were questioned by the FBI?"

"No, Jo. That's the point. *The Post* couldn't care less about keeping the facts straight. There was no FBI interview, and I know nothing about any money being used for a dirty tricks campaign. The 'secret cash fund'—their term—was unrestricted money left over from the '68 campaign. It was set aside for political polling purposes, and I never paid any attention to it."

Neither of us eats much, and Bertha's call from the kitchen signals that breakfast is over. Bob rushes out, leaving half a piece of graham toast on his plate. Later, I cut the article out of the paper and slip it into my growing scrapbook on Washington.

So much has happened recently. Bits and pieces of various news stories whirl around in my head when I climb into bed tonight. It takes forever to fall asleep, and I'm awakened at 3:00 a.m. by the strident ring of the White House phone.

Bob gropes for the receiver, and a gravelly voice on the other end apologizes for calling at this hour. As Henry Kissinger talks, his deep raspy inflections carry over to my side. He's disturbed that the North Vietnamese have gone public with the Peace Agreement, which South Vietnam has not yet signed.

Bob apologizes for the interruption and turns off the light. Flopping over onto his stomach, he is soon lightly snoring.

I'm wide awake. Staring into the darkness, I start to think about the incredibly important issues that Bob has to deal with on a daily basis. On top of managing the White House, he has to be up to speed on the Vietnam War, the presidential campaign, plans for the reorganization of the executive branch, and the status of "the New Majority," an across-the-board political alliance. Last, but not least, there's Watergate. I don't know how Bob does it.

Our alarm goes off at 6:30 a.m., and half an hour later, Henry calls again. While he and Bob talk, I take my time making the bed. I really don't want to go downstairs and face *The Post* again. On the other hand, I have to smile when I enter the kitchen. Seated in his bouncy chair, Little Oscar is laughing while our Dalmatian, Pokie, licks applesauce off his face. Bertha hands me the paper. I was right to be apprehensive. There, in large black letters, is Bob's name.

The lead article is titled, "White House Denies Story On Haldeman." In it, Ron Ziegler is quoted as saying that Woodward and Bernstein's story yesterday was an "effort to discredit individuals within the Nixon administration based on hearsay." Ron calls it "a blatant effort at character assassination...reporting such as this represents the shoddiest type of journalism."

The Post's Executive Editor Ben Bradlee replies, "We stand by our story."

I'm afraid Ron is fighting a losing battle. No matter how distorted Woodward and Bernstein's accusation is, once the story appears in print, it's almost impossible to unravel fact from fiction.

White House Hatchet Man

BOB TURNS FORTY-SIX ON Friday, October 27, and not having his name appear in print today is the best birthday present he could get. We plan to attend the National Horse Show tonight, and as we are changing for the event, he tells me that Billy Graham called to wish him a happy birthday.

Standing next to me in our bathroom, Bob plugs in his electric shaver and feels his chin for any sign of whiskers. "Billy's concerned about the effects of Watergate on Dwight and me," he says. "He told me that he'd be happy to make a statement on our behalf if we want him to."

"That's really nice!" I exclaim.

◆

THE FOLLOWING NIGHT, HANK joins us for dinner, and I realize that it's been a long time since the five of us have been together. I wish that Susan could be here, too. I cook duck *a l'orange* as a special treat. We linger at the table as Hank talks about his job at the CRP and describes his participation in a debate on the Vietnam War at Sidwell Friends School. He's sure that he was the only one there who backed the president's position, but he liked the challenge. The toughest moment was when his opponent appeared on the stage in a wheelchair. A member of Vietnam Veterans Against the War, Dudley Acker had lost both of his legs fighting in Vietnam.

"It wasn't easy," Hank says. "The students are tied up in knots over the war. My whole purpose was to make them more aware. I wanted to show them that there's another side to the story. What it boiled down to was emotion versus reason."

"Do you think you got your point across?" Ann asks.

"I think so. Kids came up to me afterward and said positive things. That's all I could hope for."

I study Hank's earnest expression and empathize with both him and Dudley Acker. *War is a terrible thing.*

◆

WE SUBSCRIBE TO THREE weekly news magazines—*Time, Newsweek,* and *U.S. News and World Report*—as well as three daily newspapers—*The Washington Post, The Washington Evening Star,* and *The Christian Science Monitor.* Between these and the network news at night, I attempt to keep up with what's going on. When I read in *Time* that Dwight Chapin admitted to hiring Segretti, I don't see how anyone can call it a crime. If that's the worst the press can come up with, then maybe things aren't so bad.

When Walter Cronkite mentions Bob's name on the CBS Evening News, it hurts. It's unnerving to hear him report that *The Washington Post* has charged that Segretti was part of a massive spy operation and Bob Haldeman was among those controlling funds for political intelligence. Cronkite's "father figure" image gives him enhanced credibility.

Halloween is my forty-fourth birthday. Four carved pumpkins with votive candles flickering inside them sit on our front porch. While Peter and Ann are out with friends, Bob and I man the door for the trick-or-treaters. During a lull, he opens his briefcase and takes out an oversized, gaudy-looking magazine.

"I don't want the kids to see this," Bob confides as he holds up a copy of the *Police Gazette.* At the top of its blood-red and bright-yellow cover is a grainy photo of Bob that looks like a mug shot.

"White House Hatchet Man" is written across the magazine in capital letters, and a girl in a revealing bikini fills most of the space below. "How to Get Rich in the Nudist Camp Business" is the featured story, along with "Male Birth Control."

"The article about me isn't that bad," Bob says, leafing through the pages. "It doesn't even mention Watergate."

Ads for men's stretch wigs and moneymaking machines flip by, and eventually Bob comes to a two-page story about himself. "Here, let me read you some of it... 'Perhaps no man in American history has been closer to a president. Wherever Nixon goes, Haldeman is there or in extremely close contact by phone or radio… Organization is Haldeman's talent, and he knows how to use that talent. President Nixon will be its beneficiary."

The doorbell rings, and Bob stuffs the magazine back into his briefcase.

"Don't tell Mom about this," he says, walking over to the door. "I'm not sure how she'll react to my being featured in *The Police Gazette*."

Reassuring him that I won't say anything, I watch as Bob offers candy to a small Raggedy Ann. *The "White House hatchet man" is thoroughly enjoying the moment.*

Ripping the Place Apart

November 1972

SOUTH VIETNAM CONTINUES TO oppose the peace agreement, and North Vietnam suspends its negotiations. In a televised campaign speech, the president affirms that the US won't be forced into an agreement by an election deadline. Peace must include the return of our POWs, as well as an accounting of our MIAs. McGovern hits back hard and accuses Nixon of lying and deceit.

Three days before the election, I fly to California on *Air Force One* with Bob. The president and first lady plan to vote in San Clemente and then return immediately to Washington. Everyone on board expects Nixon to win by a landslide, and there's a feeling of euphoria as we stop for rallies in North Carolina and New Mexico.

I spend Election Day with my parents. Setting up folding TV tables in the den, the three of us eat dinner while we watch the returns. True to the predictions, Nixon takes an early lead, and by 9:00 p.m., McGovern concedes. Not long afterward, Bob calls from the White House.

"Well, we clobbered them," he reports. "Massachusetts was the only state we didn't carry, which is a real mandate for the president's New Majority. No presidential candidate has ever won every state but one."

At 1:00 a.m., Bob calls again. Groping for the receiver, I try to answer the phone quickly before the ring awakens my mother and dad in their room. Bob's voice sounds fresh and cheery, although it is 4:00 a.m. his time.

"Just checking in," he says. "Chuck Colson and I spent the last two hours in the president's EOB office, where the three of us were discussing the returns. It got so late, we ordered bacon and eggs from the Mess for an early breakfast."

Bob is clearly jazzed up, a side of him that I don't often see. After hanging up, I lie in the dark thinking how different he sounded. So boyish, so excited, and so eager to share what he had been doing.

Six out of ten Americans vote for the president, and on Wednesday, November 8, Nixon's win is carried in banner headlines across the country. When I return to DC, I expect to find Bob in the same exuberant mood, but he's not. Preoccupied with plans for Nixon's second term, he's driven and impatient. He tells me that he expects this month will be the most intensive month he's ever experienced. I'm glad he told me what to expect.

Bob is right. During the month of November, he's home only seven nights. He's on the road constantly, and for fourteen days he's holed up at Camp David with the president. In an endless succession of meetings, he, John Ehrlichman, and others focus on the reorganization of the executive branch.

A customary review of all presidential appointments is part of the job, which includes everyone who serves at the pleasure of the president. This means the cabinet, the diplomatic corps, and the White House staff. Nixon's sweeping demand for all of them to submit resignations is criticized as being unduly harsh and insensitive. The press reports that it has "a chilling effect on White House morale" and refers to the "imperial presidency."

As chief of staff, Bob is the one carrying out the directive, and his method is described as "ruthless." He explains that reorganization is necessary to make the government operate better. He's quoted as saying, "The president's going to rip the place apart and put it back together. Bang, bang."

The cartoonist Jim Berry sees the lighter side in all of this and draws the president at his desk, talking to his dog, who is seated across from him. "I'm glad Bob Haldeman let you see me," Nixon is saying, "even if it was a brief visit, King Timahoe!" Berry sends the original cartoon to Bob, who frames it for his office at home.

◆

ON SATURDAY, NOVEMBER 18, after spending a week at Camp David, Bob calls to say that he'll be home for the day tomorrow. He wants to make the most of it and asks me to buy the ingredients for him to fix dinner. The last time we were together as a family was a month ago.

Unfortunately, our family time fizzles out after church. The calls start coming in and never stop. All too soon, Bob melds with the White House phone, and the children and I are tiptoeing around the house. Following a quick pick-up dinner, he leaves for another week of seclusion at Camp David. In his briefcase is a yellow pad with seven pages of handwritten notes.

I know this intense planning is necessary to accomplish everything the president wants in his second term, but I still can't believe the demands it puts on Bob's time. At J. Walter Thompson, he worked regular hours and had a month off each summer. We used to eat dinner with the children at 6:00 p.m. every night, and he was always home on the weekends. More importantly, he never brought his work home with him.

In Bob's absence, the Australian Embassy buys our home for their deputy chief of mission, who is a bachelor. Although we're one step closer to moving, I have yet to find a house in Georgetown. On November 21, Maxine Cheshire writes a column in the "Style" section of *The Washington Post* titled, "Haldemans Sell House, Looking Again."

> Presidential assistant H. R. (Bob) Haldeman has sold his house in the exclusive suburb of Kenwood...but he is planning to move to Georgetown, not out of Washington. The controversial Haldeman's Georgetown purchase plans seem to indicate that he does not expect to be among those leaving Washington in the staff changes now underway at the White House.

With the Nixons at Camp David for Thanksgiving, our family celebrates the holiday with the Ehrlichmans at their home. Reverting to being dads, John and Bob enjoy being with their children. The time together gives everyone a much-needed break from the tension of the past weeks.

The following day, Peter and Bob's suggestion of moving to Georgetown finally becomes a reality. On November 24, at 3:30 p.m., our broker shows me a brand new, three-story, red brick townhouse. With its four bedrooms, full attic, and attached garage, 3402 R Street is perfect. The large cherry tree in the center of the small patio clinches the deal, and I can hardly wait to have the rest of the family see it. When they do, everyone is thrilled, except Hank, who continues to question why we would want to live in such a "funky neighborhood."

◆

A FEW DAYS LATER, Bob calls from Camp David, and as soon as I hear the tone of his voice I know that something is very wrong.

"Just want you to know that I had a talk with Dwight this afternoon, and I told him that he would have to resign. There's no way around it; his connection to Segretti ties Dwight indirectly to his dirty tricks."

I'm floored. "Oh, Bob, are things really that bad? That must have been so hard on both of you. Will Dwight have to leave right away?"

"Not immediately. I think that we can ride things out for a while longer."

"Dwight's such a nice guy," I say, desperately wanting to say something meaningful.

"I think he understands why he has to go, but it's very, very tough on him," Bob explains. Then, his voice breaks. "I hope I never have to go through an experience like that again. It was horrible."

It's heart-wrenching to hear Bob talk this way. He's always so capable of controlling his emotions and dealing with things impersonally. But this is Dwight, one of Bob's closest friends.

December 1972

ON THE FIRST DAY of December, our broker turns over the keys to our new home. I'm excited but overwhelmed. We couldn't have picked a worse time to move. Bob is deluged with work, and both his sister and mother plan to visit us. Christmas is coming up, which will be followed by a week-long family vacation in Palm Springs and then the inauguration.

Fortunately, the Australian Embassy won't take possession of our house in Kenwood until the end of February, which gives me three months to get everything done. The most immediate need is the townhouse, where I have to select kitchen appliances, carpeting, window treatments, and paint for the interior.

Flawless

A S THE HOLIDAYS APPROACH, our social life picks up. On the few occasions that Bob is home, we attend the lighting of the National Christmas Tree, a candlelight tour of the White House, and White House Church. At the White House dinner in honor of the new cabinet, the president asks Bob to give the toast to Vice President Agnew. It's a thrilling moment, and when I tell Non how well Bob spoke, she attributes it to his father, who was a skilled toastmaster.

On December 14, Vietnam is back in the headlines in a big way. When the North Vietnamese make it clear they have no intention of returning to the Peace Talks, the president issues an ultimatum. Either they resume negotiations or "suffer the consequences." When they don't comply, the US conducts the most intensive bombing campaign of the war. The press labels it, "The Christmas Bombing," and one columnist calls Nixon "a maddened tyrant, who's conducting a war by tantrum."

On December 21, the fourth day of heavy air strikes over North Vietnam, three B-52s are shot down, and Hanoi claims that US prisoner of war camps were hit. Although it's a crucial time at the White House, Bob manages to come home early to keep a commitment he made to Ann. As soon as he enters the house, he takes off his coat and tie and heads for the kitchen. Slipping on his blue-and-gray-striped apron, he takes over as chef and proceeds to barbecue hamburgers for eight thirteen-year-old girls. Bob's wholehearted effort contributes to the success of our younger daughter's slumber party.

Non is with us for our last Christmas in Kenwood. Before sitting down to our traditional turkey dinner, we light the candles on the large German whirly-gig in the center of the table. Activated by the heat, its carved wooden figures begin to rotate slowly. At each person's place, a red candle burns on top of a pear coated with cream cheese. Following a moment of silence, we blow out the candles. Although we reminisce about our three years in Kenwood, we spend more time enthusiastically discussing the inauguration and our next four years in Georgetown.

The day after Christmas, former president Harry S. Truman dies at the age of eighty-eight, and the Nixons fly to Independence, Missouri, to pay their respects to Mrs. Truman. The bombing resumes full force, and three days later, the North Vietnamese concede. They agree to return to Paris for the Peace Talks, and the president orders a halt to the American air offensive. Many speculate that this might be the end of the war. We are vacationing in Palm Springs with the family when we hear the news. Everyone cheers.

January 1973

ON TUESDAY, JANUARY 2, Bob, Peter, Ann, and I return to Washington on the new *Air Force One*, an updated version of the old Boeing 707. With the exception of the crew and the flight attendants, Nancy and Ron Ziegler and the four of us are the only people on board, and we can sit wherever we want. All of the seats are still covered with white protective sheets.

Nixon's second inauguration will take place in three weeks. A stack of invitations to various inaugural events awaits us when we arrive home. In DC, barriers and grandstands are already being put in place, and I feel the excitement as I drive back and forth to Georgetown.

The Pentagon Papers trial finally gets underway in Los Angeles. Daniel Ellsberg faces charges of theft and conspiracy for stealing the papers and giving them to *The New York Times*.

Although Bob's name crops up in the news again, the stories focus on his personal life, not Watergate. In *The Evening Star*, Betty Beale writes, "...Thus, the man called the squarest member of Nixon's staff is moving to the artiest section of town. There is simply no telling what will happen from here on in during the president's second term."

In *The Washington Post*, Maxine Cheshire comments on Bob's tennis, reporting that he and John Ehrlichman "played doubles in two businesslike sets with the emphasis on exercise not banter." Various photos of Bob on the court, dressed in his tennis whites, are featured in *Time* and *Newsweek*, as well as several newspapers.

Little Oscar surprises us with his first tooth, but Bertha has a bigger bombshell to drop. In the midst of helping me sort through china and bric-a-brac that I plan to give away, she announces that she's leaving us. A week later, she and Little Oscar drive away in Big Oscar's truck. I can't envision our life without her.

With Bertha gone and the inauguration fast approaching, I feel the pressure of the move even more. A light beige carpet has been installed throughout the townhouse. The blinds are up in Peter's room, and the painter is halfway through applying the first coat of Navajo white to the living room walls. Today, the Secret Service arrives to put in a security system, which includes an on-site alarm in our entry. When it goes off, the clanging is horrendous. This happens three times, and the men are stumped. It's the pugs. Every time one of them goes through the doggy door in the basement, it sets off the alarm. Eventually, the problem is fixed, and our home is secure. The dogs can use their doggy door without creating panic throughout the neighborhood.

◆

HOWARD HUNT PLEADS GUILTY, and two days later, McCord and Liddy are convicted of conspiracy, burglary, and wiretapping. When Judge Sirica says that there is still much that we don't know about Watergate, I'm not sure what he means. With all that is going on right now, however, I don't give it a second thought.

It's overcast and windy on Inauguration Day, Saturday, January 20. As we did four years ago, everyone gets bundled up for a cold morning outside. Non and the children go in one direction; Bob and I, in the other. On the inaugural platform, the atmosphere is relaxed and friendly. We chat with some of the dignitaries and wave to others. It's a familiar scene, and I enjoy myself.

Everything proceeds exactly on schedule. Looking presidential and proud, the president delivers his final inaugural address. "…We shall answer to God, to history, and to our conscience for the way in which we use these years."

Once again, I'm aware of being a part of history on this special occasion. However, it's different this time. I know Nixon is sincere, but for some reason his words don't soar and sing as they did four years ago. I expect to catch a quotable line like, "Until he has been part of a cause larger than himself, no man is truly whole," but there isn't one. I miss the euphoric feeling that Bob and I experienced before, when we stood on the brink of the most thrilling adventure of our lives.

Following the swearing-in, Bob and I have lunch with Non and the children in Bob's office. A steward from the White House Mess takes our order, and we eat at a small table that has been set up by the window.

Later, we attend the inaugural ball at the Kennedy Center. The music is loud, and the room is packed. I struggle to protect my black velvet ball gown from getting crushed, and Bob and I slip out early. When he climbs into bed, I ask him how he would describe this week of inaugural festivities.

"Flawless," he says, turning off the light.

I am restless and can't get to sleep. *The execution may have been flawless... but the inauguration was missing something. What was it?* It finally comes to me. *The passion.*

1,461 Days Left

O N JANUARY 23, THE president makes the announcement that everyone has been waiting to hear. In a brief statement at 10:00 p.m., he tells the world that a settlement has been reached in the Paris Peace Talks. In four days, a cease-fire will go into effect which will guarantee the return of our prisoners of war and the right for South Vietnam to determine its own future. Twenty-three years after the US first sent funding and military support to the French in Vietnam, this divisive war is over. The toll is great. *So many lives lost, so many heartaches, so many tears. Now it's over...*

After the announcement, Bob's mood is upbeat, and he is more relaxed than I've seen him since the election. He accompanies the Nixons to Florida for a long weekend of rest and relaxation. Peter, Ann, and I join him in Key Biscayne, where we attend a special service honoring the cease-fire on January 27. Seated in the local Presbyterian Church, I am overcome with emotion as the bells ring at exactly 7:00 p.m. (midnight Greenwich Mean Time), joyously proclaiming that the fighting has stopped. I feel so honored to be a part of this gathering at such a historically significant moment. There isn't a dry eye when we stand and sing, "America the Beautiful." At the end of the service, no one wants to leave. Sensing a special connection, we smile and warmly greet strangers as we walk out.

"It was neat to see the president so happy," Bob says, opening the car door for me. "His only regret was that he wasn't able to share this moment with LBJ." Former president Lyndon Baines Johnson passed away five days ago.

The next morning, while the children study inside the villa, Bob and Larry work on the porch. Instead of unwinding and enjoying this moment in the sun, Bob is berating Larry over details related to the reorganization. As I lie on the beach in front of them, I can't help but overhear his sharp words. I wince.

Later, when I run into Larry in the downstairs hallway, I decide to tell him frankly what's on my mind. I've never done that before.

"I'm sorry Bob's being so rough on you, Larry. As we both know, he probably doesn't even realize how cutting his remarks are."

"Don't worry, Jo. I'm used to it, and I don't let it get to me." Larry smiles and seems to be at ease.

"I think he's critical because you're so capable," I continue. "He has such high expectations, and he knows that he can depend on you. He's just impatient to get things done…hang in there."

"I will," Larry assures me. "Bob's an incredible guy to work for, and I have the highest respect for him."

Before we leave Key Biscayne, Bob shows me a special calendar that the president plans to give to the members of his cabinet. It's a countdown from January 20, 1973, to January 20, 1977, four years from now. Each date includes the corresponding number of days remaining in the Nixon presidency. The inscription inside the handsome leather cover reads, in part:

> Every moment of history is a fleeting time, precious
> and unique. The Presidential term, which begins today,
> consists of 1,461 days…no more and no less. Each can be
> a day of strengthening and renewal for America, each can
> add depth and dimension to the American experience…

Although there has been a turnover in the staff for this second term, Bob seems entrenched in his position as chief of staff. *One thousand, four hundred, sixty-one days remain. It seems like a very long time.*

◆

ON JANUARY 30, DWIGHT Chapin resigns from the White House. Although he has accepted the position of director of market planning for United Airlines, it must be a difficult transition after serving as deputy assistant to the president of the United States. I think of him and his family all day. It's hard to face Bob this evening when he comes home. He never mentions the resignation.

Time *magazine, April 30, 1973.*

PART THREE

WATERGATE

What's Going to Happen, Will Happen

February 1973

I**N THREE WEEKS WE** will move, and my big concern is the lack of space in the townhouse. Our downstairs playroom overflows with bric-a-brac to give away. A few items have been put aside to donate to Ann's school fair, and a junk dealer will pick up what's left.

Although news of Watergate investigations continues, I have not seen Bob's name in the paper for three months, and I hope that, with our new home and the beginning of Nixon's second term, we are off on a fresh start.

On February 7, the Senate approves the creation of a seven-member committee to probe the Watergate allegations and report back to the full Senate within the year. It will be headed by Senator Sam Ervin.

The next morning is dark and stormy, and our dining room is dreary. Bob flicks on the lights as I bring in the coffee and fresh orange juice. He takes one slice of buttered graham toast, and it's a bran muffin for me.

"Jeez," Bob says under his breath. Holding up the front page of *The Washington Post*, he points to his picture in the center of the page. I stand motionless. The headline reads, "Senate Votes Watergate Probe," and I wonder why Bob's picture is there. A feeling of exasperation sweeps over me. *After all that time, why now?*

"Well, it looks like Woodward and Bernstein are back at it," Bob says. "They've managed to tie me into their latest story." Spreading the paper out in front of him, he continues. "According to them, sources say that I 'actively assisted in efforts to get the Senate to shift the focus of the investigations away from the widespread allegations of a White House-led campaign of spying and sabotage in 1972.'"

Bob looks down and skims over the article.

"Is there more?" I hesitate to ask.

"Yeah," he says. "I'm mentioned again. They say Senator Ervin intends to probe into charges beyond the Watergate bugging, including Segretti's activities. According to them, my assistant Gordon Strachan gave Segretti's name and telephone number to Liddy."

Outside, the sky is black, and the rain is coming down in wild gushes. The bleak weather provides the perfect backdrop for the drama unfolding inside.

Bob continues, "The committee might call on White House aides to testify, and Ziegler says that the administration will cooperate if the investigation is handled in a nonpartisan way."

My head jerks up. "Does that mean that *you* will have to *testify*?"

"I'm not sure." Bob folds the paper back up. "It depends on whether or not we are covered by executive privilege."

The panes of the bay window rattle as rain splatters against them. Glancing at his watch, Bob hurriedly pushes back his chair and stands. It's late, and we don't have Bertha to shout from the kitchen when the White House car arrives. The two of us rush out to the front hall, where he struggles to put on his raincoat. His left arm gets tangled in the sleeve, and I help him straighten it out.

Pausing at the front door to put up his umbrella, Bob turns to me. "No use worrying, Jo. What's going to happen, will happen." His voice is low and resigned.

What's going to happen, will happen. The words stay with me throughout the day. I'm still turning them over in my mind when Ray, the used furniture dealer, loads my giveaways into his truck. For a fleeting moment, I wonder why we're making this move. *Newsweek* is right when it describes Watergate as, "that great gummy fungus that refuses to curl up and die."

◆

THE "GUMMY FUNGUS" CONTINUES to spread, and the stories about Bob keep coming. On February 13, his name appears on the front page of *The Evening Star.* In an article titled, "Top Nixon Bodyguard Ousted by Haldeman," White House correspondent Helen Thomas writes that the chief of the White

House Secret Service was fired, following a rift with Presidential Assistant H. R. Haldeman.

A subsequent article in *Newsweek* gives more details. At a campaign rally last summer, Robert Taylor of the Secret Service threatened to arrest Bob when he tried to lower a restraining rope to make the president more accessible. Taylor was replaced, and his supporters called his removal, "Haldeman's revenge."

In an emotional scene on Valentine's Day, twenty former POWs return to the US after years of captivity. Watching on TV, I cry as Commander Jeremiah Denton steps onto American soil and states publically, "We are honored to have had the opportunity to serve our country under difficult circumstances. We are profoundly grateful to our commander in chief and to our nation for this day. God bless America."

Although Bob is gone the first three weekends in February, he helps with the move when he can. He makes occasional runs to Georgetown with the car full of paintings, lampshades, and breakables, and he draws a grid of our attic to maximize its storage space. By numbering our packing cartons and designating them to correspondingly numbered places in the attic, he assures me that I will know exactly where everything is.

Thursday, February 22, is moving day. The bitter cold and the dark storm clouds don't seem to faze the movers. Working fast and furiously, they get the job done before it starts to pour. Jeanne Ehrlichman and Nancy Ziegler drop by to see our new home and volunteer to make up the beds.

The townhouse has three stories, and we make use of every inch of space. Peter's bedroom is on the first floor and looks out on the street. It has a brick fireplace in the corner and is roomy enough for him to set up a small indoor hothouse, which was a Christmas present from my parents several years ago. He tells us that he wants to grow wax begonias.

The living room, kitchen, and dining room are on the second floor. On the third level, there are three bedrooms. The master bedroom is the largest, and I claim the walk-in closet with a window overlooking R Street as my dressing room/office. Ann plasters the walls of her room with posters of African animals and baby seals. She puts her parakeet's cage near the window so Amos can talk to the birds outside in the cherry tree. Bob uses the third bedroom as his office. In the attic, the movers arrange the boxes according to Bob's grid.

After the peace and quiet of the suburbs, I'm surprised that our family has no trouble adjusting to the activity and noise of city life. There's a constant stream of traffic on R Street, enhanced by police sirens and the wailing cry of ambulances. Western High School is a block away, and groups of boisterous students pass by our house every morning and afternoon.

Bob leaves for the White House fifteen minutes later than he did in Kenwood, and he only has to take three steps to get from our front door to the curb. To get to school, Peter and Ann have a two-block walk to Wisconsin Avenue and a short bus ride. With Montrose Park, Dumbarton Oaks, a Safeway, a delicatessen, and several restaurants nearby, there's not much need for a car.

It's wonderful to have Bob home with us for our first weekend in Georgetown. But when I hear that John Ehrlichman is at Camp David with the president, I am apprehensive. *Why isn't Bob with them?*

On Sunday, February 25, Jack Anderson writes an article for *The Washington Post* titled, "Backstage With H. R. Haldeman."

> The man who manipulates the backstage wires at the White House, H. R. Haldeman, is becoming entangled in his own cross wires. Specifically, the Watergate case. Haldeman takes his orders, of course, from President Nixon… Haldeman exercises his power from behind the scenes, carefully staying in the darkest part of the president's shadow… Senate investigators and FBI agents alike have followed the Watergate tracks right up to Haldeman's door, but can't get past his bright, young assistants.

Anderson cites Dwight Chapin, Jeb Magruder, and Gordon Strachan as being completely loyal to Bob, but they have ties to either Segretti or Liddy. He quotes a former White House aide as saying, "Haldeman is completely pragmatic. There is absolutely no idealism in this man's soul." Another aide is quoted, "Haldeman looks like a boy scout, but he's a pirate." "But," Anderson writes, "all agree that Haldeman subordinates himself for what he considers to be the good of Richard Nixon."

Chip, Chip, Chip

March 1973

A FTER LIVING IN GEORGETOWN for several weeks, I fall into a pleasant routine. I meet friends for lunch, play tennis, drive Ann out to Potomac for her weekly riding lessons, walk the pugs, and volunteer at the City Hall Complaint Center. Occasionally, Bob takes a break in the afternoon, and I meet him and the Higbys for tennis on the White House court. At night, we attend functions at the White House, as well as the State Department. At the annual Gridiron Club dinner, the press roasts the administration, and Bob reports that most of the jokes were about Watergate.

As the war winds down, the last American killed in the fighting is buried at Arlington National Cemetery. In his message to Congress, the president requests tax relief for the elderly, help for parents with children in private schools, compulsory health insurance, and better legal services for the poor. Occupying Wounded Knee, South Dakota, two hundred members of the Oglala Sioux Tribe demand a Senate inquiry into the government's treatment of them. In New York City, a pornographic movie titled *Deep Throat* is ruled obscene.

The Senate Judiciary Committee holds hearings on the confirmation of L. Patrick Gray as director of the FBI. While being interrogated, Gray admits that John Dean sat in on FBI questioning during the Watergate investigation and that he gave Dean raw FBI files. Because of his ties to Howard Hunt, Chuck Colson resigns from the White House and returns to his private law practice.

The stain of Watergate keeps spreading, and when I see a close-up of Bob's face on the March 19 cover of *Newsweek*, I shudder. With steely, gray green eyes, he's intently staring straight ahead. A diagonal, red banner at the top says, "Nixon's Palace Guard." I knew that Bob had been interviewed for the story, but I had no idea he would be so prominently featured. Five full pages are devoted exclusively to him, describing him as, "glowering out at the world from under a crew cut that would freeze Medusa... His admirers, who include most of the people who really matter in Richard Nixon's government, regard him as a genius at a thankless trade—probably one of the best ever."

The article is a mixture of good and bad. It opens with, "Harry Robbins Haldeman is, as he once cheerfully put it, Richard Nixon's son of a bitch," and concludes, "Mr. Nixon needs a Haldeman and without him would have to produce another... The hardest judgment of Haldeman is that he is sometimes loyal to a fault. 'He's earned every enemy he's got,' says one of them, a Republican congressman. 'I'd say he's a good man to have on your side.'"

I'm caught off guard when I read, "[Haldeman] would no doubt even leave Mr. Nixon if leaving would serve his interests—if, say—the Watergate imbroglio someday demanded another sacrifice and Haldeman happened to be in the line of fire."

Bob leave the White House? I don't know why Newsweek *would even suggest such a thing. Is this really a possibility? It would be devastating for Bob. What would he do if he couldn't serve his president? And what would his staff and the president do without him?*

Chip, chip, chip. The press is subtly chipping away at Bob's image. They want to bring him down. Patrick Anderson summed it up perfectly: "A president's aide can attain power and glory, but the power is precarious, and the glory may become tinged with notoriety, for there are many dangers inherent in his position."

◆

AT A PRESS CONFERENCE, Nixon warns North Vietnam that there will be serious consequences if its troops continue to infiltrate South Vietnam. Although the cease-fire is in place, both North Vietnam and South Vietnam have violated it. In answer to questions about Watergate, the president states that no one in the White House was involved in the break-in. He has told his staff to cooperate with the Senate Select Committee on Presidential Campaign Activities by submitting their sworn statements in writing. They will not have to appear in person.

Senator Sam Ervin, chairman of the Committee, complains that he can't cross-examine a piece of paper and threatens to arrest anyone who refuses to testify. When Bob's mother hears this, she calls in alarm. I do my best to reassure her that her son will not be going to jail.

Distance magnifies the stories that our families hear and read about, and I try to convince them that our lives are normal. I used to write them long weekly letters, but lately I've been calling Mom and Non every morning. The sound of my voice buoys them up.

Mother loves to hear about the family. Non is more interested in Watergate and insists that we cancel our subscription to *The Washington Post*. I confirm that Martha Mitchell really did tell the press that the president's denial of a meeting with her husband was a "God blessed lie."

"No, Non, she's not crazy, just a little kooky."

When I run into the other White House wives, I notice that we are more guarded in our conversation than we used to be. Watergate is a touchy subject, which we avoid. I feel for Susie Chapin and Patty Colson, whose husbands have resigned. It's awkward to be with Jeanne Ehrlichman and Gail Magruder, who, like me, have husbands who are frequently mentioned in the news. Dolores Higby is the only one to confide in me. She calls John Dean a "snake," which she says is "just a hunch." She keeps coming up with theories about the break-in, and her current one is that Dean knows more than he's divulging. Given the current situation, I'm hesitant to approach Lucy Winchester about the docent program for the White House wives, and I decide to put it on hold.

I wish I better understood what is happening, and I occasionally try to raise the subject of Watergate with Bob. The best time to approach him is at breakfast, when he's focused on the latest news reports. I find ways to ask questions, but as soon as I get the Haldeman look, I back off. To my friends, I'm sure that I appear calm and confident, but each new development makes me feel less secure.

◆

ON FRIDAY, MARCH 23, Bob's White House calendar shows 1,401 days remaining in the Nixon administration. It's a warm, sunny morning, and Bob's packed suitcase sits next to the front door. Wearing his blue blazer instead of a suit, he is dressed informally for the presidential trip to Florida.

"I bet you're glad to get out of here," I say.

"I am," he says. "I hate all the leaks and rumors. If I had my druthers, I'd have the White House staff go before the grand jury and tell everything we know."

Not long after Bob departs, a new Watergate story breaks. Judge Sirica releases a letter from James McCord, the former security consultant at the CRP who was found guilty at the break-in trial. In the letter, McCord writes that political pressure was applied to the defendants, who were told to plead guilty and remain silent. McCord denies that the break-in was a CIA operation and claims that perjury occurred during the trial. He also states that there are others, not yet identified, who were involved in the Watergate operation. The press calls the letter a "bombshell."

"McCord really stirred things up today." Calling from Key Biscayne later, Bob sounds exhausted. "And on top of that, the *Los Angeles Times* is reporting that Dean and Magruder knew about the bugging in advance of the break-in."

"Really?" I ask. "Do you think they did?"

"I haven't the foggiest notion."

Bob usually isn't at a loss, and I'm concerned. "How are *you* doing?"

"Okay, I guess. But this stuff never stops coming. *Somehow* the White House has got to get on top of it. Right now, it's 'subject A' for the president. He hauled me in for a five-hour meeting as soon as we got here. I'm beat."

Over the next several days, Watergate progresses. Jeb Magruder resigns, the federal grand jury reconvenes to hear new Watergate charges, and Martha Mitchell tells *The New York Times* that someone is trying to make her husband "the goat."

◆

ON MARCH 30, I return home from spending a week visiting Susan in Minnesota and my sister's family in Colorado. I am disappointed to find that I just missed Bob. He has left a note, saying that he stopped by to repack before flying to California.

It's a relief when NBC opens its evening newscast tonight with a report on farm prices, not on Watergate. A film clip of reporters gathered in front of a brick townhouse follows, and my attention is diverted by an exchange with Ann about her homework. Not until John Chancellor says, "Associated

Press reports that James McCord told the Senate Watergate Committee today that H. R. Haldeman *must* have been aware of plans to bug the Democrats," do I take note. The brick townhouse on the television screen in front of me is our home.

The front door opens, and Bob steps out. Carl Stern reports, "McCord apparently has no proof that people like Haldeman, Mitchell, and Dean are involved." Bob makes his way through a batch of reporters to the curb, where a White House car is waiting.

I can hardly wait to talk to him, and the minutes drag until he calls an hour later. "Well, McCord's done it again," he says. "Beats me what he's talking about, but he sure had the press fired up when I left the house today."

"I know. I just saw you on TV with all those reporters."

"Yeah. I couldn't even bring my suitcase with me. If I had, it would have started a whole new round of speculation by the press as to where I was going."

"You're kidding."

"No, I'm not. Terry O'Donnell picked it up later."

After Bob hangs up, I watch a repeat of the scene on the eleven o'clock news. When we moved to Georgetown a month ago, I thought Watergate was starting to fade. Instead, it's been one revelation after another.

Chip, chip, chip.

◆

AT THE END OF the month, the North Vietnamese release the last of the American POWs. After eight years, their prison, the "Hanoi Hilton," is empty. Comet Kohoutek, with its long plasma tail, is discovered and nicknamed the "comet of the century." Bill Walton leads UCLA to its seventh straight NCAA basketball title. In support of the American Indian Movement, Marlon Brando turns down the Oscar for best actor in *The Godfather.*

It Was the Best of Times, It Was the Worst of Times

April 1973

ON SUNDAY, APRIL 1, I awake to a glorious day. The cherry tree in the patio is on the verge of bursting into full bloom, and from our bedroom window all I can see are masses of tiny pink buds. Once again, I wish Bob were here to experience this moment with me. However, he's been gone more than he's been in town, and the two of us have yet to enjoy a relaxed time in our new home.

As on most Sundays, I watch the weekly broadcast of *Face the Nation* this morning. Lowell Weicker is being interviewed by a panel of journalists. He is one of seven members on the Senate Watergate Committee, and I'm anxious to hear what he has to say. It doesn't take long to find that I don't like him. Not only is he pompous, but he has strong, negative, preconceived ideas about Nixon.

When the Senator self-righteously proclaims, "H. R. Haldeman directed a master plot of sabotage and espionage in the White House," I'm angry. His statement is totally irresponsible, and I lose all respect for him.

Bob is upset when he calls the next day. "That nut Weicker had no proof when he made those charges, and he's not man enough to admit that he was wrong. Senator Ervin called and personally apologized. He said that there's no evidence whatsoever linking me to the bugging."

"I don't see how Weicker could say something like that," I say, trying to keep my voice steady.

"It's typical…just Weicker being Weicker…doing his usual political grandstanding…pure histrionics."

"So what happens now?"

"Actually, it gives me a good chance to go public. I could release a statement that would cover every conceivable thing I might be accused of and then follow it up with a tough interview. Like…" Bob stops to think. "Like, I could go on television and have Dan Rather ask me a lot of hardball questions."

"Are you serious?"

"It'd be better than just sitting around having people take potshots at me. The only problem is I'm not sure if this is the best timing." Bob is clearly frustrated. "The grand jury is meeting, and the Senate Watergate hearings are coming up."

Over time, Weicker's charges fade, and Bob drops the idea of releasing a statement and doing an interview. In the Pentagon Papers trial, Daniel Ellsberg finally testifies, three months after the opening statements were given.

On Wednesday, April 11, with 1,380 days remaining in the Nixon presidency, a leak from the grand jury brings Watergate a step closer. Reportedly both Dwight Chapin and Gordon Strachan testified in closed hearings that Bob had agreed with their proposal to approach Donald Segretti about being in charge of "dirty tricks." When I ask Bob about the story, he shrugs and says that he has no memory of Segretti's name being mentioned; consequently, he has no recollection of authorizing him for the job.

"I approve countless actions on the recommendations of others," Bob explains, "and I can't possibly keep track of all the memos I sign."

◆

SEATED AT MY SMALL desk in my dressing room/office, I read the Christian Science daily Bible Lesson. Outside, a light spring rain dampens the street and sidewalk. These moments of quiet study sustain me. As I put my books away, I pause to study the framed photo of Bob on the desk. Gripping the tiller of his Sunfish, he is looking over his shoulder at the camera. The blue and yellow sail hangs listlessly behind him. Studying the smiling, tan figure in the faded red trunks, I'm reminded of our sail five years ago when the wonder and excitement of a future in Washington consumed us both. Bob had been so confident of his managerial abilities—so hopeful of serving the one man he felt would make an outstanding president.

With all that he faces, his confidence has never faltered, nor has his loyalty to Nixon. Knowing Bob, I'm not surprised.

◆

ON SUNDAY, APRIL 15, for the first time since we moved two months ago, Bob enjoys a relaxed day at home. I love living in Georgetown, and I'm anxious to share its amenities with him. After attending services at the Georgetown Christian Science Church, we take a long walk in Montrose Park, which is only three blocks from our townhouse. When we return, we settle in the living room with the Sunday papers. With her dog, Dottie, at her feet, Ann is curled up reading *A Tale of Two Cities.*

It doesn't take Bob long to discover an article mentioning him. This time, *The Sunday Star* has a whole page on Haldeman in its first section. Titled "Nixon's 'No Man,'" it features a large cartoon figure of Bob guarding the door to the Oval Office. He's dressed in a Prussian-style uniform. His chest is covered with medals, and there are fancy epaulets on his shoulders. I start to read.

> The mystery man of the Nixon administration is Harry Robbins Haldeman… Bob Haldeman is the White House centurion… He is the unchallenged boss of a White House and executive office staff that, by Civil Service Commission reckoning, numbers more than 6,000 persons—everyone from Henry A. Kissinger to the lowliest GS-3 file clerk…
>
> One of the few intellectuals around Mr. Nixon is quoted as saying that 'Haldeman is extraordinarily quick to assimilate information and incredibly well organized. Haldeman has a capacity that I've never seen matched to think ahead and to be ahead of people. If I had to name the most interesting man in this administration, I would name Haldeman. He is the intense application of a unique talent on behalf of a president.'
>
> It is axiomatic in American politics that the opposition tries to damage the president by attacking his key assistants. Haldeman's role as Mr. Nixon's hatchet man has made him a prime target.

"Quite an article," I comment, handing the paper back to Bob.

"How about the part where it says that my assistants are afraid of me…and that I have a curt and frosty manner?" Bob asks, smiling.

Ann looks up. "*You*? 'Curt and frosty,' Dad?"

Before Bob can acknowledge his daughter's remark, the White House phone rings. It's the first time it has rung all day, and Bob takes the call upstairs in his study. When he doesn't appear again until dinner, I'm hopeful that there will be no more interruptions. However, as we are dishing up pork chops, applesauce, and artichokes, he gets another call. This time, the conversation is brief.

"The president wants to meet with John and me at seven thirty," Bob says. "Sorry, Jo. This means I've gotta eat fast."

"Not again," Ann complains. Giving her father her rendition of the Haldeman look, she adds, "You're never home anymore, Dad."

With half his dinner still on his plate, Bob excuses himself from the table. Grabbing his jacket, he calls goodbye from the entry below. I hear the front door click open—then, click closed. As Ann and I finish eating, the candles in the two silver candelabras give off a soft, flickering light. She tells me that *A Tale of Two Cities* is one of her favorite books. Quoting, she begins with the opening lines, "It was the best of times, it was the worst of times…"

The words resonate. It's as if they were describing my world today.

It's close to midnight when Bob gets home, and I have already gone to bed. A car door slams, and a few minutes later, I hear footsteps on the stairs. Bob has been gone almost five hours, and I wonder what could have kept him so long at this time of night. The only thing I can think of is Watergate. *Please let me be wrong.*

Bob slips quietly into the room. Propping myself up on one elbow, I greet him. "Hi. What's up?"

"It's Watergate, and for the moment, things don't look too good."

Falling back onto my pillow, I feel as if the wind has been knocked out of me. *Is Bob saying that there's more to come? What now?* He sits on the bed and removes his shoes while he talks.

"Earlier tonight, the president met with John Dean, who told him that Ehrlichman and I may face some major problems. Dean thinks that we could be charged with obstruction of justice."

"Why?" I ask. "How?"

"I may be vulnerable because I had leftover campaign money sent to the CRP, and it was used to pay the Watergate defendants."

"But you said that you had nothing to do with that money once it was turned over to the CRP."

"I didn't, but I guess there's more out there than I realized. I'm not a lawyer. John Dean is, and tonight he really laid it on the line." Bob twists his fraternity ring around and around on his finger as he talks. "Dean thinks John and I should take leaves of absence while we deal with this." He pauses to look at me for my reaction. "But you've got to remember, Jo, no matter what we do, there's every reason to believe that all of this can be worked out."

A leave of absence? I can't imagine Bob's taking a leave of absence, especially when Nixon's second term is just getting started. Doesn't a leave imply guilt? Does this mean that Bob has to clear his name for something he didn't do? How long would a leave last? Would it be with or without pay? Would we have to move? Move? Not again…we've lived in Georgetown for only two months.

When Bob climbs into bed, neither of us says anything. It's as if speaking would only bring on more heartache. I finally fall asleep, only to be awakened by the ring of the White House phone. It's almost 1:00 a.m., Monday morning. *I hate that phone.*

"Yes, Mr. President," Bob answers. Nixon does most of the talking, and Bob hangs up. Shrugging helplessly, he turns to me. "The president thinks that Ehrlichman and I should get a lawyer."

I'm taken aback. *It is the best of times. It is the worst of times…*

A Super-Major Watergate Day

SPRING COMES TO GEORGETOWN overnight. Everywhere I look there are tulips, azaleas, dogwood, lilac, forsythia, and cherry blossoms. The tree in our patio is covered with pink flowers. The weather is warm, and Wisconsin Avenue is jammed with tourists, students, and hippies. A strong aroma of incense, mixed with the scent of food and car fumes, fills the air.

In the news, the Supreme Court upholds the right of a school teacher to remain speechless during the Pledge of Allegiance. At the Pentagon Papers trial, Daniel Ellsberg claims that rather than "stealing" classified documents from the Pentagon, he "transferred them to a different branch of the government…" The World Trade Center opens in New York City. Israel celebrates its twenty-fifth anniversary, and Americans bound for the celebration sail under heavy security aboard the *Queen Elizabeth II*. In Washington, the Watergate Complex is now included in all city tours.

On Tuesday, April 17, I attend the state arrival of Prime Minister Giulio Andreotti of Italy on the South Lawn. I'm deeply moved by the pomp and ceremony of the occasion, but something is gnawing at me. I keep thinking about Bob and all that must be going on behind the scenes in the West Wing.

At a press conference, Nixon announces that White House personnel will appear before the Senate Watergate Committee, with the right to assert executive privilege. However, current and former senior administration officials will not be granted immunity.

When Bob comes home tonight, I sense that something is up. It's late, and he seems to be distracted. We help ourselves to leftover pork chops and cold artichokes and carry our plates, along with tall glasses of iced tea, into the dining room.

After pausing for a moment of silence, Bob speaks. "Today was a major Watergate day. Ehrlichman and I were in and out of the Oval Office all day."

I wait for an explanation, but it's clear that Bob doesn't want to go into any details right now. We finish dinner and do the dishes. As we're turning off the lights and going upstairs to get ready for bed, he finally blurts out, "Actually, today was a *super*-major Watergate day."

"What do you mean?" Bob's words send out a red flag. He never uses such exaggerated terms in talking about his work.

"It's just that the president spent the whole day discussing Watergate with Ehrlichman and me. He couldn't get beyond it. He kept asking for advice from other people, and then he'd rehash everything all over again with us. He went back and forth. The upshot was, John and I ended up meeting with a lawyer this evening."

It's dark, and my hand gropes for the banister of the stairs. "You've met with a lawyer?"

Bob is right behind me. "Yeah. A guy named John Wilson was recommended to us. He's the best. We decided to share our legal fees and ask him to represent both of us."

"You have the same lawyer?"

"Yes. The president thinks that John and I are both vulnerable. He keeps talking about the need for the two of us to take leaves of absence or..." Bob clears his throat and swallows. "Or resign."

"Resign?!"

"Yeah."

Resign? What happened to the leave of absence? My mind goes blank. It's like a black pit; there's nothing there. I struggle for the appropriate words.

"You'll make the right decision when the time comes, Bob." My voice is low and surprisingly steady. "I'm glad that you and John are getting good legal advice. Whatever you decide to do, just know that I believe in you."

"I know that, Jo."

Together, the two of us pause at the landing. I can feel Bob's closeness in the dark. His hand brushes against mine as we turn and walk across the hall into our bedroom.

It's hard to fall asleep, and when I finally do, I'm jarred awake at midnight by the phone. Bob flicks on the light, and I slide down under the covers. It's the president. *Doesn't he ever sleep?*

Bob listens, gives a faint-hearted laugh, and agrees to "keep the faith." The conversation moves from this evening's state dinner to Watergate. It goes on and on, and by the time Bob hangs up, I'm almost asleep.

"Well," he says, turning off the light. "Dean's obviously trying to save himself, and the president thinks that he'll probably get immunity."

In no time, Bob is asleep. But I'm wide awake. *What does this mean? Keep the faith? A lawyer? Leaves of absence? Resignation?* Night thoughts start to build up in my mind, and I know I must counter them.

◆

ALTHOUGH NOTHING CHANGES IN my daily routine, on Wednesday morning, April 18, I feel jumpy and apprehensive. After yesterday, I realize that I have no idea what to expect. I fix breakfast and feed the dogs. Bob leaves, and then Ann. With Hank back at UCLA and Peter in Minnesota with Susan, I'm alone. The house is quiet. Too quiet.

I watch the clock. Mother and Non will be expecting to hear from me around ten o'clock, and I'm not sure what to tell them. Before dialing, I hesitate. I want to be as up-front as possible about what is going on, but there are some things that I'd rather not share until they become certain. The family devours everything the press reports. They know that Bob might have to testify before the grand jury and/or the Senate Watergate Committee. This morning, I decide not to tell them about the lawyer. Hopefully, I'll never have to mention the possibility of Bob's taking a leave of absence…or worse still… resigning. Knowing that distance magnifies their concerns, I try to be positive and reassuring.

Tennis and a luncheon date help to distract me, but when Bob calls late in the afternoon, my concerns grow. "John and I are choppering up to Camp David with the president. We'll be spending the night, and I won't be back until sometime tomorrow."

That's all I know. However, the arrival of a swarm of reporters at our front door confirms that something big must be up. They refuse to leave, even though I tell them that Bob isn't here. *If only he would call.* The press must think that I know things they don't. On the other hand, I think they know more than they are saying. By nightfall, I feel trapped in the house. Each time

I walk by a window, I duck, hoping that no one outside can see me. Ann asks what's going on, and I tell her that I don't know.

When I go to bed at 11:00 p.m., there are about twenty reporters chatting directly below my dressing room window. In a last ditch effort to get rid of them, I pick up the phone and ask the White House operator for the press secretary.

"I'm so sorry you've had to deal with this, Jo," Ron Ziegler apologizes. "Those guys just won't let up. Simply tell them that Bob's at Camp David. You won't have to say anything else. That should get them off your back."

Ron's advice works. The reporters leave, but instead of going back to bed, I spend a long time gazing out the window looking at the moon through the masses of cherry blossoms. At the base of the tree, a frog croaks somewhere in the tulips.

◆

THURSDAY MORNING, APRIL 19, is windy. When I step outside to get the paper, a gust blows cigarette stubs and candy wrappers along the sidewalk in front of me. It's trash from the reporters last night. I've heard nothing from Bob, and I assume the press hasn't either, or else they'd be back again today.

Ann appears for breakfast with dripping wet hair after her shower. When she's ready to leave for school, I walk with her to the corner. A blast of wind whips at her uniform, and she struggles to hold her skirt down. Watching her cross Wisconsin Avenue to the bus stop, I'm touched by the normalcy of the scene. *This is what I should be focusing on—our children, our home. Instead, it's Watergate.*

Throughout the day, the wind continues to reinforce my unsettled feeling. At dinnertime, I hear from Bob's secretary, who tells me that Bob's on his way home. Pat's cheery greeting gives me no clue as to what has taken place over the past twenty-four hours.

After dinner, Bob finally opens up. As we are doing the dishes, he tells me that nothing was resolved at Camp David, although he and John spent the whole time discussing Watergate with the president. He describes last night's dinner as "painful."

"Did you talk about taking leaves or resigning?" I ask, handing Bob a skillet to dry.

"We talked about both, but the president can't decide. He doesn't want to let John and me go, and yet he's been told that if nothing else, it's an embarrassment to keep us on."

Why can't the president just make up his mind? What Bob tells me is frustrating, and I can only guess how hard this must be on him. "How can you stand all this uncertainty?" I ask.

"I can't. It's counterproductive to be spending so much time going round and round. John and I met with our lawyers this afternoon, and you'd be interested to know that they don't think we should leave."

"That's good," I say, wiping off the stove burner where some bits of corned beef hash had splattered. *At least someone is taking a firm stand.*

Bob goes up to his office to make some phone calls. Before he comes to bed, I hear him recording the day's events in his journal. My heart goes out to him. I love this strong, disciplined man. *How difficult it must be for him to describe the agonizing uncertainty of these days.*

◆

THE *MINNEAPOLIS TRIBUNE* FEATURES an interview with Susan on its front page. In the article, she is quoted as saying that her father is "a fun guy." I'd like to think that this helps to soften Bob's image, but at this point, I'm not sure that it makes any difference.

Before flying to Key Biscayne to spend Easter with his family, the president meets with members of his cabinet and tells them, "We're going to clear up Watergate." In an attempt to make up for all that Bob and John have been going through, he suggests that they spend Easter weekend at Camp David with their families. He tells them to include their assistants and their wives, Larry and Dolores Higby and Todd and Suzie Hullin.

The presidential retreat provides a welcome haven. The days are sunny and warm, and at night, the sky is chock-full of stars. The tulips are in full bloom in the meticulously planted flowerbeds. Attentive stewards in red blazers take care of all our needs.

While Bob and John spend time researching the facts for their lawyers, the rest of us attempt to keep the weekend upbeat and fun. Everyone dyes eggs, and I "plant" my traditional gumdrop tree. On Saturday night, Larry pulls out all the stops and produces Joe's stone crabs from Miami Beach, Florida.

The morning of Easter Sunday, April 22, Suzie Hullin leaves surprise Easter baskets on the doorstep of each of our cabins. Bob and John hide eggs for our egg hunt, and in Laurel, one long table is set for breakfast. After consuming eggs, bacon, ham, waffles, pancakes, and corned beef hash, we gather up the Sunday papers and settle on the terrace outside.

The Washington Post has four different Watergate stories on the front page, and *The Washington Star* features Bob in its headline. As soon as Jeanne sees it, she holds up the paper and exclaims, "Whoa, take a look at this."

"Probers Eying Haldeman." The large, black letters practically leap off the page. According to the article, the grand jury is looking into a possible connection between Bob and payments made to the Watergate defendants. The story also mentions John as a likely target of the grand jury probe.

As we speculate on the ramifications of these latest disclosures, a steward announces that the president is calling. After talking to him, Bob and John report that their options don't look good.

"At least the president favors our taking leaves rather than resigning," John adds.

As difficult as it is to talk about this, everyone has an opinion. As Bob and John openly discuss their fate with their families and their assistants, I'm deeply saddened. Spending Easter weekend at Camp David should be a happy time for them. And yet here they are, fighting for their survival.

Following an egg hunt in the woods, Dolores suggests that we take a walk around the perimeter of the camp. The men lead the way, with their wives straggling behind. Absorbed in my thoughts, I try to prioritize Bob's three options: status quo, leave of absence, or resignation.

I reason, and I rationalize, but no matter how I approach it, the pros and cons of each of the three choices balance out. There is no clear-cut answer, and I can appreciate the president's dilemma. Bob says that if it appears to be in the president's best interest for him to resign, he will do so. Right now, at least, he doesn't think that his resignation is inevitable.

◆

BOB AND JOHN REMAIN at Camp David until Monday, while the rest of us return home Sunday night. Memories of our Easter weekend together linger as I unpack, but they are bittersweet compared to my twenty previous visits. Over the past four years, I've spent fifty-three days at the presidential retreat. Now I wonder if I will ever be going back.

Bob gets home in time for dinner on Monday night. He looks weary and says that he and John spent the day getting background material for the lawyers. They discussed strategy for taking leaves of absence. Just as we finish eating, he gets a call, which he takes in his office. It's a long conversation. Stepping into our bedroom afterward, he leans against the doorframe. *What is it this time?*

"That was Ziegler, calling from Key Biscayne," Bob says. "The president asked him to inform me that a leave is not a viable choice. He thinks that I should submit my resignation."

"Oh, no," I blurt out. Then, I pause to think about the circumstances of the call. "*Ron* is the one to tell you that you should resign?" My tone denotes disbelief. "Couldn't the president have had the decency to tell you himself?"

"It's not that simple, Jo," Bob says, sitting down in one of the captain's chairs at the round table. "As you know, the president has trouble dealing with personal situations like this. It's easier for him to rely on someone else to convey the bad news." He swivels around and gazes out the window. His voice sounds wistful when he adds, "The funny thing is…that 'someone else' has always been me. Tonight, it's Ron…and I feel sorry for him. The poor guy had a terrible time trying to tell me."

"What about John?"

"The president wants both of us to resign. I had to tell John."

"Bob, how *could* you? How did he take the news?"

"He pretty much came unglued. He doesn't think that he's as vulnerable as I am, and he kept saying how unfair it is."

"It *is* unfair. This whole ghastly mess is unfair."

With that, the discussion is over. *Is this how it all ends? Bob and John are going to resign without even talking with the president?* As we climb into bed, I wonder if Bob is as upset with Nixon as I am. Probably not. As soon as the light is turned off, he's snoring.

We'll be Eaten Alive

I SPEND A RESTLESS night and awaken early Tuesday morning, April 24, to find Bob already on the phone in his office. Before leaving for the White House, he steps outside on the patio where I'm feeding the dogs.

"Ron called again," he says.

"What'd he say *this* time?" I'm still upset at the way things were handled last night.

"The president hasn't made up his mind after all."

"I can't believe it," I exclaim. "So what happens now?"

"Everybody has a different idea. Ehrlichman thinks that the president should fire Dean and that I should take a leave of absence. He would stay on the job but be prepared to take a leave if it becomes necessary. I'm just waiting to see how it all falls out."

As if to confirm John's opinion, the cover of *Time* features cartoon figures of Nixon and six men in the administration tangled up in wiretap equipment. Bob and John Dean are two of the six, but John Ehrlichman is not. In the upper right corner, a yellow banner proclaims, "Watergate Breaks Wide Open."

The seven-page article hardly mentions Bob, except to say that he's being hopelessly compromised

> ...if only because many of the men in the deepest trouble at one time or another reported to him... It is Haldeman's duty as chief of staff to protect the president from such disasters; instead his shop played a big hand in creating the debacle... One man moving most frantically to clear himself was John Ehrlichman, who has long worked intimately with Haldeman and thus could be tainted... It would be tragic if Richard Nixon's considerable

achievements as president were coupled in history with
the sordid business of Watergate…

Over the next couple of days, Bob says that all their time is consumed
with Watergate discussions and that the president continues to vacillate on
whether he and John need to take leaves or resign. I don't see how they can
continue on like this much longer. Bob and John are scheduled to meet with
the US attorneys and the chief counsel for the Senate Watergate Committee
next week. They will also be meeting with the grand jury, as well as other
congressional committees looking into Watergate.

On April 26, a new disclosure at the Pentagon Papers trial keeps Watergate
on the front page. Testimony reveals that, in 1971, two of the Watergate
defendants, Hunt and Liddy, broke into Daniel Ellsberg's psychiatrist's office in
an attempt to get information on Ellsberg's mental state. The judge in the trial
orders the prosecutor to find out who hired them.

The next morning, Acting FBI Director L. Patrick Gray resigns, stating
that he destroyed documents at the direction of Ehrlichman and Dean. Bob
tells me that the president is going to Camp David tomorrow to work on a
major Watergate speech, which he will give Monday night.

"At this point, the president expects John and me to request voluntary
leaves," Bob says.

"Really, Bob?" I don't see how my husband can take this. *At what point
will it end?*

On Saturday, April 28, a large group of noisy reporters gathers on the
sidewalk outside our townhouse. Our newsboy is daunted by their presence.
Instead of leaving our paper at the front door, he tosses it over the back fence.
Later, a sympathetic friend is so intimidated that she asks me to walk around
the block to pick up a plant she left for us. When I discover that the large
fern in the middle of the sidewalk is heavier than I expected, I agree to let a
considerate reporter carry it home for me. Another reporter cracks a joke.

"Mrs. Haldeman, does the fern have bugs?" he asks. "Get it? Bugs?"

Although everyone laughs, there's an ominous feeling in the air. I can't
put my finger on it, but it's here, and I'm sure the press senses it as much as I
do. Their commentaries speculate about what the president is going to do and
suggest that Haldeman and Ehrlichman will have to go. Clearly, the situation
is worsening. I try not to react to the rumors and innuendos, while clinging to
the faint hope that the president might change his mind again.

Putting everything aside, Bob and I go out for dinner and a movie. He appears to be in good spirits, and I try hard to relax and enjoy the evening.

On Sunday morning, April 29, I retrieve *The Washington Post* from under the azaleas in the patio. Using my apron to wipe off bits of dirt, I read that John Dean reportedly is ready to swear that he gave both Ehrlichman and Haldeman progress reports on the cover-up. Pressure is growing for the president to replace the Justice Department lawyers with a special prosecutor, and there is more speculation about removing Bob and John.

"Boy," Bob says at breakfast. "As soon as the president reads all this stuff, he'll want John and me to come up to Camp David immediately."

"What do you mean?" I question.

"He'll want our resignations."

"I thought you said he wanted you to take leaves of absence," I comment weakly.

"Things are moving too fast in the other direction," Bob says. "Either way, I'll be out of the White House." He stands and walks over to the kitchen window, where he looks down at the reporters mingling on the sidewalk. "It's time for me to tell our families that I might have to take a leave of absence. Then they'll be prepared in case I have to resign."

As usual, Bob has covered all of his bases. His decision is clear to him, and he's in control. However, I feel lost and empty, as if I've run out of gas. I'm glad that we're going to church this morning. I need to turn to a greater power to sustain me.

True to his word, as soon as we get home, Bob calls our three out-of-town children, as well as our parents. I try not to think about the future. To keep busy, I make Bob's lunch—cottage cheese, canned pineapple, Ry-Krisp, and iced tea.

The White House phone rings, and I instantly assume it's that dreaded call from Nixon. The conversation is surprisingly brief.

"The president wants John and me to chopper up to meet with him at Camp David at one thirty today." Bob's steady eyes and unruffled demeanor are reassuring.

When the White House phone rings again, I fight to stay composed.

"That was Ron," Bob says. "He's at Camp David, too. The president now feels very strongly that John and I should volunteer to resign."

My heart does a nosedive down to my stomach, and my voice is weak. "Is this it?"

"I'm afraid so," Bob confirms. "Ron said that the president figures we'll be eaten alive if we take a leave of absence."

He puts on his blazer and turns to me. Our eyes meet. He gives me a tender hug, and we kiss. Stepping out of our bedroom, Bob nearly collides with Ann in the hall. Wearing faded jeans and a baggy sweatshirt, she's clutching a basketball and is in a hurry to leave.

"I'm going to the park," she says.

"Hey, 'Awful Annie,' wait a minute," Bob says, using his nickname for her, a play on *Little Orphan Annie*. "I'm taking off, too, and I want to tell you something before I go." Ann stops on the landing, and Bob walks over and puts his hands on her shoulders. "There's a good chance that I'm going to have to take a leave of absence from the White House."

"Are things that bad?" Ann asks.

"Yes, they are," Bob acknowledges. "They're pretty bad."

Bob leans down and wraps his arms around his daughter and the basketball at the same time. My heart is breaking as he follows Ann downstairs. Father and daughter step outside together. The press surrounds them. Putting her head down, Ann charges through the crowd and makes her way down the sidewalk. Bob climbs into the waiting White House car and is driven away.

I'm alone. Even the press is gone. I anticipate a long, agonizing wait, so I try to keep busy with mundane chores. I clean up Bob's untouched lunch, pay bills, catch up on the ironing, walk the dogs, sew a button on Bob's shirt, and sweep up the trash left by the reporters. In the late afternoon, I'm straightening up the living room when the ring of the White House phone startles me. I reach for the receiver and then draw back. Standing motionless, I eye the white instrument on the table in front of me. *If I don't answer it, I won't hear any bad news.* On the fourth ring, I give in. Gripping the receiver, I slowly bring it to my ear.

"Good evening, Mrs. Haldeman." The voice of the White House operator is both cheery and respectful. "Mr. Haldeman is calling from Camp David and would like to speak to you."

All of a sudden, Bob is on the line, and my heart is pounding. He tells me that he just finished meeting with the president. "It's just what I expected," he says. "The president asked John and me to submit our resignations. There's no turning back this time."

Keep talking, Bob. If you expect me to say something, I don't think I can. Keep talking.

"I'll be home before long," Bob continues as if this were any normal day. "Will you call the children and our parents and give them the news?"

"Of course." My reply is steady, but my hand is shaking. "I'm so sorry, Bob. I hope you're all right. I love you." *Is that all I can say? There's so much more. So much more.* After hanging up, I stand and stare at the phone. Tonight, this constant intruder into my life has finally had the last word.

The fact that Bob asked me to contact our families is a lifesaver. Instead of breaking down, I have to maintain my composure. When I talk to Susan and Hank, both of them are concerned over how their dad is coping. Neither divulges much about his or her own feelings. Peter asks a slew of questions about the future. Bob will tell Ann when he returns.

I catch my parents at Bay Island, where they are spending the weekend. As soon as I explain that I have news from Bob, both of them want to be on the line at the same time. This involves a long wait, while Dad comes in from planting a gardenia bush at the side of the house. I can hear Mother reminding him to leave his shoes outside. When I tell them about the resignation, they both express deep concern for Bob and his feelings. Their strong support helps to steady a gnawing ache that's starting to grow in my stomach.

I take a deep breath. The next call is the hardest, and I've left it until the end. As I dial Non's number, I picture her at the desert in her house at Smoke Tree. Soon the sun will disappear behind Mount San Jacinto, and long shadows will extend from the grapefruit trees to the swimming pool. Wherever she is, her West Highland terrier, Perky, will be at her side.

The phone rings twice. "Hello." The way Non says "hello," it always comes out in bird-like chirps.

"Hi, Non…I just heard from Bob. He's still at Camp David with the president and John Ehrlichman, and he asked me to call you." I wait for my mother-in-law to say something, but she doesn't. She knows me too well and senses what's coming. "Bob's not taking a leave of absence after all," I blurt out. "He and John are resigning."

Silence.

"Non, are you there?"

"Of course, I'm here, Jo," she answers. I think she's annoyed that I would even question her not staying on the line. "I've been thinking about Bob ever since he called this morning," she says. "I can't imagine what the president will do without him. Who will replace him?"

"I have no idea," I reply. "I don't think the president has even thought about that yet."

"Well, now more than ever, we must stand by our president. He needs our full support." Non is emphatic, and suddenly it becomes clear that she's the one encouraging me, rather than the other way around.

"You're right," I say. "Nixon's giving a speech tomorrow night. Be sure and watch it. I'm sure he'll be talking about Bob and John."

"I can't think of two finer men than the two of them," Non continues. "The president was so fortunate to have both of them in the White House. Do you think they can get their side of the story out now?"

"I hope so. I know Bob would like to go public in some way. I'll call you as soon as I have anything to report."

"You better, Jo, and be sure and tell Bob that I'm so very proud of him." Non pauses. "Remember, it's not 'all *will* be well'...it's 'all *is* well.'"

"All *is* well," I repeat and hang up. I have nothing but admiration for Bob's mother. I know her heart is breaking, but she won't give in. She's a fighter.

The Final Journal Entry

I T'S DARK WHEN I hear a car door slam. The front door opens, and I rush downstairs to meet Bob.

"Hi," he says, standing motionless in the entry.

"Oh, Bob," I cry out, as I wrap my arms around him.

He holds me tight and mumbles in a tired voice, "Onward and upward."

"Everyone in the family knows, except Ann," I tell him. "She's up in her bedroom."

"I'll talk to her now," Bob says.

I follow Bob up two flights of stairs, where he lightly knocks on the door of our thirteen-year-old daughter's room. He goes in and closes the door behind him. From the master bedroom across the hall, I can hear their muffled voices and then a burst of tears from Ann. Tonight, she discovers that her father is not invincible.

A call from Nancy Ziegler diverts my attention. In a shaky voice, she explains that Ron just told her about the resignations, and she is devastated. She had no idea that Ron was at Camp David. Before leaving two days ago, he told her that he would be working on "a highly sensitive matter." He had asked her to pack an extra suit for him.

After talking to Nancy, I have a strong desire to call Jeanne. We haven't talked since Pat Gray resigned as acting director of the FBI after claiming that her husband John and John Dean had instructed him to destroy documents. My hand rests on the receiver of the White House phone. It's so easy to ask an operator to get Mrs. Ehrlichman on the line, but I decide to wait. This is a private time for both of us, and we need to share it with our families. We can talk later.

As I get ready for bed, I can hear Bob dictating the events of this fateful day in his diary. His voice is low and steady. I can't make out what he's saying, and I don't try. He'll tell me when he's ready.

Later, lying next to me in bed, Bob starts to talk. "Well, it was a pretty rugged time for all three of us at Camp David. At first the president wanted to meet with John and me at the same time, but I told him he should talk to us separately. I was first. I rode a bike over to Aspen, while John waited in Laurel. When I arrived, the president was already in terrible shape emotionally. He shook my hand..." Bob's voice trails off and is almost inaudible when he adds, "...That's the first time he's ever done that."

I groan. The formality of shaking hands is so typical of Nixon's social awkwardness. *How bitterly poignant that handshake with Bob must have been...*

"The president wanted to show me how beautiful the tulips were, so we stood out on the porch for a while. When we went inside, he told me that he had done a lot of praying and that this was the hardest decision he's ever had to make."

"Oh, Bob," I say in a hoarse whisper.

Bob continues, "The president got pretty sentimental. He said that John and I are the two best men he knows. I assured him that, although I disagreed with his decision to let us go, I would do everything I could to implement it."

This is so characteristic of Bob. As soon as he knows that something is inevitable, he accepts it and moves on. "When did the president tell John?" I ask.

"Right after he met with me. I rode the bike back, and John walked over to Aspen. He was there about half an hour, and then the two of us worked on our letters of resignation."

Moonlight filters through the cherry blossoms, softly lighting the room. I study Bob's face. He is lost in thought, and there is no frown. "Did you see the president again?"

"Yeah. He asked John and me to come back to Aspen about five thirty. After reviewing our letters, he called in Bill Rogers, who listened to us read them out loud. Bill made a couple of corrections, and then the whole thing was over. That was it. As of tomorrow afternoon, John and I will no longer be working in the White House."

I lie very still, fighting back tears. From Bob's composed tone, I can tell that he's not bitter, and he doesn't feel sorry for himself. He's reconciled and accepts his resignation as a fact of life. I'll do everything I can to stand by him and support him. I love this strong, self-possessed man. There will be tough days ahead, but we'll get through them.

I try hard to believe that "all *is* well."

◆

APRIL 30, 1973. IN so many ways, this morning starts out just like any other day. Our newspaper lands with a thud on the slate terrace in the patio. The happy chatter of Amos, Ann's parakeet, comes from her room. Down one flight of stairs, the fern (without bugs) sits on a blue-and-white Chinese garden stool. Next to it, the pugs are stretched out in a patch of sunlight streaming in through the French doors. The smell of fresh coffee comes from the kitchen, and in the dining room, the table is set for breakfast. Outside, sleepy-eyed reporters are starting to gather on the sidewalk. Several of them set up campstools, and it's obvious that they plan to stay until they find out what's going on. Some clutch Styrofoam cups of hot coffee and pass around bags of donuts. Three of them start tossing a Frisbee. Although I cling to the familiarity of the morning scene, I know that today will be unique. *Like no other day I have ever experienced.*

Wearing a tan suit, Bob steps into the kitchen to say goodbye before leaving. His composure and confidence reassure me. Stooping down to give Ann an extra-long hug, he tells his daughter, "When news of my resignation gets out this morning, you have to be brave." Ann's eyes glisten with tears as she nods.

Next, Bob turns to me. I wrap my arms around his neck, and I don't want to let him go. Gently releasing my grip, he reassures me. "I'll be okay, Jo." Then he adds lightheartedly, "Well, off to another day at the office."

A sea of curious reporters surges forward as soon as he steps outside. Smiling, Bob makes a few mundane remarks before climbing into the car. As the black Mercury pulls away from the curb and heads for the White House, the reporters turn and start directing questions at me. I shake my head and close the door. *If only they knew what is coming.*

I'm not used to dealing with a situation like this, and it's as if I am in a fog. I can't think straight. My feet feel like they have two heavy weights holding them down, and it's an effort to get through my morning chores. After Ann leaves for school, the house is deadly quiet, and I'm terribly aware of being alone.

My mind still won't focus, and I find myself wandering from room to room. First, I check on Peter's wax begonias. Then, I rearrange some magazines on the coffee table in the living room and run my fingers along the keys of the piano. Absent-mindedly counting the steps as I go upstairs, I poke my head into Bob's office. His White House calendar is on the desk. On today's date, under the number 1,361, Bob has written a single word. "Resignations." He is 1,361 days short of completing the most exciting, challenging, and rewarding job he could ever hope to have.

Patrick Anderson wrote, "The president, when he leaves office, has at least been president; the assistant, when he leaves has been—what? A man who stood in the shadows of power, who played a mysterious role in a complicated process, a man who got little credit for his successes and ample blame for his mistakes, a man who will seem a braggart if he seeks credit, but whose good works will soon be forgotten if he does not." *Bob won't seek credit. That's not his style. And, in the climate of Watergate, his "good works" will never be remembered.*

I don't fight the tears as they flow down my face.

By 10:00 a.m., I've pulled myself together enough to make my daily calls to Mother and Non. Although I had every intention of bolstering them up, they are the ones reassuring me. In the kitchen, I look out the window to check on the reporters. They are bored, and two of them are helping my neighbor unload plants for her garden. They still don't know about the resignations.

11:00 a.m. The time has come. Ron Ziegler is announcing the resignations of Bob, John, and Attorney General Richard Kleindienst, and the firing of John Dean. Tonight, the president will address the nation.

Bob's career at the White House is over. Instead of the customary promotion or recognition that has always come so naturally, he is out of a job.

The ring of the White House phone jars me. It's Henry Kissinger calling to tell me how sorry he is to hear about Bob. His voice is solemn, and his words are sincere. They mean the world to me right now.

♦

AT DINNER TONIGHT, BOB talks matter-of-factly about his final day at the White House. "This morning, when John and I told the senior staff we had submitted our resignations, they were really caught off guard. Later, Billy

Graham, Ted Agnew, and John Connally called me. Each of them thought that it was the right move."

As 9:00 p.m. approaches, Bob turns on the television. "The president was in terrible shape today," he says. "I hope he can make it through his speech."

Watching Bob settle back in the chair and put his feet up on the ottoman, I realize that he's never been home when Nixon has addressed the nation. *Bob doesn't belong here. He should be at the White House, conferring with the president's inner circle of advisors. How can this driven man bear the thought of not being needed?*

Suddenly, we see Nixon seated at his desk in the Oval Office. There's a bust of Lincoln on one side of him and a picture of his family on the other. The camera zooms in closer, and my immediate reaction is negative. The setting is too exact and looks staged. I don't like the carefully placed bronze sculpture and the precisely angled photograph. *Everything's wrong. This whole situation is a nightmare. I'm not sure I can watch this.*

"Good evening," the president begins. "I want to talk to you tonight from my heart on a subject of deep concern to every American." He continues for five long minutes without mentioning Bob. I nervously twist my engagement ring around and around on my finger. *Could it be that the president has changed his mind about the resignations?*

"Today, in one of the most difficult decisions of my presidency..." *I can't look. I close my eyes, and I want to cover my ears.* "...I accepted the resignations of two of my closest associates...Bob Haldeman and John Ehrlichman—two of the finest public servants it has been my privilege to know."

The speech is hard for me to track. The words fade in and out as I make an effort to follow them. At last it is over, and Bob's resignation is official. No more drama or indecision. What had to be said was said, but Nixon's words seemed trite to me. They were window dressing, like the bust and the photo on the desk. I'm left with a hollow feeling in my stomach.

Bob stands and stretches. "Not one of the president's finer efforts," he says, with his arms extended. "He's clearly shaken...I should give him a call."

Picking up the receiver, he asks to speak to the president. He waits, and then his look of expectancy dissolves. I watch in dismay as he hangs up. With his fingers still resting on the White House receiver, he says, "The president's not taking calls."

Not taking calls? I can't believe it. At this heart-wrenching moment, I want to cry out, "You owe this to my husband, Mr. President. Forget your little jokes about my drinking problem. For the past five years, Bob has put you before everything else in his life. His dedication and loyalty have never wavered...not even now. Talk to him, Mr. President. Talk to him."

Bob goes up to his study, and I call the families. I'd give anything to avoid these conversations, but I mask my emotions and play-act at being rock solid and positive. I give Non an evasive answer when she asks if Bob has talked to the president.

At 10:00 p.m., the White House phone rings just as I'm coming upstairs. Bob answers it in his study, "Yes, Mr. President." I'm glued to my spot on the landing and feel compelled to listen.

"Well, the resignations are behind you now," Bob says matter-of-factly. "I know it's tough, but it's time to move on."

How can Bob be so calm?

"I'm sorry that Cap's the only cabinet officer you've heard from. I think it's because the White House operators are telling people that you aren't taking calls." Pause. "No, sir, I can't do that. I know that I've always checked on the reaction to your speeches in the past, but tonight that's not possible."

Another pause. "I'm sorry, sir. All my connections to the White House have been severed. You'll have to get someone else to follow up."

I'm shocked. I feel like bursting into the room and asking Bob why he doesn't get mad. I am amazed that even now his respect for the presidency supersedes everything else, and he refuses to be critical of Nixon's insensitive request.

I move into our bedroom as soon as Bob starts to dictate his daily journal. Tonight, April 30, 1973, will be his final entry after four years, three months, and ten days. I'm sure he's relieved. He never liked the added chore of recording the events of his day, but he stood by his commitment to do it.

Emotionally drained, both Bob and I fall asleep shortly after going to bed. At midnight, the White House phone rings, and Bob gropes in the dark for the receiver. It's the president again, still upset at the reaction he received to his speech. The conversation is brief, and Bob's last words are, "Yes, sir, I'll keep the faith."

I don't want to hear this. I bury my face in the pillow and let out a muffled groan. For the life of me, I can't comprehend how the president can be so oblivious to Bob's feelings. This is the end for Bob, and yet all Nixon tells him is to "keep the faith." The remarkable thing is, Bob gets it. He understands his president and accepts him unconditionally.

An Outsider

O N TUESDAY, MAY 1, Bob is without a job. The alarm goes off at 6:45 a.m., just as it always does. Our bedroom is already filled with sunlight, and the air is warm and fragrant. I open the window as wide as it will go. Outside, tiny green leaves are starting to replace the blossoms on the craggy boughs of the cherry tree. In the patio below, *The Washington Post* lies in the tulip bed. I can hear the reporters assembling out in front.

"I hate this humidity," Bob mumbles, and I instantly regret doing anything that might make his morning more difficult than it already is. I close the window and turn on the air conditioner.

Bob plans to go into the White House later today to remove his personal things from his office, but first he spends time alone in his study reading the Christian Science Bible Lesson. Until he moved to Washington, this had been part of his daily morning routine.

Without a car and driver, Bob asks me to take him to the White House. I have to back out of the garage slowly to avoid the reporters, who crowd around his side of the Thunderbird. He smiles as he repeats, "No comment." I study him while we are waiting for the signal to change at Pennsylvania Avenue. With his American flag pin in his lapel, he grips his briefcase on his lap and stares straight ahead. For some reason, I envision him as a resolute little boy, clutching his lunchbox on the first day of school.

Oh, Bob. You remind me of the day of your swearing-in. With your raised right hand and hopeful expression, I saw you then as a naïve, trusting Boy Scout. Does anyone else ever see you this way?

When I return home, the reporters have left, and the house feels different. I turn off the air conditioner and open the windows. Although the air is hot and humid, I'm cold. I go up to Bob's study. It's comforting to be in this well-organized, functional room. Everything is in its place. A White House memo pad sits on the desk with a black Pentel pen next to it. Bob's religious books are neatly piled on the end table by his big chair. His favorite quote from Nixon's first inaugural address hangs on the wall in its gold frame.

"Until he has been part of a cause larger than himself, no man is truly whole."

If Bob's cause is the Nixon presidency, does his resignation affect his sense of accomplishment? Does he consider himself "truly whole" now? If not, will he ever?

Throughout the day, Watergate continues to capture most of the news. The Senate passes a resolution calling on the president to appoint a special outside prosecutor. Ron Ziegler apologizes to *The Washington Post* for criticizing its stories on Watergate. There's a startling new disclosure in the Pentagon Papers trial. It is reported that John Ehrlichman was told about the break-in at Ellsberg's psychiatrist's office immediately after it took place. Pressured to explain why he didn't do anything about it, John becomes the center of a lot of media attention.

In the afternoon, Susan arrives home for a short visit. I wish it could be under happier circumstances, but she seems to be taking things in stride. In five days, she will leave for a three-week tour of England with my mother and father, who are taking her on the trip as an early college graduation gift.

With Hank in California and Peter still in Minneapolis, I miss our two sons at dinner tonight. I wish our whole family could be together, but that rarely happens these days. Before eating, we bow our heads for a moment of silence.

"How'd things go at the White House today, Dad?" Susan asks, as soon as we start to eat.

"Not great," Bob responds. "When John and I got to our offices, there were FBI agents posted at our doors."

"The FBI?" Ann asks. "Why?"

Liberally salting his pot roast, carrots, and potatoes, Bob explains. "The president was advised to put guards on all of our files. He wants to avoid any possible charge of destruction of evidence. When I started to enter my office, the agent stationed outside wouldn't even let me take my briefcase in with me. He said that it could be used to smuggle something out."

"*You?*" I exclaim. "Smuggle things out of your *own* office?"

"Yeah. Len Garment—the new White House counsel—had to come and check me out before I could leave. He had me read out loud some of the papers I was taking with me to prove that they were personal. One was a list of Bible quotes."

"That must have been awkward," I comment.

"I guess it had to be done," Bob says. "But it was really embarrassing for the poor FBI guy."

"Did you see the president?" Susan asks.

"Yeah. He passed by my office on his way to a meeting in the Cabinet Room. Although he had ordered the guards, it upset him when he actually saw the FBI agent at my door. He sort of pushed the guy against the wall. But then he came back later and apologized."

Bob tells us that all of his notes and memos are to be removed from his office and kept under lock and key in a storage space across the street in the EOB. From now on, he will need the FBI's permission to access them. This will make it extremely difficult for him to prepare for his upcoming sessions with the grand jury, as well as several congressional committees and the US attorneys.

I'm saddened to hear how quickly things have disintegrated. Tonight on the *CBS Evening News*, Roger Mudd states in his commentary that the only winners in Watergate so far are the thirty-six lawyers. It's obvious "that great, gummy fungus" *Newsweek* called Watergate is still refusing to "curl up and die."

◆

THE NEXT MORNING, MAY 2, I get up early. It's Bob's second day out of office, and the reality of what this means is beginning to sink in. From now on, he will be answering to his lawyers, instead of the president. He'll be concentrating on his legal defense, rather than participating in Nixon's vision of the future— reorganizing the executive branch, strengthening the ties between the United States and China, limiting nuclear arms, reforming welfare, creating an environmental protection agency, and producing the bicentennial.

Instead of planning for the future, Bob will be delving into the past. He will have to familiarize himself with all of his former actions. This will entail reconstructing hundreds of hours of discussions and meetings, and he will have to search through pages and pages of notes, calendars, schedules, phone logs, and memos.

Questions flood my mind. My first concern is financial. *What will we do for income? When will Bob be able to work? Who will hire him? Will we have to move?*

Then, my questions become more mundane. *What will Bob do around the house all day? How will his being home affect our relationship? Will he expect me to get his lunch? Who answers the phone? Who gets the car?*

I should know better than to waste my time worrying. Bob is also awake early, and as usual, he has it all figured out. He plans to get up at 6:45 a.m. every day, and after breakfast, he'll devote an hour to the study of Christian Science. When he's home for lunch, he wants to eat by himself and would like me to stock up on cottage cheese, Dole canned pineapple slices, and Ry-Krisp crackers. We will share the phone, as well as the Thunderbird.

Although he won't be able to get a job until Watergate is behind him, Bob tells me that we have no immediate financial concerns. He expects to be gone a lot. He will be testifying at congressional hearings and the grand jury, as well as conferring with his lawyers. To prepare for these meetings, he will work both at home and the EOB, where he will go through his files.

With a full day of appointments today, Bob takes the car, and I stay home with Susan. In the news, John Connally calls Watergate a "silly, stupid, illegal act" and announces that he's switching to the Republican Party. *U.S. News and World Report* has a big spread on John McCain's first person account of his ordeal as a POW in North Vietnam for over five years. And there's speculation on who will replace Bob as Nixon's chief of staff.

"No one's replacing me," Bob tells us at dinner. "The president plans to act as his own chief of staff."

"How can he possibly do that?" I question.

"He can't...but he won't admit it," Bob says.

In the middle of dessert, Bob receives a call from the president, who wants to meet with him right away. Quickly changing into his dark green blazer, gray slacks, and a Repp tie, Bob grabs the car keys from the kitchen counter and says goodbye to Susan, Ann, and me.

"I thought you couldn't go back to the White House, Dad," Ann calls after him.

"You're right. I don't have an office, and I can't just walk into the White House like I used to," Bob replies from the doorway. "But tonight, they'll give me a special clearance."

It hurts to hear this exchange between Bob and our younger daughter. *How quickly things can change. Two days ago, he was managing the entire White House staff. Now he has to be specially cleared.*

Bob doesn't return until almost 10:00 p.m. Before joining me in the living room, he heads for the kitchen, where he scoops up a heaping tablespoon of coffee ice cream.

"Well, I finally convinced the president that he had to get Al Haig as his chief of staff," he says, licking the ice cream around the edge of the spoon to form a rounded mound. "Al's the only one who can do the job. Plus, he has a good working relationship with Henry."

"I'll bet that's a relief," I say, but my heart isn't in it. I'm glad that Bob feels comfortable about his replacement, but it's not easy for me to accept someone else as the president's chief of staff. *That's Bob's job.*

The phone rings, and I'm pleasantly surprised to hear Jeanne Ehrlichman's voice. The last time we talked was a week before our husbands resigned, and I'm anxious to find out how she and her family are coping.

"It's all so unfair," Jeanne begins. There's no lilt to her voice, which isn't like her. "John doesn't think he deserves any of this, and it's really been hard on the rest of us. Don't you find that's true with Bob?"

How do I answer? Bob has never expressed any resentment. "The resignation was difficult for him to accept, but now he's trying to move on. I just wish I knew where all of this will lead us. I feel like I'm in limbo." John's bitterness makes me appreciate how positive Bob has been.

"I don't know about you, but I've stopped following Watergate," Jeanne says.

"How can you do that? Watergate's the only news there is."

"I've stopped watching TV, and I don't read the papers. The latest reporting on the break-in at Ellsberg's psychiatrist's office was the last straw for me." Jeanne's voice cracks. "John was furious when he first heard about the break-in. We were vacationing at Cape Cod, and I remember him yelling over the phone at Hunt and Liddy. He demanded to know what made them do such a thing. There must have been seventy-five other ways to discredit Ellsberg.'"

"Oh, Jeannie, I'm so sorry."

"I blame those two guys," Jeanne says. "That break-in was Hunt and Liddy's idea, and it was stupid. Just plain stupid. If it had never happened, I think John could have survived."

Jeanne is so distraught, I hardly recognize her. She has always been so upbeat. I'm glad she didn't see the editorial in *The Washington Post* this morning, which questioned why Ehrlichman didn't turn Hunt and Liddy over to the authorities as soon as he was told about their break-in.

John Chancellor's commentary on NBC tonight is even worse. I cringe when he states that out of over two million federal employees, Haldeman and Ehrlichman are by far the most unpopular and that "there was dancing in the halls of Congress" when their resignations were announced.

It's not easy to hear something like this, but my reaction is different from Jeanne's. I'd rather know what's being said than be oblivious to it.

Wax Begonias

BOB AND I AGREE that summer is as good a time as any to cut our ties to Washington. We can spend July and August in Newport and use that time to make the transition back to Los Angeles. Hopefully, during those months, I'll be able to find a house and get Peter and Ann enrolled in schools. Logistically, this makes sense, but the thought of it is daunting. We have lived in Georgetown for only two months, and Bob and I have shared only one normal day in our townhouse. I don't want to sell it, and I really don't want to face another move.

Reluctantly, I call our realtor to list our home. She is surprised to hear from me, but she has a client who might be interested in a short-term lease. The newly-appointed Secretary of the Army Howard "Bo" Callaway and his wife want to rent in Georgetown while they look at homes. The thought of renting rather than selling is appealing. It would give me more time, and I wouldn't have to cut all my ties to Georgetown.

Barbara wants to show the house as soon as possible, but she has one condition. No reporters. She tells me that she is intimidated by them and refuses to come if they are around.

"Whenever Bob's at home, the press will be here," I tell her. "When he's gone, you're safe." I don't mention the guy on the motorcycle who gives a Nazi salute and shouts, "Heil, Haldeman," every time he rides past the house.

I thought the press would go away after Bob resigned, but that's not the case. The Haldeman name and photos of the family repeatedly appear in newspapers and magazines. On Sunday, May 6, we are followed to church by a slew of reporters and photographers. Connie Chung of CBS even attends the service, where she sits in the balcony and takes notes.

In a story about Bob's and John's resignations in *The Daily Bruin*, Hank is quoted as saying that his father was active on the UCLA campus in "a managerial way." The story says that as a student, Bob was described as, "Happy Harry, the guy with the horrible haircut, who was the main cog in UCLA's greatest Homecoming Week."

In an interview with *The Minneapolis Star*, Susan is quoted as saying, "It hurts to know that people will recognize the Haldeman name, and no matter what happens, Watergate will linger in their minds." Characters in the *Doonesbury* comic strip poke fun at Bob's career in advertising, and *The Washington Evening Star* pointlessly prints a photo of me stepping out of our front door. The caption reads, "Mrs. Joanne Haldeman, wife of H. R. Haldeman, picks up her paper from the doorstep." *Newsweek* has a photo of Ann leaving for school. Her hair is wet from her shower, and her wrist is wrapped after a fall from a horse. When Winzola McLendon asks to interview Jeanne and me for the August issue of *McCall's Magazine,* the two of us turn her down.

Bob and John are on the cover of the May 7 issue of *Newsweek*. Wearing dark glasses, the two of them look like hoods. The black-and-white photo contrasts with a jarring red background, and large white letters across the top proclaim, "The White House in Turmoil."

Anyone associated with Watergate is fair game for the press, and many stories are based on nothing more than rumors and leaks. Confidential testimony is frequently divulged by the FBI and Justice Department, as well as the congressional committees. The lawyer author Louis Nizer writes, "I fear McCarthyism in reverse. People are being perhaps destroyed by headlines, where there are as yet no proven facts before a jury in a trial… This is a time to be cautious…"

Investigative journalism takes on a life of its own, and *The Washington Post* is awarded the Pulitzer Prize for its Watergate reporting. Bob Woodward and Carl Bernstein are the nation's newest heroes.

◆

MY MOTHER AND FATHER stay with us for three days before leaving with Susan on their trip to England. The townhouse has limited space, but we manage to fit everyone in. With Peter in Minneapolis, my father can stay in his room. Although the fluorescent light in Peter's hothouse remains on all night, Dad takes it in stride. As a member of the Bel-Air Men's Garden Club, he appreciates his grandson's interest in horticulture.

This is not the case when Susan sees the hothouse. Pulling me aside, she asks, "Do you know what Peter's growing?"

"Wax begonias," I tell her.

"I think you're wrong, Mom. I'm almost positive it's marijuana."

My first reaction is to laugh, but when I tell Bob, he's horrified.

"Marijuana!" he exclaims. "Good Lord, Jo, the last thing I need right now is to have someone discover that there's marijuana growing in my house!"

Bob removes one of the plants and places it in a wax paper sandwich bag. The next day, he gives it to Larry to have it checked out by the White House.

Over the next few days, Bob meets with the grand jury. "It's crazy," he says, sounding frustrated. "The prosecutors have access to all of their files whenever they want, and I'm supposed to answer every question by memory. It's like the Inquisition."

After waiting three days, Bob is informed that the "wax begonia" plant is marijuana. Bob wants to flush all of the plants down the toilet, but there are too many of them. He has enough on his mind, so I assure him that I will dispose of them.

The timing is ideal. The trash is scheduled to be picked up the following morning, and I dump the plants in one of the containers before wheeling it out to the curb.

At breakfast, Bob is mortified when he hears my solution.

"I don't believe it, Jo," he says, giving me the Haldeman look. "You got rid of the marijuana in the *trash*? With all those reporters right there? Where do you think they're going to throw their paper cups and soft drink cans? In the trash—along with their cigarette butts and half-eaten donuts. All it takes is one reporter to discover the marijuana, and I'm finished."

I dash over to the kitchen window and peer down at the street. Bob is right. Reporters are all over the place, and in front of them are the trash containers. *Will they lift the lids and discover the marijuana?* My palms are sweaty, and I'm glued to the window. I don't leave my post until the trash truck has come and gone. *At last, I can breathe.*

◆

"Good grief. Now what?" Bob asks, holding up a section of *The Sunday Star* with his picture on the front page. It shows him leaving our house, carrying his briefcase.

At the other end of our dining room table, I'm caught taking a bite of bran muffin. I can't imagine what this latest round of publicity is about. Bob scoots the paper in my direction, and the headline jumps out at me, "For This Haldeman Briefcase." I start to read the article aloud:

"'The briefcase in which Bob Haldeman, the powerful boss of the White House and human door to President Nixon…carried his papers will be auctioned off May nineteenth at the National Cathedral School for Girls…'"

"I thought we donated tickets for the presidential box at the Kennedy Center," Bob interrupts.

"We did, but I also gave the school a lot of stuff when we moved. I guess your old briefcase was in the pile of giveaways." Taking a swallow of coffee, I continue. "The article states that the briefcase not only bore the initials H. R. H. in gold, but the inside dividers had labels 'guaranteed to stimulate the imagination' such as 'Current,' 'File,' 'Hot,' and 'Destroy.'"

"That's ridiculous," Bob exclaims. "I never labeled my files like that."

"It does say that the school scratched off your initials and removed the labels." Reading further, I laugh. "Oh my gosh, it says that the school might have raised hundreds of dollars on your briefcase if the initials had been left on it."

"Just what I need," Bob mutters, standing to clear his dishes.

Poor Bob, it never seems to end.

The Ervin Show

THREE MONTHS AFTER ITS creation, the Senate Select Committee on Presidential Campaign Activities—also referred to as the Watergate Committee or the Ervin Committee—releases a tentative list of thirteen witnesses. My heart falls when I see that Bob is one of them. The hearings will be held three mornings a week, starting at 10:00 a.m. The three major networks will split live coverage of the event, and at night, PBS will show taped highlights. Bob and I plan to spend every moment we can watching them. When Non arrives for a brief visit before leaving on a tour of Russia, she becomes completely absorbed in the proceedings and wants to cancel her trip. Assuring her that it will be three weeks before he and John will be called to testify, Bob finally convinces her to go.

On Thursday, May 17, the "show" begins. The "stage" is an ornate caucus room in the Russell Senate Office Building. Seated at a long table, seven senators, four Democrats and three Republicans, are the "stars." Staff members sit behind them, along with the chief counsel, the chief minority counsel, and their assistants.

The "superstar" is Chairman Samuel J. Ervin of North Carolina. His gavel is a beautifully carved wooden mallet from a North Carolina Cherokee Indian, which he uses freely to maintain order. When he speaks, his sagging jowls and overly active eyebrows command attention. In a slow, Southern drawl, he declares that he's determined to uncover all the facts.

"No one will be spared…whatever his station in life may be," the seventy-six-year-old Democrat declares. "Those men who broke into the Democratic offices at the Watergate were in effect breaking into the home of every citizen of the United States."

That night, I drop Bob off at the EOB to go through his files in preparation for his future testimony. Impounded by the FBI, his papers are stored in a small, hot, stuffy room on the fifth floor. Bob has access to them by appointment and under the constant supervision of a camera and a Secret Service agent, who keeps a record of every document Bob reviews. While in the room, Bob is not permitted to take notes—or copy or remove any of his papers. He has to try to commit what he reads to memory, then step out in the hallway and reconstruct it on a notepad as best he can. He spends much of his time going in and out.

After taking Ann to a friend's house for a sleepover, I drive to the EOB to get Bob. I have no idea when he'll appear, but I don't mind waiting. The night air is warm, and the full moon casts long shadows across the EOB's towering gingerbread façade. Finally, Bob comes out. It's after midnight. Pausing at the top of the stairs, he clutches his briefcase in his right hand and walks slowly down the granite steps. His shoulders are slightly humped, and his brow is furrowed.

"Tough night?" I ask, as he slips into the passenger seat.

"Yeah," he says. "The heat was so unbearable in that room I even felt sorry for the Secret Service guy who was there with me." Bob stretches. "Sorry to be so late. I couldn't leave until I had everything the lawyers wanted."

I start the car and head up Executive Avenue, the short road that runs between the EOB and the White House. Yawning, Bob continues, "Actually, it was pretty interesting. I made two stacks of papers. One was half an inch high, and the other was over a foot. The small stack was Watergate related stuff. The other stack was everything else from the past four and a half years." He gives a little laugh. "It's obvious that I didn't spend a lot of time worrying about Watergate when I was in the White House."

With the windows down, a rush of warm air fills the car. The night is gentle, smoothing away the rough edges of the past couple of days.

"Did you know that the full moon and warm weather bring out the kooks and criminals?" Bob asks, interrupting my thoughts.

"No," I say. *What in the world made him think of that?*

"The Secret Service guy told me," Bob explains. "Another thing I realized tonight is that the combined staffs of both the Ervin Committee and the prosecutor's office is one hundred seventy-two people, and they are all working against me... One hundred seventy-two to one aren't very good odds."

"You're right," I agree, sadly. As I turn onto Pennsylvania Avenue, a cloud passes over the moon, briefly diminishing its brilliant glow.

◆

OVER THE NEXT COUPLE weeks, the Senate Watergate hearing continues. Like everyone else, Bob and I are glued to the TV. The first witnesses to testify are the policemen and detectives who responded to calls to investigate a burglary at the Democratic Headquarters in the Watergate Complex early in the morning on Saturday, June 17, 1972. Next, the committee hears testimony from three of the seven people involved in the burglary. Rubber gloves, walkie-talkies, electronic surveillance equipment, and duct tape are tools of their trade, along with clandestine drop-offs and code words. A bus conductor's change dispenser was used in making calls from a pay phone booth located near the Blue Fountain Inn on Route 355. Three secret meetings took place at the "second overlook of the George Washington Parkway on the Virginia side." Money was transported in a hotel laundry bag.

The more we see of the hearing, the more ludicrous it seems. Someone describes it as "part morality play and part comedy." The witnesses are odd characters, whose stories unfold like a Keystone Cops movie. It's "The Ervin Show," and I can't imagine Bob's having a part in it.

Ron Ziegler tells the press that the president rarely watches television and isn't following the hearings. Nixon gets most of his information from news summaries, and furthermore, he's too busy planning for the Soviet Summit. Ron makes it clear that the president and Henry Kissinger are also absorbed in the ongoing struggle to keep the Vietnam Peace Agreement on track.

Polls show that 77 percent of Americans believe the president should *not* resign. Archibald Cox takes a leave of absence from Harvard Law School to become the Watergate special prosecutor. Former attorney general John Mitchell and former secretary of the treasury Maurice Stans are indicted in the Vesco case, which entailed alleged bribery in the form of campaign contributions. John Dean declares that he will not be made a "scapegoat," and the Pentagon Papers trial ends in a mistrial after eighty-nine days. The judge states that government misconduct made a fair trial impossible and cites FBI wiretaps, as well as the break-in at Ellsberg's psychiatrist's office. All charges against Daniel Ellsberg are dismissed, and the courtroom erupts in loud cheering and clapping.

On May 22, the president releases a four-thousand-word statement, which he hopes will clear up his part in Watergate. In it, he denies having any prior knowledge of the break-in, as well as any awareness of, or participation in, the cover-up. He explains that he directed Bob Haldeman and John Ehrlichman to ensure that the Watergate investigation wouldn't expose either an unrelated CIA operation or a separate White House Special Investigative Unit.

On Thursday, May 24, it pours rain all day. As I drive along E street and pass the White House, I catch a glimpse of workmen sloshing around in the mud erecting a large tent on the South Lawn. Tonight, President and Mrs. Nixon are hosting a black-tie gala in honor of the prisoners of war. Bob Hope, John Wayne, and Sammy Davis Jr. will provide the entertainment for the 1,300 guests, including 500 POWs. As the largest event to ever take place at the White House, it is being billed as "the most dazzling party in White House social annals."

This is one party Bob would love to attend. The prisoners of war are his true heroes, and he admires their patriotism, loyalty, and pride. Instead of being present at the White House, however, he spends his evening at home. Exhausted after a full day of giving depositions, he removes his blazer and tie and slips into a worn, navy blue cardigan with two moth holes in the right sleeve. Joining me in the kitchen, he shows me a note he received from the president. Nixon's scrawl fills the small piece of White House stationery, and I feel for Bob as I read the heartrending words.

> *Dear Bob,*
>
> *As I sit here preparing remarks for the POWs I realize this day would never have come without your steadfast support and also John's. The nation, the POWs, and I shall always be in your debt.*
>
> *RN*
>
> *P.S. We shall come out ok in the end.*

"You wouldn't believe how much of a hassle it was for the president to get this to me," Bob says. "He had Manolo hand-deliver it to Larry, who said that Manolo had tears in his eyes. He was pretty emotional about the whole thing."

Under Siege

BOB FOLLOWS THE SENATE hearings as much as he can, but he has many demands on his time. These include interviews with the grand jury, the special prosecutor, and the Ervin Committee staff, as well as the US attorney's office and two other congressional committees. To prepare himself, he's either reviewing things with his lawyers or on the fifth floor of the EOB, going through his files. Hanging over him is the thought that if he fails to remember things correctly, he faces the possibility of perjuring himself.

When our realtor shows our house, I prefer not to be around. With little enthusiasm, I do what's necessary to get ready to leave. I pack up winter clothes that we won't need in California, get estimates from moving companies, and write out instructions and phone numbers for the prospective renter. When a Los Angeles broker calls to say that she has the perfect house for us in Hancock Park, I tell her that I'm not interested right now.

I'm not happy about leaving Washington.

June 1973

THE CHIP, CHIP, CHIP of Watergate continues. Both *The New York Times* and *The Washington Post* report that John Dean has alleged that the president knew about the cover-up. Dean also claims that at a meeting last March, Nixon asked how much the Watergate burglars would have to be paid to ensure their silence. Dean had replied, "About a million dollars," and the president had responded that "it would be no problem."

I shudder when *Newsweek* states that the grand jury is going to indict Haldeman, Ehrlichman, Mitchell, and Magruder. Another article in the magazine, titled "Family Fallout: Painful Days," talks about the effect of Watergate on the families.

> They never mixed with outsiders much, even in the best of times. The men who followed Richard Nixon to Washington generally kept to themselves—shunning personal publicity, socializing occasionally with one another, spending most of their free time quietly at home with their wives and children. Now, in the shadow of Watergate, these quintessentially Nixonian families are suffering through a painful period of notoriety and stress. And it seems a condition for which they were left largely unprepared by their previously sheltered existence.

> "It's so tragic," says one Nixon campaign veteran who knows many of them. "These were a bunch of young family men on their way up. They had everything going for them, and now their lives have been wrecked."

> Some old friends seem to avoid the shadowed Nixon men and their families like the plague. "We wouldn't think of going to see them," says one former employee of the CRP. "If you ever knew anybody these days a link is attempted. There is so much paranoia and guilt by association."

It's hard to see our close-knit Nixon team breaking up as the stain of Watergate spreads. Fearing that even a simple phone call might be misinterpreted, our lawyers advise us not to talk to one another. Any one of us could be accused of participating in a conspiracy or a cover-up. As this distancing grows, I think a lot about the effect that Watergate is having on the people I know. I wish that I could communicate with Nancy Ziegler, Gail Magruder, Susie Chapin, Dolores Higby, and of course, Jeanne.

I feel compelled to write a letter of support to these women. I want to reassure them that the Nixon team continues in spirit and that no one should feel abandoned. Not knowing what to do with the letter, I place it in the back of my desk drawer. A week later, I show it to Bob and ask him if I should send it to the *Washington Post*, as an open letter to the wives of Watergate. Bob agrees with the idea, but first he wants to run it by his lawyers for their approval.

Both John Wilson and his partner Frank Strickler strongly advise me not to send the letter. It could have legal repercussions for Bob later. Frustrated, I empathize with Gail Magruder when I watch the Watergate hearing. She is almost in tears as her husband, Jeb, struggles to answer tough questions about his knowledge of the Watergate break-in.

"Don't even think about talking to Gail," Bob says, anticipating what I'm going to say.

"All I want to do is to take her a plant," I tell him.

"Are you crazy? The press is all over the place."

When I entreat him one more time, Bob hesitates, and then reluctantly gives in. With no reporters in sight, my five-minute drop-off goes without a hitch. However, I feel like a criminal as I sneak up and deposit a small violet plant at the Magruders' front door.

I don't like living like this. It's not natural. My world seems to be turning upside down, and I don't like it.

◆

ON JUNE 9, SECRETARIAT wins the Belmont Stakes by a whopping thirty-one lengths. The large chestnut colt becomes the first Triple Crown champion in twenty-five years. The Supreme Court turns the issue of obscenity over to the states, and in Tokyo erotic prints by Picasso are censored before being exhibited.

In Washington, there's a two-week break in the televised Senate hearings. During this time, the weather turns hot and humid. The reporters in front of our home shed their coats and roll up their shirtsleeves. Instead of playing Frisbee, they sit on campstools in the shade. When our newspaper sails across our back fence and lands on top of the tulips, I don't care. The flowers have long since wilted. A canopy of green has replaced the cherry blossoms, and the pugs stretch out in the shade on the cool slate below.

Before leaving Washington, I would like to personally thank the White House operators. Although the White House phone has been my nemesis these past four years, these women are my heroines. Handling an average of fifty thousand calls daily, they are always pleasant and unruffled. Part technician, part diplomat, and part detective, they can tactfully track down anyone, anywhere.

Bob makes the arrangements for our visit to the sub-basement of the EOB. Here, a handful of operators work the switchboards in eight hour shifts in two small, windowless rooms. When Bob and I introduce ourselves, no one's face looks familiar, but I recognize each voice. There is an unspoken bond between us, and saying goodbye is a painful process for me.

Our realtor informs us that the Callaways have decided to rent our home for the summer. Although I'm relieved not to have to move our things out, there is still a lot to do. I begin by making inventory lists of our china, linen, and silver. As soon as we make arrangements to turn over the house on June 15, I read about it in Maxine Cheshire's column in *The Washington Post*.

> Others involved in the Watergate probe may wait to see what the future holds before deciding to uproot their families, but former presidential aide H. R. Haldeman and his wife already are making plans to move back to California when school is out... The family has been virtually under siege with reporters and photographers camped on their doorstep.

Reservations?

OUR DEPARTURE FROM WASHINGTON will be divided into two phases. First, Peter and Ann will fly to California. The following day, Bob and I will leave for Minnesota, where we will attend Susan's graduation. While I work on the travel arrangements for the children, I tell them to pack enough clothes to last at least three months. I check on flight schedules, buy tickets, and coordinate the arrival time with Bob's sister, Betsy, who will meet the plane at LAX. Ann's parakeet needs a special permit to travel in the cabin, and the pugs require reserved spaces in the baggage section. They must be sedated before the flight, which entails making meatballs out of dog food with pills inside them.

On Thursday, June 14, Bob spends his final day in a meeting with Sam Dash, chief counsel for the Senate Watergate Committee, while I take Peter and Ann to the airport. Six suitcases, two flight bags, three dog kennels, and a birdcage are lined up on the sidewalk outside our front door. Reporters watch in fascination as we struggle to get everything loaded into a taxi and a borrowed station wagon. At Dulles, it takes two porters with trolleys to transport our belongings to the check-in counter.

Nothing is easy today. The pugs are leery about taking their meatballs, and an American Airlines representative is suspicious of Peter's bulging flight bag. When she discovers a plastic bag half-full of water with two goldfish in it, a supervisor is called. Eventually, the airline allows Peter and Ann to board with the two fish and one bird. With the three pugs in the baggage section, I've completed "phase one" of our departure from Washington.

Bob shows up later in the evening, following his five-hour meeting with Sam Dash. He looks haggard, but he still has to pack and review some paperwork. Before going to bed at 1:30 a.m., he finds me outside on our patio.

"It's the middle of the night, Jo!" he exclaims. "What on earth are you doing?"

"I want the garden to look nice for the Callaways," I explain. "I'm replacing the dead tulips under the cherry tree with geraniums."

Shaking his head, Bob goes back upstairs. It's our final night as official residents of Washington, and this crazy scene is not what I ever anticipated. Here I am outside gardening by moonlight, while Bob wanders around barefoot in his pajamas. I picture the Ehrlichmans comfortably ensconced in their home in Virginia, and I'm envious. I know the press has been hard on them recently, but at least they don't have to pack up and leave right now.

What little sleep I get is fragmented, and I awake on Friday morning feeling out of sorts. I will miss this town. Birds are twittering in the cherry tree outside, the sun is shining, and warm air is wafting in through the open bedroom window. Happy memories flood my mind, and for a brief moment, Watergate isn't in the picture.

At 8:30 a.m., Larry arrives in a borrowed White House station wagon to take Bob and me to National Airport. As Larry loads our suitcases into the back, Bob makes a last minute run through the house. When one of the few remaining reporters asks for a statement, Bob tells him, "Once the truth is known about Watergate, it will be clear that I was not involved in either the bugging or the cover-up."

At the end of the block, I turn and look back. The red brick townhouse is like many others in Georgetown, but this one was our home for four brief months, and I loved it. Larry drives slowly, giving Bob and me a chance to say our silent goodbyes to Washington. Before crossing the Fourteenth Street Bridge, we pass the White House, and I watch as Bob's and Larry's heads turn in unison to look. Nothing is said, and I can only imagine what each of them must be feeling.

The terminal is crowded, and there are long lines. Bob and I have not traveled together on a commercial flight in five years. While he looks for a porter to help with our five suitcases and two carry-ons, I wait in line at the Northwest Orient check-in counter. At last, it's my turn, and the agent requests our tickets.

Tickets?

I reach into my purse, and as I'm fumbling around, the agent asks in what name I made the reservations.

Reservations?

Not until this very moment does it dawn on me that I have neither reservations nor tickets. I wrote down the flight information, but in the confusion of getting the children off, I never followed through. Bob and the porter arrive with the suitcases just as the agent informs me that the plane is full. There's a waiting list, and there is no way we can get on this flight to Minneapolis.

"Sorry, Mr. Haldeman, I wish I could help," the agent says, looking right through me as if I didn't exist. "I'd be happy to book you on our three fifteen flight, if that works for you and Mrs. Haldeman."

Suddenly, Bob and I are on center stage. Not only do the people in the ticket line recognize us and know what the problem is, but everywhere I look I see the Haldeman name. Virtually everyone is reading the early edition of *The Evening Star,* with banner headlines proclaiming, "Focus Shifts to Haldeman." Testifying with limited immunity at the Senate Watergate hearing yesterday, Jeb Magruder said that he had attended meetings to approve Liddy's plans for the bugging and the break-in. He stated that all plans had gone to Haldeman's aide, Gordon Strachan. Upon hearing this, Senator Ervin concluded that Haldeman must have known about the break-in.

Haldeman. Haldeman. Haldeman. Bob's name appears everywhere. *And I have let him down in the worst possible way. I wish I could dissolve. Disappear. Vanish.* There's not a thing I can do, except to say I'm sorry. I steel myself for the Haldeman look, but it's not there. Instead, Bob's eyes are soft and steady, and he tells me not to worry.

"You've had a lot on your mind recently," he says. I nod. The agent issues the tickets.

Calmly assuming control, Bob calls Susan from a pay phone to give her our new arrival time. He suggests that he and I have lunch in Georgetown at the Gourmetisserie, which is within walking distance of our townhouse. We can wait at home until it's time to return to the airport.

Retracing our steps through the terminal, we check our luggage in three lockers. Bob flags a taxi, and for the second time this morning, we drive by Washington's monuments and the White House. After lunch, we walk home, where I hesitate on the sidewalk before stepping inside. Although we left only a couple of hours ago, the house looks different. I feel like an intruder. In the living room, I sit on the edge of the couch and try to read one of the magazines that I had meticulously arranged on the coffee table earlier. Eager to make a call, Bob heads straight for the phone in the kitchen.

"Hey, Larry," he says, "you won't believe what happened at the airport." While Bob gives a detailed description of why we aren't on the plane, I fall back on the couch and try to block it out.

On the drive back to National Airport, our taxi passes the monuments and the White House for the *third* time. Our check-in at the Northwest Orient ticket counter goes smoothly, and an airline agent personally escorts us out to the plane. She points to two seats in the first row. The seat across the aisle is being held for a VIP passenger who turns out to be the Democratic senator from Minnesota, Hubert Humphrey. When he boards, he cordially shakes hands and is remarkably interested in and supportive of Bob. Although the two of them talk nonstop during the entire flight, they never mention the 1968 presidential election, when Humphrey was defeated by Nixon.

The following day, Bob and I attend the graduation ceremony at the University of Minnesota. Seated high up in a packed stadium, we can't even find Susan in the mass of students below. Fortunately, Bob discovers that we can use the zoom lens on his movie camera to get a close-up view of our daughter receiving her B.A. in history. We are proud of our summa cum laude graduate, who begins her summer job tomorrow, working at the local Burger King.

Sunday, June 17, 1973, is the anniversary of Watergate. *Was it only one year ago that I was in Key Biscayne, reading about a bizarre break-in at the Watergate? How would I ever have known that it would have such a devastating effect on our lives twelve months later?*

Although our flight to California is the last leg of our official departure from Washington, Bob will be making many return trips. Not only will he be meeting with his lawyers and giving depositions, but he'll be testifying at the Senate Watergate hearing next month.

Newport will be our base for the next three months. During this time, my job will be to find a home in Los Angeles, enroll Peter and Ann in school, and sell the townhouse. Both Bob and I could easily get discouraged with our situation, but we have our faith. I cling to one of my favorite quotes, "To those leaning on the Sustaining Infinite, today is big with blessings."

The Elusive Mr. Haldeman

TWO HOURS AFTER LANDING at LAX, we are walking across the bridge onto Bay Island. Pulling a two-wheeled cart filled with our suitcases, we follow the path past the center green, the caretaker's house, and the tennis court. The carriage lamp in front of #11 is lit, and the tomato-red golf cart sits next to the fence with its battery being charged. Sounds of happy voices come from the open windows. Mom, Dad, Peter, Ann, and my sister with her four children are expecting us.

As usual, dinner is a lively affair. In order to accommodate eleven of us, two extensions have been added to the dining room table. The sun is setting, and the musty-yellow café curtains and the half-shutters above them are pulled back. The rose garden outside is in deep shade, but the tips of the tall eucalyptus trees are highlighted in a golden glow.

At the head of the table, my father stands. His chair makes a scraping sound as he pushes it back across the rough, linoleum-tile floor. "I'd like to propose a toast," he says, raising his glass. "Please join me in welcoming home Bob and Jo."

◆

WITH THE CHAOS OF Washington behind us, I anticipate enjoying the summer without the press, but that's not possible. Reporters become frantic when they can't find us. Not knowing that we are spending the first half of the summer on Harbor Island, they rent boats and hover offshore from Bay Island. A front page news story appears in the *Daily Pilot,* speculating about our whereabouts. A large photo of #11 is featured above the headline, "Haldeman, Kin Hidden in Newport—Somewhere." The article accuses the "elusive Mr. Haldeman" of deliberately hiding. In the meantime, Bob goes unnoticed, blithely sailing his Sunfish around the reporters' boats each afternoon.

When our location is finally "discovered," a photo of the house on Harbor Island appears in the *Los Angeles Times* with a caption reading, "Haldeman's Hideaway Uncovered." A local resident is quoted as saying, "Bob Haldeman sure has caused a lot of trouble," but the reporter hastens to add, "The neighbor would not elaborate."

A few days later when Bob receives a call from the Associated Press, I ask him what it was about.

"Just a rumor," he responds evasively.

"What now?" I press.

"Apparently, I've committed suicide."

◆

NIXON RECEIVES A MAJOR setback when Congress passes the Case-Church Amendment, which forbids all US military activity in Southeast Asia unless the president secures congressional approval in advance. This ends direct US military involvement in the Vietnam War and ties Nixon's hands. The hawks predict that it is an open invitation to the Communists to invade South Vietnam. Watergate is also moving in the wrong direction. It is now being investigated by the General Accounting Office, along with the Ervin Committee, four other congressional committees, the FBI, and several grand juries.

The Senate Watergate hearings continue on Monday, June 25, with John Dean testifying. Public interest is so high that all three television networks carry his testimony live. Bob, the children, and I watch it at #11 with my parents and my sister, Gay, and her family.

Seated at a table facing the senators, Dean looks young and serious. Clearing his throat, he leans forward to get closer to the microphone. "To one who was in the White House, and became somewhat familiar with its inner workings," he begins, "the Watergate matter was an inevitable outgrowth of a climate of excessive concern over the political impact of demonstrators, excessive concern over leaks, an insatiable appetite for political intelligence, all coupled with a do-it-yourself White House staff, regardless of the law."

I squirm uncomfortably in my chair. While I don't like what Dean says, I wonder how much of the climate in the White House reflected Bob's unwavering demand for perfection. I look over at him. Seated in a black Windsor chair in the living room, he's busily taking notes on a yellow pad.

Reading in a flat monotone, Dean implicates Mitchell, Magruder, and Colson. His opening statement is 245 pages long, includes forty-six supporting documents, and lasts seven hours. Occasionally adjusting his thin, tortoiseshell glasses, Dean doesn't hesitate to speak against the president of the United States and claims that Nixon took part in the cover-up. The thirty-four-year-old former White House counsel states that he dealt with the president mostly through John Ehrlichman and Bob Haldeman and accuses them of being "the prime orchestrators of the cover-up."

"Dean's desperate," Bob says calmly as he writes. "He's trying to save himself by pointing the finger at John and me. This is the only way he can get immunity. He has to come up with a plausible story to impress the federal prosecutors."

The Senate Watergate Committee's questioning of Dean lasts four days. Giving precise answers, he never falters as his perfectly coifed wife looks on. Seated directly behind him, Maureen is praised by the press, who refer to her "steady gaze and glamorous air." As I watch, I try to picture myself seated in that same room next month when Bob is scheduled to testify.

After Dean's appearance, columnist Stewart Alsop writes in *Newsweek*, "To continue to believe that President Nixon was wholly innocent of any involvement in the Watergate cover-up requires, by this time, a major act of faith… If the pro-Nixon witnesses, or Mr. Nixon himself, can extricate the president from the web John Dean has woven, it will be a miracle."

I worry about the effect of Dean's testimony on public opinion. I hope people won't prejudge Bob before he has a chance to testify. When I see a cartoon of Bob and John Ehrlichman fending off Dean, it reminds me of something that Patrick Anderson wrote. "The aide will almost certainly develop an enemy or two among his fellow staff members, his rivals in the harem."

July 1973

IN JULY, BOTH GREECE and Afghanistan proclaim new republics, and the Bahamas declare independence after three hundred years of British rule. The US Senate approves an amendment that will allow the construction of the Alaskan pipeline. Both the Senate and the House pass the War Powers Resolution, which restricts the president's power to commit the United States to any armed conflict unless there is a declaration of war by Congress. Another blow to Nixon.

By the middle of the month, the reality of our new life starts to sink in. Although Harbor Island is "home" right now, I spend much of my time in Los Angeles, looking at schools and houses. Bob is commuting back and forth to Washington. Whenever the Callaways are out of town, they invite him to stay in the upstairs study of our townhouse, where he has his desk, files, and a daybed.

On Tuesday evening, July 10, he calls from his study. In the course of our conversation, he confides in me that he just finished listening to one of the White House tapes. I'm dumbfounded.

"How'd you get it?" I ask. "I thought the tapes were top secret."

"They are," Bob says. "But the president wanted to refresh his memory of a meeting in the Oval Office. He told me to take the tape home and then summarize it for him."

"Why you? You don't work for him anymore. Is it even okay for you to have that tape?"

"Of course. The tapes belong to the president, and he can do whatever he wants with them. Besides, tonight isn't the first time I've done this. I listened to one last April, too."

Bob doesn't go into any further detail, and soon we are discussing a house I saw today.

Nixon Bugged Himself

A S THE TIME FOR Bob's appearance at the Senate Watergate hearing draws nearer, he spends a weekend being "prepped" by his brother Tom and his cousin Bill Haight. Bill is a trial lawyer, and both he and Tom hurl a variety of tough questions at Bob. *Do John Dean, John Mitchell, and John Ehrlichman prepare this way, too? They are all lawyers. They probably don't need the extra drill.*

On Monday morning, July 16, Bob and I turn on television to watch the testimony of Alex Butterfield. After being sworn-in, Alex starts to read his opening statement, beginning with how he got his job at the White House.

"It was at the time of the transition," he states. "I was serving as the senior US military officer in Australia, and I was amazed to get a call from my old friend Bob Haldeman, who was in New York. He wanted to talk to me about working as some sort of assistant to the president."

Bob leans forward in disbelief. "That's not true!" he exclaims. "I never contacted Alex about a job. He was the one to approach me. He sent me a long letter specifically requesting the position."

Neither Bob nor I can imagine why Alex would lie, but the exchange that follows is even more unnerving. "Mr. Butterfield, are you aware of the installation of any listening devices in the Oval Office of the president?" Chief Minority Counsel Fred Thompson asks.

Listening devices? Bob and I look at each other. *Will Alex reveal the existence of the White House taping system?* There's a stunned silence among the Committee members, spectators, and the press. All eyes are focused on the tan, handsome, forty-seven-year-old witness. Alex doesn't flinch.

"I was aware of listening devices." Long pause. "Yes, sir."

With his words virtually ricocheting off the tall marble columns in the staid Caucus Room, Alex clasps his hands in front of him and leans forward. In a steady voice, he explains that the devices were installed in both the Oval Office and the president's EOB office. The recordings were made for historical purposes, and only a handful of people know about the existence of the taping system. Bob is one of them.

Alex concludes, "I only hope that I have not by my openness, and by my adherence to all instructions received to date, given away something which the president planned to use at a later time in support of his position."

"The president can declare executive privilege to protect the tapes," Bob says. "And Alex knows that."

Outside, a thick layer of fog descends on Newport, and the mournful call of the foghorn carries across the bay. Bob's pen glides swiftly across his yellow pad, and my mind races. *This is one more incident where Bob has been named as one of the prime people involved. And not only did he know about the tapes, but he listened to two of them.*

I slump back in my chair.

The next morning, Alex's disclosure is the lead story nationally, and the headline "NIXON BUGGED HIMSELF" covers the entire front page of the *New York Post*. Most Americans want the tapes turned over to the Ervin Committee and/or the special prosecutor. John Connally is among the few who favor destroying them, and he tells Bob that the president should build a bonfire in the Rose Garden and invite the press to film the tapes as they go up in smoke. Although the president has only 40 percent public approval of the way he's handling the situation, he refuses to release them. *John Connally is right. Burn the tapes as soon as you can.*

On Friday, July 20, Nixon returns to the White House after being hospitalized with viral pneumonia for the past eight days. Officially greeting his staff in the Rose Garden, he acknowledges rumors of his resignation and calls them "poppycock."

"…let others wallow in Watergate," he says. "We're going to do our job."

◆

AT LAST IT'S TIME for John Ehrlichman, and then Bob, to appear before the Ervin Committee. Bob and I fly to Washington, but once we are there, we part ways. Wanting to be near his personal papers and files, Bob stays in his office at our townhouse. I join Kathleen Bell at her lovely home on Dexter Street. I have fond memories of sailing in the Virgin Islands with her and her husband George, who has since passed away.

On Monday, July 23, John begins his testimony. Gathered around the TV in the Bells' den, Jeanne, Bob, Kathleen, and I are served coffee and pastries by Lucille, the housekeeper. With its spring green walls, bright, chintz-covered chairs, and many bookshelves, the cozy room is comforting at a time of nervous tension.

Remembering how self-assured John was during his mock trial at Stanford Law School, I'm confident he will do well this morning. But I have reservations, too. Although he is good-natured and has a wicked sense of humor, John can be cocky. I worry that he might become abrasive when the senators question him.

"I didn't cover up anything to do with Watergate," John emphatically declares in his opening statement. "The vast percentage of my working time was spent on *substantive* issues and domestic policy. About one half of one percent was spent on politics, the campaign, and the events with which you have been concerning yourself as a committee."

John is grilled by the Committee for five days. During that time, he makes it clear that he's angry about being secretly recorded by the president. He testifies that he wants the tapes to be made public, in order to confirm what he has said. Most of the senators' questions deal with John's role in the break-in at Ellsberg's psychiatrist's office and the "Plumbers Unit," an investigative team led by Hunt and Liddy to prevent leaks.

Senator Ervin's hokey way of speaking visibly irritates John, who is usually affable and outgoing. When John's jaw juts out, he appears to be snarling, and a commentator refers to his "look of defiance." Not only is he combative in his answers, but so is his lawyer, John Wilson, who is representing both John and Bob. Wilson exchanges verbal blows with Senator Ervin over the president's power to protect national security.

In summarizing, John says, "I do not apologize for my loyalty to the president, any more than I apologize for my love of country."

It's clear that John's demeanor grated on the committee, the public, and the press. One journalist describes him as, "alternately scornful, disputatious, circumlocutory, condescending, and quite without apology for anything." Jeanne had wanted to accompany John to the hearings, but he was concerned that the atmosphere was too hostile. I think her presence might have helped to soften his image.

How will Bob be judged when he testifies? When Joseph Kraft refers to John's "maniacal arrogance," I worry. Bob and John are so often linked together. *Might Bob, with his crew cut and Germanic image, also be perceived as "maniacally arrogant"?* Bernard Levin writes in *The London Times,* "The Senate hearings are like an inquisition, and the witnesses are having their cases prejudged without any of the safeguards of true legal proceedings."

Mr. Inside

O N MONDAY MORNING, JULY 30, I wake up early after a restless night. Now that the moment is here, it seems surreal that Bob will be testifying this afternoon. Sunlight seeps through the closed shutters in Kathleen's guest bedroom. Washington is already hot and muggy, and the air conditioner has been running nonstop throughout the night. Susan arrived several days ago, and as I watch her sleepily disentangle herself from her twisted bed sheets, I think about our children. Throughout this whole ordeal, they have taken each day in stride. How Bob will be judged after these hearings is questionable, but whatever happens, neither he nor I ever want to lose the love or respect of Susan, Hank, Peter, and Ann.

Hank arrived last night, and all of us agreed that he and Susan should attend today's hearing with their father. If all goes well, I will join Susan and Bob tomorrow.

In the afternoon, John, Jeanne, Kathleen, and I settle in the den to watch the proceedings. When the Senate Caucus Room flashes onto the TV screen, I stiffen up in anticipation. As soon as I see Bob raise his right hand and swear to tell the truth, I relax. Standing rigidly erect, he tucks in his chin and stares straight ahead. His demeanor is respectful and confident.

Before giving his opening statement, Bob turns to confer with John Wilson, who is seated next to him. Only five feet, four inches tall, the seventy-two-year-old lawyer is well respected and has a reputation of being exceptionally able.

Bob's pace is slow when he starts to read. He praises the White House staff and those who served with him. "They were the most outstanding, most dedicated, and most able group of people with whom I have ever been associated...or ever hope to be associated."

With assurance, Bob states that the president "raised questions about Watergate from time to time during the period of June through the election." He takes a moment to look at the senators. "The president's interest consistently was to get the facts and to get them out." The steady drone of his voice reminds me of those nights when I would hear him dictating his daily journal onto a cassette.

In referring to the White House investigation of Watergate, Bob pauses. "And it now appears...we were badly misled by one or more of the principals, and even more so, by our own man, for reasons which are still not completely clear."

This is as close as Bob gets to blaming John Dean, and when he concludes, I think his opening statement came across as honest and nonjudgmental. *The Washington Post* concedes that "the man, who has been endlessly portrayed as Bad Guy No. 1 in the Watergate plot...was as amiable as a bowl of warm pudding, despite all of the prior testimony about his Prussian managerial style."

The following morning, I'm apprehensive about attending the hearing. Dressing simply, I wear a pleated, off-white skirt and dark-green, cotton blouse. It's too hot to take a sweater or a jacket. By the time I reach the packed Senate Caucus Room, I have a bad case of nerves. Susan and I pause in the doorway to let our eyes adjust to the harsh glare of the camera lights. With its twelve marble columns, ornate ceiling, and four giant crystal chandeliers, the room is larger than it appeared on television. Tension and excitement fill the air as we take our reserved seats in the first row of spectators. Several rows in front of me, there are two empty leather chairs at a table covered with a brown felt cloth. On the table are two microphones, a pitcher of ice water, and two glasses.

Bob enters the room with John Wilson at his side. Smiling, he waves to Susan and me as one of the spectators in the rear calls out, "Good luck, H. R." Looking poised and confident, he takes his seat at the table. From where I sit, I see only the back of his head, his bristly crew cut, and his hunched shoulders.

I know that Bob is determined to tell the truth. As he testifies, it's obvious that he's trying to answer the questions directly and specifically. Aware of the risk of committing perjury, he has been advised by his lawyers to respond, "I don't recall," rather than speculate.

The Committee is indignant that Bob has had access to two of the presidential tapes. Claiming to be outraged, they demand to know why a private citizen was given that privilege, while elected government officials were not. Senator Ervin is suspicious. Jabbing at the air with his bony index finger, he wonders if the president and Bob selected only those portions of the tapes that they thought would be helpful to the White House.

In commenting on his recollection of what he heard on the September 15, 1972, tape, Bob states that his notes show that, "President Nixon had no knowledge of, or involvement in, either the Watergate affair or the subsequent efforts to cover up."

Senator Howard Baker from Tennessee questions Bob on his "accuracy of recollection" regarding the March 21, 1973, tape. In an earlier statement, Bob quoted the president saying, "There is no problem in raising a million dollars, we can do that, but it would be wrong."

"Now how sure are you, Mr. Haldeman, that those tapes in fact say that?" asks Senator Baker.

"I am absolutely positive that the tapes—"

"Did you hear it with your own voice?" Senator Baker interjects.

"With my own ears," Bob confirms. "Yes."

Later Senator Weicker questions Bob, bringing back bitter memories of his interview on *Meet the Press* when his arrogance and unsubstantiated accusations of Bob had incensed me. Shifting his six-foot, six-inch frame, Weicker leans forward.

"I think that…both you and I would agree that this went far beyond just a few men breaking into the Watergate…. It has revealed a situation both within the Committee to Re-Elect the President and within the White House, whereupon everything that was touched was corroded."

Bob straightens up. Choosing his words carefully, he speaks slowly. "I will not, in any way, shape, or form ever accept that allegation or contention. I think that does a grave disservice to the country even to state it. And I apologize immediately for having responded with that amount of vigor."

The tone of Bob's voice is deliberate. I don't detect any anger, only sincerity and conviction.

August 1973

BOB SPENDS THREE DAYS being grilled by the Committee. He remains unruffled and self-assured, but there are times when he answers that he can't recall, or when he qualifies his answer as being to the best of his recollection. When he

Jo and Bob at President Nixon's second inauguration.
January 20, 1973.

John and Jeanne Ehrlichman at the second inauguration.
January 20, 1973.

March 19, 1973

Nixon's Palace Guard

50 cents

Newsweek

*Presidential Aide
Haldeman*

Cover of Newsweek *dated March 19, 1973.*

Bob filming the presidential motorcade in Atlantic City, New Jersey. June 1971.

Bob in the redecorated villa before learning of the Watergate break-in. The Key Biscayne Hotel, June 17, 1972.

Bob in the new Laurel cabin. Camp David, October 1972.

Jeanne Ehrlichman holds up The Sunday Star, *featuring Bob in its headline. Camp David, Easter Sunday, April 22, 1973.*

Cover of Newsweek *dated May 7, 1973.*

Jo and Bob with Senator Hubert Humphrey.
Flight from Washington to Minnesota. June 1973.

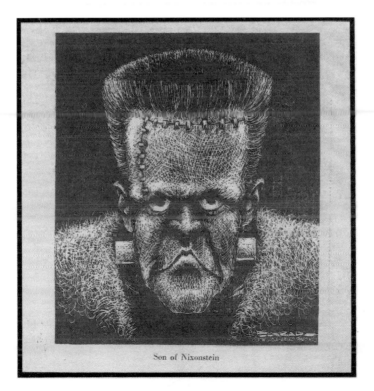

Son of Nixonstein

Paul Conrad's cartoon in the Los Angeles Times. *August 1973.*

Jo and Bob on the porch at #11 Bay Island. September 1973.

*Bob and his new puppy, Rufus,
at Smoke Tree Ranch.
Palm Springs, October 1973.*

Cover of Newsweek.
March 11, 1974.

Jo reading about Watergate in the International Herald Tribune. *Nice, France, July 1974.*

Jo celebrates her 46th birthday in the defendants' room.
U.S. District Courthouse, Washington, DC, October 31, 1974.

Courtroom artist Freda Reiter presents Bob with her sketch of him at the Watergate trial. November 1974.

"The Three Hams." The chief Watergate prosecutor, Jim Neal, presents a Christmas ham to Bob's lead defense attorney, John Wilson. December 1974.

Bob poses with the hookah in the Arabian tent bedroom. Alexandria, Virginia, October 1974.

John Ehrlichman, seated on zaisu, enjoys Bob's birthday cake. Alexandria, Virginia, October 27, 1974.

Peter, Susan, Ann, and Hank celebrate Christmas during the Watergate trial.
Arlington, Virginia, December 25, 1974.

View from car while being towed after a breakdown on the 14th Street Bridge.
Washington, DC, December 27, 1974.

Jo and Susan look on as Bob addresses the press after the Watergate trial verdict.
U.S. District Courthouse. Washington, DC, January 1, 1975.

Herald Examiner *headline dated February 21, 1975.*

*Mike Wallace interviews Bob at home for 60 Minutes.
Los Angeles, March 1975.*

*Bob meets with the press following the Nixon/Frost interviews.
In front of the Haldeman home. Los Angeles, May 1977.*

The Haldeman family, following Susan's graduation from UCLA School of Law.
June 19, 1977.

Jo on her 49th birthday at the Visitors Center at Lompoc Federal Prison Camp.
October 31, 1977.

Jo with flowers from Demetrius, an inmate at the prison camp.
The Parkers' house in Santa Ynez, June 1977.

Bob on a town pass.
Hans Christian Andersen State Park.
Solvang, April 28, 1978.

Jo in front of the Coldwell
Banker Larchmont office.
Los Angeles, August 1977.

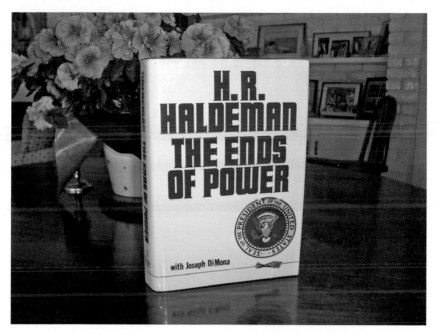

Bob's book, The Ends of Power. *February 1978.*

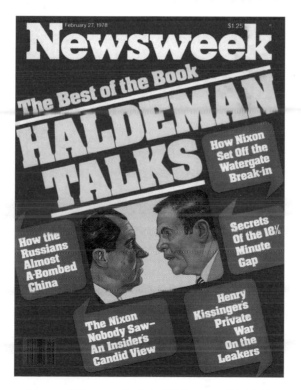

Cover of Newsweek *dated February 27, 1978.*

Jo and Bob at the Parkers' house. Thanksgiving Day, 1978.

Bob's release from the prison camp. Herald Examiner, *December 20, 1978.*

does, the seven senators act as if they don't believe him. Their posturing and exaggerated words of disbelief frustrate me. It's hard to respect them when they act so superior. The *Minneapolis Tribune* has a cartoon of Bob raising his *left* hand, saying, "My name—to the best of my recollection at this point in time—is H. R. Haldeman."

On the whole, the press gives Bob high marks. *Life* magazine describes him as, "the picture of neat propriety in his brush cut and flag lapel pin." He is portrayed as, "more polite than his reputation for being hard-nosed led the senators to expect."

In one article, there is a brief reference to me. "Stamped on the strong face of Jo Haldeman, married twenty-four years and mother of nearly grown children, were the habits of reserve and deep personal discipline to be expected in the partner of Nixon's relentless chief of staff."

In comparing the Haldeman style with the Ehrlichman style, William Shannon writes:

> They had been known in their days of White House power as "the Germans," "the Berlin Wall," or "Mr. Outside" and "Mr. Inside." John D. Ehrlichman, who had a gift for small talk and made himself available occasionally to members of the press and of Congress, was regarded as the more affable "Mr. Outside." H. R. Haldeman, his UCLA classmate, once said, "Every president needs an SOB. I'm Nixon's." Tireless in his attention to detail, tyrannical to his subordinates, implacable in his acquisition of power, Haldeman was the inaccessible "Mr. Inside."
>
> In their successive appearances before the Committee, however, they reversed their public images: Ehrlichman, coming on like gangbusters, hostile and combative; Haldeman, all soft deference and prep school manners.

Son of Nixonstein

WHEN BOB AND I return to California, it's not the welcome home I expected. We are greeted by a vicious cartoon that virtually leaps off the editorial page of the *Los Angeles Times*. In heavy black ink, Bob is portrayed as an evil-looking, crew cut Frankenstein. Paul Conrad, the noted cartoonist, has drawn him with bolts protruding from his neck and a jagged scar cutting across his forehead. His grim face scowls out from a black background, and the caption reads, "Son of Nixonstein."

As soon as I see the humiliating portrayal, I'm overwhelmed by the power of a cartoon. Without words, the single image makes an indelible imprint in my mind. I don't want the children to see it and cram it into the trashcan. I cry, and my tears come from embarrassment and shame.

I never thought it would happen, but Bob has become notorious. His name and face appear not just in the news, but in hair salons, ice cream shops, and delicatessens. There's "Haldemint Ice Cream," "Haldeman's Hot Potato Salad," and the "Haldeman Cut," a Bob Haldeman crew cut for women. In *Doonesbury*, the nationally syndicated comic strip, Mark Slackmeyer's biography of Bob reads, "Los Angeles is a lonely town to grow up in, especially if you're a small boy named H. R. Haldeman."

When people hear me say my name or see it on a check or charge card, they recognize it and often question if I'm any relation to *the* Haldeman. In West Los Angeles, some irate residents of Rustic Canyon want to change the name of Haldeman Road. The area was developed in the early 1920s by the Uplifters Club, who used it as a ranch. As a prominent member of Uplifters—along with his close friend, L. Frank Baum, author of the Oz books—Bob's grandfather, Harry Marston Haldeman, had a street named after him. Fondly remembering her dating days with Bud, Harry Marston's son, Non is heartsick over the proposed name change. She cherishes her memories of visits with the family at their house on Haldeman Road.

Here at Newport Beach, a recently updated local map gets Bob and John Ehrlichman mixed up. A large arrow swoops down on Bay Island and identifies it as the location where "John Haldeman stayed in seclusion."

The *Queen* tour boat now includes a stop offshore from #11. When the wind is right, it carries the captain's voice up to the porch. "The white house with the blue shutters is where Watergate figure H. R. Haldeman lives. Look carefully, and you might see him." The passengers' heads simultaneously turn and look in our direction.

When a barber convinces Bob to let his hair grow, the press writes endless tongue-in-cheek stories about it. There's "Haldeman's Head With Hair," "Taking a New Look," and "Haldeman Involved in Scalp Cover-up." A few columnists even speculate that Bob is trying to change his image. Before and after photos of Bob appear in *Newsweek,* which reports that it's "all part of a hairy deal between father and son," referring to Bob's agreement with Hank to let his hair grow, as soon as Hank cuts his.

It's not easy to live with the fallout from Watergate, but nothing can compare to the guilt and sadness I feel when I see Peter's name on his new Newport Beach Public Library card—"Peter Haldeaux."

◆

ON TUESDAY, AUGUST 7, live television coverage of the Watergate hearings ends after thirty-five days of testimony from thirty-seven witnesses. They held the nation spellbound for 325 hours. Only two major figures in the Nixon White House did not appear: Charles Colson, who pleaded the Fifth Amendment, and the president, who declined the invitation.

Although the "biggest soap opera of all time" is finally over, the grand jury is still looking into Watergate, and the press is quick to prejudge the men being called to testify. The coverage is so unfair that even the liberal commentator Daniel Schorr expresses doubt about it on the CBS Evening News.

> This past year, a new kind of journalism developed, and
> I found myself doing on a daily routine some things I

would never have done before. There was a vacuum in investigation, and the press began to try men in the most effective court in the country. The men involved in the Watergate [affair] were convicted by the media, perhaps in a more meaningful way than any jail sentence they will eventually get.

On August 15, the president gives his second major speech on Watergate. Denying a role in the cover-up, he admits abuses by his subordinates. There isn't a day that goes by without a story about the Nixon White House. Secretary of State William Rogers resigns and is replaced by Henry Kissinger. Vice President Agnew is under investigation for alleged conspiracy, extortion, bribery, and tax fraud. Judge Sirica orders the president to turn over to the Justice Department the tapes of nine specific meetings related to Watergate. Nixon refuses. John Ehrlichman is indicted with three others in connection with the break-in at Ellsberg's psychiatrist's office. Jeb Magruder pleads guilty to a one-count indictment of conspiracy to obstruct justice, defraud the US, and eavesdrop on the Democratic National Headquarters. And when John Mitchell walks out on Martha, she tells the press that the stories about her receiving psychiatric care are "goddamned lies."

Although I have found an English Tudor house in Hancock Park that both Bob and I like, the purchase is contingent upon the sale of our townhouse. Until we have a qualified buyer, Bob and I will continue to live at #11, while Peter and Ann stay with friends in the city in order to attend their new schools. It's frustrating.

The Attic and the Puppy

September 1973

IN SEPTEMBER, THERE'S A noticeable change on Bay Island as summer residents pack up and head home. The days are shorter, and the ground is covered with large, dry sycamore leaves. At #11, the clothesline is empty, and the beach equipment is stored in an upstairs closet. Susan leaves for UC Berkeley's Boalt Hall School of Law, and Hank returns to UCLA as a junior. Peter enters the eleventh grade at Harvard School, his father's alma mater. And Ann is in the ninth grade at Marlborough, the alma mater of her mother, sister, grandmother, and various aunts. With our children gone, the beach house is a lonely place. Bob and I are the only ones left—along with three pugs.

October 1973

THE TOWNHOUSE SELLS IN mid-September, and on Tuesday morning, October 2, a large Allied van arrives at 443 North McCadden Place with our furniture. With Bob's help, the move-in is completed by nightfall. Three months after leaving Washington, our family is united under one roof, and Peter and Ann can enjoy the privacy of their own bedrooms.

Back in our old neighborhood, surrounded by family and friends, I find that it's easy to slip into the same lifestyle I had five years ago. Before long, I'm serving on both the Harvard School Mothers' Club Board and the Salvation Army Advisory Board. Bob and I become active in our church, and each of us teaches a Sunday School class.

When Bob isn't in Washington, he spends most of his time in his upstairs study. The room isn't large. His desk, daybed, chair, and ottoman take up most of the space. Bookshelves line one wall, and his guitar case leans against them. The three windows in the corner overlook our small, kidney-shaped swimming pool, as well as the canopy of a large Brazilian pepper tree in our backyard.

Bob's autographed photos of prominent national leaders hang on the wall, along with Nixon's inaugural quote. To these, he has added his collection of framed political cartoons lampooning him. There's no room for the large portrait of Nixon, and it ends up in the attic, safely wedged between two boxes of Christmas decorations.

"From now on, slacks and blazers are as dressy as I'm going to get," Bob says, passing me in the hall. In his arms is a mound of suits. Each one is on a wood hanger in a tan plastic bag, clearly identified in large black print – Navy Blue, Olive Green, Pinstripe, Tan, etc. The suits go into the attic with Nixon, and I wonder when I will see any of them again.

◆

FINANCIALLY, WATERGATE HAS BOB trapped in limbo. Until he knows whether he's going to be indicted by the grand jury, he can't get a job. In the meantime, we're living off his J. Walter Thompson retirement fund and income from our investments. Bob figures this will cover us in the short run, and he writes me a monthly check so I can pay our daily living expenses. He pays the school tuitions, taxes, and mortgage payments. His legal bills are mounting, and I worry.

Before we left Washington, when Nixon suggested that Bob and John could work at the Nixon Foundation, the two of them turned him down. There was also discussion of a deal with *Reader's Digest* to write about Nixon's first term in the White House, but Bob wasn't interested.

"If I ever do any writing, it'll be a book," he says. "It'll be about the president's accomplishments. Not Watergate…but the *rest* of the Nixon story…like China, détente with Russia, welfare, healthcare, and tax reform. All that stuff that the president never gets any credit for."

Bob soon realizes that writing a book is in fact the best way for him to make money. It's a monumental task, but he's disciplined and makes himself do it. After breakfast each morning, he goes up to his office, where he spends an hour studying the Christian Science Bible Lesson. Then he picks up a yellow pad and a pen and starts writing.

With time at home, Bob decides to get a dog. Claiming that pugs "don't count as *real* dogs," he researches the subject and comes up with the perfect breed—the Rhodesian Ridgeback.

Once Bob finds a litter, however, there's a snag. The breeder refuses to sell a puppy to someone who is unemployed. Fortunately, he's an avid Nixon supporter, and when he realizes who Bob is, the breeder quickly changes his mind. Bob returns home with the pick of the litter, as well as a collar, leash, and two bags of kibble.

With a soulful look and a long, wagging tail, "Rufus" joins our family. Handsome and smart, the gangly puppy is devoted to Bob. Soon, the two of them are inseparable. Curled up in a spot of sunshine on the carpet in Bob's office, Rufus doesn't move until Bob takes a break for lunch. In the late afternoon, they emerge again. This time, it's for obedience training in the driveway.

The Saturday Night Massacre

IN WASHINGTON, THE NIXON White House continues to unravel. After admitting to his role in the payment of "hush money" to the Watergate burglars, John Dean pleads guilty to obstruction of justice. Pleading nolo contendere to one count of income tax evasion, Vice President Agnew resigns, and a judge sentences him to three years' probation and a $10,000 fine. Nixon nominates House Minority Leader Gerald Ford to succeed Agnew.

With still no word from the Watergate grand jury, Non moves ahead with her plans to give a welcome home party in honor of Bob and me. It's black tie, and I look forward to wearing my second inaugural ball gown.

On October 12, the Los Angeles Country Club is abuzz as two hundred guests gather for a reception and a sit-down dinner. Following a dessert of individual hot chocolate soufflés, Non steps up to the microphone and introduces her son. With his longer hair and deep tan, Bob looks handsome. He gives a brief summary of his experience at the White House and the effects of Watergate and then asks for questions.

In response to one about the tapes, he says, "I have always supported the president's position on nondisclosure of privileged material, but I have no doubt that if and when the tapes are made public, President Nixon and I will be fully exonerated. As I told him, the tapes are our best defense."

I hope Bob is right about the tapes. It's reassuring to know that he is convinced that they will prove his innocence. I'm glad when he tells the guests that he wants to go on record publicly with his side of the story. "But," he adds, "It must be at the right time and to the proper authorities."

When asked about the five civil lawsuits pending against him, Bob's response is lighthearted. "It would appear that I'm involved in a new government recreational program designed to keep the unemployed occupied."

Meanwhile, the tapes create a major problem for Nixon. The president offers to have Democratic Senator Stennis review and summarize the tapes that have been requested by the special prosecutor. Archibald Cox refuses the offer, and things reach a climax. Nixon asks for Cox's resignation. Cox refuses. On Saturday night, October 20, the president orders the attorney general to fire Cox. Rather than carry out the order, both the attorney general and the deputy attorney general resign. In a wild night of great confusion, the solicitor general, the third-ranking official in the Justice Department, reluctantly agrees to take over and fires Cox.

Throughout the evening, I keep the TV on and watch with alarm as the networks keep breaking into their programs with updated bulletins. John Chancellor begins his broadcast by telling us that the "country is in the midst of what may be the most serious constitutional crisis in its history."

"Nothing even remotely like this has ever happened," he says. "In my career as a correspondent, I never thought I would be announcing these things."

I'm anxious to hear from Bob, who is in Washington. When he finally calls, it's late at night.

"What's going on?" I ask. "It sounds awful."

"It *is* awful," he agrees. "The president's being chewed to death from every side. Haig called this afternoon to talk about the situation, and I agreed with him that drastic action was the only way for the president to save himself."

I am concerned that Bob supports taking "drastic action," and I am surprised to hear that the White House is still seeking his counsel.

Tonight's events soon become known as the "Saturday Night Massacre." Calling Nixon a "madman and a tyrant," the press plays it for all it is worth. Senator Kennedy claims that it was a reckless act, done by a president "who has no respect for the law and no regard for men of conscience."

◆

FOUR DAYS LATER, THE president vetoes the War Powers Resolution, calling the bill "unconstitutional and dangerous."

The Tapes, the Tapes, the Tapes

November 1973

ON NOVEMBER 1, THE president appoints a new special prosecutor. Leon Jaworski is a sixty-eight-year-old Democrat who voted for Nixon. Two weeks later, the House allocates one million dollars to begin an impeachment process. *It's sad. Just one year ago, the president won the election by the largest number of votes in history.*

On November 7, Nixon receives another setback when Congress overrides his presidential veto of the War Powers Resolution. A few days later, Nixon tells a group of Associated Press managing editors that he has never profited financially from public service. Justifying himself, he adds, "People have to know whether or not their president is a crook. Well, I'm not a crook."

The media and political cartoonists pick up on the president's unfortunate remark. Every time I see something about it, I find it hard to believe that this is the same man who spoke with such eloquence and inspiration at his first inauguration. I think of the quote hanging on the wall of Bob's study, and I'm disheartened.

The dispute over the tapes continues. The president cites national security as a reason for not turning them over, but he agrees to release edited transcripts. When I hear that the conversations might contain both swearing and racial slurs, I become apprehensive. On the other hand, Bob steadfastly maintains that the tapes will vindicate him.

When an 18½–minute gap is discovered in a recording of a discussion that took place in the Oval Office on June 20, 1972, only three days after the Watergate break-in, it creates more mistrust. My heart sinks when I hear that the conversation was between the president and Bob. *Why is it always*

Bob? Why couldn't it have been John Dean or even John Ehrlichman? The press suggests that Nixon and Bob could have been discussing a cover-up. Questions are raised. Was the tape accidentally erased? Did someone tamper with it?

"I can guarantee you that the president and I were *not* talking about any cover-up," Bob assures the family over Thanksgiving.

Seated on chaises by Non's pool at Smoke Tree, six of us are discussing Conrad's cartoon in today's *Los Angeles Times*. It shows the president and Bob conferring, but there are no words in the conversation balloons. When we ask what could have caused the gap, Bob speculates that it might have been the president himself.

"He's so mechanically inept," he explains.

Several days later, Rose Mary Woods tells Judge Sirica that she made a "terrible mistake," and she is responsible. She forgot to remove her left foot from the pedal of the tape player when she took a phone call. As hard as she tries to demonstrate what took place, however, it appears to be physically impossible. People doubt that she is telling the truth.

The tapes, the tapes, the tapes. That's all I read about these days. They are even the subject of a sham notice in *The Harvard Daily Bulletin* at Peter's school.

> Members of The Cassette Tape Recording Club are advised to see Peter Haldeman if they can't attend a meeting scheduled for seventh period.

My heart goes out to our son.

December 1973

STILL NO WORD FROM the grand jury. In South Vietnam, the fighting continues without US participation, and the Communists quickly take over two-thirds of the country. The Nobel Peace Prize is awarded to both Henry Kissinger and Le Duc Tho, founder of the Indochinese Communist Party. An Arab oil embargo creates an energy crisis in the US, resulting in long lines at gas stations across the country. Congressman Gerald Ford is sworn in as vice president.

Only twelve months ago, we were still living in Kenwood. Bertha was working for us, and Watergate was being described as "that great, gummy fungus." Although our life has changed substantially since then, our celebration of Christmas remains the same. Bob hangs strands of colored lights around our outside entrance, while I decorate the tree in the living room.

Dressed in tuxedos and long dresses, fifteen members of the extended Haldeman family arrive for Christmas Eve dinner and gifts. On Christmas morning, my parents join us for breakfast. Mom's contribution is a tray of broiled grapefruit doused with brandy and brown sugar. Along with our stockings and presents, there's a gift for each of the three pugs, as well as for our newest addition, Rufus.

We spend the week after Christmas at Smoke Tree with Non. To accommodate seven adults and thirteen grandchildren, the garage has been converted into a dormitory for the boys. The driveway at Rock 12 is filled with bikes, and the American flag hangs limply from the flagpole.

Following dinner at the Ranch House on New Year's Eve, we stroll back to Non's house. The dark forms of cactus line the road, and the stars shine brilliantly. Bob searches for Orion. The moon reflects off the snowy peaks of Mount San Jacinto, and the air is cold. I link arms with my husband and dig my other hand into the warm, wool lining of my jacket pocket. *It's a different world here at Smoke Tree, and I am at peace. No one reacts to the Haldeman name. No one judges us.*

January 1974

IN JANUARY, THE UNANSWERED question of the 18½–minute gap in the White House tape is turned over to the grand jury. The cover of *Newsweek* features a cartoon of Nixon, Bob, and Rose Mary Woods posed as the Greek statue of Laocoön and his sons. Instead of serpents entangling them, it is the tapes.

Following Kissinger's "shuttle diplomacy" in the Middle East, Egypt and Israel reach an agreement on troop disengagement, and the president receives a much-needed boost in the polls. In his State of the Union address, Nixon names the energy crisis, welfare, and mass transit as the major domestic issues plaguing the country. He states that one year of Watergate is enough and implores the country and Congress to turn to more urgent matters. *I hope he can convince the American people that his ability to govern hasn't been damaged.*

February 1974

ON FEBRUARY 25, THE House Judiciary Committee formally requests the White House to produce recordings of forty-two Watergate-related conversations between the president and members of his administration. When it's reported that the thirteen men and eight women on the grand jury are probably going to indict several key Nixon aides, I hate to hear Bob say that he assumes that he is one of them.

"I think it's inevitable, Jo. And, if I'm indicted, I'll have to go to trial in a few months."

A week later, when we are washing the dishes after dinner, Bob tells me that he talked to a former bank officer who served eight months in Lompoc Federal Prison.

"Why?" I ask, completely caught off guard.

"I wanted to find out what to expect if I have to go to jail."

"Don't talk like that, Bob. You are *not* going to jail."

"Well, that remains to be seen. I thought it was a good chance to get some firsthand information on a prison camp here in Southern California. The guy said that it wasn't as bad as he expected. He was treated well, and the time passed quickly."

I don't want to hear this. While Bob dries a colander, I scrub an iron skillet in a sink of soapy water. *Prison.* I scrub harder. Not only do I want to get rid of the bits of fried liver and onions, but I want to scrub away any thoughts of an indictment, trial, or *prison.*

"Aren't you being a little premature?" I ask, handing Bob the clean skillet.

"I'm just being realistic, Jo."

The Long Wait is Over

March 1974

UNTIL BOB'S RESIGNATION a year ago, nearly everything in his life had gone his way. He was surrounded by a loving and supportive family, was in excellent health, and had no financial problems. Bright and capable, he quickly rose to the top in advertising. As White House chief of staff, Bob reached the pinnacle of his career. Exuding confidence, he was driven and demanding. Now he spends his days waiting to hear if he will be indicted.

On March 1, the long wait is over.

I'm with Bob in his study when his phone rings. Although the conversation is brief, he takes notes. He winces slightly and avoids looking at me. I know that it can mean only one thing.

Slowly putting down the receiver, Bob says, "That was John Wilson. The grand jury just handed down seven indictments, and I'm one of them."

I grip the back of the desk chair for support. I've had so much time to prepare myself for this moment, yet my knees feel as if they might buckle. "Oh, Bob..."

"The seven are—Mitchell, Ehrlichman, Colson, Strachan, Mardian, Parkinson, and me."

"Who are Mardian and Parkinson?"

"Lawyers for the CRP. Each of us is charged with conspiring to obstruct justice." Bob's voice is controlled, matter-of-fact. "And then there are individual charges on top of that."

"What are yours?" I'm not sure I really want to know.

"In addition to conspiracy to obstruct justice, mine are obstruction of justice and three counts of perjury."

So many? What do these terms mean? What exactly did Bob do?

The phone rings. "It's Wilson again," Bob mouths. "I'll fill you in on everything later."

As I turn to leave, I look back. Everything in this room imparts memories of Washington. Most of all, Nixon's inaugural quote. Today, the words blur as I try to make them out.

"Until he has been part of a cause larger than himself, no man is truly whole."

The quote, which has always seemed so noble, sounds almost ordinary. Right now, I don't even know what the cause is.

On my way downstairs, I stop to look out the window. Reporters and photographers are already assembling on our lawn. They remind me of sharks, milling around waiting for their prey. Bob joins me in the front hall. Reaching for the handle on the heavy oak front door, he says that Wilson told him that he should meet with the press. He is to answer all of their questions with, "no comment."

Dressed in his standard khaki pants and rumpled button-down shirt, Bob doesn't bother to change. He leaves Rufus inside with me and steps outside. The door closes behind him, momentarily separating his world from mine.

I can't think straight, and random thoughts fill my brain. *How can Bob possibly deal with the media right now? What are they asking him? Why didn't he change his clothes? He looks so grubby. I hate those suede Wallabee shoes.*

The door opens, a photographer's flash goes off, and Bob steps back in. His shoulders sag, and his frumpy clothes make him look tired. I wrap my arms around him, and he holds me close. Neither of us says anything.

How did we ever reach this point? What on earth went wrong?

Bob returns to his study, and I don't see much of him for the rest of the day. He's on the phone constantly, but he promises to go over everything later with the children and me. I'm relieved to see how relaxed he is when he and Rufus finally make their appearance in the kitchen. He even starts making dipping sauces for the beef fondue we are having for dinner.

Hot oil pops in a small pot in the center of the breakfast table. Turning down the flame, Bob looks over at Peter, Ann, and me. "I'm sure you have lots of questions, but first I want to make one thing very clear. I believe that I am innocent. I have never knowingly done anything illegal or morally wrong."

Bob stabs a piece of meat with a long fork and puts it in the hot oil. "You should also know that what the press calls a 'cover-up' and the grand jury calls

a 'conspiracy to obstruct justice,' I have always considered 'containment.'"
He pauses to twist his fork in the oil and then continues. "The White House
experienced many flaps besides the break-in, and it was my job to minimize
any fallout. In this case, I worked to contain the fallout from Watergate. I don't
think that I ever broke any law, and I look forward to proving my innocence
in court."

"What about the specific charges against you?" Peter asks.

"I was indicted for *obstructing* justice and *conspiring* to obstruct justice,"
Bob says. "The grand jury believes that I authorized the direction of money
to the Watergate burglars and the destruction of evidence. This is based on
John Dean's claim that I told my assistant Gordon Strachan to destroy wiretap
evidence—which is a flat-out lie. It's also based on the fact that I authorized
the transfer of three hundred fifty thousand dollars from a special fund in
the White House to the Committee to Re-Elect the President—and that
I participated in conversations about the burglars' requests for money. The
grand jury believes that I was aware of the payment of money out of that cash
fund—which I was not. I am also charged with three counts of perjury."

"So, they think that you lied, Dad?" Ann asks, helping herself to a mixture
of horseradish and soy sauce.

"Perjury is *knowingly* making a false statement, which I absolutely did not
do," Bob explains. "I was determined to tell the truth at the Senate hearings,
but it's obvious to me *now* that in trying to reconstruct my notes on the March
twenty-first tape, I got confused. I testified that the president said that it would
be wrong to raise money for the Watergate burglars, when in fact he used
those words in the context of granting them clemency. It was an accidental
misstatement on my part. It was not intentional."

"Why can't you just explain that you made a mistake?" Ann questions.

"Because I was asked if I were *sure* that the president said it would be
wrong to raise the money, and I told the senators that I was *absolutely positive*.
The grand jury concluded that I had deliberately lied to mislead them. They
also believe that I lied two other times. Once, when I testified that no one in
the White House was aware that funds were being used to pay the burglars
until March 1973. And another time, when I told the senators that I didn't
think there was any reference to Magruder's committing perjury on the March
twenty-first tape."

Bob patiently answers our questions. He knows that the children and I are apprehensive about the future and scared at the thought of his going through a trial and possibly going to prison. In time, the flame goes out under the fondue pot, but no one wants to leave as long as Bob is talking. He explains that the next step will be his arraignment in a Washington court. The charges will be read, and he will enter a plea of not guilty. At that point, he will have to report to a probation officer and forfeit his passport. He tells us that a trial won't be for several months. If he's found guilty, the next step is an appeal process.

When I climb into bed later tonight, my head is spinning. Next to me, seemingly calm and confident as ever, Bob works on a crossword puzzle before turning off the light.

"Goodnight, Bob," I say. "I love you."

"I love you, too."

◆

THE REPERCUSSIONS ARE IMMEDIATE. The media calls the grand jury's action, "the most sweeping single indictment of former government officials in US history." The Haldeman name is prominently featured in the news releases, and Bob's mother pastes every story she sees into her growing scrapbook. Even with all the negative publicity, her faith in her son never falters. When he tells her that he plans to make a public statement, Non is thrilled.

On Monday, March 4, Bob holds a press conference on our front lawn. This time, he asks me how he looks before stepping out to meet with the reporters. Wearing gray slacks with a freshly ironed, white button-down shirt, plaid tie, and dark green blazer, he gets my wholehearted approval. His small American flag is in his left lapel.

As soon as the front door closes behind him, I dash upstairs to the landing where I can look down on the scene below. Grabbing Bob's movie camera, I kneel on the window seat and press the lens against the leaded window to film the event. Rufus climbs up next to me, and a photographer takes a picture of the two of us peering out. It appears in the paper the next day along with Bob's statement, "I'm completely proud and completely appreciative of the opportunity to serve under President Nixon, one of the greatest presidents this country has had."

✦

ON SATURDAY MORNING, MARCH 9, Bob appears in the courtroom of Chief US District Judge John J. Sirica for his arraignment. Home alone, I think of him constantly and keep looking at the clock, wondering what's happening.

The phone rings, and I rush to get it. "The whole process took less than five minutes," Bob reports. "The seven of us were advised of our constitutional rights, the charges were read, and we all pleaded 'not guilty.'"

"Oh, Bob…"

"The worst came after we left the courthouse. A lot of hippies were lining the sidewalk just waiting to heckle us. That was not pleasant. They booed us and carried signs saying, 'Sieg Heil' and 'Throw away the keys.'"

It's a vivid scene, and I can't get it of my mind. The courthouse is only three blocks away from the White House, and yet the two are worlds apart.

When I hear that jury selection will begin six months from now, the thought of a trial is daunting. I have no idea what it will be like, and I fear the verdict. If Bob is found guilty, I'm told he could be fined $16,000 and face five years in prison for each of the five counts. *Twenty-five years in prison… This is beyond anything I could ever imagine.*

◆

THINGS CONTINUE TO CRUMBLE around Nixon. So far, Haldeman, Ehrlichman, Mitchell, Colson, Mardian, Parkinson, and Strachan have been indicted. Dean, Magruder, and Segretti have pled guilty to various crimes. In New York, Mitchell and Stans are on trial for obstruction of justice and perjury in connection with political contributions. In Washington, Dwight Chapin is under indictment for perjury. I can hardly keep up with the names and cases. Some are good friends; others, I've never met. Some I feel sorry for; others, I'm not so sure. I empathize with most of them and their families.

In mid-March, it becomes public knowledge that the grand jury named the president as an unindicted coconspirator in the Watergate cover-up. Senator James Buckley of New York says he doesn't see how Nixon can survive and calls for his resignation. The staunchly conservative Republican declares that an impeachment trial would turn the Senate into "a twentieth-century Roman Coliseum."

Nixon doesn't buckle under. In a press conference, he states, "While it might be an act of courage to run away from a job that you were elected to do, it also takes courage to stand and fight for what you believe is right, and that is what I intend to do..."

Bob rallies in support of the president. He's adamantly opposed to Nixon's quitting and shows me the short note he wrote to him. He quotes Pat Nixon's words to her husband in 1962, when he was considering resigning from the Eisenhower ticket:

> You can't think of resigning. ...if you, in the face of attack, do not fight back but simply crawl away, you will destroy yourself. Your life will be marred forever and the same will be true of your family, and particularly, your daughters.

In addition to the Watergate trial, Bob also has been named as a defendant in a slew of civil lawsuits:

> The Socialist Workers Party is alleging that Mitchell, Ehrlichman, and Haldeman violated its rights through wiretapping and mail surveillance.
>
> Jane Fonda is suing Nixon, Ehrlichman, and Haldeman for alleged violation of her rights through surveillance of her antiwar activities.
>
> Morton Halperin, a former Kissinger aide, has filed a suit against Kissinger, Ehrlichman, and Haldeman, charging that his civil rights were violated through wiretapping.
>
> Lastly, fourteen young people in Charlotte, North Carolina, have filed a suit against two advance men, the local police department, the Secret Service, and Haldeman. They claim that Bob instructed the security personnel at a Billy Graham rally to force out anyone they thought might demonstrate against the president.

Although the government picks up part of the tab on these civil suits, Bob still has to prepare for them and testify. This costs money, and with no income coming in, he proposes creating a defense fund. The thought of asking our friends for money disturbs me, and I disagree with the idea. It's hard to argue with Bob, particularly under these circumstances, but this time I tell him how I feel.

Expletive Deleted

April 1974

IN EARLY APRIL, BOB is asked to be a speaker at the annual gathering of the Young Presidents' Organization University in Acapulco, Mexico. With a trial pending, he needs to get court approval to leave the United States. Permission is granted, but Bob's not allowed to discuss Watergate or anything related to it.

"Half the people here simply want to see what he looks like and how he handles himself," a YPO leader tells the press.

Governor Ronald Reagan of California gives the keynote address, and Bob's talk is titled, "A Night with H. R. Haldeman." Appearing on a panel afterward, he freely answers questions. When asked if he and President Nixon were ever "chums," he responds, "No, but neither of us sought such a relationship or permitted it. It would have gotten in the way of an extremely good working relationship."

Bob predicts that the president will come out of this ordeal stronger than ever. "Not only will he unify the people behind him, but he will regain his credibility."

Bob's unwavering support for the president clashes with the resentment that John Ehrlichman feels. In an article appearing in the *Los Angeles Times*, Kenneth Reich writes that John believes he was deceived by Bob and Nixon, both of whom knew about the installation of the White House taping system.

Seated at the breakfast table, Bob reads the article out loud, while I make Ann's lunch for school. It pains me to hear that John has expressed "disenchantment with Nixon in private," and that he has had "something of a falling-out with his longtime friend and colleague, former White House chief of staff H. R. Haldeman."

"You know better than to believe everything in print, Jo," Bob says. "The only thing that's changed is that John and I both agree that we should each have our own lawyer. He'll get someone else, and I'll keep John Wilson and Frank Strickler."

"Is John mad at you?" Ann asks, taking her lunch bag from the counter.

"He's upset because he didn't know about the tapes when we worked at the White House," her father explains.

"Why didn't you tell him?"

"The concern was that if John and others had known, it would have affected their conversations."

"But you knew, Dad...and the president knew."

"Actually, I forgot," Bob says. "And I'm sure the president did, too. The tapes were for his personal use, and there was no need for anyone else to be aware of them. They were never meant to be made public."

◆

THE TAPES CONTINUE TO be a major issue. Following a request by the House Judiciary Committee for everything that's relevant to Watergate, the White House announces that the president will respond with a major speech. On Monday night, April 29, Bob and I watch in the family room as Nixon tells the country that he's turning over 1,200 pages of edited transcripts of private White House conversations. Pointing to several piles of bound folders on his left, he says that he realizes "these conversations will provide grist for many sensational stories in the press."

Puzzled, I look over at Bob. He remains fixed on the president, who goes on to explain. "I have been reluctant to release these tapes, not just because they will embarrass me and those with whom I have talked—which they will—and not just because they will become the subject of speculation and even ridicule—which they will—and not just because certain parts of them will be seized upon by political and journalistic opponents—which they will. I have been reluctant because in these and in all the other conversations in this office, people have spoken their minds freely, never dreaming that specific sentences...would be picked out as the subjects of national attention and controversy. …Never before in the history of the presidency have records that are so private been made so public."

When the speech is over, I feel defeated. In his third major speech on Watergate, the president has stated that there's reason to be concerned about what's on the tapes.

"Are you worried, Bob?" I ask.

"Nope," he says.

In the days following the release of the transcripts, I think about Bob's complacency. The media jumps right in, and soon snippets of conversations are being quoted out of context. These are candid and at times offensive. The term "expletive deleted" appears occasionally, leaving a lot to speculation.

Several major *pro*-Nixon newspapers call for the president's resignation in their editorials, while others go as far as endorsing his impeachment. Even the minority leader in the Senate, Republican Senator Hugh Scott, describes the White House discussions as, "deplorable, shabby, disgusting, and immoral." Joseph Alsop, a columnist usually friendly to the president, compares the atmosphere in the Oval Office to "the back room of a second-rate advertising agency in a suburb of hell."

It's disheartening to hear these descriptions coming from pro-Nixon supporters, and I'm embarrassed as I read portions of the transcripts. I worry about the effect of the "expletive deleted's" on other family members. Mother and Dad hide their discomfort by never mentioning the tapes or the transcripts. Non remains proud of her son and has no trouble defending the conversations. The children never bring up the subject.

Clearly frustrated, Bob says, "Look, Jo, Kennedy and Johnson taped conversations in the White House, and I can assure you that they didn't sound any different from ours. It's the way men talk. These were private discussions never meant to be made public."

Seeing my doubtful expression, he continues, "If only you and everyone else could listen to the hours and hours of tapes where the president discussed national and international affairs, then you'd see how truly presidential he can be. Unfortunately, *these* transcripts deal *only* with Watergate. In them, you see us at our absolute worst. We were in the middle of a major crisis, and we were floundering."

Giving an apologetic half-smile, Bob admits that their efforts to deal with Watergate were far from admirable and their language may have been crude at times.

May 1974

SHORTLY AFTER THE TRANSCRIPTS are released, they are published in paperback. Now that anyone and everyone has a copy, they are the subject of many lively discussions. When the Ehrlichmans join Bob and me for a five-day vacation in Palm Springs, we spend hours bemoaning their release. Jeanne and I are concerned about the negative impact of the less-than-presidential conversations. John continues to be upset that he had no knowledge of the taping system. Bob reminds us that it was installed to provide the president with an accurate record of what was said for his memoirs.

Bob is frustrated that the release of the transcripts has created a great distraction. The focus should be on the more important things the president is trying to accomplish. I'm more discouraged now than I have been in the past. I find nothing redeeming about the tapes, and I wish the president had destroyed them.

Although Nixon proposes comprehensive national health insurance in a radio address, it goes nowhere, and his public support continues to erode. By the end of the month, the House Judiciary Committee is warning the president that his refusal to turn over the actual tapes, rather than the edited transcripts, "might constitute a ground for impeachment." When Nixon doesn't comply, the Supreme Court agrees to review the matter.

Dwight Chapin is sentenced to ten to thirty months in federal prison. My heart breaks for him and his family. I know that it is extremely hard on Bob as well.

The Smoking Gun

June 1974

INDICTED WITH BOB THREE months ago, Charles Colson pleads guilty to obstruction of justice and is sentenced to one to three years in prison and a $5,000 fine. The president's popularity takes an unexpected upswing when he returns from a "triumphant" world tour. In Cairo, Nixon and President Anwar el-Sadat sign an accord in which the US will supply Egypt with nuclear technology. After attending the twenty-fifth anniversary of NATO, Nixon flies to Moscow, where he and Soviet Chief Brezhnev hold a third summit meeting and embark on a series of arms negotiations. As long as Nixon concentrates on foreign affairs, he gets high marks, fueling speculation that he might be able to regain his stature after all.

Sometimes I forget that there are other stories in the news. Mikhail Baryshnikov, the Soviets' premier ballet dancer, defects to the West, and former chief justice of the Supreme Court Earl Warren dies. After being abducted last February, Patty Hearst, heiress to the Hearst publishing fortune, is being held captive by the Symbionese Liberation Army. The Environmental Protection Agency orders gas stations to have at least one pump with unleaded gas, and string bikinis are the latest craze.

When Non asks me to join her and five of her grandchildren, including Ann, on a whirlwind American Express tour of Europe, I look forward to spending the month abroad. As we move from country to country, I'm amazed to see how little the Europeans care about Watergate. Invariably, they believe that the American public is overreacting.

July 1974

Non and I stay abreast of the news by reading the *International Herald Tribune*. In Nice, France, it's disheartening to see a picture of John Ehrlichman on the front page. Sitting on the boardwalk overlooking the Mediterranean, I read that he was convicted of conspiracy and perjury in the Ellsberg psychiatrist office break-in trial. I have tried not to think about Watergate on this trip, but reading this brings it all back. Suddenly, I feel very far away from home.

As soon as I return to Los Angeles, Watergate is front and center. The House Judiciary Committee approves three articles of impeachment, charging President Richard Milhous Nixon with obstruction of justice, abuse of power, and contempt of Congress. The last president to have impeachment proceedings brought against him was Andrew Johnson, 106 years ago. The Supreme Court rules that the president cannot claim executive privilege for the tapes, and he must surrender those that were subpoenaed.

Calling the Watergate scandal, "a shameful episode in the history of this country," the judge in the Ellsberg break-in trial gives John Ehrlichman the harshest sentence yet meted out—twenty months to five years. I feel John's pain when I read a description of his reaction in *The Nation*.

> Ehrlichman momentarily lost his usual steely grip on himself. Standing glumly erect as he listened to the judge's words, Ehrlichman returned silently to the witness table and reached out to steady himself on the back of his chair, then slowly sank down into his seat.

Former presidential lawyer Herbert Kalmbach goes to prison for six to eighteen months for campaign violations. Former secretary of the treasury John Connally is indicted on charges of bribery, perjury, and conspiracy.

In the meantime, Bob has found an agent and is working on a partial manuscript to submit to a New York publisher. He and Hank Saperstein hope to get a million dollar advance. When nothing materializes, Saperstein publicly admits, "It's not easy to promote a book about the Nixon White House by someone who's under indictment." His comment is discouraging, but Bob takes it in stride and continues working on his manuscript. I don't see how he does it.

August 1974

IN AUGUST, SUSAN IS clerking for an attorney in Red Wing, Minnesota, and both Hank and Peter are working in Los Angeles. Ann joins Bob and me and the four dogs at Bay Island for the month.

When my parents arrive at #11 for the weekend, the routine never varies. We hear the slap of Dad's flip flops as he works around the house and walks back and forth to the dock, checking on his boat. From the front porch comes the sound of Mom snapping off the ends of the string beans that we'll have with tonight's leg of lamb dinner.

On Friday, August 2, Judge Sirica sentences John Dean to prison for one to four years for his admitted role in the cover-up. Three days later, a big Watergate story breaks. The White House releases three more tape transcripts of conversations held in the Oval Office and the EOB on June 23, 1972, six days after the break-in. In one of them, Bob and Nixon discuss getting the CIA to tell the FBI to "turn off" its investigation into "the Democratic break-in thing."

The transcript reportedly links the president and his chief of staff to the "initial stages of the cover-up," and public reaction to it is strong. *Is this as bad as it sounds? How will it affect Bob's case?*

Outside, the wind is blowing, creating white caps on the bay. I know Bob would love to be out sailing, but he's deluged with phone calls. When there's finally a lull, he joins me on the porch.

"Don't jump to conclusions, Jo," he says, aware of my concern. "You've got to remember that the president and I were trying to keep the investigation from getting into other areas that had nothing to do with the break-in."

Although Bob remains calm and self-assured, I am not. It becomes clear that the president has two options—resign or fight impeachment charges on the floor of the Senate. In no time, this June 23, 1972 tape becomes known as the "Smoking Gun."

Is it possible that a conversation between Nixon and my husband *could bring the presidency to an end?* I am stunned.

I Do Not Want to Go to Jail

TENSION CONTINUES TO BUILD, and the weather changes. Tuesday, August 6, is hot. There's not a breath of wind, and the bay is as smooth as glass. The deadly calm feels ominous. Seeking relief from the heat, I set up a beach chair under an umbrella close to the water. Before long, Bob joins me. We're alone, and I can tell that he has something important on his mind.

"Ziegler just called," he begins. "He's sure the president's going to resign."

"Oh, no..." I catch my breath.

"I hope to talk to him before he makes up his mind. But first, I'd like to get your opinion."

"Yes?" I can't imagine what Bob is thinking.

"I plan to ask the president for a pardon. What do you think?" Bob avoids looking at me, focusing instead on two boys in kayaks having a water fight.

"A pardon?" I repeat. His suggestion comes as a surprise, and I need to collect my thoughts.

"Yes, a pardon...I do not want to go to jail." Bob enunciates each word precisely.

"You won't go to jail!" I blurt out. "You can't!" The thought of Bob's being sent to prison is abhorrent to me. Yet, I hesitate answering him.

Why? Why do I question Bob's asking for his own pardon? I think it's because I believe he's innocent. And the only place for Bob to prove his innocence is in a court of law. To pardon is to forgive someone for an offense. Doesn't asking for a pardon imply guilt?

"So?" Bob asks, glancing over at me.

I brush some sand from my arm. Looking up, my eyes meet his. *I owe it to him to respond truthfully—even though I can't fully explain my feelings.*

"A pardon would be extraordinary, Bob. If the president granted you one, all the uncertainty and fear that we're experiencing now would be gone. We could get on with our lives." My voice is firm, but now it falters. "It's just that... that...I feel you should not ask for your own pardon. To me...it implies your acceptance of guilt. Let someone else request it."

For a long while, Bob says nothing. Absentmindedly smoothing out an area of damp sand beside him, he uses a seashell to draw a set of ascending connected straight lines that resemble stairs.

At last, he speaks. "Actually, I was thinking that as his final act in office, the president should pardon everyone connected to Watergate and grant amnesty to all the Vietnam War draft dodgers. By dealing with the whole shebang in one fell swoop, he'd clear the slate for Ford." Bob studies his design and adds a few more "steps." "It may seem self-serving, but I honestly feel that the president would be doing the nation an enormous favor."

The more Bob talks, the more resistant I become. I tell him that I don't think the country would accept Nixon's granting both a general amnesty and blanket pardons. The president is under attack, and emotions are too raw right now.

Bob isn't persuaded, and our conversation peters out. Rubbing sand over his drawing, he tosses the shell into the water and heads back to the house. When I walk into the living room later, I find him talking on the phone to Al Haig. Explaining that he wants to discuss blanket pardons and amnesty with the president, Bob is put on hold. As he waits, I go into the bedroom to change into shorts and a polo shirt. The silence continues, and I start to tense up. Finally, I hear him say, "Thanks, Al. I understand." There's a click as he places the receiver back on its cradle.

I may question the premise for Bob's call, but it hurts me deeply to see him denied access to Nixon. Within minutes, he places other calls. He talks to his lawyers, John Ehrlichman, and Dwight Chapin, explaining to each of them his proposal to grant universal pardons and amnesty. John agrees to contact Julie Eisenhower and Rose Mary Woods, both of whom might be helpful in getting through to the president.

For the rest of the day, I feel out of sorts. Seeking support, I call my father. As a lawyer, he's greatly respected and noted for being fair and nonjudgmental.

"I don't understand your position, Jo," Dad says. "I've already written the president, asking him to give Bob a pardon. I think Nixon owes it to him, and Bob shouldn't hesitate to ask for one."

I'm taken aback by my father's answer. It causes me to have second thoughts. Bob and I are in agreement on most issues, and I am generally supportive of him. But in this case, I feel as if I am undermining him. I don't like to be in this position, and I wish I knew what to do. *What to say…*

◆

AT 7:30 A.M. THE next morning, the home phone rings while Bob and I are eating breakfast. When I answer it, a White House operator informs me that the president would like to speak to Mr. Haldeman. Bob takes the receiver and settles on a high stool next to the kitchen wall phone.

"Good morning, Mr. President," Bob begins, reminding me of all the times I've overheard this greeting in the past. "No, sir, it's foggy here." There's a long pause. "Yes, sir…I understand if you feel that you have to resign, but I think you're making a serious mistake." Bob's voice is firm and decisive. "However, if this is your decision, you know that I'll do everything I can to support you."

Shifting his position on the stool, Bob swings around so that he's facing the window in the upper half of the Dutch door. Outside in the turning basin, a small boat with three fishermen in it is anchored off the seawall. Each time they cast their lines, ripples move in graduating rings across the still water.

"Mr. President, there is one point that I would like to raise with you," Bob continues, slowly twisting the telephone cord around his left index finger. "I firmly believe that you should exercise your constitutional authority to grant pardons… Yes, sir…to all those who have been charged with any crimes in connection with Watergate. *And* I also think that you should grant amnesty to the draft dodgers at the same time. In wiping the slate clean, pardons should go hand in hand with amnesty."

Don't do this, Bob.

Bob doesn't falter. "For the sake of the country, and especially for the sake of your successor, I think it's imperative that you bring all of this to an end. I realize that my request is a minor point compared to what you're now facing, but I'd like to follow it up with a written recommendation as soon as possible." Bob presents his case as if it were a run-of-the-mill White House memo. It's cut and dried, impersonal. "I'll do that," he says, "and I wish you all the best… Yes, sir… Good luck, Mr. President."

Giving a heavy sigh, Bob hangs up the receiver and then stands and stretches. "Well, it's all over," he says, and his voice is hoarse. "Without congressional support, the president feels he can't govern the country. He's going to resign tomorrow."

"I'm so sorry, Bob. So very sorry." I can only wonder what must be going through Nixon's mind right now. So many memories…so many shattered hopes and dreams. Tentatively, I ask, "Do you think the president will grant the pardons and amnesty?"

"I doubt it," Bob says. "But it was sure worth the effort."

As soon as he finishes his breakfast, Bob gets back on the phone. In his race against the clock, he does everything he can to pursue his objective. First, he calls John to see if he's made progress in contacting Julie and Rose. Then, he asks his lawyers to send a memo immediately to the White House on the subject of pardons and amnesty. His last call is to update Al Haig on what's going on.

I sense that Bob is starting to act desperate, and it's more than I can bear. Stepping outside, I'm engulfed in a low layer of early morning fog. Everything is damp, and I can taste the salt in the air. At the side of the house, the American flag droops on the flagpole. Bob's Sunfish looks desolate on the beach, where he left it two days ago.

In an attempt to work off my frustration, I start sweeping the porch. Watching the sand disappear between the weathered wood planks gives me a sense of satisfaction. At least, I'm in control. The glass door slides open, and Bob steps out. I'm surprised to see him when he has so much going on.

"What's up?" I ask.

"I just got a call from the FBI," he says.

"What do you mean? Why?"

"One of their agents in Boston received an anonymous tip. Apparently, someone's planning to kill me tonight."

The broom slips out of my hand, and Bob catches it.

"Don't worry, Jo. It's not a big deal."

"Murder's not a big deal?" I ask weakly.

Bob grips my shoulders and looks at me. "I'm sure it was just a crank call. Everything's under control. Mr. Joyce, from the FBI's LA office, told me that he has already contacted the Newport Police. They should be arriving any minute."

"The police are coming?" I can't believe what Bob is saying. "The police are coming to Bay Island?"

Within the hour, Bob's protection arrives in force. Three Newport policemen appear to stake out the island, a Coast Guard boat cruises back and forth in front of our house, and a police helicopter hovers overhead. By noon, the island is swarming with activity. Bewildered-looking neighbors congregate in little groups, trying to figure out what's going on. All the attention exasperates Bob, who finally convinces the police to call off the boat and the helicopter.

"I can't just ignore this," Lieutenant Jim Spears says. "I'm leaving three plainclothes policemen here overnight. One will be stationed at the bridge, and the other two will be somewhere on the grounds. Don't worry. They'll be gone by eight tomorrow morning. I promise."

Meanwhile, rumors of the president's pending resignation are rampant, and several reporters show up at our door. At the same time, Peter calls from Los Angeles to report that the press is also gathering outside our home. He puts two of the reporters on the line, and I hear Bob tell each of them, "No comment."

The phone rings again. It's John Wilson confirming that Bob's memo requesting blanket pardons and amnesty has been delivered to the president. A neighbor taps on the door and breezes in. Oblivious to all that's going on, she proceeds to tell me how much she admires our family and presents me with an oversized green leather scrapbook of pugs. *Pugs? Of all times, why now?*

I am touched and thank her profusely. By nightfall, however, I have another concern. It's the policemen stationed on the island. It's a cool, foggy night, and at ten o'clock, I ask Ann to help me make gingerbread, while I put on a pot of coffee.

"Good grief. What's going on?" Bob asks, stepping into the kitchen.

"Mom thinks the policemen will get cold," Ann explains.

Bob shakes his head in disbelief. "I'm going to bed. The two of you are nuts."

Resignation and a Pardon

WHEN I STEP OUTSIDE to get the paper the next morning, the brick walk is damp from the heavy fog. Hesitating, I pick up the *Los Angeles Times*. Today—Thursday, August 8—is one day I'd rather not see the headline. But there it is: "Nixon Resignation Appears Imminent." I scan the article as I walk back inside.

> Nixon buckles under GOP pressure… Not enough support in the Senate to escape conviction if impeached by the House… Vice President Ford briefed by Nixon's chief of staff…

It is reported that the president will address the nation tonight to announce his resignation. *How can any of us understand the tremendous inner pain Nixon must be feeling? It's such a sad way to end his career in government. He was so proud, and he accomplished so much.*

Bob spends the day on the phone, still pushing for last-minute pardons and amnesty. I try to keep busy around the house, but what I really want is to be by myself. Late in the afternoon, I go for a sail in Hank's little Sabot. The sun is finally out, and its warmth feels good. I'm alone, and memories of Richard Nixon flood my mind. Some are personal; some, presidential.

I envision Nixon as a candidate, wildly waving his hands above his head in a "V for victory" sign. I see him as president, confidently striding down the steps of *Air Force One* to shake hands with Chou En-lai on Chinese soil. And I'll never forget the sight of him as the proud father of the bride, beaming as he escorted Tricia down the aisle in the White House Rose Garden.

For me personally, there's the memory of all of the White House receiving lines where Nixon would grip my hand and ask about my "drinking problem."

He loved his little joke. It was his anchor in an insecure world of social amenities and small talk.

Tonight, Bob, Ann, and I gather in the living room to watch Nixon give the last formal speech of his presidency. Promptly at 6:00 p.m., the president appears on the TV screen. Seated at his desk in the Oval Office, he looks up and gives a forced smile. In his lapel is a small American flag. Reading slowly and deliberately, he begins.

"This is the thirty-seventh time I've spoken to you from this office. Throughout my public life, I have always tried to do what was best for the nation."

Nixon tells us that without congressional support, he cannot continue as president. "With the disappearance of that base…there is no need for the process to be prolonged."

Then Nixon says the words that must be the most difficult he has ever had to utter. "Therefore, I shall resign the presidency effective at noon tomorrow."

I look over to see Bob's reaction. He doesn't flinch; he's engrossed in the speech. The president continues, "By taking this action, I hope that I will have hastened the start of that process of healing which is so desperately needed in America."

Referring to his inaugural address, Nixon reminds us of his promise to dedicate himself to the cause of peace. After mentioning his accomplishments, he concludes, "…To have served in this office is to have felt a very personal sense of kinship with each and every American. In leaving it, I do so with this prayer, 'May God's grace be with you in all the days ahead.'"

The president's image fades, and I check my watch. It took only sixteen minutes for Nixon to announce the most significant decision of his presidency.

Slowly rising from the couch, Ann addresses her father. "I'm really sorry, Dad."

Bob steps out on the porch, and I follow. The two of us stand in silence, side by side, looking at the bay. It's the Thursday night "beer can race," and a dozen sailboats glide by. Their giant, colorful spinnakers balloon out in front of them. In the distance, the hills are turning pink in the light of the setting sun. The sight of the slowly turning Ferris wheel at the Fun Zone is strangely poignant.

I feel empty. Not bitter, just terribly sad.

◆

AT 6:30 A.M., ON August 9, 1974, Bob and I are back on the couch again. This time, we're here to watch live coverage of the president's departure from the White House. The minute the Nixon family steps into the East Room, the US Marine Band plays "Hail to the Chief" for their last entrance. Three hundred members of Nixon's staff are gathered to say goodbye. Many are crying.

Standing at a podium, Nixon starts out awkwardly. He lacks his usual rigorous self-control and gives in to his emotions. Fumbling in describing the virtues of government service, he adds that in his administration "no man or no woman ever profited at the public expense or the public till."

The president's speech is disjointed and rambling. Squirming uncomfortably, I shift positions. While Nixon talks, I study the somber expressions on the faces of Tricia, Eddie, Julie, David…and…Pat. Poor Pat. Her eyes are swollen from crying, and yet there she is standing at her husband's side looking brave. I feel sorry for her. *Should I have made an effort to reach out to her long ago when Jeanne Ehrlichman expressed concern? Probably not. If there was going to be a personal relationship, it would have had to come from the president or Pat.*

Nixon goes on and on. He's almost irrational. He talks about his father and mother and finally concludes by saying, "Always give your best; never get discouraged; never be petty. Always remember, others may hate you, but those who hate you don't win unless you hate them. And then you destroy yourself."

At last, it's over. I'm relieved. It was truly painful to watch.

The scene changes to the South Lawn, where President and Mrs. Nixon are boarding the helicopter for Andrews Air Force Base. From there, the two of them will transfer to *Air Force One,* which will fly them across the country to California. At 12:00 p.m. Eastern time, Gerald Ford will be sworn in as the thirty-eighth president of the United States. At that exact moment, Richard Nixon will become a private citizen, and *Air Force One* will take on a new identification. Without the president on board, it officially becomes *SAM 26000.*"Well, that's it," Bob says in a resigned voice as he turns off the television. "Richard Nixon now has the dubious honor of being the first president in our country's history to resign." Bob shrugs and gives a weak smile. "In spite of everything, I'll always be proud to have served under him."

I find it difficult to be enthusiastic about President Ford's acceptance speech. It hurts to see how positively it's received. Referring to "a great new era," and "returning honor to the presidency" after "our long national nightmare,"

Ford casts shame on the Nixon administration, and I worry about how it reflects on Bob. I'm afraid that people will associate him with the "nightmare," when there was so much more to the Nixon presidency.

> As the aide departs from the White House, bloody but not quite bowed, he must watch with envy as the new president's team marches in—crisp, confident, eager to clean up the mess in Washington, to get the country moving again.
>
> —*The Presidents' Men* by Patrick Anderson

September 1974

BOB'S TRIAL HAS BEEN continued until next month. We return to Hancock Park, and the four children return to their various schools—Susan at Boalt Hall School of Law for her second year; Hank, a senior at UCLA; Peter, a senior at Harvard School; and Ann, a sophomore at Marlborough.

On September 8, thirty days after being sworn in as president, Ford grants Nixon a "full, free, and absolute pardon for all federal crimes he committed or may have committed." Explaining that "Richard Nixon and his loved ones have suffered enough," Ford adds that a fair trial by jury wouldn't be possible and that a presidential pardon will spare the nation any additional grief in this "American tragedy."

I believe the pardon is in the country's best interest, but public reaction to it is mixed. In general, it follows party lines, with many Democrats expressing outright anger. They want Nixon to stand trial, and some even accuse Ford of striking a deal with the former president. Republicans generally support the pardon. A number of our friends are annoyed that Nixon got off scot-free, leaving Bob and all the others to suffer the consequences.

"President Ford had no choice," Bob tells his mother and me during dinner at the Los Angeles Country Club. "To save the presidency, he *had* to pardon President Nixon. Nothing would have been accomplished by dragging him through the mud." A waiter sets down a plate of macaroons, and Bob takes two. "A trial would have been a big feeding frenzy for the media."

The day after Nixon is pardoned, the White House announces that it "has under study the issue of pardons for those accused or convicted of Watergate crimes." My heart skips a beat. *Maybe…just maybe…this is it. And best of all, a pardon would be coming from a third party. I'm excited. Bob won't have to face a trial. He can get a job and pay off his legal fees. The press will leave us alone. Our lives will finally return to normal.*

"Don't hold your breath, Jo," Bob advises. "President Ford hasn't acted yet."

A week later, Ford offers conditional clemency to the Vietnam War deserters and draft dodgers, but there are no pardons. Watergate is still dragging us along. On top of everything else, Bob's prospects for publishing a book dry up. After contacting fourteen publishers, his agent tells him that he won't be representing him any longer.

"The president's resignation put a lid on things," Hank Saperstein says. "Besides, Nixon's going to write his own memoirs. Who'd want to read Haldeman's version, if he could get Nixon's?"

Where does that leave Bob? He needs lawyers, and lawyers cost money. Household expenses, mortgage payments, and tuition for the children's schools cost money, too. Although he assures me that he gets some income from investments, I'm not sure where we stand financially.

"What are you going to do?" I ask, stepping out on our patio. Sunshine streams through the craggy branches of the Brazilian pepper tree in the center of the garden, and at its base, colorful pink and white impatiens are in full bloom. Bob is working at the glass-topped wrought iron table, with Rufus stretched out in the sun at his feet.

"I hate to tell you this, Jo, but at this point, my only option is a defense fund," he says. "I know how you feel about it, but take a look at this." Rummaging through a pile of papers, he pulls out a letter asking for contributions on Bob's behalf. It's signed by Z. Wayne Griffin, a well-known Los Angeles businessman and a friend of the family.

As much as I hate the idea of asking for money, I reluctantly agree. "You've got to do it, Bob." I see no other way out. The next day, Wayne sends his letter to 1,500 of his business associates, along with a financial fact sheet.

Friction Benefits Me

WHILE MEDIA HYPE OVER the upcoming Watergate trial grows daily, I'm only slightly aware of other world news events. After ruling in "opulent splendor" for fifty-eight years, Haile Selassie, emperor of Ethiopia, is unseated in a bloodless coup. Cyclone Fifi hits Honduras, killing ten thousand people. Alexander Haig is appointed NATO commander in Europe, and Betty Ford undergoes surgery for breast cancer.

Reporting one negative story after another, the press keeps pounding Bob. Woodward and Bernstein quote sources as saying that his request for a pardon was "threatening" and "tantamount to blackmail." When the two reporters write that Bob implied he would send Nixon to jail if he didn't get a pardon, Bob's lawyer publicly refutes the article. It's a valiant attempt by John Wilson, but I doubt if it does any good. *No one will read it. No one cares.*

Parade magazine states that "many White House observers accuse Haldeman of contributing to the fall of his boss by isolating him, abusing power, refusing to permit dissent, and surrounding himself with arrogant, ruthless, untruthful, paranoidal, subservient aides."

In his *San Francisco Chronicle* column, Herb Caen reports that Bob was "coldly" told that he would not be charged for dinner at Chez Panisse, because the restaurant wouldn't accept "tainted money." In reality, when Bob, Susan, and I were at Chez Panisse, the manager enthusiastically welcomed us and insisted that our dinner was "on the house." Bob left a generous tip.

In one newspaper, Jeanne Ehrlichman and I are described as "single-minded and ambitious like their husbands; never a part of Washington social life; and always aloof, close-mouthed, and mysterious... Official Washington, which never particularly liked them, gives both women high marks in their hour of trial."

It's been a long time since I have read anything positive about Bob. The press has built him up as such a villain that I don't see how he's ever going to get an objective trial.

◆

BOB PLANS TO BE in Washington for jury selection, which is scheduled to begin on the first of October. Although Susan has already started classes, she is going to take the term off. She wants to support her father by attending the trial and will take advantage of the unique opportunity to observe his lawyers at work.

I will join Bob and Susan when the actual trial begins. Knowing that it could last up to four months, I decide to split my time between Washington and Los Angeles. I plan to spend two to three weeks in Los Angeles, then two to three weeks in DC. That's a long time to be gone from home, and I don't like the thought of being so far away from the children. Hank lives independently, but I have to arrange for a housekeeper to stay with Peter and Ann. Neither they nor I are happy with this arrangement. I'm glad that they will be in school most of the time and that their grandparents are here to check on them.

When it comes time to pack, Bob has to resurrect his suits and winter clothes from the attic. Neatly arranging stacks of folded shirts, sweaters, and ties, he packs two suitcases. His suits go on hangers in a garment bag.

"This trial's going to be a charade," he says, when I enter our bedroom. "I don't know why I'm even packing for it. Sirica's a lousy judge, and it'll be impossible for me to get a fair deal."

"Why do you say that?" I ask.

"Sirica's not very smart. He's opinionated and doles out harsh sentences. People call him 'Maximum John' for a reason."

Bob's negativity is uncharacteristic and disturbs me. This trial is the greatest challenge that he's ever had to face, and it's important for him to think positively. The poem, "Friction Benefits Me," by Elena Goforth Whitehead is helpful to me, and I slip it into his suitcase. It reads in part:

No life is free of conflict and abrasion,
But I select the metal of my mold.

My attitudes are of my own persuasion,
Disturbed and hurt, or calm and self-controlled.

October 1974

IN ORDER TO PREPARE for the trial and find a place to live, Bob flies to Washington a few days before jury selection begins. A friend lends him a car, and in no time, he has rented a townhouse in Alexandria, Virginia. Unlike in political campaigns, Bob calls every night. I look forward to his report, but it's not like being there with him.

On the first day of jury selection, the judge orders a separate trial for Gordon Strachan. A photo of Bob arriving at court appears in the *Los Angeles Times*. The paper predicts that Nixon will cast a large shadow over the proceedings but will probably never appear personally. John Ehrlichman has subpoenaed the former president as a defense witness, and the prosecution wants to question Nixon about the tapes.

The *Times* also reports that there are "cracks in the once solid front of the White House 'twins'—Haldeman and Ehrlichman," who may break with one another. John is supposedly "seething" over the tapes and is convinced that Bob and the president "deliberately kept him in the dark and frequently discussed him behind his back." I hope that the story is exaggerated. I'm anxious to talk to Jeanne about it.

It takes the prosecution and defense lawyers eleven days to select a jury of nine women and three men. Susan arrives in DC in time to hear the judge give the jury instructions.

The trial is set to begin on Monday, October 14. With my heart in my throat, I say goodbye to Hank, Peter, and Ann and leave for Washington.

The New York Times/John Daly Hart

H. R. Haldeman testifying in his own defense. His lawyer is John J. Wilson, left. Judge is John J. Sirica.

Bob Haldeman testifying in the Watergate Cover-up Trial, November 29, 1974.
John Daly Hart, The New York Times

PART FOUR

THE TRIAL

An Arabian Tent and the Courtroom

IME MAGAZINE RANKS THE Watergate trial as "one of the ten or so most important events in the American presidency." Identified in court as *Criminal Case No. 74-110 United States of America v. John Mitchell, et al.*, it has five defendants: John Mitchell, H. R. Haldeman, John Ehrlichman, Robert Mardian, and Kenneth Parkinson. I've never met Mardian or Parkinson, the former assistant attorney general and the former counsel for the Committee to Re-Elect the President. I don't know why these five men are linked together. It compounds the case for each of them and is unfair.

If only Bob could stand trial alone.

It's intimidating to think about what lies ahead, but I love being back in Washington. I'm curious to see the townhouse that Bob rented in Arlington. When he stops the car in front of the three-story brick residence at 216 Wilkes Street, I'm pleased. A brick sidewalk is lined with trees whose bright yellow leaves shimmer in the early evening light. We are two blocks from the Potomac River, where a cluster of small boats lies at anchor in a protected harbor.

Although the scene is vintage New England, the interior of our new home is contemporary. Susan calls it a "bachelor pad," and Bob seems anxious to get my reaction. I can see why, as the three of us walk from room to room. There is a floor-to-ceiling fish tank in the living room, and the dining room has no windows. In keeping with its Japanese décor, the table is two feet off the floor with Japanese legless chairs, or *zaisus*. The master bath is black from top to bottom, and the coup de grâce is the master bedroom. It's an Arabian tent. Fabric with wild patterns of black, brown, and white swirls is draped from the center of the ceiling to the tops of the walls and then down to the floor, concealing the windows and doors. The carpet is white fur, and a smoky mirror covers the wall behind a king-sized mattress, which sits on the floor. Three over-sized pillows have been randomly placed around the room, and a three-foot tall, brass Turkish hookah stands in one corner. There is no other furniture.

"I hope you won't have nightmares," Bob says, giving a hopeless shrug. Groping the sheets that cover the door, he tries to find his way out. When he does, I follow.

October 14, 1974—Trial Day One

ON MONDAY MORNING, OCTOBER 14, I'm disoriented when I awake. Everything seems surreal. It's hard enough to accept the fact that Bob will be a principal defendant in a major criminal trial today, let alone that the two of us have just spent the night completely enclosed in futuristic brown, black, and white swirls.

The day gets off to a slow start. As I get up, I come face to face with myself in the huge mirror. I look tired and frazzled and immediately begin to worry about the impression I will make in court. Crawling around on all fours, Bob helps me make up the bed. Susan joins us for breakfast in the Japanese dining room, where I discover that stockings and heels don't make it easy to sit on a *zaisu* on the floor. The air is hot and humid when we step outside, but my hands are cold and clammy. I wish I felt more confident about what to expect in court.

Our transportation is an older model Checker cab, which a friend has lent us until we can buy a used car. When traffic slows to a crawl on the Fourteenth Street Bridge, Bob gets antsy, and his fingers nervously tap on the steering wheel. One block from the Capitol, he turns into the parking lot for the United States District Courthouse on Constitution Avenue. Spectators line the sidewalk, and a few of them snicker as we walk past. In the lobby, we take the escalator to the second floor and proceed down a long hall. Bob points to a closed door on the right.

"Over the next few months, we'll be spending a lot time in that courtroom," he says. "That's where the Honorable Judge John J. Sirica presides."

I tense up and grip Bob's arm for assurance. Across the hall, we enter a suite of three rooms which has been made available for the defendants and their attorneys. Bob and his lawyers have staked out the middle room, while the others use the larger and smaller rooms on either side. There are tables and chairs, a couple of desks, and a red, Naugahyde couch. Sunlight streams in through large south-facing windows that overlook the entrance to the building.

As soon as Bob, Susan, and I enter the room, John Ehrlichman and John Mitchell break away from their groups to greet me. After exchanging hugs, I tell them that I miss their wives. John M. jokes about his lonely life after his divorce from Martha, and John E. tells me that he and Jeanne have sold their house in Virginia and have moved back to Seattle.

Bob introduces me to Bob Mardian, Ken Parkinson, their wives, and the other lawyers. At 9:20 a.m., a marshal appears and asks everyone to follow him into Courtroom Two. The casual conversation subsides, and we collect our things and walk across the hall. With an uneasy sense of foreboding growing with each step, I keep my head down and focus on the granite floor. For a fleeting moment, I'm not sure if I want to be here after all.

Sirica's courtroom is crowded and buzzing with excitement as our group enters. Bob explains that the public sits on the left and the press and court artists are on the right. The trial will not be televised. We make our way down the aisle to the first two rows on the left, which are reserved for the families and friends of the defendants, witnesses, and attorneys. Glancing at his watch, Bob leaves to join his lawyers, and I take one of the few remaining seats in the second row.

Everyone around me is talking. They act as if this were a fun event. Reporters scrutinize our side of the room, and when their eyes rest on me, I straighten up. Although I feel insecure and alone, I try to appear confident. I focus on what is going on directly in front of me inside the rail.

I spot Susan sitting on a bench near a table where her father and John Wilson are conferring. I will be looking at the back of their heads during most of the trial. To the right are the other four defendants' tables. Centered on the back wall, the judge's seat faces the courtroom, with the court reporter and clerks in front of it. The prosecutors' table is in front of the jury box, which lines the left wall. In the far left corner, the witness box looks isolated and lonely.

At 9:30 a.m., the clerk's voice cuts through the chatter. "Will you all please rise." Susan looks over her shoulder and gives me a reassuring smile. A door in the back opens, and the stooped figure of Judge Sirica enters. I'm surprised to see how small and unimposing he is. As soon as he takes his seat, I expect the action to start, but it doesn't. Without the jury in the room, the lawyers haggle over legal issues, and the preliminary proceedings last for two hours.

At 11:30 a.m., the jury is finally called in, and I lean forward to get a better view of the nine women and three men who hold my husband's fate in their hands. I can feel a knot in my stomach as I search their faces for a revealing expression, but there is none. Each of them looks stoic and serious, and I wonder what they are thinking. According to a recent poll, 84 percent of the people in Washington are convinced that Mitchell, Haldeman, Ehrlichman, Mardian, and Parkinson are guilty.

At the prosecutors' table, Associate Special Prosecutor James Foster confers with four of his assistants. One of them stands and introduces himself to the court. Richard Ben-Veniste has a shock of jet-black hair and is wearing rimless glasses. He looks young and acts pompous, as he explains to the jury that it's his job to give the government's opening statement.

"The opening argument is like showing you the cover of a jigsaw puzzle box," he says. "When you see what the picture looks like, it will be easier to put the pieces together."

Ben-Veniste begins by describing the early morning break-in at the Democratic headquarters in the Watergate. The easel beside him holds a chart titled "The Cast of Characters," and I cringe when I see Bob's name on it. Ben-Veniste weaves an incriminating web as he works his way through a series of activities that occurred over a two-year time span. At every opportunity, he repeats the words "illegal" and "immoral." His voice drones on, and my head nods. To force myself to focus, I pull a steno pad out of my purse and start taking notes.

At 12:20 p.m., we adjourn for an hour and a half lunch break. The defendants, their lawyers, and family members return to the defendants' rooms. With an array of legal documents spread out on the table, Bob's three lawyers—John Wilson, Frank Strickler, and Ross O'Donoghue—decide to work through the break.

Bob, Susan, and I walk to Barney's, a nearby delicatessen, to get takeout lunches for the six of us. On the way back, we stop in front of the courthouse to watch a group of reporters in shirtsleeves playing football on the lawn. We exchange smiles, and a photographer from *The Washington Post* scurries over to take our picture.

The afternoon drags as Ben-Veniste goes through his chronology of events. To stay alert, I start taking notes again. Each time Bob's name is mentioned, I mark it with an asterisk. There are three asterisks:

*Magruder told Bob that burglars were caught in the Watergate.

*On Bob's orders, Strachan destroyed evidence in both his and Bob's files.

*Bob controlled a secret cash fund.

Concluding his remarks, Richard Ben-Veniste tells the jury, "Keep your eye on the ball following the evidence. You will find beyond any reasonable doubt that these defendants are guilty."

"The government must prove what it has said," Judge Sirica adds. "Just remember, the prosecution's opening statement isn't evidence." Court is adjourned at 4:35 p.m. It's been a long first day, but the upside of it is that I better understand what to expect in court.

Had by His Boss

THIS MORNING, THERE'S A large photo of Bob, Susan, and me on the front page of *The Washington Post*. All three of us look happy. I show the paper to Bob, who is trying to eat breakfast in our Japanese dining room. Struggling to get his legs under the table, he has knocked his placemat askew.

At the courthouse, a sense of camaraderie prevails in the defendants' rooms, and I enjoy talking with Bob Mardian and Ken Parkinson, as well as their wives. At 9:45 a.m., the jury is called into the courtroom, and John Ehrlichman's lawyer stands. Bill Frates is the first defense lawyer to give an opening statement. This can be done before or after the prosecution presents its case. Bob's and John Mitchell's lawyers have chosen to wait.

There's a hushed silence as people wait to hear what Frates has to say. *Is John really going to split with Bob and blame the president?* Frates' voice rises and falls in a steady cadence. Then, slowly and deliberately, he states, "President Richard Nixon deceived, lied, and misled John Ehrlichman...to save his own neck."

The words are sharp and angry. They leave no doubt as to what course John will be taking, and I feel as if a giant wall has come between him and Bob. I look for a reaction. John is bent over an artist's pad in deep concentration, and his pencil moves rapidly. Bob is leaning over his table, intently writing on a yellow pad. Neither of them looks up.

Frates continues. "President Nixon, who knew the full story, withheld it from Mr. Ehrlichman and prevented his recommended disclosure of the facts.

John Ehrlichman was forced to resign in order to take the heat. In simple terms, he was *had* by his boss."

Had by his boss? This is so different from John's testimony at the Senate Watergate Committee. At that time, he didn't know about the existence of the White House tapes, and he told the senators that he didn't apologize for his loyalty to the president any more than he apologized for his love of this country.

The jurors show no emotion, and I desperately want to know what they're thinking. "Stiff like martinets," I write. I wish I knew more about them. Bob tells me that when they were asked if they recognized any of the defendants during the selection process, one of the women had pointed to him. "I recognize that one," she had said. "But now he looks like a movie star."

Following a long discussion at the bench between the lawyers and Judge Sirica, Bob Mardian's lawyer stands to give his opening statement. Short and paunchy, David Bress gets off to a slow start. He becomes indignant and loses me as he goes on and on. I don't see how the jury can keep track of his presentation any better than I can.

When we leave the courthouse this evening, Susan vents her frustration. "It's ridiculous, Mom. Each of the five defendants expects the jury to track his side of the story, but that's impossible. Sirica won't let them take notes, and it's completely unrealistic for him to tell them that by being attentive they will remember everything."

As I prepare dinner, I keep thinking about John Ehrlichman's opening statement. It raises a lot of questions. *Was Bill Frates successful in portraying Nixon as the bad guy? If so, will it make the jury more sympathetic toward John? How will this affect Bob's case? I haven't noticed any change in his relationship with John, although the two of them don't spend much time together. They are with their lawyers virtually every minute.*

John Wesley Dean, III

October 16, 1974—Trial Day Three

I T'S POURING RAIN ON the third day of the trial. Clutching umbrellas, Susan, Bob, and I put our heads down and trudge from the parking lot to the courthouse. On our way, we pass a long line of people waiting to be admitted to the morning session. Only a few have umbrellas or raincoats. Most of them are soaking wet.

"Looks like everyone wants to see Dean take the stand today," Bob says as he steps to the side, attempting to avoid a large puddle.

John Wesley Dean, III, the thirty-five-year-old "hero" of the Senate Watergate hearings, is the government's star witness. With his amazing memory and precise recitation of details, he will provide the foundation of the prosecution's case, along with the White House tapes and transcripts.

Dean, tapes, and transcripts—it's a powerful combination. As I think about it, a gnawing feeling grows in the pit of my stomach. I wonder how the team of defense lawyers plans to discredit it. The tapes and transcripts will speak for themselves. Not only will the jurors *hear* Nixon and his aides intimately talking in the Oval Office, but they will be able to *read* every word. Using only those portions of the tapes that they want to emphasize, the prosecution will repeat them over and over, driving home each and every point.

Ken Parkinson's lawyer, Jake Stein, is first on the court agenda this morning. "Salt and pepper hair combed straight back," I write as Stein walks over to the lectern and arranges a stack of green note cards. His quiet, personable way of speaking makes his presentation easy to follow. I like him. Compared to Bill Frates and David Bress yesterday, Stein's opening statement is simple, clear and concise.

When I return to the courtroom after the break, I have to push my way through hordes of people to find a seat. The public benches are packed, and there are excited whispers about Dean's imminent appearance.

"John Wesley Dean, III." Jim Neal, the chief prosecutor, calls the government's first witness.

The name hangs suspended in the long silence that follows. Along with everyone else, I focus on the left door in the honey-colored, wood-paneled wall behind the judge. Nothing happens. We wait, and I watch the clock. At 11:22 a.m., the door opens, and a slight young man enters the room. Compared to Jim Neal's husky physique, the former presidential counsel looks bland and frail.

Frequently clearing his throat, Dean speaks directly to the jury as he answers Neal's questions. He gives a detailed description of a series of events in which he participated after the Watergate break-in. "Articulates his words precisely," I write. "Gestures a lot with his right hand. Long, slender fingers."

After lunch, there's a flutter of excitement when a chic, young woman enters the courtroom. Her platinum blonde hair is slicked back into a tight bun. "It's Maureen Dean," the woman behind me whispers in awe. The jurors show no reaction.

Removing oversized dark glasses, Maureen takes a seat on my bench. Glancing from her to her husband, I find my emotions churning. I'm angry with Dean, who sits there so complacently telling his story. I blame him for withholding information from Bob and the president. I blame him for putting his own self-interest first.

The scratchy sound of chalk on paper brings my attention back to the trial. Across the aisle from me, the court artists are sketching Maureen. Three of the artists have contraptions on their heads to hold their binoculars in place while they draw. The fourth wears a cartridge belt to hold her felt tip pens.

Dean's flat voice drones on throughout the afternoon. After the break, Maureen slips in next to me. The two of us stand together when Judge Sirica enters, and I can feel people staring at us. While the lawyers gather at the bench and the jury is out of the room, I introduce myself to Maureen and ask how she's doing.

"Okay," she replies. "I'm living temporarily with a friend in Chevy Chase. John's been in prison a little over a month, and I've only seen him three times. I hope Jim Neal will let me talk to him during the breaks."

In her beige wool skirt, tight black sweater, and gold jewelry, "Mo" looks sophisticated, and I have trouble picturing her visiting her husband in prison. A year ago, John pled guilty to obstruction of justice and received a sentence of one to four years. Instead of being incarcerated, however, he is being held temporarily at Fort Holabird as part of the government's "witness protection program." Located in Baltimore, Maryland, this "safe house holding facility" is a convenient place for the prosecutors to meet with him to discuss their strategy.

It's still raining when court adjourns. After a long, trying day, Bob and I retire early. When the doorbell rings at 10:00 p.m., it wakes us up. Startled, Bob throws back the covers and crawls out of bed. Feeling his way along the wall, he gropes behind the hanging sheets to find the intercom. I can hear him fumbling with the lever of the speaker.

"Who is it?" he asks groggily.

"I'm from the 'Style' section of *The Washington Post*," a woman's voice pleasantly explains. "Will someone please come down?"

"No," Bob answers emphatically, and there's a click when he releases the talk switch.

"Never?" the voice asks plaintively.

"Never," Bob repeats and turns off the speaker. I can hear him shuffling across the fur carpet, struggling to find the bed.

Thud. Something heavy hits the floor. "Damn!"

"Are you all right?" I call out. Bob sounded as if he were in pain. I can't see a thing in this tent.

"It's that stupid hookah. What a ridiculous thing to have in a bedroom!"

The heavy brass stand landed on Bob's bare foot, and I feel for him. And yet I'm so tired right now, it strikes me as funny. Suddenly, everything is funny. Not only this, but the Arabian tent, the fish tank, the Japanese dining room, the Checker cab, the late night visit from the journalist, and even the trial. I duck under the covers to suppress my snickers. It all seems so surreal. *What on earth am I doing here?*

Bedlam

A s Bob, Susan, and I walk to the defendants' rooms on the morning of the trial's fourth day, my heart falls. Dozens of shopping carts filled with white plastic bags line the marble hallway. Inside each bag is a headphone.

"I guess today's the day that we *get* to listen to the White House tapes," Bob says sarcastically.

At 10:15 a.m., the jury is called in, and Judge Sirica explains that a conspiracy is two or more persons who get together to knowingly accomplish an illegal act or a legal purpose by illegal means. John Dean takes his seat in the witness box. I look for Maureen, but I don't see her. During the break, John Wilson makes a point of telling me not to sit next to her if she comes today, because it sends the wrong message to the jury. I agree, but I have no control over where Mo decides to sit.

At 11:35 a.m., I write a single word in capital letters in my steno book, "BEDLAM," as members of the prosecuting team wheel in the shopping carts and haphazardly distribute headphones, along with transcripts of the tapes. Eager to get them, people shout out and raise their hands. The solemnity and dignity of the courtroom instantly changes into a circus-like atmosphere. In the end, everyone receives a white plastic bag. Not just the judge, jury, alternates, lawyers, defendants, and clerks, but family members, friends, reporters, artists, and the general public, as well.

There's a rustling of plastic as we remove our headphones from the bags and examine them. The monstrous, tan, cup-like ear pads are mounted on wide headbands, each of which has a long, twisty cord connected to it. After plugging this into a round metal outlet on the floor under our seats, we are instructed to listen to a ten-second test tape.

"Weird sight!" I write as I look around the room. John Ehrlichman's headphones are askew; Judge Sirica is still struggling to figure out how to put his on; John Wilson's look like a bonnet on his pink head; Bob's hair is slightly out of place; and the artists have their headphones perched on top of their binoculars. In the witness box, John Dean calmly looks over the transcript. His headphones are precisely in place.

When everyone is set, the courtroom becomes silent as we strain to make out the conversation on the first tape. The judge, jury, prosecutor, defendants, and their lawyers have been given transcripts to follow along. For those of us who don't have transcripts, the scratchy sounds and exaggerated background noises on the tape make it difficult to distinguish who is talking and what is being said. A pen grates on paper; a coffee cup clatters in its saucer; a chair squeaks; and a cough explodes in my ear.

The tape goes on for about an hour. In a discussion that took place on September 15, 1972 in the Oval Office, Dean gives a progress report on the Watergate investigation to the president and Bob. It's an odd sensation to hear their voices, and I feel like an eavesdropper. I also find that the swearing isn't nearly as bad as I feared it might be. With the exception of an occasional "damn," there are very few four letter words, and I never hear the "f" word. The term "expletive deleted," used in the transcript, is far more suggestive than the actual language.

Late in the afternoon, both Dean and the jury are excused, and there's a long discussion at the bench about calling Nixon as a witness. Although both the government and John Ehrlichman have subpoenaed him, Nixon's lawyer says the former president won't be able to appear for several weeks. He has been suffering from a flare-up of the phlebitis that has plagued him for many years.

Intense, Tedious, and Boring

October 18, 1974—Trial Day Five

Aᴇᴡ ᴏꜰ ᴛʜᴇ spectators hiss at John Ehrlichman this morning as he walks into the courthouse. It's hurtful to see this, and I look away. In court today, John Dean will be subjected to more of Jim Neal's direct examination. Standing at the lectern, the forty-six-year-old native of Tennessee addresses his star witness in a pleasant, Southern drawl. As he talks, he flips through the pages of a large loose-leaf notebook, which contains a multitude of yellow index tabs. His presentation is mesmerizing. To my surprise, I find that Neal has a certain folksy charm and is less abrasive than some of the other lawyers.

Later in the day, listening to the March 21, 1973, tape, I hear John Dean tell the president, "We have a cancer…within…*close* to the presidency that's growing." I pay close attention when Nixon says that "it would be wrong" to grant the Watergate burglars clemency. This is where Bob is supposed to have perjured himself at the Watergate hearings. He had *mistakenly* stated that the president had used those words, "it would be wrong," in discussing the payment of money, instead of clemency. I hope that the jury can see this as a mistake and won't regard it as an intentional lie—perjury.

When court is adjourned this evening, I find it hard to believe that we have completed the first week of the trial. On the drive home, I take stock of my reactions. *The court process can be incredibly intense, as well as tedious and boring. One moment, I'm afraid and apprehensive; the next, I'm laughing and enjoying the fellowship. Bob Mardian's opening statement is forgettable; Ken Parkinson's is memorable. Richard Ben-Veniste is brash; Jim Neal is a "straight talker." The tapes are extremely difficult to follow; the transcripts are inaccurate;*

and the "expletive deleted's" aren't as bad as I had expected. John Dean has an uncanny recall of the minutiae, and his testimony comes across as believable. It's difficult to face John Ehrlichman after he blamed the president and split with Bob. The benches are hard, and I hope Maureen Dean won't sit next to me.

◆

OVER THE WEEKEND, I catch up on the news. In Rabat, Arab heads of state call for the creation of an independent Palestinian state. Former president Nixon is in critical condition following an operation to prevent a blood clot from traveling to his lungs. President Ford and Secretary of State Henry Kissinger agree that escalating oil prices will lead to a worldwide depression. Racial violence breaks out in Boston's public schools, and Ford denies the governor's request to call in the National Guard. Defending his pardon of Nixon, Ford tells a House panel that there was "no deal."

October 22, 1974—Trial Day Seven

TODAY IS COOL AND crisp. Although a chilly wind penetrates our light coats as we walk from the car to the courthouse, Bob is in no hurry. When a young boy with a Polaroid camera asks to take his picture, he stops to pose. Autograph seekers hound him, and he obligingly signs "H. R. Haldeman" on whatever they give him.

Wearing a beige suit, John Dean takes his place in the witness box for the fifth straight day. At one point in his testimony, he quotes Bob: "Once the toothpaste is out of the tube, it's hard to get it back in."

After lunch, Jim Neal finally winds up his direct, and John Wilson is the first defense lawyer to cross-examine Dean. Bob's lawyer is raring to go, and his shiny, bald head is flushed in anticipation. I soon become apprehensive. After asking each question, Wilson wanders back to his table and then whips around and interrupts Dean's attempt to respond. Speaking in a flat, controlled voice, Dean has a wide-eyed, innocent look and remains unflappable. I find Wilson's theatrics disconcerting, and I worry that the jury may find them offensive.

Using a red felt tip pen to record my personal feelings, I write, "Dean maintains his cool…even when admitting he had concealed evidence after telling authorities for months that he had disclosed everything."

When Wilson belabors a point, Sirica tilts back in his chair and says, "Awright, let's get on with this."

"But, Your Honor," our crusty bulldog snaps back, "I've sat around here for five days waiting for this opportunity." John Wilson has known Sirica for over forty years and is aware of his "Italian temper." Apparently, one of his strategies is to provoke the judge into making a legal error that could be grounds for a mistrial.

I have trouble keeping track of Wilson's points, and I wish that he would follow up on the tapes. *Why doesn't he reinforce Bob's innocence and clarify his motives? He makes everything so drawn-out and complicated.* Feeling let down, I write one word when Wilson is through with his cross-examination: "TEDIOUS."

When we return to the defendants' rooms, I lag behind as Bob and the other lawyers gather around John Wilson to congratulate him. I'm surprised when Susan approaches me and admits that she, too, was disappointed. It's nice to have someone with whom I can share my thoughts, but we are careful about keeping our opinions to ourselves. Wilson is considered to be the best trial lawyer in Washington. His reputation is impeccable, and Bob's future depends on him.

October 23–25, 1974—Trial Days Eight–Ten

ON WEDNESDAY, OCTOBER 23, Bob tells us that Jim Neal approached John Wilson about a possible plea bargain. "I told them that it would be very hard for me to consider a plea," Bob says, "unless someone can show me that I did something illegal."

John Dean spends three more days being cross-examined by the other four defense lawyers. During this time, he confirms that he borrowed money from the $350,000 that Bob had transferred from the White House to the CRP. With no sense of wrongdoing, Dean states that he used the money to pay for his honeymoon and a new patio. I'm amazed and look over at Maureen to see her reaction. She doesn't flinch.

Friday is Hank's twenty-first birthday, and he's celebrating in California without us. I miss him and wonder when our family will be together again.

◆

TWO DAYS LATER, IT'S Bob's forty-eighth birthday, and John Ehrlichman joins us for dinner. Struggling to lower his large frame onto the Japanese *zaisu,* he jokingly asks Bob if he can't afford chairs.

"If you think that's bad, try sleeping in an Arabian tent," Bob counters.

Throughout the evening, both men are relaxed and chatty, but neither one mentions the trial. Although their legal defenses differ, as well as their perspectives on Watergate, it's obvious that they don't want these divergent views to affect their friendship.

As I watch the two of them interact, I'm reminded of how positive Bob has been throughout this whole ordeal. He's under as much pressure now as he was in the White House, but he is handling it differently. He is patient in court, remains upbeat, laughs a lot, and is more than willing to help out at home. His faith is upholding him, and I know that everything will be all right. No matter how this trial ends.

October 28, 1974—Trial Day Eleven

THE COURTROOM IS PACKED on Monday when the government calls its second witness, the infamous Howard Hunt. Considered the mastermind behind the Watergate break-in, Hunt is a former CIA agent. Wearing a rumpled, double-breasted, gray pinstripe suit, his stooped figure looks bedraggled. His voice is almost inaudible. I write, "sounds as if he has some teeth missing."

"When I was released from prison last January," Hunt testifies, "I had planned to reconstruct my life. However, in the spring of this year, I began to read the transcripts of the White House tapes, and I felt a sense of rude awakening. I realized that *these men* were not worth my continued loyalty…I resolved to make the hard decision to testify to the entire truth."

The derogatory reference to "these men" hurts. Although Bob has never met Hunt, I'm sure the jury doesn't realize it and has already linked the two of them together.

When court adjourns, I remain seated on the bench, staring at the empty witness chair. Hunt's testimony was damaging to Bob, and the sad memory of his slouched body has a lingering effect on me. I had expected to see a self-possessed, dispassionate CIA agent. Instead, I found a broken man. The last thing I write for today is, "I feel great compassion for this tragic figure."

October 29, 1974—Trial Day Twelve

IN ITS OCTOBER 29 issue, *People* magazine has a positive article about Bob, which is particularly nice to see after so much negative publicity.

> ...H. R. "Bob" Haldeman, forty-eight, has remained the most resolutely cheerful.... [He] still chats easily with spectators, and unflinchingly autographs copies of Woodward and Bernstein's *All the President's Men.* His newly modish hairstyle and modest sideburns have further softened the bristling, tough-guy image dating from his days as Richard Nixon's principal assistant.... [He] is considerably sustained by the unflagging support of his family, especially his wife, Jo, and his eldest daughter, Susan, twenty-three.... Susan dropped out of law school to attend every minute of the trial... The family has been... using borrowed cars and taxis to get to the courthouse.

On the other hand, John Molloy of *The Washington Star* writes one of the strangest articles about Bob.

> Haldeman was smart to get rid of his crew cut. It was typically fifties and sent out a message of those times when the blacks experienced great racial prejudice. In Haldeman's case, the crew cut said to the blacks, "I'm prejudiced."

If there's one thing I'm learning, it's that journalism isn't objective. It's filled with the biases and subjective opinions of the reporter. In the future, I don't think that I will ever accept a news article at face value.

Jeb Stuart Magruder

October 30, 1974—Trial Day Thirteen

L AST WEEKEND, WE BOUGHT a used 1969 Toyota. The little, yellow sedan doesn't have as much character as the Checker cab, but it's ours. Bob loves using its stick shift, which he has to do frequently on this morning's heavy commute across the Fourteenth Street Bridge. The air is warm and humid, and below us the Potomac River smells pungent and fishy. I'm hot in my black turtleneck sweater and tweed skirt. The skirt is itchy, and I notice that I already have a snag in my left stocking. I dislike having to dress up every day and wish that I could occasionally wear pants.

Jeb Stuart Magruder is the government's third witness. Sentenced to ten months to four years, Jeb is being held at Fort Holabird as part of the witness protection program, along with John Dean.

At thirty-four, Jeb joined the White House staff as special assistant to the president. During the 1972 presidential campaign, he moved over to the CRP as its deputy director. I know him personally and am anxious to hear his testimony. His youth and look of boyish innocence make it difficult to believe that he was convicted of perjury and obstruction of justice.

"Jeb's testimony flows easily," I write as Jill Volner, one of the young assistant prosecutors, questions him for the second day. "More personable than John Dean." When Jeb freely admits to lying to the FBI and the grand jury, as well as concocting the cover story for the break-in, he sounds glib. The more he talks, the more superficial he appears.

"Jeb's told so many different stories, he's unable to distinguish fact from fiction," Bob says during our lunch break. "His testimony's all over the place."

In the hallway, I run into Gail. Jeb's pretty wife is wearing a bright, periwinkle-blue suit, which complements her blue eyes. As soon as I see her, it's as if Watergate had never put a constraint on our friendship. Gail reminds me of the time I left a violet plant on her front porch, and I tell her about my attempt to write an open letter of support to the Watergate wives. She talks freely about how much her life has changed. She visits Jeb at Fort Holabird every day, and last week was their fifteenth wedding anniversary.

"It must be hard on you to watch Jeb testify," I say.

"Not particularly," Gail quickly replies. "You soon realize that it's all a game that the lawyers are playing with the defendant's life. You learn to accept it, and you do what you have to."

Gail's detached attitude surprises me. She's tougher than I expected. As the afternoon proceeds, Jeb links all five defendants to Watergate, and it's clear that his testimony will spare no one. He makes an effective witness for the prosecution.

On the way home this evening, Bob needs to review his files at the EOB. As we turn into the parking lot at the White House south entrance, I am beset by strong feelings of déjà vu. *How many times in the past have I parked my car here? How many times did I climb those back stairs to Bob's office?* This evening, it's different. Not only do we have to wait for the White House police to scrutinize our temporary passes, but we are not allowed to get out of the car until a member of the Secret Service is available to escort us across the street to the EOB.

Once we reach the fifth floor, the agent accompanies Bob into the attic room. Susan and I wait outside in the hot, stuffy hall for over an hour. She reviews her trial notes, while I try to read. At one point, we are allowed to peek inside the room. I see bare light bulbs suspended from the ceiling, a desk, chair, file cabinets, security camera, and two motion sensors. Bob has to sign in or out every time he goes through the door.

Walking back to the car, Bob chats nonchalantly with our security escort. In front of us, the White House is bathed in the soft light of an almost full moon. It looks majestic and grand. Memories flood my mind, and it's a deeply personal moment. *I wish so much that things had turned out differently.*

October 31, 1974—Trial Day Fourteen

TODAY IS MY FORTY-SIXTH birthday, and even with all he has on his mind, Bob remembers. In a drab conference room, surrounded by empty bookcases, files, and packing boxes, he and his legal team present me with a cake and sing "Happy Birthday."

An Island and a Monument

November 6–20, 1974

I HAVE BEEN IN Washington for more than three weeks, and I miss Hank, Peter, and Ann. It's not easy to live with our family split up like this; I want to go home. With things proceeding slowly in court, Bob agrees that it's a good time for me to take a break. I plan to return in time for John Wilson's opening statement.

On November 6, I fly to Los Angeles for a much anticipated two-week stay. Once I settle in, it's easy to slip into my old routine. I am happy to be back with family and friends, and the days pass quickly. When the time comes for me to return to Washington, the hardest part is once again leaving Peter and Ann with the housekeeper.

Bob and Susan meet me at Dulles, and from there we drive to Arlington, Virginia. The townhouse in Alexandria was sold while I was in California, and Bob has rented a small, two-story brick home at 722 Cleveland Avenue. Although it only has two bedrooms and one tiny bathroom, I prefer it to the bachelor pad with its bizarre décor. Pointing to a vase of flowers on a table in the living room, Bob tells me that our landlady gave it to him, with a note saying that he adds class to the neighborhood.

In the master bedroom, there's a small desk with Bob's papers and books piled on it. Here, he reviews his legal documents and reads the Christian Science Daily Lesson. The poem I gave him, "Friction Benefits Me," is propped up against the desk lamp.

November 21, 1974—Trial Day Twenty-Nine

IT'S OVERCAST AND COLD this morning, and I expect to see snow when I push aside the ruffled white curtains at the bedroom window. Instead, there is nothing but a few barren trees and piles of dry leaves.

I find it's hard to adjust to being back in court, and I have trouble concentrating. It's frustrating to hear that John Wilson probably won't be giving his opening statement for another week. This means that I could have stayed in Los Angeles longer.

While we're listening to a tape of a conversation between Bob, John Ehrlichman, and Nixon, a reporter in the press section laughs and is reprimanded by the federal marshal. Annoyed, I glare at the reporter. He returns my look with a smart-alecky grin.

I'm out of sorts all morning, and things don't get any better in the afternoon. With the jury out of the courtroom, John Wilson reacts when the judge rules against him.

Pouting, he glowers at Sirica. "That's for my error bag, Judge, and it's already bursting at the seams."

"You mean your wind bag," Jim Neal fires back. "Actually, it's for your 'ferty bag,' which is two pounds of manure in a one-pound bag."

Everyone laughs, and Wilson quickly responds, "I've been listening to this product of the Moonshine District of Tennessee for eight weeks now, and I'm getting tired of it."

I'm irritated. The lawyers are fiercely competitive in everything they do and say, and their one-upmanship often comes across as pure theatrics. They play to the press and the public. This trial has serious consequences for the five defendants, and it disturbs me when the lawyers seem to lose sight of this.

As soon as court is adjourned, I'm anxious to leave. Feeling discouraged, I stop and quietly remind myself of the "Friction" poem. *"My attitude is of my own persuasion."* Am I going to allow myself to be *"disturbed and hurt"* or do I remain *"calm and self-controlled"*?

◆

I WELCOME THE WEEKEND. On an unusually balmy Sunday afternoon, Bob, Susan, and I take off for Theodore Roosevelt Island. The tiny eighty-eight-acre patch of land in the middle of the Potomac River is an ideal place for the three of us to get away from the stresses of court. Following a dirt path through the naked woods, we don't do much talking. In this serene spot, the only sign of the outside world is the rumble of airplanes above as they approach and depart National Airport. The trial seems very, very far away.

Before returning home, we pay a visit to the Lincoln Memorial, which is a sharp contrast to the solitude of Roosevelt Island. Surrounded by crowds of noisy, enthusiastic tourists, I stand at the base of our sixteenth president's towering, seated figure. Across the Reflecting Pool, the Washington Monument is bathed in the pinkish glow of the setting sun. Experiencing the same sense of peace I had earlier, I find the view both beautiful and moving.

Don't Be Absurd, Jo

November 25, 1974—Trial Day Thirty-One

THIS MORNING, THE PROSECUTION finally rests its case. While the lawyers for Ehrlichman, Mardian, and Parkinson believed that it was more effective to give their opening statements before the prosecution's case, the lawyers for John Mitchell and Bob decided to wait until now.

At 3:50 p.m., Bill Hundley addresses the court on behalf of John Mitchell. Calling John the fall guy for Watergate, he tells the jury that, "Mr. Mitchell's loyalty and belief in his president kept him from blowing the whistle on the Nixon White House." It's late, and I note that the jurors don't appear to be paying attention. Hundley's words seem to be lost on them. I hope the jury will be more alert when John Wilson gives his opening statement tomorrow.

On the way home tonight, we drop the Toyota off at the dealership to repair a loose engine mount. Returning to the house in a rental car, we discover that the washing machine is broken. Things are not going well.

November 26, 1974—Trial Day Thirty-Two

THE COURTROOM IS PACKED this morning, and there's a noticeable air of anticipation. When the jury enters at 10:00 a.m., I take out a fresh steno book and fold back the cover. All eyes are on John Wilson as he slowly walks over to the lectern and puts down a single legal pad. Whistling to himself, he pulls over a file cabinet filled with backup material. Bob's lawyer has everyone's undivided attention.

"May it please the court, ladies and gentlemen of the jury..." John speaks deliberately as he outlines what he plans to include in his opening statement. Separating his chronology into chapters, he begins.

"Chapter One: Before the Break-In; Chapter Two: Shortly after the Break-In; Chapter Three: The Need for Money..." Soon the chapters start to blur, and the chronology drags. The courtroom is especially hot, and I can't concentrate. No one can. Across from me, an artist yawns, and in the jury box, a juror's head nods. After the break, half of the reporters don't return.

"Mr. Haldeman did not enter into a conspiracy and did not intend to enter into a conspiracy..." Wilson concludes at 11:30 a.m. and sits down.

I'm at a loss. In the beginning, Bob's lawyer had a captivated audience, but I'm afraid he lost them with his long, confusing presentation. There was too much detail. Even if the jurors had been allowed to take notes, I don't think they could have followed him. Most of them look bored.

This afternoon, when John Mitchell takes the stand for his direct examination, things don't get any better. Wearing a brown suit, brown tie, and yellow shirt, he looks frumpy. His voice is faint, and he doesn't have his usual twinkle. In contrast, Bill Hundley is hurried, and his words are jumbled. Headphones are distributed, and we are subjected to another tape.

"J. M. should use a mike," I write. "The room is too hot, and juror number four is asleep."

At 4:15 p.m., court adjourns. It has been a disappointing day, and I want to leave as soon as possible.

On the way home, my feelings get the best of me. Turning to Bob, I blurt out, "I wish *you* could have given your own opening statement. You don't mince words, and you speak to the point."

"Don't be absurd, Jo," Bob replies. "You know absolutely nothing about legal tactics. John Wilson really knows his stuff, and I'm darn lucky to have him as my lawyer."

I can understand why Bob feels this way. It's essential for him to believe in his lawyer and to agree with his tactics. I spoke without thinking and regret being critical.

November 27, 1974—Trial Day Thirty-Three

WHEN I STEP OUT to get the paper this morning, the thermometer shows only twenty-eight degrees, and there's a layer of ice on the front walk. In an article about the trial in *The New York Times,* I read that Wilson's opening statement was "long and low-keyed."

In court, yesterday's lackluster performances are noticeably replaced by the vitality of the chief prosecutor as he strides up to the lectern. Baiting John Mitchell with a slew of cutting remarks, Jim Neal begins his cross examination. His attack lasts four hours and is so intense he doesn't even pause when he accidentally knocks over a glass of water. With water spreading across his papers and running down the side of the lectern, Neal calmly finishes up.

◆

THERE IS NO COURT on Thanksgiving, November 28, and for the first time I can remember, we aren't having a turkey dinner. Instead, Bob, Susan, and I have meat patties, lima beans, and cottage cheese in our little dining room.

No one knows where we will be at Christmas, but I'm determined to have our family together at that time. I make reservations for Hank, Peter, and Ann to fly to DC if the trial is still going on. Bob, Susan, and I have reservations to return to California if it's not.

Bob's Day in Court

November 29, 1974—Trial Day Thirty-Four

FRIDAY MORNING, I WAKE up with butterflies in my stomach. Today, Bob will be called to testify. The word is out, and the line of spectators at the courthouse is already long. People nudge each other as we walk past, and press photographers jostle to take Bob's picture. He is relaxed and stops to sign autographs.

So much is riding on Bob's testimony today. While he seems to be enjoying himself, I can feel a knot tightening in my stomach.

In the defendants' rooms, I'm surprised to see Jeanne Ehrlichman. She tells me that she plans to be here for both Bob's and John's testimonies. The courtroom is packed. I want to find a good seat, but I end up off to the side in the second row, where I can't even see the witness box. Recognizing my dilemma, a friend of John Mitchell gives me his seat on the front bench.

At 10:50 a.m., John Wilson calls Bob to the stand for his direct examination. Leaning forward, Judge Sirica asks Wilson, "I take it you're not going to make an opening statement?"

"I hope everyone remembers that I already made one," Bob's lawyer tersely responds.

Following this exchange, Bob is sworn in. He looks clean-cut and handsome in his Repp tie and Phelps-Wilger suit with his little American flag in the lapel. Gripping the edge of the bench, I'm more nervous than I thought I would be. I desperately want Bob's honesty, loyalty, and competence to come across. I love him, and I want others to see my husband as I know him.

Whistling softly to himself, John Wilson adjusts his heavily magnified glasses and walks over to the lectern.

"Mr. Haldeman, can you tell the court where you reside in Los Angeles?"

Bob's expression is blank. Following a long pause, an embarrassed smile spreads across his face. I'm mortified. *Could it be that he's forgotten our address?* Richard Ben-Veniste snickers.

Finally, Bob speaks. "Sorry," he apologizes. "I've moved around a lot recently. My home address is four-four-three North McCadden Place."

Answering the rest of Wilson's questions without hesitating, Bob succinctly describes the structure of the White House staff, as well as his job as chief of staff.

"I had no independent schedule of my own during my four and a half years in the White House," he explains. "I operated as the one person who was totally available to the president at all times, day and night."

As the day progresses, Ben-Veniste does his best to create a distraction by posturing and trying to look bored. He languishes in his chair, while Wilson questions Bob about the FBI and the CIA. Assistant Prosecutor Jill Volner yawns and looks at her watch. Bob ignores their theatrics and continues to hold the jury's attention. He denies having any involvement in raising hush money for the Watergate burglars. He tells the jury that he did not authorize the destruction of documents, nor did he intentionally seek to obstruct justice.

At one point, Ben-Veniste objects. "That's a leading question, Your Honor."

Wilson fires back, "I haven't asked a leading question in four hours, and that's a pretty good track record."

Mr. Hoffar, one of the jurors, straightens up and intently follows this exchange. He appears to be amused by Bob's lawyer, which I hope is a good sign.

When court is adjourned, I want to throw my arms around Bob's neck and congratulate him, but he is quickly surrounded by lawyers. It's been a long day, and I was impressed with my husband. His answers were clear, and I don't see how anyone can fault him. In my daily call home, I give our families a glowing report of Bob's first day on the stand.

The next morning, *The New York Times* reports, "Mr. Haldeman appeared confident and spoke in an eager manner, leaning forward and speaking close to the microphone."

December 2, 1974—Trial Day Thirty-Five

BOB'S MOTHER AND BROTHER arrive over the weekend in the middle of a violent thunder storm. Their plane is buffeted by lightning and torrents of rain, which is a frightening experience for everyone—except Non, who is so focused on Bob and the trial she remains undaunted by the weather.

This morning, it's still raining hard. As Bob, Non, Tom, Susan, and I slosh through puddles on our way to the courthouse, we are hit by a heavy gust of wind. Stepping into the foyer, four of us look totally bedraggled. But not Bob. Every hair is in place.

"Does your barber travel with you?" Tom quips.

Bob laughs. "With a little time and hairspray, you, too, could have the same effect."

In the courtroom, I take a seat between Non and Tom in the front row. When Bob comes in with his lawyers, he smiles at us, and Non excitedly jabs me with her elbow. Jim Neal comes in late, having been delayed by the storm. When he sits down at the prosecutors' table in front of us, Non nudges me again. Every time she moves, her charm bracelet jangles noisily. People are starting to look at us, and I feel conspicuous. Non is oblivious. The jury enters, and when one of the jurors looks in our direction, Non excitedly whispers, "I think that woman knows that I'm Bob's mother."

"Shhh," Tom says, "You're attracting attention, Mom. Take off your bracelet."

After Bob is seated in the witness box, John Wilson steps up to the lectern. In typical fashion, he softly whistles as he leans down to organize some papers in the large file box next to him.

"Why's he whistling?" Non asks.

"I don't know. It's a habit he has," I whisper.

Continuing from where he left off last Friday, Wilson proceeds with his direct examination of Bob. Time drags. He loses me when he quotes from various conversations, memos, and tapes.

"Etc…etc…yawn," I write.

"What's the relevancy of this?" Ben-Veniste asks, leaping up from his seat.

"If Mr. Ben-Veniste will sit down for five minutes, he'd learn the relevance," Bob's fiery lawyer retorts.

"Your Honor? May I ask Your Honor a question?" Bob interjects.

"No," Judge Sirica snaps back. "Wait for counsel."

Following a few more exchanges between Wilson and Ben-Veniste, Sirica scowls. "I'm not going to let you engage in these little side remarks. We used to have a judge here who would say something once, and if you didn't abide by it, you would be on your way to that little jail behind this court." The judge pauses, and his voice becomes stern. "Do you understand what I mean?"

Tom gives me a surprised look, and his mother leans over and whispers, "Is it always like this, Jo?"

"No, Non," I tell her. "It's *not* always like this."

When court adjourns for lunch, Bob's sister joins us. We have been expecting Betsy since early this morning, but her red-eye flight from Los Angeles was delayed by the storm.

Back in the courtroom, John Wilson does a good job of wrapping up his direct, and I'm less critical of him. After spending all morning on tedious testimony, he is able to capitalize on it. He ends by asking Bob a series of questions. Did he knowingly enter into a conspiracy? Did he intend to enter into a conspiracy? Did he intend to obstruct justice? Did he intend to conspire with John Mitchell or John Ehrlichman to give false testimony?

Bob looks directly at his lawyer and each time answers, "No, sir, I did not."

Four Days of Cross-Examination

L ATE IN THE AFTERNOON, it's Richard Ben-Veniste's turn to cross-examine Bob. He stands and places a thick, black three-ring notebook on the lectern. With red tabs marking points of reference, it's intimidating.

"Please give 'yes' or 'no' answers to my questions, Mr. Haldeman," Ben-Veniste begins.

"Yes, sir," Bob acknowledges.

"How many people were you chief of?"

A grin flashes across Bob's face. "I can't answer that with a 'yes' or a 'no.' I must explain."

"Good for you, Bob," Non says under her breath.

Ben-Veniste's questions come fast. "Did you have an interest in detail?" "Who were your assistants?" "Did you determine who went in to see the president?" "You were very close to Mr. Nixon? No question about that."

"No question about that," Bob confirms.

"You agreed to tell the grand jury everything you knew, Mr. Haldeman, and yet you never mentioned anything about the White House tapes. Was it your hope that they wouldn't be revealed?"

"It was not a matter of my hopes," Bob replies, looking straight at the jury. "I was under orders from the president of the United States not to disclose the taping system. Those were my instructions."

There are times when Bob can't remember a specific conversation or date, and he has to answer, "I can't recall." When he does this, Ben-Veniste rolls his eyes in exasperation.

Throughout the afternoon, Bob remains unruffled by the assistant prosecutor's questions and theatrics.

December 3, 1974—Trial Day Thirty-Six

SIRICA'S COURTROOM IS SO crowded, the marshal has to ask some people to move in order to accommodate our family. At 9:40 a.m., the jury is called in, and Bob is seated in the witness box. Looking pleased with himself, Ben-Veniste sizes up his audience and approaches the lectern. With an exaggerated flair, he fingers a red tab and opens his black notebook to where he left off yesterday. Focusing on the White House tape transcripts, he reads selected portions of conversations out of context, which distorts their meaning. Then he summarizes Bob's answers, deliberately drawing the wrong conclusion.

"Weren't you concerned that the money you had transferred to the CRP showed a direct link between the burglars and the CRP?" Ben-Veniste asks.

Bob tries to respond, but Ben-Veniste interrupts him. "Sir, I'm not through," Bob says, looking up at the judge.

"All right, let him finish," Sirica instructs the assistant prosecutor.

When Bob takes his time explaining, Ben-Veniste puts his head down in despair and leans against his file cabinet.

"Your Honor," he states, "I'm not getting to ask too many questions. I told the court that I would be through by Wednesday, but that won't be the case if Mr. Haldeman continues to give such long answers."

Ben-Veniste is not happy. With the jury out of the room, he complains to the judge, "Mr. Haldeman's answers are wandering up and down the lot. They're breaking up the rhythm of my cross-examination."

"I don't care if this interferes with his rhythm," Wilson interjects.

"If Mr. Haldeman were charged with verbosity, he'd certainly have to plead guilty," Jim Neal counters.

Court is adjourned for lunch. Returning from McDonald's, we overtake the marshal on his way back to the courthouse. Next to him is a short man with a black fedora pulled down over his face. He is stooped over, and his hands are stuffed into the pockets of his heavy black raincoat.

"How were the Big Macs?" Tom asks good-naturedly.

The two men smile as we walk past them.

"Do you know who that was?" Bob asks.

Tom grins. "A member of the Mafia?"

"Nope," Bob says. "His Honor, Judge John J. Sirica."

It's cold in the courtroom when we return, and the jurors look more alert than they did earlier. As Bob answers a question about the $350,000 in the

White House fund that was transferred to the CRP, Ben-Veniste impatiently walks up and down in front of the jury.

Bob stops talking and stares at him. "Sir, I will wait for you."

Returning to the lectern, Ben-Veniste replies, "I'm listening."

At another point, Ben-Veniste questions that payments to the Watergate break-in defendants were made for "humanitarian reasons."

Admonishing the jury not to place any emphasis on the judge's questions, Sirica asks, "Why did you use the term 'humanitarian reasons,' Mr. Haldeman?"

"I doubt that I did," Bob replies.

"Doesn't the payment of any funds to the defendants bother you?" Sirica questions.

"Very much so," Bob says. "Particularly in recent months."

There's laughter, but the man seated behind me doesn't think the remark is funny. I hear him mutter under his breath, "I don't know if I want to stay and listen to this Haldeman guy continue to lie."

I clench my hands and feel my knuckles tighten. This man has no knowledge of the facts, and I resent that he can be so quick to pass judgment. I'm concerned that Bob can come across so believable to me, and yet that's not the case with others. I worry about how the jurors see him.

Ben-Veniste is increasingly frustrated as Bob modifies his answers. "I can't recall... I can't answer that when you take little bits and pieces out of the transcript... I just don't see it that way... I have to go back to explain... I didn't use that tone of voice."

When we are walking to the parking lot after court, Bob complains that the worst thing about the trial is having to be respectful to Richard Ben-Veniste.

"It takes everything I've got to address him as, 'sir,'" he says dejectedly.

December 4, 1974—Trial Day Thirty-Seven

"Good morning, members of the jury," Judge Sirica says on the thirty-seventh day of the trial. Once again, Non, Betsy, Tom, and I are seated in the family section on the bench, and Bob is in the witness box. Richard Ben-Veniste is at the lectern. This time, he's clutching the tape transcripts, which are bulging with notes held in place by paper clips.

"In respect to the tapes, Mr. Ehrlich...er...Mr. Haldeman," he begins, correcting himself.

Bob glances at John and cocks his right eyebrow to mimic John's typical quizzical expression. John smiles and returns the look.

The assistant prosecutor quotes from the March 21, 1973, tape, zeroing in on the president's remark, "It would be wrong." Nixon was referring to granting clemency to the Watergate burglars, but Bob mistakenly testified at the Senate hearing that the remark, "It would be wrong," was in reference to raising a million dollars for the burglars.

As Bob explains his error, Ben-Veniste drums his fingers on the lectern and repeatedly looks at the clock. When Bob concludes, the assistant prosecutor asks him if he took notes during the meeting.

"I may have," Bob answers. "But I don't remember seeing them, and I can't find them, so maybe I didn't take notes."

"Was it hard to access your files, Mr. Haldeman?"

"Access wasn't hard," Bob replies. "The difficulty was in trying to review my papers with two or three Secret Service agents always in the room with me. They were constantly talking, making phone calls, and smoking, and as my wife will testify, I don't work well under those conditions."

The jury looks in our direction, and Non nudges me. "He's talking about you, Jo," she whispers.

Returning from the morning break, I write in red in my notebook, "Morning was tedious. Bob seemed subdued. BV's aggressiveness probably paid off... *if* the jury was following."

Things are slow as the morning drags on, and several jurors look sleepy. There are long lapses of time while Ben-Veniste pauses to look over a transcript. Reading portions of it out of context, he then asks Bob to verify conclusions that are contrary to Bob's recollection of the events.

John Wilson objects, and Judge Sirica states that if the defendants want the full tape played, they can do so at the time of their rebuttal.

"That's unfair," Non says in a loud, agitated whisper. Betsy and Tom nod in agreement.

Looking in our direction, Sirica scowls. "I realize some members of... out in the audience don't like my ruling. But that's the way it is. Everything's settled. Let's proceed."

At lunch, Bob and Susan caution me that the judge's remarks about "the audience" were directed at our family. I explain that it's hard not to react when the prosecution is allowed to make so many distortions and Bob is denied the opportunity to correct or clarify them.

In the afternoon, the jury is alert and seems to be paying close attention to Bob's answers. During the break, the court clerk tells him that he has never seen a witness hold the jury's attention like he did.

"You always make everything so clear," Non says. "I don't see how anyone can believe those awful things 'Bona-testy' keeps saying about you."

"It's Ben-Veniste, Mom," Tom interjects. "Ri-chard Ben Ven-is-te."

On the news tonight, ABC opens with a picture of Bob, Susan, and me standing at a side door of the courthouse. "Haldeman's difficulties began when he tried to get in a little used side door," the commentator states. I have no idea what he's talking about, but, as always, it has a negative spin.

December 5, 1974—Trial Day Thirty-Eight

RICHARD BEN-VENISTE'S CROSS-EXAMINATION OF Bob continues for the fourth day, and the jury seems to be paying close attention. Ben-Veniste continues to distort the transcripts by reading selected passages. When Bob answers the questions, he takes his time and speaks with authority.

"Are you finished?" Ben-Veniste asks at one point.

"The answer to your question is, 'no,'" Bob responds.

Sirica repeatedly allows the assistant prosecutor to make long statements and won't let Bob explain or clarify. In my notebook, I write, "This is becoming an inquisition."

John Ehrlichman's lawyer asks to the approach the bench. When Sirica says, "No," Bill Frates requests that the record reflect the denial. The judge relents. "All right, approach the bench."

"FRUSTRATION!!" I write in red. "I'm on the verge of getting up and leaving…"

After Ben-Veniste completes his cross-examination, three of the other defense attorneys question Bob. John Wilson waives his right to redirect examination. At 11:20 a.m., Bob is finally excused. Other than a few character witnesses, his defense has concluded.

Next, it's John Ehrlichman's turn.

John Daniel Ehrlichman

THIS AFTERNOON, WE HAVE a change of pace when Ehrlichman's lawyers call Charles Wendell Colson to the stand as a "court witness." The forty-three-year-old former White House special counsel pled guilty to obstruction of justice and received a sentence of one to three years. He is being held temporarily at Fort Holabird, along with John Dean and Jeb Magruder. This is Chuck's first public appearance in court, and as a court witness, his credibility is not vouched for by any of the parties in the case. Both the defense and the prosecution are apprehensive about what he might say.

When Chuck takes the stand, the defendants' concerns are justified. His testimony is damaging to all five of them. If anyone is pleased, it's the chief prosecutor. Beaming, Jim Neal exclaims, "If Mr. Ehrlichman's other witnesses are like Mr. Colson, I'd be inclined to bring them all in here myself."

Mary McGrory writes in her column in *The Washington Star,* "Even Richard Nixon's long-suffering, erstwhile press secretary was moved to call [Charles Colson] 'a cobra.' Why a defense lawyer would call [him] from prison and set him loose at the Watergate conspiracy trial is unfathomable. The results were predictable. All of the defense [lawyers] were practically jumping on their chairs to get out of his path."

Chuck's testimony is a blow to John's defense, which receives another setback when Sirica rules that Nixon will not be called as a witness in this trial. John has always believed that the former president's testimony is indispensable to his case.

December 9, 1974—Trial Day Forty

ON MONDAY MORNING, WE stop on the way to court to mail our Christmas cards. I didn't write any personal messages this year. Our lives are so public everyone knows what has been going on.

Non, Betsy, and Tom flew back to California over the weekend, and I miss them. As Bob, Susan, and I walk through the parking lot, we pass two young men exchanging autographs.

"I'll trade you two Ehrlichmans for a Haldeman," one of them says.

In court, the lawyers spend most of the morning arguing among themselves while the jury is out of the room. When John takes the stand in the afternoon, I'm seated next to Jeanne. In order not to distract her during his testimony, I don't take notes.

Slouching in the witness chair, John looks dumpy as he peers over his rimless glasses. At the same time, his lawyer, Bill Frates, seems unprepared and ill at ease. Throughout his direct examination, he often changes subjects and interrupts his client. His "long list of rock bottom" twenty witnesses disintegrates, and the tapes he wants to submit as evidence can't be played until a technician arrives.

During the afternoon break, Jeanne tells me that she worked all weekend trying to organize John's papers, but there was only so much she could do. "Bob had plenty of time to prepare," she says, "but John didn't. As soon as he was found guilty in the Ellsberg trial, he had to start all over again on this one. John was a broken man when he walked into Sirica's courtroom." I try to be encouraging, but there's not much I can say. The situation is awkward.

Leaving the defendants' rooms this evening, Bill Frates sums it up when he jokingly admits, "I should have gone to med school...if I could have gotten in."

December 10, 1974—Trial Day Forty-One

JEANNE'S WORDS STAY WITH me, and I can only imagine how hard this trial must be on her. While Bob appears calm and collected, Jeanne describes John as emotionally wrung out. She admits that he seems to be distancing himself from her. While Bob and I are closer than we've been in a long time, the two of them appear to have stopped functioning as a team.

This afternoon, Bill Frates continues with his direct examination. He isn't as nervous as he was earlier, and he makes fewer untimely side remarks and jokes. Wearing a blue-gray suit, blue shirt and dark blue tie, John looks more put together than he did yesterday. The courtroom is completely silent as Frates guides John through his waning days at the White House and asks him to describe his last meeting with Nixon.

"The president asked Bob Haldeman and me to come up to Camp David together," John says in a low, unsteady voice. "After we arrived, he called Bob to meet with him at his cabin first. Then, it was my turn."

Following a long pause, John's face flushes, and his voice cracks. "Nixon and I talked on the terrace for a while, and then we moved inside. He said, in substance, that this was a very painful conversation for him. He was obviously very emotionally upset."

Frates interrupts. "How could you tell?"

"Because the president broke down at one point and cried."

Reliving this experience is agonizing for John, but he keeps going. "The president said that I had been, or tried to be, his conscience. I replied that I hadn't been as effective as I would have liked. He said that, on reflection, my judgment was correct." John stares at the wood railing on the witness box and then looks over at the jury.

"Nixon asked if there was anything he could do for me, and I said that sometime I would like him to explain to our children…" John stops. Unable to complete his sentence, he reaches for a cup of water. "Excuse me," he apologizes. "I'm sorry."

"Mr. Ehrlichman, would you like me to call a brief recess?" Sirica asks.

In an attempt to compose himself, John removes his glasses. "Excuse me," he repeats.

His eyes fill with tears, and I can't look at him. I'm overcome with sympathy, and at the same time, I'm uncomfortable. It's hard to see a grown man cry. Bob is looking down, and I wonder what he's thinking.

The judge calls for a twenty-minute break. The jury exits, filing by the slumped figure in the witness box. John looks the other way.

When court continues, Frates tries to change the subject, but John interrupts him. "It's important for me to finish my last sentence," he says, clearing his throat. "When the president asked if he could do anything for me, I told him that he could explain to my children…" He stops again, and there's another long, agonizing pause before he can continue, "…explain to my children…*why* he was asking me to leave." John studies the jury and then adds, "That basically was the end."

Staring at a crumpled candy wrapper under the bench in front of me, I feel confused and uncomfortable. This isn't the John that I knew. I always thought of him as the Rock of Gibraltar. Smart and confident, he definitely had an air of cockiness. He was also sensitive and seemed to have the ability to balance the demands of the White House with the needs of his family. John was the only person I ever thought I could to turn to if I needed to talk to someone about my relationship with Bob. *Maybe I didn't really know him. Has he changed? Is Jeanne right when she says that John is a broken man?*

At this moment, I feel so very, very sorry for him. And for Jeannie, too.

From One Ham to Another

December 11, 1974—Trial Day Forty-Two

TODAY, I START ON my third steno book. Between its gray-green cardboard covers, there are eighty blank pages, and I can't imagine how or when this saga will end. Note-taking continues to keep me focused in court and helps me retain what transpires. As I review what I have written, it reinforces my conviction that there is no way this can be a fair trial. Without permission to take and refer to notes, it's impossible for the jury to track and remember the individual cases of the five defendants.

The first thing I write this morning is, "Susie had dinner last night with Jamie Wyeth." The son of Andrew Wyeth, the well-known American artist, often attends the trial where he sketches people and scenes. His drawing of Susan is a remarkable likeness.

◆

AFTER JOHN EHRLICHMAN'S DISPLAY of emotion yesterday, I'm apprehensive about his cross-examination in court today. When he takes his place in the witness box, however, he looks composed. His jacket is unbuttoned, and he's leaning back comfortably in his chair.

Gathering up his papers, Jim Neal exudes an aura of confidence as he walks over to the lectern. Using John's own words as ammunition, Neal repeatedly asks him if he wanted to get the truth out as Watergate developed. On one occasion, Neal quotes John as saying, "umm humm, umm humm," as if he were agreeing with the president.

Interrupting, John says, "I'm not sure I said, 'Umm humm,' in quite the way you 'umm hummed' it."

"How did *you* 'umm humm'?" asks Neal.

"I made a noise that was essentially noncommittal."

In several instances, John aggressively counters Neal's attack with caustic remarks, but he also compliments him. He tells the chief prosecutor that he's artful, and he appreciates the job that Neal is doing. "And you're doing it very well," he adds.

At the end of the day, I write, "I believe John is coming out better on the cross than he did on the direct."

◆

OVER THE NEXT COUPLE of days, the lawyers for Bob Mardian and Ken Parkinson present their cases. Although I hardly know these men, I continue to take extensive notes. It's hard to stay engaged, and every now and then, my head nods. *How alert is the jury?*

◆

IT'S THE WEEKEND, AND Bob, Susan, and I buy our Christmas tree. When we return to our home in Arlington, Bob builds a fire in the living room fireplace, using wood he received as a gift from one of his lawyers. With a light snow falling outside, the three of us string garlands of popcorn and cranberries to go on the tree, along with red and white candy canes. Bob tapes a yellow paper star on the top. It sits at an angle.

December 17, 1974—Trial Day Forty-Six

HANK IS THE FIRST of our children to arrive in DC for the holidays. On Tuesday, I'm eager to have him join me in court, where Sirica is on the warpath, "Tyrant," I write, explaining to Hank that the judge wants things to move along faster. Word is, he has plans for a cruise at the end of December. There's no indication that the trial will be over by Christmas, and the jury turned down his suggestion that they sit on Saturdays.

In the defendants' rooms, the atmosphere is relaxed, and there is more socializing than usual. Hank is surprised at all of the camaraderie. At one point, Ken Parkinson's mother tells Bob that one of her friends *swears* he wears a toupee.

"Nope," Bob replies, placing a chair directly in front of her and sitting down. While the other defendants and their lawyers gather around, he leans forward and asks her to test her friend's theory.

Yanking hard on a few strands of Bob's hair, Mrs. Parkinson enthusiastically declares, "It's real!" The rest of us cheer.

December 18, 1974—Trial Day Forty-Seven

IN DECEMBER, GOVERNOR NELSON Rockefeller is sworn in as vice president, filling the vacancy created when Gerald Ford became president. The national jobless rate rises to 6.5 percent, the highest level of unemployment since 1961. In London, a bomb explodes in Harrod's, causing considerable damage. An earthquake in Pakistan kills 4,700 and injures 15,000. At the age of eighty, one of radio's most enduring stars, comedian Jack Benny, dies.

At the trial, the esprit de corps in the defendants' rooms continues, and on December 18, Jim Neal suddenly appears. Sporting a sheepish grin, he's clutching a big cigar in one hand and cradling a Virginia baked ham in the other. Everyone swarms around him.

"From one ham to another," the chief prosecutor says, presenting the ham to John Wilson.

"I can't believe how laid-back everybody is," Hank comments.

"It'll be different tomorrow," his father tells him. "It's Neal's turn to crank up the heat."

Artfully Weaving the Web

December 19, 1974 — Trial Day Forty-Eight

I T'S SNOWING. OUTSIDE, IT'S a gentle world of white, as tiny flakes silently fall to the ground. Inside, Sirica's courtroom is packed, and the anxiety mounts. After forty-seven days and eighty witnesses, it's time for Jim Neal's closing argument. As Hank and I take our seats on the bench, I can't help but compare the relaxed atmosphere of yesterday to the stress of this moment. Today, there will be no jokes about toupees and hams, no back-slapping or big cigars.

The action starts after lunch. Moving swiftly and efficiently, the chief prosecutor arranges large, yellow charts on an easel. "Mr. Neal," Judge Sirica comments, "You're so eager to get started, you're like a race horse at the gate."

At 2:50 p.m., the jury is called in. Looking serious in a gray three-piece suit and blue shirt, Neal faces the jurors. "After twelve weeks, I'm sure you know who I am," he begins. "I stand up here today to represent the United States of America… Perjury, obstruction of justice and conspiracy to obstruct justice are all involved in this case… I'll tell you what this was about. It was too much money…"

Giving a scathing denunciation of "defense attempts to pass off hundreds of thousands of dollars paid to the Watergate burglars," Neal talks about "hush money." He tells the jurors, "There has been an effort to beguile you, repeated over and over again,"

Neal then lights into Bob. "In one of the saddest chapters in the two-hundred-year-long glorious history of the United States, defendant Haldeman has a conversation with the then-president in the sanctity of the White House."

After reading from the transcript of the meeting between Bob and the president on June 23, 1972, Neal quotes Bob's explanation of the attempt to use the CIA to obstruct an FBI investigation, "It was to avoid political embarrassment."

"What a lie!" Neal shouts. "Can you imagine?"

A shiver runs through me, and Hank asks if I'm okay. I didn't realize how much I would need him for moral support. His presence is reassuring.

Neal thumbs through a large stack of index cards. "Now let's see what Mr. Ehrlichman said on the stand," he says sarcastically. "Mr. Ehrlichman just sat there. Do you really believe that he didn't know what was going on? He knows what's going on twenty-four hours a day. You can tell from his demeanor."

The chief prosecutor grips everyone's attention. He points an accusatory finger. He pounds the lectern. His face expands and contracts like rubber during his various mood changes. One moment, he's pensive; the next, concerned; then, angry. With a dramatic flourish, he flips the pages of his chart, and the jurors lean forward to get a better look.

This is Jim Neal at his best. Using every ploy he can, he artfully weaves the web that is the government's case.

Court is adjourned at 5:10 p.m., and I remain motionless on the bench. Having taken seven pages of notes in small print, I feel emotionally and physically drained. "I'm worried," I confess to Hank. "Jim Neal's a real spellbinder. I think he captivated the jury with all that drama and sarcasm. How can anyone top him?"

Hank stands and stretches. "Let's hope John Wilson will in his final argument tomorrow."

December 20, 1974—Trial Day Forty-Nine

JOHN WILSON IS ONE of Washington's best trial lawyers, and today we are counting on his passion, self-confidence, and expertise to convince the jury of Bob's innocence. And yet, today of all days, Wilson announces that he's tired. I am upset. I don't understand why he didn't pace himself better.

My frustration grows throughout the morning as Jim Neal continues to hammer away at each of the defendants in his final argument. Explaining that the 3,700 hours of White House tapes are unique in the history of litigation, he uses selected portions of them to scorn Mitchell, Haldeman, and Ehrlichman.

"You have heard the voices of three of the defendants," Neal says. "You have heard them talk as the cover-up begins to crumble. You have heard them scramble for position and develop lines and scenarios." Dropping his voice, he continues, "Tragically, these conspiratorial conversations have happened in the hallowed halls of the White House, where once strode such giants as Jefferson, Jackson, Lincoln, the two Roosevelts, Eisenhower, Kennedy."

Next, Neal compares the quotes of Lincoln and FDR to one of Nixon's. "With malice toward none and charity for all," he recites in a revered tone. "We have nothing to fear but fear itself," he states dramatically. Then, he throws up his arms and says indifferently. "Give 'em an *hors d'oeuvre*, and maybe they won't come back for the main course."

Watching his performance, I cringe and look over at my son, who is seated on the bench next to me. Although nothing in the tapes is new to Hank, I'm uncomfortable having him hear Neal quote the president in such a demeaning way. Absorbed in the chief prosecutor's summation, he seems to be intently following every word.

Later, Hank leans over and whispers, "Neal's going light on Parkinson. I'll betcha Ken's going to get off."

When we adjourn for lunch, I have a lot of frustration bottled up inside of me, and I'm not eager to mingle with the other defendants. Meeting up with John Wilson in the hall, I can no longer contain my feelings.

"John," I say, looking down on Bob's lawyer who is a couple of inches shorter than I am, "I don't mean to be speaking out of turn, but please consider making your final argument short and simple. Just stress Bob's innocence. Please don't complicate things."

A hand grips my shoulder, and Bob gently pulls me away. He shakes his head, indicating that he disagrees with what I'm saying. His confidence in his lawyer never seems to waver, and I immediately regret interfering.

The courtroom is cold when we return. At 1:29 p.m., John Wilson steps up to the lectern. The jury is seated, but several reporters are still straggling in. Although Wilson whistles under his breath and acts confident, I'm apprehensive. His final statement has to be clear and convincing. The jury has to understand it and believe it.

Wilson begins by complimenting the jurors on their attention and recognizing their sacrifice in serving. "Trial lawyers are the surgeons of the law," he explains. "My approach this afternoon will be different from that of my illustrious opponent. I want to start out in a haphazard fashion."

Haphazard fashion? Oh, no. This is exactly what I had feared. What's next? Slumping down on the bench, I try to follow as Wilson refers to the Handbook of Jury Instructions and the Precepts of English Law. The jurors stare blankly ahead. Jim Neal pours himself a glass of water.

"Having gone over these abstract principles," Wilson continues, "I now want to discuss in chronological order the conspiracy charge against Mr. Haldeman."

I straighten up. Perhaps, he can pull this off after all—but that doesn't happen. Starting with the Watergate break-in on June 17, 1972, Wilson rambles on for two and a half hours. I have eight pages of notes written in small print, including:

> *Juror 2 is asleep... Wilson has lost me... He knows the case too well... Goes into too much detail... Confusing... Oh, dear... Heck.*

At 5:00 p.m., court is adjourned for the weekend, and I close my notebook. I look over at Hank, who shrugs his shoulders in resignation. Without saying anything, the two of us stand and walk out of the courtroom together.

◆

ON SUNDAY, DECEMBER 22, Peter and Ann arrive for a week's stay over the holidays. For the first time in three months, our whole family is together and I feel complete. Although our small two-bedroom house is a tight squeeze, we make it work. The biggest challenge for Bob and me is sharing the one bathroom with our four grown children.

December 23, 1974—Trial Day Fifty

THE TOYOTA IS TOO small for the six of us, so once again, we borrow the Checker cab to transport everyone to court. Bob and I are enormously proud of our children. It's special to have all four of them attending the trial today, and I enthusiastically introduce our newest arrivals to the defendants and the lawyers.

In the courtroom, Frank Strickler, John Wilson's partner, gives the closing argument on Bob's three perjury charges. Although I think his presentation lacks punch and won't be remembered, both Peter and Susan say it's effective. When we adjourn, Judge Sirica wishes the jury a Merry Christmas, and John and Jeanne dash out the door to catch a cab to the airport. They plan to spend the holiday with their five children at home in Hunts Point, Washington.

◆

COURT IS RECESSED FOR two days. On December 24, we wrap gifts, attend the 5:00 p.m. Christmas Eve service at St. John's Episcopal Church in Washington, and return home for a traditional turkey dinner with all the trimmings. Before going to bed, we put our presents under the tree and place our socks on the hearth. Later, Bob and I play Santa, filling them with a variety of goodies purchased at the last minute from the local drugstore. Unfortunately for me, my small Peds sock liner holds very little.

Christmas is different this year. But somehow it works. It doesn't matter what the circumstances are, as long as the six of us are together.

December 26, 1974—Trial Day Fifty-One

COMING DOWNSTAIRS ON THURSDAY, December 26, I feel as if Christmas never happened. Dressed for court, I walk past the living room, where the tree is the only indication of yesterday's celebration. Its needles are starting to turn brown, and the paper star is missing. Hank has taken off to ski at Vail, and Ann plans to visit a friend for the day.

As soon as I enter the defendants' rooms this morning, I miss John Wilson's commanding presence. Bob tells me that he's getting some much needed rest at The Homestead, a resort in Virginia. The jury is called in at 9:45 a.m., and Bill Frates stands to give John Ehrlichman's closing argument. Jeanne is seated next to Peter and me.

"I want to record this for our children word for word," she says, taking out a pad and a pen from her purse.

Frates talks, and Jeanne writes like mad all morning. After lunch, he is still talking, and she is still writing. Sirica looks impatient and tells the jury, "It doesn't look like we will finish today. If we sit late, we can get rid of as many arguments as possible."

Did the judge really say that? In front of the jury? At least they turn him down, and court adjourns at 5:15 p.m.

A Jar of Jam

FRIDAY, THE COURTROOM IS packed. Ann and I have to share a small space on the bench, while Peter sits on one of the chairs that have been set up in the aisle. The morning is spent on Parkinson's final argument.

After lunch, the government presents its rebuttal. I can feel my heart pounding as Richard Ben-Veniste stands. For some reason, Bob has been singled out, and the thirty-one-year-old assistant prosecutor will be delivering a separate rebuttal against only him. Jim Neal will follow, taking on the other four defendants. I'm on edge. Ben-Veniste's cockiness and self-importance annoy me, and I don't want Peter and Ann to be subjected to his degrading remarks about their father.

Taking his place at the lectern, Ben-Veniste deliberately pauses to adjust his glasses. "I speak for the young, who have a stake in justice," he begins. "I have great respect for John Wilson, who if he were here now—instead of taking his vacation a little earlier than the rest of us—would have a twinkle in his eye." His comment is snide and unnecessary.

Facing the jury, Ben-Veniste has his back to Bob. In a voice laden with sarcasm, he compares Bob to a little boy who gets caught with jam on his face.

"Here's the jam, ladies and gentlemen," he exclaims. "It's on Mr. Haldeman's face. It's on his hands, and he can't get it off."

Every time Ben-Veniste cites more evidence against Bob, he repeats the story of the boy and the jam. As the jurors turn to look, I know they visualize Bob smeared with bright red strawberry jam. Ben-Veniste paints a vivid image that captures the imagination, and I'm chagrined. *Do our children really have to hear this?*

At the end of half an hour, Ben-Veniste concludes his rebuttal. With a self-satisfied expression, he slowly turns and walks back to the prosecutors' table. During the break, a crowd gathers in the hall, and I have trouble getting past it. When I see what the attraction is, I'm sickened. Standing in the middle of an admiring group of journalists, Richard Ben-Veniste is grinning. Obviously enjoying the attention, he raises his right hand high above his head for all to see. In it, he holds a jar of jam.

Late in the afternoon, it's Jim Neal's turn to deliver the rebuttal against the other four defendants. Hunched over the lectern, he addresses the jury. "It's no fun casting stones," he says, "but to keep society going, stones must be cast. People must be called to account."

Speaking for four hours, the chief prosecutor varies his tone of voice. Soft and deliberate on some occasions; at other times, loud and vigorous. As always, he's a spellbinder, but compared to his final argument earlier, what he says today seems somewhat confusing and rushed.

"Everyone blames John Dean," Neal concludes. "But Mr. Mitchell also blames Mr. Colson. Mr. Ehrlichman blames the president. Mr. Mardian blames the White House. And…" He pauses. "Mr. Haldeman really can't recall enough to blame anybody." People around me snicker under their breath.

After fifty-two days, everything has been covered: the opening statements, the testimony of witnesses, twenty-two hours of taped conversations, the final arguments, and the rebuttals. *Some of it was boring. Some of it was fascinating. And so much of it was frustrating. At last, it's over.* On Monday, the case will go to the jury.

Leaving the courtroom, I feel weak. Ben-Veniste's stinging accusations about the jam and Neal's exaggerations stay with me. I take them personally and become obsessed with one objective—to get out of this building as quickly as possible. Desperate to be alone, I give no thought to Bob and the children. Putting my head down, I plow through the crowd.

"Mrs. Haldeman," Jim Neal calls out, stopping me in the hall. He extends his hand and locks eyes with me. "I want to wish you well…no matter what the outcome might be."

The heartfelt message from Bob's adversary catches me off guard and puts my emotions over the top. Fighting to hold back tears, I'm more determined than ever to get away. Peter catches up with me and tries to offer me his arm.

I turn away and step onto the escalator.

Once outside, I come to my senses and realize what I have done. Desperate to leave the courthouse, I thought of no one but myself. Finally, the tears come… I can no longer hold them back.

By the time Bob and the three children find me, I have my emotions under control. I try to make amends with Peter, but he keeps his distance. It's been a trying day, and no one feels like talking. The five of us pile into the Checker cab with one thought in mind, to get home as quickly as possible.

Bob turns the key in the ignition, but nothing happens. He tries again, but the engine won't turn over. He checks under the hood and reports that the battery is dead. People ignore us as they get into their cars and drive away. Everyone has enough problems of his or her own.

Winding his scarf around his neck for protection against the bitter cold, Bob leaves us to get help. An hour passes before he returns, and when he does, we can't believe what we see.

"Dad's in a cage!" Ann exclaims. "He's a *prisoner!*"

Obtaining the assistance of two policemen, Bob has returned with them in their patrol car. Unfortunately, the only seat available is the one in back behind a plate of steel mesh. His doors have no inside handles, and an officer has to let him out. They jump start our battery, and at last, we are on our way home.

Halfway across the Fourteenth Street Bridge, the Checker cab stalls in the middle lane of heavy, rush-hour traffic. With cars whizzing past us on both sides, it's too dangerous to get out. There's not a thing we can do, except to sit here and wait to be rescued.

Ann prints "SOS" in large letters across the fogged-up back window. After a short wait, a small pickup truck comes up behind us and slowly pushes us over to the center guard rail, before driving away. Once again, we wait. Eventually, a tow truck with blinking, red emergency lights comes to our rescue.

Attaching a huge hook to the front bumper of the Checker cab, the driver uses a crane to hoist us up to a forty-five degree angle. With our front wheels completely off the ground, the only thing we can see is the hook and the flashing red lights. Eyeing her father sitting helplessly behind the wheel, Susan smiles. "You look ridiculous, Dad."

"This whole day's been ridiculous," Bob responds. "I've been smeared with jam, imprisoned in a police car, and hauled away by a tow-truck."

The Checker cab gives a lurch, and our heads bob in unison. With that, the bizarre scene suddenly becomes hilarious. Giving in to our pent-up emotions, the five of us burst out laughing.

◆

WITH THE TRIAL WINDING down, Bob and I use the weekend to prepare for our return home. We put Peter and Ann on a flight to Los Angeles, return the rollaway bed and linens that we borrowed, advertise the Toyota, follow up on the repair of the Checker cab, and notify our landlady that we'll be leaving soon.

The Jury Deliberates

December 30, 1974—Trial Day Fifty-Three

BY THE TIME BOB, Susan, and I arrive at the courthouse on Monday, I'm resigned to accepting whatever happens next. This morning, Judge Sirica will give his instructions to the nine women and three men. Then, it will be their responsibility to work through the complexities of each of the five defendants' cases and reach just conclusions. I can only hope that they will take their time doing this.

In court, I look for a positive sign as the jurors take their seats in the jury box. Their expressions remain stoic. The marshal stands and tells us, "If you want to leave you must do it now. No one will be permitted to enter or leave during his Honor's instructions."

Adjusting his reading glasses, Judge Sirica swivels around in his chair to face the jurors. He compliments them on their attention and begins by defining the word, "verdict." "'Ver' from *veritas*, truth; 'Dict' from *dictum*, speak".

"To find any of the defendants guilty, you must all agree that sometime during the conspiracy, if only for one day, the defendant willingly took part in just one of the forty-five overt acts cited in the indictment."

Sirica's instructions go on for two and a half hours, and I don't see how the jury can possibly remember any of it. "You are searching for the truth," the judge concludes. "Let it be a verdict that will fulfill your duty and do justice to your conscience."

At 12:30 p.m., the jury is excused to deliberate. The case is in their hands, and I feel both anxiety and relief. Everyone agrees that deliberations will take at least a week, and I'm torn between the anticipation of getting a verdict and the dread of hearing what it will be.

Back in the defendants' rooms, there's a noticeable change in the atmosphere. Newspapers, books, crossword puzzles, and playing cards appear out of nowhere. We talk louder, laugh harder, and drink more coffee. Pam Parkinson passes around a plate of homemade cookies. John Mitchell puffs on his pipe, and others light up cigarettes. Susan and I play double solitaire.

At 2:00 p.m., we are called back into court. The jury has requested individual copies of the indictment, and we are told that Mr. Hoffar, a retired fifty-seven-year-old superintendent of park police, is the foreman. I'm encouraged. I think he likes John Wilson, which might help Bob. At 5:45 p.m., we trudge back into the courtroom again. It's freezing. This time, the jurors have requested the transcripts of John Mitchell's testimony at both the trial and the grand jury, as well as the trial testimony of John Dean and two other government witnesses.

Judge Sirica explains that it's not his practice to let the jurors have copies of testimony in the jury room and that it would take a court reporter about three weeks to read the requested material in open court. The judge denies the request. He tells the jurors that they must rely on their own recollections of the testimony.

At 6:00 p.m., the jury is excused, and court is adjourned. We can go home.

December 31, 1974—Trial Day Fifty-Four

THIS MORNING, THE PRESS is out in full force in anticipation of a verdict. Campers, stations wagons, walkie-talkies, televisions, telephones, lights, and cameras line our path as Bob, Susan, and I walk from the parking lot to the courthouse.

In the relaxed atmosphere, John Wilson pauses outside the defendants' rooms to autograph a tape transcript for Fred Graham, a CBS newscaster. Back from his vacation, John is in high spirits and invites Fred into the room for a chat. Soon, Freda Reiter, the court artist, wanders in, followed by a reporter who says he heard that coffee is available. This is more than Bob can take. Giving a helpless shrug, he moves into the smaller room to get some privacy.

In the afternoon, the defendants are called back into the courtroom, where Sirica announces that the jury has requested the June 23, 1972, and the March 21, 1973, tapes, both of which include Bob. *This can't be good.* I squirm uncomfortably on the bench.

Although it's drizzly and dark when we come out of the courthouse this evening, we are met by a glare of lights and lots of activity. I grip Bob's arm tighter as we dodge newscasters, cameramen, and electricians.

Tonight is New Year's Eve. All I want is to spend a quiet evening at home with Bob and Susan. Our dinner is interrupted, however, by a reporter at the front door, who wants to confirm that we are celebrating with the Ehrlichmans. Pointing to the personalized license plates on the Checker Cab parked in front, he's convinced that Jan Evans' initials stand for John Ehrlichman. Bob finally convinces him otherwise, and he leaves. We are in bed with lights off by 10:00 p.m.

We Have a Verdict

January 1, 1975—Trial Day Fifty-Five

ON THIS FIRST DAY of the New Year, the weather is beautiful, crisp, and sunny with a few puffy clouds. Because it's a holiday, there isn't any traffic, and we arrive at the courthouse early. The halls are empty, and neither the escalator nor the elevator is in service.

The jury has been deliberating for a day and a half, and we expect this to be another long day of sitting around. I read the paper, while Bob gets into a serious game of bridge. With an overwhelming amount of information to consider, the jurors have two more requests: a list of the documentary evidence and Judge Sirica's instructions on perjury law.

At 4:30 p.m., I yawn and look at my watch. It's almost time to go home. Bob smiles as he plays his last card and makes a "small slam." At that moment, the door to the hall opens. The court marshal steps into the room, and his words shatter our relaxed camaraderie.

"We have a verdict."

At first, no one moves, and faces go blank in disbelief. When we are told to report to Judge Sirica's courtroom immediately, Bob's lawyers close in on him. He and I are separated, but we make eye contact across the room. His gray-green eyes are soft and steady. They tell me that he's in control. He mouths the words, "Don't worry. I'm okay."

Before I know it, both Bob and Susan are gone. I'm surrounded by people pushing toward the door. I can feel my heart pounding. *It's the verdict, Jo… the* verdict. *It's too soon. Stay calm. What if I cry?* My thoughts are all over the place. As I'm fumbling in my purse for a hankie, Jeannie appears. Her presence grounds me. Together, we walk across the hall into the courtroom.

Bob is seated at his table with his lawyers; Susan is nearby. Jeanne and I sit on a bench in the second row. Pam Parkinson is on the other side of me. The room is icy cold, and I shiver. Jeanne leans over and lightly grips my arm. Her hand is warm and reassuring. Across the aisle, reporters stampede to get seats, and the press section fills up quickly. Behind me, there are only seven spectators in the section reserved for the public. No one—absolutely no one—expected such an early verdict. My body feels like a dead weight, but I straighten up and try to sit tall.

The jury is called in. Clutching a large brown envelope, John Hoffar leads the way.

"Have the jurors reached a verdict?" the clerk asks.

"Yes, we have," Mr. Hoffar confirms, handing the envelope to the marshal. He passes it to the clerk, who takes it to the judge.

After checking its contents, Sirica hands the envelope with the verdicts back to the clerk, and the defendants are told to stand. Court Clerk James Capitanio starts to read, "The United States of America v. John Mitchell, Harry R. Haldeman, John D. Ehrlichman, Robert C. Mardian, and Kenneth W. Parkinson. Criminal case number seven-four-one-one-zero..."

With his hands clasped in front of him, Bob stares straight ahead. I can't see his face. As much as I would like to forget the scene in front of me, I know I never will. All I care about is Bob. As the clerk reads his name and the five charges against him, I close my eyes.

"Count One [conspiracy to obstruct justice]—Guilty."

No, no, no...

"Count Two [obstruction of justice]—Guilty."

Stay strong, Jo. I clench my fists, and my nails dig into my palms.

"Count Seven [perjury at the Senate hearing, regarding knowledge of funds used for blackmail or "hush money"]—Guilty."

Swallow... Take a deep breath.

"Count Eight [perjury at the Senate hearing, regarding the president's statement, "It would be wrong"]—Guilty."

I'm cold and numb.

"Count Nine [perjury at the Senate hearing, regarding a reference to Jeb Magruder's committing perjury]—Guilty."

It's over. I open my eyes. Everything is the same. Bob hasn't moved. He's all right.

Repeating the word "guilty" fifteen times, the gray-haired clerk reads the charges against the other defendants. Only one person is found innocent, Ken Parkinson, the forty-seven-year-old lawyer for the CRP. Judge Sirica thanks the jurors for their work and wishes them a "Happy New Year."

People start to move. Next to me, Pam Parkinson is overcome with relief. Her face turns white, and she looks as if she might faint. My arms automatically reach out to support her. I hear myself tell her how happy I am for her and her family. Dorothy Mardian gives the "Bronx cheer," and the press looks in our direction. I hope they don't think that I did it. As we file out of the courtroom, Bob Mardian remains slumped in his seat with his head in his hands.

Back in the defendants' rooms, I rush to the phone to deliver the news to our families, but it's too late. Non, Mom, Dad, Hank, Peter, and Ann already know. The moment the verdict was read in court, the Rose Bowl game was interrupted for a special announcement. I'm heartsick. *What a terrible way for our children and families to find out about Bob.* I assure them that we're all right and will be home soon.

Outside, it's as if Mother Nature were upset. The sky suddenly turns black, and a freak storm comes from out of nowhere. The drama of the scene is eerie. The wind blows in great gusts, and rain lashes across the windowpanes. Inside, the conviviality is gone. Although forever bonded by this life-shattering experience, each of us is already moving on. Keeping our thoughts to ourselves, we methodically pack up our things to clear out of the rooms.

At an impromptu press conference in the hallway, John Ehrlichman says, "If there ever has been a 'political trial' in this country, this was it." With Jeanne standing beside him, he states that he's confident that his conviction will be overturned based on the fact that he was denied Nixon's testimony.

When we leave the courthouse, heavy drops of rain sting as a fierce wind blows them across my face. I'm not prepared for this. Along with the other defendants, we are swallowed up by the press. I'm aware of noise and confusion as reporters and photographers push and shove to jockey for position. They keep shouting one question over and over: "What will you do now that the trial is over?"

John Mitchell pauses before stepping into a waiting limousine. With his pipe clenched between his teeth, he replies, "I'm going to the moon, I think. It's the best place."

Hugging his wife, Ken Parkinson grins. "I'm going home and taking a hot bath."

"This is not a happy occasion," Jim Neal tells a cluster of reporters. "We prosecuted as fairly as we could and as vigorously as we could...and..." He pauses. "I just don't have anything more to say."

Bob faces a battery of microphones. With Susan and me next to him, he states, "There is only one human being in the world who knows with absolute moral certainty the truth concerning the charges against me, and I know legally and morally that I am totally and absolutely innocent. I have the full conviction that ultimately the truth will be known."

When asked what he will do now that the trial is over, Bob replies, "I will proceed with the process of appeal, moving through the judicial system."

As we step away from the microphones, a savage gust of wind rips at my hair. Above us, dark clouds shift positions and angrily swirl around. The shouting and the jostling seem to intensify. It's a nightmare. I tell myself that I'm not a part of it. I'll wake up, and everything will be normal. *Normal? What is normal? I don't know anymore.* Susan's arm steadies me.

Bob guides the two of us through the unruly crowd.

Bob Haldeman returns to Lompoc Federal Prison Camp after furlough,
September 1978.

PART FIVE

PRISON

Mike Wallace Interview

January 1975

I N WORLD NEWS, COMMUNIST troops launch a new full-scale offensive against South Vietnam. Although the aggression is in violation of the Paris Peace Accords, the US does not retaliate. China reelects Chou En-lai as prime minister at its first meeting of the National People's Congress.

In its first issue after the trial, *Time* reports that "most of the mysteries of Watergate have been resolved, and the nation can now begin to leave Watergate to the historians."

I don't see it that way. Watergate is far from being resolved. Bob is a convicted felon, and we are going to be living under the shadow of Watergate for a long time. The appeal process alone could take over two years. Bob's lawyers have already submitted a request for a retrial on the grounds that the jurors may have broken their sequestration and read the newspaper or watched TV.

On January 8, Judge Sirica surprises everyone by reducing the sentences of the prosecution's star witnesses to "time served." John Dean and Jeb Magruder are given their freedom in exchange for their testimony. Non voices what we all are thinking when she says that it's unfair to have Dean and Magruder walking around as free men while her son waits to be sentenced.

Three days later, it's an odd feeling for Bob and me to be meeting with a probation officer in our home. I serve Mr. Westman coffee and sweet rolls during the two-hour interview, while he asks questions about our states of mind, our financial situation, and the burden prison will place on our family. His soft-spoken, courteous demeanor puts both Bob and me at ease.

"I believe in my husband's innocence," I tell him. "But I'm prepared for the worst."

Bob is sincere and straightforward as he talks about our home life and finances, as well as his reactions to the trial, incarceration, and the future. Mr. Westman tells us that his report will be sent to Judge Sirica and suggests that I write a letter on Bob's behalf. Determined to choose the right words to describe Bob's ability, loyalty, and love of community and family, I spend hours working on it. I conclude by telling Sirica that I can find nothing redeeming about Bob's having to serve time in prison.

As Bob and I pick up the pieces of our former life, I find it hard to focus on my daily routine. Every time Watergate is mentioned in the news, it's a constant reminder of how unsettled things are. Throughout the month of January, I cling to the positive and try to work through the negative. When John Wilson files for an acquittal based on Nixon's failure to testify at the trial and the massive pretrial publicity, I wonder if there is still hope for Bob.

February 1975

ON FRIDAY, FEBRUARY 21, Bob is in Washington for his sentencing. It's a cold, dreary day, and I feel so alone. The two of us have been together so much recently, it's hard to be separated at this crucial time. When the phone rings, I'm not far from it. I hesitate before picking up the receiver. *Do I really want to hear what Bob has to say? It's all so final.*

His voice sounds upbeat and matter-of-fact. He's in a hurry, and the conversation is brief. "Sirica gave Mitchell, Ehrlichman, and me two and a half to eight years. Mardian got ten months."

"Oh..."

"It could have been worse, Jo. Take care. I'll see you tomorrow."

Bob is right. It could have been worse. Two and a half to eight years is a lot better than the maximum of twenty-five years, but it still means that he will be going to prison.

Deep in thought, I stand motionless at the kitchen window. The gardener is hosing down the driveway, but I'm not focused on him. Rufus comes over and nudges me. *Bob doesn't belong locked up. What good does it serve? Who benefits? My husband is not a criminal.*

This evening, the *Herald Examiner*'s banner headline shares Bob's fate with the rest of the world. "WATERGATE 'BIG 4' GET PRISON TERMS." The next day, John Wilson tells the press, "Whatever Bob Haldeman did, so did Richard Nixon. Nixon has been freed of judicial punishment, yet Bob Haldeman has had to endure agony and punishment by trial and conviction."

John Ehrlichman's request to work with the Indians in New Mexico instead of going to prison is denied. John Mitchell informs the press that his sentence could have been worse—life with Martha.

March 1975

IN MARCH, FOLLOWING A powerful North Vietnam offensive in the Central Highlands of South Vietnam, the South Vietnamese army retreats in chaos, leaving nearly sixty thousand dead or missing.

Not in a position to seek outside employment, Bob continues to work on his book, which emphasizes the goals and accomplishments of the Nixon presidency. He still has no agent or publisher, and I wish I could help financially. The fact that I have no job skills troubles me.

Just when our income situation is looking pretty bleak, Bob receives an offer from CBS to do a five-and-a-half-hour interview with Mike Wallace. It will be videotaped in our living room and aired on *60 Minutes* on March 23 and March 30, two consecutive Sunday nights. Bob is pleased. Not only will he receive a substantial amount of money, but he will have the opportunity to get his story across in his own words.

Filming for the interview begins on Monday morning, March 3, when a TV crew sets up a battery of lights and cameras in our living room, and makeup artists take over the patio. At the last minute, Mike Wallace and Bob take their seats in two Windsor chairs in front of the fireplace. Mike is dressed in a dark gray suit and tan Italian loafers. Bob is wearing his tried-and-true blue blazer, gray slacks, and black shoes. Both men have red ties.

Watching from the upstairs landing, I peer down on the scene through the dark wood balustrade with Rufus beside me. I'm fascinated by Mike's technique as an interviewer. Rather than ask questions, he makes statements and then looks puzzled. Stating that Charles Colson thought Henry Kissinger was unstable at times, Mike raises his eyebrows and looks at Bob.

"President Nixon never thought that Kissinger was unstable," Bob replies. "Henry had monumental talents. It was just that at times, he was difficult to deal with."

"Bill Safire wrote that your detestation of the press was as great as Nixon's," Mike states, looking pained.

Bob smiles. "I did not detest the press. My realistic evaluation of them as an adversary was not detestation."

Mike leans forward and comments on Ron Ziegler's statement that the White House handled Watergate badly.

"I would agree, but I don't know 'the why.'" Bob confirms. "Richard Nixon had a good team. I do feel that I used bad judgment in the way I handled Watergate. It was a woeful lack of perception on my part."

Mike glances at a yellow pad containing his notes. "I understand that Pat Nixon was appalled at the White House tapes and that she blamed you for them."

"I doubt Mrs. Nixon said that," Bob replies. "I never talked to her about the tapes. They were installed on her husband's orders."

Finally asking a direct question, Mike asks Bob why he didn't burn the tapes.

Calmly folding his hands in his lap, Bob says, "At one time, the president discussed that with me, but my strong opinion was not to destroy them. Obviously, this was another one of my errors in judgment. I believed the tapes would be invaluable, and I continued to believe that they would prove my innocence."

Mike recalls that Bob once told him that Nixon was one of the *weirdest* men ever to sit in the White House. Mike raises his eyebrows in concern.

"He was a complex, paradoxical man," Bob says. "The more you know of a complex man, the more perplexing you find him. President Nixon's whole make-up goes in two directions…very public, very private. He's tough in the abstract, soft in the specific. In some ways, he was cold. But in some ways, he was very warm, very emotional…sentimental."

Mike asks Bob who he thinks is "Deep Throat."

Bob shrugs. "I haven't thought much about it, but my best guess is Mark Felt. I assume it was someone in the FBI, and Felt was the associate director at the time.

Every now and then, Mike stops the filming either to be briefed by his staff or to collect his thoughts. He ruins several "takes" by using profanity. Bob has no notes and remains poised and unflappable.

When the interviews are over, I compliment Bob on his composure, as well as his clear, concise answers. He shows me a list of ten objectives that he had written down earlier. One of them is to "raise *each* question to a higher philosophic plane."

The two *60 Minute* interviews get extremely high ratings, but CBS is criticized for paying a convicted felon. In a two-page story titled, "Haldeman Comes Out of his Shell to Claim a $25,000 TV Pearl," *People* magazine states, "Recently, H. R. ('Bob') Haldeman, Nixon's master intriguer, picked up a fast $25,000 without ever leaving his own living room…" Bracing myself for another round of negative publicity, I wish others could see the side of Bob that I do—his close family ties, dedication to church, strength of character, and sense of humor.

I Find a Purpose

April 1975

O N APRIL 21, PRESIDENT Thieu resigns, and nine days later, the capital of South Vietnam falls. The sight is heartbreaking as hundreds of local civilians frantically try to flee Saigon. With twelve provinces and more than eight million people under the control of North Vietnam, the war is over.

Fifty-eight thousand Americans lost their lives. *For what?*

Former president Nixon remains isolated in San Clemente, where he is working on his memoir. Reportedly, his spirits are good, despite the fact that he has high blood pressure and needs to take anticoagulant drugs to fend off any recurrence of his phlebitis.

May 1975

SEEKING A COLLABORATOR FOR his book, Bob approaches John Toland, the noted author of *The Rising Sun.* When he is turned down, it seems to affect me more than it does Bob. While he immediately starts working on other possibilities, I sit and stew. *Why aren't things moving forward? If only there were something that I could do.*

On a damp, foggy morning in May, I'm home alone. Despondent, I drop down on the couch in the family room. Yesterday, this room was filled with noisy tenth-graders, as Ann and her friends worked on their class banner. Today, the room is lifeless and ominously quiet. Sitting motionless, I stare out at the garden.

My thoughts are random and self-centered. *Why isn't it sunny? I'm cold. Why did Bob and I ever buy this couch? The fabric is itchy, and the blue plaid pattern is ugly. I hate my life right now. Friends think that I am strong, but I'm not. I have nothing worthwhile to offer.*

Startled by Rufus' wet nose nuzzling me, I catch myself. I know better than to waste my time feeling sorry for myself. I need to put my trust in a higher source. I repeat the words of a hymn:

O Lord, I would delight in Thee,
And on Thy care depend;
To Thee in every trouble flee,
My best, my ever Friend.

June–August 1975

PETER'S GRADUATION FROM HIGH school on Friday, June 6, is a happy occasion. Filled with pride, Bob and I watch as he receives his diploma from Harvard School.

NBC does a special report on Watergate on August 9, the anniversary of President Ford's first year in office. Twenty-one men in the Nixon administration have been sentenced to prison. When I hear that John Ehrlichman has walked out on Jeanne, I am shocked. My mind is flooded with the many happy memories our family has shared with John, Jeanne, and their five children. Although she referred to him as a "broken man" at the trial, I never thought things would go this far.

From press reports, I think I would hardly recognize John now. Sporting a "salt and pepper beard," he lives in a rented adobe house in Santa Fe, New Mexico. Described as leading a bohemian lifestyle, he writes novels and provides pro bono legal help for the Pueblo Indians.

October 1975

THINGS CONTINUE TO BE on hold in Bob's life. He still doesn't have a collaborator or a publisher, and nothing has materialized in the appeal process. The possibility of his going to prison is becoming more of a reality with each passing day. Periodically, he meets with his lawyers in Washington, but mostly he works on his book. Setting aside large chunks of time for research, he has accumulated stacks of yellow pads filled with notes written in longhand.

I feel for Bob. It is hard to see him working so diligently on a book without any interest being shown by a publisher. And it's hard waiting to hear on his appeal. I am increasingly frustrated. With Bob not employed, we have no money coming in, and I desperately want to contribute. It bothers me to continue living as if nothing has changed. My life seems so superficial.

The days drag. Even the children aren't around much. Susan and Hank both live on the west side of town and attend UCLA. She has transferred from Boalt, and he's a senior, working part-time for Mike Curb Productions. Peter is a freshman at Vassar College, and Ann, the only one of our children now living at home, is a junior at Marlborough.

November–December 1975

I FINALLY FIND A purpose. After attending an all-day church seminar, I drive home with an old high school friend. Lucy Ann Bell is the top residential real estate broker nationally for Coldwell Banker. She tells me that she has been searching for an assistant, and I mention that I'm looking for a job that will be both meaningful and lucrative. Before long, we both realize that our needs have been met, and the two of us agree to team up. Before working for her, however, I must pass the California Real Estate Exam and get my license. Bob is pleased to hear about my prospective job, and he gives me a real estate course for Christmas.

I'm eager to start the weekly classes at Anthony Real Estate School in Hollywood, and I am confident that I will make a difference in Lucy's life—and in Bob's. *I feel good about myself.*

Appeal Denied

January–March 1976

IN THE NEWS, PREMIER Chou En-lai dies at the age of seventy-eight. Former ambassador to China George H. W. Bush is sworn in as director of the CIA. A subway system is opened in the nation's capital.

During the first three months of 1976, I spend my days either in class at Anthony School or studying. I'm determined to get a perfect score on the California real estate test.

When the movie *All the President's Men*, starring Robert Redford and Dustin Hoffman as Bob Woodward and Carl Bernstein, is released, Bob and I are anxious to see it. Trying to avoid being recognized, we slip into a small neighborhood theater for an afternoon matinee. It's hard for us to experience the unraveling of the Nixon administration all over again, but fortunately Bob isn't featured much. On the whole, it's an entertaining movie. I'm sure the film will become a classic, keeping the story of Watergate alive for future generations.

April 1976

ON APRIL 2, DWIGHT Chapin is released from the Federal Prison Camp in Lompoc, California, after serving nine months. Two weeks later, I pass the real estate test and treat myself to a banana split. The following day, I report to work at the Hancock Park office of Coldwell Banker as Lucy's assistant. I'm given a desk of my own, right up front, directly behind the receptionist. Under Lucy's tutelage, I show houses to her clients, go on caravans, hold open houses, attend office meetings, write ads, and organize her files. I learn by doing and am busier than I've ever been. I have no time to think about myself.

Only a month after joining Lucy, I'm left in charge of her business while she takes off for a week's vacation in Hawaii. Working long hours and foregoing regular meals, I follow up on her many deals and consummate the sale of five homes in five days. It's a whirlwind experience, in which I learn far more about real estate than I ever did at Anthony School.

Bob is proud of my accomplishments. While I'm rarely home and I worry about his spending so much time working alone in his upstairs office, I am grateful to have my job. It's demanding, gets me out, and provides income.

Summer 1976

OUR COUNTRY CELEBRATES ITS two hundredth birthday on the Fourth of July. In New York, fifteen tall ships sail up the Hudson River, and in Washington DC, a million people cheer during the fireworks when "1776–1976 Happy Birthday USA" lights up the sky.

Red, white, and blue pinwheels line the brick walk at #11, and streamers, flags, a cutout of Uncle Sam, and other patriotic decorations festoon the house. When Bob's family arrives, Daddy greets them in his five-foot-long Fourth of July tie. Mother wears a red costume covered in large white stars. In her extended left hand, she holds a sparkler that my sister lights, and everyone sings a rousing round of "The Star Spangled Banner."

What a bittersweet occasion this must be for Nixon. He was so looking forward to celebrating the Bicentennial during his presidency.

Unless Bob's conviction is overturned in the appeal process, he will go to prison next June. Realizing that this could be Bob's last summer at home for several years, Lucy gives me a lot of flexibility in my work schedule so I can be with him as much as possible at Bay Island.

October 1976

AS THE COUNTRY GEARS up for another election, I wonder if Bob ever longs for those high-pressure days on the campaign trail. Saddled with a slow economy and the political price he paid for pardoning Nixon, President Ford is in a tough fight for the presidency against Jimmy Carter, the governor of Georgia. A former peanut farmer, Carter is campaigning as a Washington outsider and a reformer.

The US Circuit Court of Appeals denies Bob's appeal. Although his lawyers state publicly that they intend to take the case to the Supreme Court, they tell Bob that this is a long shot. He has nowhere else to turn. *This is it. In eight months, Bob will be going to prison. I've got to keep myself on an even keel. I want to be strong for Bob and the children, as well as the rest of the family.*

On October 28, John Ehrlichman enters prison early. Convicted in both the Ellsberg and Watergate trials, he will serve his two sentences concurrently. It's heartbreaking to watch him on TV as he enters Swift Trail Federal Prison in Tucson, Arizona. However, a call I receive from Jeanne affects me more. John has told her that he wants a divorce. I am speechless.

The David Frost Interviews

November 1976

O N NOVEMBER 2, WITH only a two-percentage-point lead in the popular vote, Jimmy Carter narrowly defeats President Ford.

While Bob continues to struggle to find an agent and a publisher for his book, John Dean's memoir, *Blind Ambition*, is released and immediately appears on the bestseller list. In it, the former counsel to the president presents his side of the Watergate story. Portraying himself as a victim and pointing the finger at others in the White House, Dean also admits to wrongdoing. My emotions are too raw for me to read it.

January–February 1977

JAMES EARL CARTER IS sworn in as the thirty-ninth president of the United States on January 20. In his inaugural address, Carter pledges "to aid Americans in regenerating a spirit of trust." As an example of that spirit, he and his family break tradition during the inaugural parade and walk down Pennsylvania Avenue to the White House.

Following the inaugural events on television, I keep thinking about "what could have been." Without Watergate, Nixon would be retiring from office today. If he had been able to complete two full terms as president, he could well have attained a working coalition of the New American Majority, ended the Vietnam War, brought about prosperity without inflation, and achieved a generation of peace in the world. Without Watergate, Bob would be returning to Los Angeles as a well-respected businessman after an eight-year stint as chief of staff of the White House. Presumably, there would have been no lack of interesting job offers, as well as speaking engagements and opportunities to serve on both community and corporate boards.

As it is, Bob is a convicted felon with no means of support and an uncertain future. *I know his name will always be associated with Watergate.*

March–May 1977

IT'S REASSURING TO SEE how polite and supportive strangers generally are when they see Bob. He even has his own rooting section at the UCLA basketball games. Whenever he raises his arm during halftime, a group of students across the court stands up and cheers.

Bob tells me about an experience he had in the coffee shop at the Miami Airport. He was eating lunch when all but one of the waitresses excitedly rushed out of the restaurant. When Bob asked what was happening, the remaining waitress told him that H. R. Haldeman had been spotted in the terminal.

Envisioning the scene, I laugh. "Did you tell her who you were?"

"No," Bob replies. "We just chatted about how exciting it was."

◆

WITH NO WORD YET on the Supreme Court appeal, I'm becoming more resigned to the fact that Bob will have to go to prison. In the meantime, after being out of the public eye for almost three years, former president Nixon goes public in a big way. He agrees to be interviewed by David Frost, a thirty-eight-year-old British journalist and media personality.

The first of the four shows airs on May 4, and Bob is eager to hear what the president has to say. His expectations are high, and he doesn't want to wait for the delayed broadcast on the West Coast. Instead, he listens "live," as Rob Odle, former staff assistant to the president, holds the phone up to his television set in Alexandria, Virginia.

When Bob comes into the kitchen later, I can tell that he's not pleased. "The interview focused on Watergate, and it's really bad," he says. "The president put the blame on Ehrlichman and me."

My heart sinks. *Why? Why would Nixon turn on Bob and John?* Frustrated, I plunge a knife into a potato I am cutting up to add to the corned beef cooking on the stove.

When the interview is shown on the West Coast, Bob and I watch it in the den as we eat dinner. Although he had warned me, I am taken aback. Not only does Nixon blame the cover-up on his two aides, but he claims that his only guilt was in not firing Haldeman and Ehrlichman earlier.

I feel for Bob, who is sitting on the couch next to me taking notes. "There's no way the president can sever himself from John and me," he says. "The tapes are proof of that. He was part of every discussion we had about saving and protecting his presidency."

As soon as the interview is over, my father calls. Although he has always been a staunch Nixon supporter, Daddy is upset, and for the first time I hear him criticize the former president. "Please tell Bob how disappointed I am with Nixon," he says. "When the chips are down, no honorable man would avoid the responsibility and loyalty due to his staff. The captain goes down with the ship. He does not leap off."

The interview has forty-five million viewers. It's the largest worldwide audience ever for a news interview. John Ehrlichman tells the press that Nixon's remarks are "a smarmy, maudlin rationalization that will be tested and found false."

Two weeks later, Nixon makes headlines when David Frost asks him about the legality of a presidential act. His response is convoluted and troubling. "Well, when the president does it that means it is *not* illegal."

On May 23, the US Supreme Court announces its decision not to hear Bob's appeal. *The door closes on any remaining hope. I won't allow myself to think about what comes next.*

In the final segment of the Nixon/Frost interview, on May 25, the former president becomes emotional and admits that he was responsible for bringing himself down. Noticeably perspiring, he says, "I gave them [the American people] a sword, and they stuck it in. They twisted it with relish, and I guess if I had been in their position, I would have done the same thing. I let my friends down. I let the country down... I let the American people down. And I have to carry that burden with me for the rest of my life."

Overall, I'm disappointed in Nixon's performance, and I don't find his wallowing in self-pity admirable or presidential. Bob puts some of the blame on himself. "The problem was we tried to present the president as one hundred percent good, while others were constantly portraying him as one hundred percent bad. In overplaying our hand, I wonder if we set the president up for the fall."

David Frost is expected to make a million dollars from the interviews, and a Gallup Poll shows 69 percent of the public thinks that Nixon is still trying to cover up. The press pursues Bob for his reaction, and he finally gives in. In a press conference on our front lawn, he waits until all of the reporters are assembled. Then, he steps up to a battery of microphones and says, "I have one brief statement. If you really want to know how I feel about President Nixon, you can find out by reading my book."

"Book?" I question, as soon as Bob steps back inside. "Do you have a publisher?"

"Not yet, but now that the president has dumped John and me, I'm going to change my approach. I've decided to write the Watergate story as I saw it. That way, I'll be able to provide some explanations and clear up some questions." Pulling off his tie, Bob drapes it and his blazer over the banister in the entry hall. "After three years of avoiding the subject of Watergate, I'm going to take it on. It's not the book that I want to write, but it will sell."

The gloves are off.

Night Thoughts

June 1977

THE PRESS RELISHES REHASHING Watergate on the fifth anniversary of the break-in, and the US Supreme Court upholds public control of Nixon's papers and tapes. In Britain, Queen Elizabeth celebrates twenty-five years on the throne with six days of pomp and pageantry. Seattle Slew wins the Triple Crown at Belmont.

On June 2, Sirica orders Bob to report to the Federal Prison Camp at Lompoc in twenty days. Steeling myself to mark the date on my calendar, I write "Lompoc" on the June 22 square and shade it in with a pencil. Now that prison is a reality for Bob, I can't bring myself to write or say that word. As long as he's incarcerated, I will refer to it as "the camp" or "Lompoc."

Bob methodically makes preparations for his departure. After wrapping up his legal affairs, he finalizes the plans for his revised book on Watergate. With Joe DiMona as his collaborator, he signs a publishing contract with the New York Times Book Company, Inc.

Before leaving for Lompoc, Bob attends both of his daughters' graduations: Ann's from Marlborough and Susan's from UCLA School of Law. His last outing is a family party in his honor given by his sister Betsy at her home in Rolling Hills.

These are poignant occasions. However, any happy memories are overshadowed by a growing anxiety when I climb into bed the night before Bob's last day at home. My uncertainty becomes magnified as soon as he turns out the light. Night thoughts take over, and I become fearful and unsure about the future. Sensing my concern, Bob patiently begins to talk me through it.

"Don't worry, Jo, I'm going to be fine. Think of prison as a work camp."

"Will you be able to call?" I ask. "I'll want to know how you're doing."

"I'm sure there's a pay phone I can use," Bob says. "And you'll be coming up for visits. We'll have lots of time to talk then."

"What if there's an emergency here at home?"

"You'll handle things just fine. I have complete confidence in any decisions you might have to make without me. Just know that it's really hard for me to walk away and leave you, and I appreciate all that you'll be doing here at home."

The two of us talk until past midnight, and I'm grateful for Bob's patience. Lying in the dark, he extends his arm and draws me to him.

◆

ON OUR FINAL DAY together, I find myself being overly helpful just to be near Bob. When he leaves for a haircut at the Larchmont Barber Shop, I have trouble holding back tears. I want him here with me so I can commit to memory everything he does—his laughter and his gestures, the way he peers over his reading glasses, how he meticulously combs his hair or toys with his spoon at the dinner table.

When Bob shows me a letter from Nixon that he received in today's mail, I'm touched. Compared to the former president's accusations on the David Frost interviews, he seems to be speaking from his heart. The note is dated June 19 and sent from La Casa Pacifica, San Clemente.

> *Dear Bob,*
>
> *As you know letter writing is not one of my major abilities. To find words adequately to express my deepest feelings for you as the day approaches when you go to Lompoc is extremely difficult.*
>
> *We all hope that somehow the scales of what is called justice will be brought into balance. In the meantime, while it is small comfort, that enormously strong faith which is yours will sustain you, coupled with the realization that as far as Pat and I are concerned you have had, do have and will always have our deepest respect, admiration & personal affection. I*

know I reflect the views of many others who had the privilege of knowing the real Bob Haldeman.

God bless you.

RN

Tonight is our last night together, and by the time we go to bed, Bob has already moved on. His clothes are laid out for tomorrow, and his Bible is on the table in the front hall, where he won't forget it. With two pillows supporting him, he's sitting up in bed, working on a crossword puzzle. His pen moves rapidly across the page. It's as if he doesn't have a care in the world, while for me it's the opposite. I can't concentrate, and *The Thorn Birds* lies unopened on my lap. Switching off the light, Bob slides down and pulls up the covers. Facing me, he sleeps on his side with his hands tucked under his chin. In no time, he's lightly snoring.

Lying wide awake, I stare at the ceiling. My night thoughts return, and this time they are more explicit. I picture a barbed wire fence, rough-looking prisoners, and guards with guns. *Will Bob fit in at the camp? He's so orderly and neat, and he likes his privacy. He's not athletic or physically fit. What if the inmates pick on him? What if the guards have a grudge against him?* I feel as if I'm slipping backward. Bob's reassuring words from last night are gone, and before I know it, I'm crying. Bob sleepily props himself up on his right elbow.

"What's wrong, Jo?"

He must be kidding. How can Bob ask what's wrong? In a few hours, I'm driving him to...to...Lompoc...the camp. That's what's wrong.

"I don't want you to go."

"I know that, but we've got to put this experience behind us." Bob's voice is firm but gentle. "I've been living in limbo for four and a half years, ever since my name was first mentioned in connection with Watergate. Going to prison is actually a step forward, because it's the *last* thing I have to go through. When this is over, we can all move forward. We will have survived. All of us will do just fine."

"I...I know we will," I say, struggling to stay composed. "I'm so sorry to act this way. It's just that... I love you, and I don't want anything to happen to you."

"Nothing's going to 'happen to me.' As I told you, it's like I'm going to a work camp, and you'll see it tomorrow when you take me. Right now, we've got to get some sleep."

His words have a calming effect, but as soon as I look at the lumpy shape next to me, I burst into tears again. I can make out Bob's face, and the more loving his expression, the harder I cry.

I have a request, and it makes absolutely no sense. "Bob, I can't look at you. It makes me cry. You've got to turn the other way."

Before turning over onto his other side, Bob tells me that he loves me, and we kiss. Now the two of us are back to back. Eventually, I fall asleep.

In the morning, I'm relieved to find that my night thoughts have retreated. I embrace the day with the calm reassurance that I am here to support Bob as he starts on this last chapter in the saga of Watergate.

The Camp

THE FEDERAL PRISON CAMP in Lompoc is 150 miles north of Los Angeles. Bob has been granted permission to travel by car instead of riding in a prison van. He's not allowed to drive, so I'll chauffeur him. The two of us will make the trip alone. Later in the week, I'll take his mother with me for the first visit. After that, the children.

In order to avoid the media, Bob decides to check in on Tuesday, June 21, a day earlier than announced. Somehow, the information gets out, and reporters start gathering in front of our house first thing in the morning. I greet them when I step outside, and I can feel their eyes following me as I walk back to the garage. I turn the key, but the car won't start. Several reporters come over and watch as I struggle with the ignition. Finally, I'm successful, and by the time Bob comes out, I'm waiting for him in the driveway. Accompanied by camera flashes and questions, he walks over to the car and climbs in.

"What's in the bag?" one reporter shouts.

Bob smiles but doesn't answer. In his hand is a small paper bag, containing his toilet case and Bible. Nothing else. They're the only personal items that he's allowed to bring with him. The facility provides clothes and linen, and later he can make a written request for things from home.

Bob doesn't have to be at the camp until 2:00 p.m., and we have allowed plenty of time to make the three-hour trip. Our drive through the San Fernando Valley is hot and dry, but along the coast, both of us are especially aware of the beauty of the ocean and the mountains. Bob lowers the passenger window and lets the cool salt air sweep through the car.

"I want to remember this," he says, taking a deep breath. When he adds that he's not sure when he'll get to see the ocean again, it breaks my heart.

In Santa Barbara, we stop for gas, followed by lunch at a Taco Bell. Seated in the shade of a yellow and red plastic umbrella, Bob finishes his iced tea and tells me that we have only sixty-one miles to go. I don't like to hear how close we are. Time is passing too quickly.

Soon, the road turns inland and goes through a pass, opening onto rolling hills dotted with clusters of poppies, lupine, and mustard. Approaching Lompoc, I'm overcome by the sight and heady fragrance of sweet peas, alyssum, and delphiniums, which are all in full bloom. Known as the "City Set in the Valley of Flowers," Lompoc is surrounded by 1,500 acres of flowers, grown only for their seeds.

In the middle of nowhere, we pass a dark green highway sign, propped up at the side of the two-lane asphalt road. With an arrow pointing to the right, it reads, "Floradale Avenue—Correctional Facility." My grip on the steering wheel tightens, and I wonder how often I will be making this drive over the next two and a half to eight years.

Before long, we come to the camp parking lot, bordered by giant eucalyptus trees. Across from it is a cluster of buildings: a three-story administration facility, two dormitories, a small, brick Visitors Center, and a chapel. Off to the side, there's a large playing field with a chain-link fence around it. The setting isn't nearly as bad as I had envisioned it, and I feel less apprehensive.

"End of the line," Bob says, stretching. "Here's where I get out."

I turn off the engine and remain seated behind the wheel. Bob leans over to give me a kiss. Turning to face him, I wrap my arms around his neck. Our kiss is brief—almost impersonal, not the way I want it to be.

"I love you," Bob says, gently releasing my clasp.

"I love you, too." My voice cracks. "Take care."

The next thing I know, the seat next to me is empty. The car door slams shut, and Bob is gone. I watch him walk away. The only sounds I hear are the crunching of gravel and the popping of eucalyptus pods under Bob's Wallabees. Wearing khaki pants, a white button-down shirt, and a windbreaker, he grips his paper bag in his left hand. Once he reaches the other side of the road, he turns and gives a final wave. He looks little and so alone.

When Bob enters the Administration Building, he will be photographed, fingerprinted, and subjected to a body search for drugs and weapons. I shudder. *Bob doesn't belong here. How can I possibly leave him?*

Somehow, I start the car and get back on the road. Feeling disconnected from my body, I'm hardly aware of the long drive home. As soon as I step into the entry hall, I'm jolted back to reality. The three pugs are barking, and Susan and Ann rush out to greet me. As we talk, I relive the heartache of this long day.

At 11:30 p.m., the phone rings. It's a collect call from Bob! *Bob? Calling me now?* Eager to hear his voice, I quickly agree to accept the charges.

"Hi, Jo. I knew you would want a report, so I called as soon as I could."

As Bob describes being processed and assigned a cubicle in the dorm, I take notes which Susan and Ann read over my shoulder. His voice sounds as upbeat as ever, and I'm relieved.

When I finally climb into bed at 1:30 a.m., I curl up with Bob's pillow and lie with my arm extended over onto his side. I have no night thoughts and fall into a deep sleep almost immediately.

Handelman, You Have a Visit

THE FOLLOWING MORNING, HENRY Kissinger calls to say he's thinking of Bob and me and wishes us well. He tells me that Bob has conducted himself with great dignity throughout this whole ordeal. When I hear the familiar German accent, it evokes strong memories of Bob, John, and Henry in their glory days at the White House, and I picture the self-confident, all-powerful Palace Guard, laughing and joking. At the time, Bob seemed invincible. He was always in control, and I can't help comparing those days to what he faces now.

When I go into the Coldwell Banker office, Lucy has already read news accounts of Bob's arrival at the camp yesterday. She understands how anxious I am to visit him and encourages me to take time off this weekend. Visiting hours are from 12:00 p.m. to 3:00 p.m. on weekdays and 8:00 a.m. to 3:00 p.m. on weekends. During daylight saving time, there are additional visiting hours from 5:00 p.m. to 8:00 p.m. on Fridays and Saturdays.

Three days after taking Bob to the camp, I return on Friday, June 24, with his mother for our first visit. Driving along the coast in her chocolate-brown Cadillac Seville, the two of us talk nonstop, excitedly speculating on what sort of life Bob is leading—who his friends are, what the food is like, and how he spends his time. We hardly take note of the beautiful coastline or Lompoc's spectacular fields of flowers. Three large, pink cardboard boxes are on the backseat. Each contains a picnic lunch, personally packed by the chef at the Los Angeles Country Club. Bruno is a fan of Non's, and he would do anything for her.

Arriving at noon, we park the car and follow the stream of families carrying picnic baskets into the Visitors Center. Non is upbeat and excited

page 416, Jo Haldeman

about seeing her son. But for some reason, I suddenly feel out of place and become filled with misgivings. *This is it, Jo. Get a hold of yourself.*

The room is crowded, and people are divided into two lines for processing. A uniformed guard is seated at a table. Checking off Non's and my names, as well as Bob's, he asks if we brought in anything illegal. As soon as we are cleared, Bob is notified over a blaring loudspeaker.

"Handelman, you have a visit!"

Non looks crestfallen. "They didn't get the name right! How will Bob know it's for him?"

"Don't worry, Non, he'll know." Looking across a paved area, I see a chain-link fence in the distance. With a pang, I recognize Bob as one of the men waiting patiently at the gate.

"Bob's coming over here!" Non exclaims. It's the same elated tone she used whenever she spotted her son at a White House event.

As soon as he steps inside the room, Bob identifies himself to the guard. "Haldeman, number one-four-eight-nine-six-three-B." I cringe.

Non and I push forward to greet him, but Bob is distracted. Guiding us toward the door on the opposite side of the room, he tells us to hurry if we want to get seats at a table in the patio.

"The guys told me that outside is the best place to be," he explains.

The three of us step out into a small grassy area, which is enclosed on three sides by the L-shaped Visitors Center and the camp chapel. The fourth side is open to the road, where a painted white line runs along the edge of the asphalt. Bob doesn't relax until we're seated at one of the picnic tables. At the other end of it, a Spanish-speaking family is busily unpacking a lunch of tamales, beans, rice, and homemade tortillas and salsa.

Eagerly opening one of the pink boxes, Bob exclaims, "Wow! This is great, Mom. Roast beef, sourdough French bread, fresh fruit, and country club macaroons! Thanks."

As we eat, Bob and his mother are both at ease and animated, while I feel restrained and out of sorts. Bob talks freely about life in the camp. He refers to the other prisoners as "the guys," and he says he would like to join a bridge group during "free time" in the afternoon. He'd also like to play tennis and plans to put in a request for me to bring him his racket.

Sharing camp stories with us, Bob describes an overly strict guard, nicknamed "Deputy Dog." He also talks about one of "the guys" who tried to blow up his mother's plane after he took out life insurance on her. Stimulated by the novelty of life at the camp, Non and Bob are chatty and lighthearted. Still unsure of myself, I remain quiet and withdrawn. I feel like the "odd man out."

Bob tells us that he lives in a multi-storied dorm with over four hundred other inmates. He is assigned a cubicle, which he refers to as his "house." A five-foot-high partition defines his personal area, which contains a bed, desk, chair, and cupboard. Bob is subjected to inspections, head counts, and demerits, or "shots." Tan khaki pants and blue oxford cloth shirts are the camp uniform. These are issued each week, along with shorts, socks, towels, and sheets. A washer and dryer are available, as well as a laundry service. Requests for certain personal items from home—such as clothing, books, sports gear, or toiletries—must be in writing. All letters and packages will be opened and approved before they are distributed.

"Before long, I'll be assigned to a job," Bob says, looking pleased. "In the meantime, I have a temporary assignment at the power plant."

"I bet they put you to work in the office," Non speculates. "You're such a good manager, and you're so organized."

Before we know it, our three-hour visit is over. The air is cooler, and wisps of fog are starting to creep across the patio. Along with the other families, Non and I follow Bob to the edge of the lawn.

"This is as far as I can go," he says, coming to an abrupt halt at the white line on the road. "I'm not allowed to step over that."

Bob's words tell it like it is, and the line is a blunt visual reminder of where he is. Non and I try to put up a good front as we kiss him goodbye, but it's difficult. Clutching our leftover picnic supplies, we join a straggly procession of mostly women and children on their way back to the parking lot. Behind us, Bob stands with his feet firmly planted on his side of the white line.

Good Days, Bad Days

DROPPING ME OFF AT my sister's house in Santa Ynez, Non faces the long drive back to Los Angeles alone. The Parkers' rambling ranch-style home is about twenty-six miles from the camp, which is an easy commute for me. I plan to spend two nights here and visit Bob on my own tomorrow. On Sunday, the children will pick me up, so we can go together.

Gay, David, and their four children live in a different world from mine. With their two Golden Retrievers, three horses, several chickens, and one unusually large pig named Piglet, it's chaos. But it's happy chaos, and I love being around all of them. It's good for me.

I'm up early the next morning, but Gay is already in the kitchen. Not only has she offered me her car for the day, but she sends me off with thermoses of hot coffee and freshly squeezed orange juice. On the way to the camp, I make a quick stop to pick up breakfast at a coffee shop in the quaint Danish town of Solvang.

I can hardly wait to see Bob, but at the same time, I remember the uneasiness I felt yesterday. Also, I'm apprehensive about being alone with him for *seven* hours. It's been a long time since the two of us have spent that much time together with no breaks. To be on the safe side, I bring Scrabble, backgammon, and two decks of cards.

When I check in at the Visitors Center, I'm pleased to hear "Haldeman" pronounced correctly over the loudspeaker. A wheelbarrow full of pink, purple, and white stock sits next to the main door, and I'm surprised to see flower arrangements on several tables in the patio. A few of the chairs even have small, colorful umbrellas attached to them. When I comment on how pretty everything looks, Bob tells me that the warden has spruced up the camp to make a good impression on any important visitors Bob might have.

As we take our seats at a picnic table, a couple of the inmates call out, "Hi, H. R.," and Bob explains that's what the guys call him. Eagerly opening the Styrofoam box with his breakfast in it, Bob spears some hardened scrambled eggs with a plastic fork, takes a bite of a jelly donut, and washes everything down with Gay's juice and coffee. Digging into the pocket of his khaki pants, he hands me a scrap of paper with a list of things he wants me to send him: his windbreaker, two sweaters, white espadrilles, and four pairs of shorts and socks. At the bottom of the page, he's added sweatpants and a zipper sweatshirt with a hood.

"Sweatpants?" I question. "You don't like sweatpants...and are you sure you want a sweatshirt with a hood?" Bob has never worn anything that covers his head. He doesn't like the feeling, and besides, it might mess up his hair.

Shrugging, he justifies his request. "The guys told me that I should have them."

The sun beats down, but it's not overly hot. The flowers on the table fill the air with a lovely, soft fragrance. We play Scrabble, gin rummy, and double solitaire. The conversation flows naturally, and the hours pass quickly.

For lunch, I drive into Lompoc to pick up fish and chips, which is one of Bob's favorites. Unfortunately, the container of malt vinegar tips over in the car, and when I hand the bag to Bob, the bottom disintegrates. The food spills out onto the ground, and with the exception of two small containers of coleslaw, our lunch is inedible.

Seeing our predicament, an inmate seated with his family at the next table comes to the rescue.

"Enjoy, H. R.," he says, dishing up two extra plates of spaghetti, meatballs, lasagna, green salad, and toasted garlic bread.

"Thanks, Luigi," Bob says, explaining to me that Luigi owns an Italian restaurant in San Diego.

I'm overwhelmed with Luigi's thoughtfulness, and I take it to heart. It shows me how well-liked Bob is, and it makes me realize how out of sorts I've been. I need to change my attitude. Instead of expecting the worst, I resolve to look for the good in this camp experience.

After we clean up, I entertain Bob with my real estate stories, and he talks about the problems he's having with his book. It's difficult for him to find the time to work on it, and it's virtually impossible for him to be alone without distractions. His publisher and collaborator are pressuring him to go into greater depth on Watergate. They want him to place the blame on others, but he's resisting.

As Bob and I talk, I feel a closeness between the two of us that I haven't experienced for a long time. I'm reminded of the time at Bay Island when my parents agonized over the condition of a frayed electrical cord. I had longed to have the same sort of mundane discussion with Bob, but he was preoccupied with the White House. This afternoon, it's finally happening. We talk about anything and everything. Nothing holds us back.

When visiting hours are up, we're still engrossed in our conversation, and I find it hard to leave. As we are reluctantly saying goodbye, one of the guys approaches us. In his arms are two huge bunches of purple and white stock, which he awkwardly presents to me with an embarrassed grin.

"Thanks, Demetrius," Bob says, clapping him on the back.

I bury my face deep into the center of the blossoms and breathe in their heavenly fragrance. Peering over the flowers, I tell Demetrius that he has provided the perfect ending to a perfect day. This time, when I step over the white line, I hardly notice it. *I just spent seven delightful hours with my husband.*

◆

ON SUNDAY MORNING, JUNE 26, I'm awakened by the Parkers' hens clucking in the barn and the smell of coffee. Lazily climbing out of bed, I feel content and cared for. I am anticipating my visit to the camp with Susan, Peter, and Ann. Hank plans to see his father next week.

On the way to Lompoc, the three children and I stop in Solvang to buy sandwiches for lunch. As soon as we pass the correctional facility sign, there's a noticeable silence in the car. Sensing the children's anxiety, I try to reassure them by taking a short drive around the camp. But my spirits plunge as we approach the parking lot. Across the road, Bob is standing behind the chain-link fence with other inmates. The sight is disturbing, and I worry how the children are going to react. Bob waves, and without hesitating, they wave back. Despite my concerns, they appear to be at ease during the check-in procedure. When the loudspeaker blasts their father's name and he has to identify himself by a number, the three of them take it in stride.

Two of the guys are saving a patio table for us, and Demetrius self-consciously hands me a large container of flowers to use as a centerpiece. As we set up lunch, I'm glad to see the children asking so many questions. The more they know about their father's situation, the less anxious they will feel.

Bob tells us that he likes his temporary job as a clerk at the power plant. Following an evaluation by the staff, he will be given a permanent job. He takes a two-mile walk around the track before and after dinner each night, but he must be in his dorm at 8:00 p.m. and 10:00 p.m. for "the count." Wednesday, Saturday, and Sunday nights are movie nights.

Pointing to his khaki pants and blue oxford cloth shirt, Bob asks the children how they like his "jail clothes." I'm puzzled. This isn't like Bob, and I'm not sure if he's trying to be funny or if he wants to shock us. In any event, the children don't react. When he requests some more personal items, I make a list in my spiral notebook: a Casio calculator, two books (*The Silmarillion* by J. R. R. Tolkien and *The Once and Future King* by T. H. White), a belt, and tennis shoes. The shoes must be ventilated, canvas Tretorns, size 12-D.

"Canvas Tretorns?" I question.

"Yes," Bob confirms. "For jogging."

"Jogging?!" the children exclaim in unison.

"You've *never* jogged," I add.

"I need the exercise," Bob says. "The guys here jog around the playing field, and they think I should, too."

Our visit goes well, until it comes time to leave. As we're packing up, Susan turns to her father and says, "This is just so frustrating, Dad. It's such a waste of time and money. It doesn't serve any purpose."

Turning to face his older daughter, Bob places his hands on her shoulders.

"Look, Sus, you know as well as I do that there are many things in life that we don't understand. This experience may appear to have no purpose, but I know that no matter how wrong or unfair it may seem, it's part of my growth and progress. Right now, this is where I am, and I plan to make the best of it." He pauses and then adds, "The toughest part for me is seeing how hard this is on each of you."

The children and I take turns giving Bob hugs. The final act of stepping across the white line is inevitable. Seeing us hesitate, Bob quips, "Hey, guys, just think of all the picnics you get to have in prison!"

The four of us laugh halfheartedly and then reluctantly trudge back to the parking lot. As we drive away, Ann rolls down her window and waves to her father. "That white line's like a ten-foot wall," she says, dejectedly.

No one talks as we head back to Los Angeles. We are tired, and each of us is lost in his or her own thoughts. When I stop for gas in Santa Barbara, however, we are brought back to our senses. It's a nightmare. The car won't start, and the attendant tells me that I need a mechanic. Today is Sunday, and there are no mechanics available. My only option is to have the station wagon towed to a garage and leave it. By the time I do this and rent a car, we've added another two hours to our drive home. It's long past dark when we finally reach Hancock Park.

In bed, I reflect back over the past three days, which seem more like three weeks. First, there was Bob, who appeared to be adjusting well. Next, Non, who as always, saw her son in the best light. Then, the children, who took their father's imprisonment in stride. And lastly, me. I think I handled some things well, and others, I did not. At times, I struggled to keep a positive attitude. Tonight, I am very tired.

◆

THE ALARM RINGS FIRST thing the next morning. Instead of reporting to Coldwell Banker, I have to return the rental car to the local agency in Hollywood. Peter will meet me there and drive me to Santa Barbara to pick up the station wagon.

Things do not go well. Inspecting the rental car, the mechanic falsely claims that I dented it in three places. Already at my breaking point, I burst into a flood of tears. Not only do I embarrass myself, but also the mechanic, the owner of the agency, and Peter. Anxious to get rid of me as quickly as possible, the owner waives the charges and escorts Peter and me out the door.

On the road, Peter and I don't talk much. I'm still trying to get control of my emotions, and the Volkswagen engine is so noisy it drowns out most of our conversation anyway. I'm content to lean back and think my own thoughts. A memory comes to mind of last Christmas, when I put a massive green bow on top of this little red Beetle, and Bob drove it to the airport to pick up Peter from college. I smile.

By the time we reach Santa Barbara, my station wagon is ready, and I'm back on the road in no time. On the way home, I stop at a Hollywood sporting goods store to buy Bob his sweatpants, hooded sweatshirt, and Tretorn tennis shoes. I'm in a hurry, but the shoe salesman is inexperienced and can't find what I need. Witnessing my frustration, a nearby customer asks why my husband doesn't buy his own shoes.

Losing my self-control, I snap, "He can't. He's in *prison*."

Tears well up in my eyes. People around me stare. I am embarrassed, and so are they. *Why would I blurt out something like that?* First of all, it's not my nature. Secondly, I vowed I would never use that word as long as Bob is at "the camp." *What's happening to me?*

The Sewer Plant and Poppies

WITH THE WEEKEND FINALLY behind me, I return to work. I love what I do, but it's exhausting. Not only are the hours long, but I'm constantly striving to emulate Lucy. When we started working together a year ago, I was her "gofer" and was paid a salary. Now I'm her partner and receive a percentage of the commission. It's a world of buyers and sellers, interest rates, mortgages, listing agreements, and sales purchase contracts. With twenty-one homes in escrow, six deals pending, and a long list of clients, Lucy is constantly on the go. She has so much business, it's almost more than the two of us can handle. Her newest listing sets a record. The white brick English home on South Hudson is listed at $900,000. I appreciate the fact that Lucy encourages me to take time off to enjoy Newport, but when I do, I feel guilty missing work. *Besides, Bay Island is not the same without Bob.*

July 1977

FRIDAY, JULY 1, is a particularly long day. I leave Newport and drive to LA to have lunch with Non and Betsy, before continuing up the coast to have an evening visit with Bob.

Before checking in at the camp, I pick up a bucket of Colonel Sanders Kentucky Fried Chicken for dinner. The weather is warm, which means Bob and I can be outside. He looks good. His hair has been "styled" by one of the inmates, and he has lost weight from jogging. The guys have told him that their wives like them to wear their own clothes rather than "jail clothes," so he's dressed in a madras shirt and blue denims that I sent from home.

Searching through the chicken for a piece of white meat, Bob looks up and casually announces that he has his permanent job now. "After a thorough evaluation of my talents, the powers-that-be assigned me to...the sewer plant."

"The sewer plant?" I ask. "That's where you work?"

"Actually, I couldn't ask for a better spot," Bob explains. "The processing basins are located in a deserted ravine not far from here, which gets me away from the camp and gives me some privacy. A prison bus drives the other guys and me out there each morning and picks us up at the end of the day. All we have to do is to run a few chemical tests on the sewage for a couple of hours, and then we have our afternoons free."

"I can't believe it," I say, trying to absorb what Bob is telling me. "I thought you'd be assigned to the office."

Bob waves away a wasp that's hovering over a leftover chicken bone. "The location's kind of pretty, and it's quiet. We have a small office with a cooktop, a refrigerator, and a washer and dryer. And best of all, there's a typewriter. My publisher's been bugging me to get the editing done on my book. Now that I have a typewriter, I won't have to write everything out in longhand anymore."

"Sounds good, but..." I hesitate. "Does it smell?"

"The odor's carried downwind, and it's not that bad." Bob pauses. "The guys call the sewer plant the 'shit house.'" Another pause. "Just think, Jo, I must have set some sort of record. In the last four years, I've gone from the White House to the shit house!" He laughs, "Hee, hee, hee."

Bob is amused at his joke, and once again, his words startle me. I don't know why he says things like, "shit house" and "jail clothes." *It doesn't sound like him. What makes him talk like this?*

Helping himself to a piece of my mother's Harvey Wallbanger Bundt cake, Bob continues. "Periodically, we have to search for drugs. When the hard-core prisoners in the penitentiary across the road think they might get caught, they put their drugs into plastic bags and flush them down the toilet." He looks over at me and adds, "Don't say anything about this to Mom when you talk to her. Just tell her that I'm a chemist and I work in an office at the disposal plant."

"I will," I assure him, knowing that no matter what Bob does, Non will be proud of him.

Between Bob's stories of life around the camp and mine at Coldwell Banker, our three-hour visit passes quickly. On the whole, it's been a good day today. Saying goodbye isn't as hard as it has been, and I'm staying nearby with the Parkers. It's still light at 8:00 p.m., and the drive along the two-lane country road is lovely. The sight of a full moon rising directly in front of me is breathtaking. I pass dairy cows contentedly grazing in lush green fields, and in the distance, Lompoc's flower beds look like a giant, multi-colored patchwork quilt. I am at peace with myself.

◆

THE NEXT MORNING, GAY helps me pack up my fancy, rattan picnic basket. The beautifully equipped Abercrombie & Fitch hamper was a wedding present, and I've finally found a way to put it to good use. It's a Saturday, and the visiting hours are longer. With the exception of the afternoon break, I'm looking forward to spending the whole day with Bob.

On the way to Lompoc, I can't resist stopping to pick a few wildflowers for Bob. By the time I reach the camp, heavy black clouds have blotted out the sun. The towering pines and eucalyptus trees surrounding the parking lot look dark and foreboding. As I'm unloading my things, it starts to rain. I make a mad dash to the Visitors Center. In one hand, I grip the bouquet of poppies and lupine, along with the hamper. In the other, I clutch my purse and a bag of games.

Inside, it's bedlam. The unseasonably wet weather has forced everyone to remain indoors. The air is thick with cigarette smoke and the odor of damp clothing. Babies are crying, and older children are working off their pent-up energy by running around the crowded room.

As soon as Bob checks in, we head for a corner, where we drag two vinyl-covered chairs together. Once we're settled, I give Bob the bedraggled wildflowers. He starts to take them and then quickly retracts his hand.

"Good grief, Jo," he exclaims. "Don't you know that it's against the law to pick California poppies?"

Embarrassed and confused, I mumble, "I…I didn't know…I'm sorry."

Bob shakes his head in disbelief. "Here I am in jail, and right in front of the guards, my wife hands me a bunch of illegally picked wildflowers. You've got to get rid of them right away."

I head for the trashcan at the far end of the room. Above it a soap opera in Spanish blares from a wall-mounted TV. I hesitate. It's hard to toss the flowers into the trash, where they land on top of a mixture of orange peels, fast food wrappers, and cigarette butts. And it's doubly hard to see Bob sitting on that cheap, red vinyl chair in the middle of all this confusion. Usually adept, he's awkwardly trying to undo the straps that hold the dishes and silverware inside our fancy picnic basket.

How can today's visit be so different from yesterday's? Nothing is going right. It's raining. I'm angry at myself for picking the flowers, and I hate this crummy room, where Bob looks so out of place. The noise drowns out most of our conversation, and we have to shout. Bob lacks his usual enthusiasm, and for the first time, he finds fault with things. He misses his privacy and complains that the camp food is institutional.

"Most of the time we only have plastic spoons to eat with," he says. "The knives and forks 'mysteriously disappear,' just like my toilet kit."

"Someone stole your toilet kit?"

"Yeah," he confirms. "Can you send me a new one?"

At 8:00 p.m., visiting hours are finally over, and everyone springs into action. Bob and I pack up and follow the parade to the side door. As families push past us, he gives me a quick kiss and hands me the hamper. Halfway out the door, I look back and call out, "I love you." I don't think he hears me.

Outside, the rain has stopped, and it's starting to clear. Walking past the damp picnic tables, I come to the white line. Instead of ignoring it, I deliberately step on it. It's a dumb thing to do, but it makes me feel better.

Things don't improve on the drive back to Newport. The station wagon breaks down again in Santa Barbara, and this time, it's a broken radiator hose. *What's going on with this stupid car? Why is all of this happening to me?* When I'm back on the road, I sing hymns to keep from feeling sorry for myself.

> *It matters not what be thy lot,*
> *So Love doth guide;*
> *For storm or shine, pure peace is thine,*
> *Whate'er betide...*

I struggle to stay awake and arrive at Bay Island well after midnight. Trying to be as quiet as possible, I push a cart containing my overnight bag and picnic supplies across the bridge onto the island. At #11, the porch light is on, and Mother is still up waiting for me. After I shower, she appears with a bowl of soup on a tray. My heart fills with affection. Her calm strength and love assure me that everything will be all right.

A Commutation of Sentence

TWO DAYS LATER, I'M surrounded by family as Hortons and Haldemans gather at #11 to celebrate the Fourth of July. Although everyone misses Bob, he sounds quite content when he calls from the camp. Explaining that the warden has allowed the press to film his cubicle and the sewer plant, he adds that the buildings were painted for the occasion.

"Did you do anything special today?" I ask.

"It was neat," Bob exclaims. "They put on a Fourth of July picnic with barbecued chicken and *free* soda pop!"

Soda pop? In thirty years, I've never heard Bob use the term "soda pop," let alone drink one. Listening to him talk, I realize that it takes very little to please him these days. Food has become the primary focus of his attention.

August 1977

IN AUGUST, THE SPACE shuttle *Enterprise* passes its first flight test in the Mojave Desert. After twenty-five years, the Volkswagen Beetle is being replaced by the Rabbit. Jackie Kennedy Onassis receives $20 million from her late husband's estate, and Elvis Presley dies at forty-two.

Between my work at Coldwell Banker, visits with Bob, and visits to Bay Island, my days are full this summer. Although I spend much of my time on the road, I find that it gives me a chance to reflect on my life. The drive along the coast is particularly beautiful, and I love the smell of the eucalyptus trees mixed with the saltiness of the sea air. There are rugged palisades on one side and the beach with its rolling waves on the other. In the distance, offshore oil rigs dot the ocean. At times, I parallel the train, and we play a game of "cat and mouse." One minute, it appears on my right; the next, it's on my left.

My mother and father take the family to Honolulu this month to celebrate their fiftieth wedding anniversary. Although there are fourteen of us, I find that it's hard to be here without Bob. The trip brings back nostalgic memories of my last visit. As a junior in high school, I sailed to Hawaii with my family on the Matson Line's *S.S. Lurline*. Bob paid his own way to join us and was with me every waking moment.

The days get hotter. At the camp, I wear a straw hat and sit in the shade, while Bob faces the sun to keep up on his tan. On several occasions, Bob asks another inmate and his wife to join us at our table. Robert is serving time for nursing home fraud. He and Bob both enjoy bridge, and as partners, they placed third in the duplicate bridge tournament. When they tell Mildred and me that they also tried to join the fire brigade, we are astonished. The two of them are older than most of the inmates and physically less fit.

"The fire brigade?" Mildred questions. "Whatever gave you that idea?"

Giving a smug smile, Robert responds, "Firefighters get private rooms."

September 1977

By September, Bob has a steady flow of visitors. In addition to scheduling visits with family and close friends, I coordinate requests from Maury and Kathleen Stans (former secretary of commerce), Chuck Colson (former special counsel to the president), John and Nell Wooden (UCLA basketball coach), Diane Sawyer (former press aide to the president), Bruce Herschensohn (former deputy special assistant to the president), and Larry Higby, Gordon Strachan, and Dwight Chapin (former aides to Bob in the White House).

Mother and Dad combine their visits with overnight stays at the Parkers, and Non drives alone to Lompoc every other week. I go every Friday, which means that I can have both lunch and dinner with Bob, as long as it's still daylight saving time. This leaves me free to work on the weekends, the busiest time in real estate.

When the station wagon breaks down for the fourth time, both Bob and I agree that it's time to replace it. Soon, I'm the proud owner of a new Ford Grenada. The four-door sedan is black and has flashy chrome hubcaps. It's fun for me, and yet appropriate for my real estate clients.

My next trip to Lompoc is a breeze. What a difference a new car makes! To my surprise, Bob has something new, too. A full, thick mustache.

"You look like...Pancho Villa," I tell him.

Bob is pleased with the comparison. "The guys who ride in the bus with me to the sewer plant encouraged me to grow it," he says, running his finger along the bushy growth of hair on his upper lip. "They think I look Mexican, like them."

As we eat and talk, Bob tells me that his publisher is pushing him to hurry up and finish the book. However, it's difficult for him to work fast. The typewriter at the sewer plant frequently skips letters, and several of its keys stick.

In the middle of our conversation, Bob abruptly excuses himself and goes over to another table, where a young inmate and his mother are visiting. He's done this before, and I don't like it. It's hurtful to be left alone after I've driven miles to be with him for such a brief time. *Why does he do it?*

When Bob returns, he gives me a ring made of highly polished, honey-colored wood. "Here, Jo. Bud made this for you in furniture shop."

Feeling sheepish for having been annoyed, I slip the ring on my right ring finger. It fits perfectly. Bud looks pleased when I thank him.

◆

THREE MONTHS HAVE PASSED since Bob entered the camp, and he can now apply for a commutation of sentence. According to his probation officer, things look encouraging. Judge Sirica is trying to get away from his "Maximum John" image and shows signs of greater compassion. Family and friends are being encouraged to write to him on Bob's behalf. In my letter to Sirica, I refer to Bob's character, his devotion to his family, and his strong reliance on his faith. I talk about the hardships we face, but I avoid pleading for sympathy.

Both Henry Kissinger and Charles Colson tell Bob that they will also send letters to Sirica. Henry is teaching at the Edmund Walsh School of Foreign Service at Georgetown University, and Chuck is setting up a Prison Christian Fellowship Program. Bob asks me to contact James Neal, too. Although John Wilson feels that it would be an imposition to ask the former prosecutor at the Watergate trial to write, Bob thinks that Mr. Neal would be happy to do it.

Judge Sirica reduces Bob's sentence from two and a half to eight years to one to four years. Sometime in May, the parole board will set his release date. At that point, Bob will have been at the camp for almost a year.

Two Birthday Picnics

October 1977

O NE OF THE THINGS I miss most about Washington is the dramatic change of color in the fall. The gray, leathery leaves on the sycamore trees that line our street in Hancock Park can't compare to the vivid crimson and gold foliage in Georgetown and Kenwood. In our backyard, the large Brazilian pepper tree isn't deciduous, and its leaves remain a dull green. Red berries appear on the pyracantha bushes at the side of the house, and buds are starting to form on the camellia plants in front.

Two un-carved pumpkins sit on our front doorstep, and my new car is parked in the driveway. I'm careful when I hand wash it. It has no smears, and its black paint shimmers in the morning sunlight. One of the best things about it is the tape player, and I buy lots of cassettes of my favorite Broadway musicals. Turning up the volume, I play them over and over as I drive back and forth to the camp. I adapt their sentimental lyrics to fit my own circumstances. In *Man of La Mancha,* Nixon becomes Don Quixote, the knight-errant who fights windmills and tries to achieve "the impossible dream." With his luxurious mustache, Bob is Sancho Panza, Don Quixote's sidekick. When the Mother Abbess in *The Sound of Music* tells Maria to "climb every mountain," I think of the gently rolling hills north of Santa Barbara. The song that's closest to my heart is "Send in the Clowns" from Stephen Sondheim's *A Little Night Music.* Its lyrics describe an upside-down world similar to the one in which Bob and I live. I'm the "one who keeps tearing around," and he's the "one who can't move." Like the character Desiree, I question, "Isn't it rich? Aren't we a pair?"

With the exception of the three pugs and Rufus, I'm the only one living at home now. Bob's office and the children's rooms are deserted and quiet. After taking the California bar exam this summer, Susan is clerking for a judge in St. Paul, Minnesota. Hank is working in the music business and lives in West Los Angeles. Peter has transferred from Vassar to the University of California at Santa Cruz, and Ann is a freshman at Stanford. Although I miss the children, it's good that they aren't here. I'm hardly ever home.

On October 25, I take Hank and his girlfriend to dinner at L'Hermitage to celebrate his twenty-fourth birthday. Heather Eaton is a lovely girl, and I am glad that Hank is serious about their relationship. He tells me that he wants his father to meet her, but he refuses to take her to Lompoc. He doesn't want "Heath" to see Bob in the camp.

When Bob turns fifty-one on October 27, he shaves off his moustache. Because he cannot receive anything that hasn't been on a list submitted by him and preapproved, we cannot surprise him with gifts. Instead, his mother, sister, and I bring him a special picnic. We prepare everything that Bob likes: duck *a l'orange,* wild rice, marinated green beans, tapioca with whipped cream, homemade oatmeal cookies, Betsy's homegrown blackberries, and Los Angeles Country Club macaroons. Although we think it might be too ostentatious to use the damask tablecloth, china plates, and silver flatware, it doesn't bother Bob. He likes it and says that it makes it seem more like a party.

Four days later, I return to the camp with my mother and Gay to celebrate my forty-ninth birthday. This time it's all of *my* favorites: corned beef sandwiches, sauerkraut, dill pickles, peanut butter milk shakes, and Mom's homemade pumpkin pie, topped off with whipped cream and honey. Bob is a good sport and eats everything, except the pickles and the sauerkraut.

November 1977

AFTER THE TWO BIRTHDAYS, I decide to replace our elegant, English picnic hamper with something smaller and lighter. At an import store, I buy a cheap, dome-shaped wicker basket, a small wooden cutting board, and a set of ugly, pea green plastic dishes. When Bob questions the color, I tell him that I had no choice.

Without daylight saving time, the camp no longer has extended visiting hours on Fridays and Saturdays. In order to make myself available to Lucy on the weekends, I plan to visit Bob every Monday. It's cold at the camp on

Monday, November 7, but Bob and I prefer to sit outside, away from the crowd. Handing him a ham sandwich, I tell him that Rose Mary Woods called the other day. "She asked about you and said that President Nixon was very blue the day you entered prison."

"Did you happen to mention to Rose how blue *I* felt that day?" Bob asks sarcastically.

After playing a game of gin rummy, I put a stack of mail on the table for Bob to go through. He scans several national news magazines and holds up one with Nixon on the cover. "You know, Jo, I think President Nixon's just as much a prisoner as I am. The only difference is *his* walls are invisible." Bob glances around the patio. "I'll tell you one thing though...I'd rather be here than where he is."

A dark cloud blocks the sun, and Bob zips up his windbreaker. "I'm convinced that Richard Nixon still has the potential for greatness. The highpoint of my career was serving in his administration. There's no doubt in my mind that, even knowing the outcome, I would still choose to work for him in Washington."

"Even with Watergate, your resignation, and... this?" I ask, looking around us at the camp.

"Even with this," Bob confirms without hesitation.

At 3:00 p.m. visiting hours are over, and I collect my things. On the drive home, I have plenty of time to mull over Bob's remarks. He said that he would still choose to go to Washington, even if it meant the same outcome. *Would I?*

Unlike Bob's response, mine is not quick or clear. Unquestionably, Washington was the experience of a lifetime for both of us. Our time in and around the White House was far more exciting and meaningful than I ever dreamed it would be. Serving as the president's chief of staff was Bob's moment in the sun, and I gladly supported him by taking a backseat. I had so many reasons to be proud of him, and I was.

But there was also a dark side. To accomplish all that he did, Bob was hard on his staff, as well as himself—and me. His total commitment to the president, together with his insensitivity, became a problem in our relationship, which we never really addressed. My insecurities as a White House wife were personal and private, and it was my nature to work through them on my own. One way of coping was to rationalize that in four or eight years we would return to Los Angeles and I would have *my* Bob back.

Then came Watergate, which brought its own very public challenges. Aware of our difficulties, our friends and family rallied in support of Bob and me. Without question, Bob bore the brunt of its repercussions, but he turned to me. As a result, our marriage was strengthened.

What if we hadn't gone to Washington? Presumably, Bob would have continued to be a successful businessman and a pillar of the Los Angeles community. We would have been financially comfortable, the Haldeman name would have been unsullied, and our family would have been spared the fallout of Watergate.

Would I have chosen to go to Washington if I had known then what the next ten years would bring? I don't know...

The Ends of Power

December 1977

ONDAY, DECEMBER 9, IS another cold and dreary day, but this time, Bob and I decide to have our picnic inside. As usual, the visiting room is crowded and noisy, and we have to huddle together in order to carry on a conversation. Bob is eager to give me an update on his book. He has finally finished it, and Tom Lipscomb, the publisher, and Joe DiMona, his collaborator, have come up with a title.

"How do you like *The Ends of Power*?" He asks, raising his voice.

In the past, I've been critical of Tom and Joe, but I'm really pleased with their suggestion. "I like it a lot," I tell Bob. "I think *The Ends of Power* makes a real statement."

"The jacket's going to be red, white, and blue. Underneath my name and the title, there'll be a replica of the presidential seal…*except,* the eagle has lost its grip on the arrows, and its left claw is empty. The arrows are lying in a bundle below."

"Sounds good," I say. "It's powerful."

"The publication date has been moved up to the middle of March," Bob continues, opening the picnic hamper. "I've got less than three months to do my final edits and clean up some of Joe's more exaggerated scenarios."

"That sounds tight. Can you make it?"

"I think so, but it'd sure be great if you could help. I wondered if you would take parts of the book with you and work on them at home."

"Of course."

I'm flattered that Bob is turning to me for help, but I'm worried about how much time I have to give to his book. Not only is Christmas practically here, but I spend long hours at Coldwell Banker. I also agreed to be interviewed by two journalists. Bob is convinced that the added publicity will help the sale of his book, and he encouraged me to talk to them. Camilla Synder is interested in my work in real estate for her article in the *Herald Examiner*. In contrast, Tommy Thompson wants to feature Washington and Watergate for his story in *The Ladies Home Journal*.

When I hear that Bob will be given a seven-day furlough at Christmas, I'm thrilled, and I want everything to be perfect for his homecoming. Before I leave to pick him up on December 21, my Christmas gifts are wrapped, our cards are in the mail, and the tree and house are decorated. I've completed my editing of *The Ends of Power*, and my interviews with Camilla and Tommy are over. In the living room, my homemade sign saying, "Welcome Home, H. R. H.," is taped to the fireplace mantle.

As soon as Bob walks through the front door, the activity in our home picks up. Hank introduces Heather to his father. Family and friends drop by for visits, and we receive many thoughtful gifts. Bob has no trouble adjusting and thoroughly enjoys seeing everyone.

On December 22, Ann is presented at the annual Las Madrinas Debutante Ball. Although Bob escorted Susan around the dance floor on her presentation eight years ago, he believes that his presence at the event this year would be too much of a distraction. Dressed in white tie and tails, Hank substitutes for his father, and Bob finds himself home alone on the second night of his furlough. The rest of the family attends the ball, and a spontaneous round of applause breaks out as Hank and Ann take center stage. I am overwhelmed, and my heart is filled with pride. It's as if everyone in the room wants to show support for Bob and our family.

On Christmas Eve, Bob takes his place at the head of the table and carves the turkey for twenty Haldemans. The following morning, my parents come for breakfast, and Bob cooks the scrambled eggs. When we open our stockings, mine is filled with little notes saying: "Good for Crest toothpaste," "Good for Kodak film," and "Good for Arpege bath powder." Unable to do any shopping, Bob has substituted notes instead. One of my gifts to him is a replacement for the collage of family photos that was stolen from his cubicle at the camp.

The day after Christmas, Susan returns to her clerkship in Minnesota, and John Ehrlichman and his oldest daughter, Jan, drop by for tea. On a Christmas furlough, John is in Los Angeles to visit his mother. He has put on weight since the Watergate trial and sports a bushy mustache, as well as a receding hairline. Relaxed and chatty, both John and Bob joke about their experiences in prison and are soon comparing "hacks" (guards), head counts, lock downs, work assignments, and the quality of institutional food. John never mentions Jeanne.

At 5:00 p.m., on Tuesday, December 27, Bob's furlough is up. Before leaving, he insists on making his favorite sandwich for lunch. Standing at the kitchen counter, he meticulously butters two slices of Weber's white sandwich bread and spreads them with cranberry sauce and mayonnaise. Next, he adds turkey and lettuce, followed by generous amounts of salt and pepper. The two of us eat at the breakfast table by the window, with Rufus and the pugs at our feet.

I walk back to the garage to get the car, while Bob pauses to wave to Ann, who is leaning out her upstairs bedroom window. Dressed in the same blue athletic suit that he was wearing when I picked him up at the camp, Bob looks as if he were going jogging. But he's not. Instead, he's going back to Lompoc, and we face another long separation. I can't help thinking about the futility of his incarceration.

Bob turns on the radio as soon as we are on the freeway. Switching from the news to country music, he starts to sing "A Boy Named Sue" along with Johnny Cash. Belting out each verse, word for word, he never misses a beat. There isn't much traffic, and I set the cruise control. Bob closes his eyes and taps his foot in time to the music. A wax paper bag slips off his lap and lands on the floor. Inside it is an extra turkey sandwich.

◆

IN THE NEWS THIS month, Vietnamese "boat people," attempting to flee from the Communists, arrive in the United States in droves. John Travolta stars in *Saturday Night Fever*, and Debby Boone's "You Light up My Life" is the current hit song. Charlie Chaplin dies at eighty-eight.

January 1978

IT'S NEW YEAR'S DAY. Three years ago today, the trial verdict was announced. Driving to Lompoc this morning, I think back to that moment, visualizing Bob in the courtroom. With his hands clasped in front of him, he stood before

Judge Sirica, never flinching as the word guilty was read five times. *So much has happened since then. We have moved on.*

It's my first visit since Bob was home on furlough, and it's tough getting back into the routine. The weather doesn't help. It's cold and rainy, preventing us from being outside. Rounding up two of the vinyl-covered chairs, Bob and I sit facing each other in the middle of the crowded Visitors Center. He goes through the mail, while I unpack the picnic hamper. I struggle to be upbeat, but Bob is relaxed and eager to talk. He tells me that he has been reassigned from the dormitory to a room. He has a Chinese roommate named Tom who is a good bridge player and doesn't drink or smoke. His only fault is that he's too respectful of Bob and acts subservient.

"Tom keeps calling me Mr. Haldeman, instead of 'H. R.' like the other guys do," Bob says. "But, I can't complain. He's good at making deals, and *that's* what prison's all about. I'm not sure how he does it. He gets oranges every morning, so we can have fresh juice. And he's even convinced some old guy to leave milk and rolls outside our door for breakfast."

Using the cutting board, Bob slices an apple and spreads blue cheese on each piece. "The guys at the sewer plant have deals, too," he says. "They sneak steaks and eggs from the kitchen and store them with the chemicals in our refrigerator. Later, we cook them on the Bunsen burner."

Bob is less eager to talk about the progress of the editing of his book. Tom, his publisher, and Joe, his collaborator, challenge every change he wants to make and try to dissuade him from cutting the parts that are speculative and titillating.

"But there's good news on the sales side," Bob says. "The serialization rights have been syndicated and bought by *Newsweek* and thirty newspapers. Tom tells me that two hundred and fifty thousand advance copies of the book have also been sold, which is the highest number ever." Handing me a slice of apple with cheese on it, he adds, "Just think, Jo, I can finally start paying off my legal fees, and the first check's going to John Wilson for forty thousand dollars."

February–March 1978

BOB TELLS ME THAT the release date for his book has been moved up to February 27 and is being kept as a closely guarded secret. "Tom and Joe are treating it like 'literary plutonium.'"

Eleven days before the official release date, *The Washington Post* strikes again.

On February 16, the paper reveals the closely guarded secret. Apparently, *The Ends of Power* was stolen from the bookbinder by a reporter, and now unauthorized excerpts appear in *The Post* under the headline, "Haldeman Accuses Nixon." *The New York Times* describes the act as, "a second-rate burglary of H. R. Haldeman's memoir of a third-rate burglary." *The Post* counters that it is under no obligation to honor the veil of secrecy. It never signed a contract for the serialization rights.

Scooping everyone, *The Washington Post* features the more sensational scenarios that Joe and Tom insisted on. Bob is criticized for his use of conjecture when writing about President Nixon, Henry Kissinger, and Charles Colson. The media frantically tries to contact him, but the Federal Bureau of Prisons issues a statement saying that he is denying all requests for interviews. I hear nothing from him and have to rely on news reports.

The following day, a gigantic headline in the *Los Angeles Times* reads, "HALDEMAN'S MEMOIRS." Under that is a smaller headline, "An Inside Look at the Nixon Presidency." Half of the newspaper's front page is devoted to articles about the book, and there are four full pages of excerpts and photos inside. I've never seen the paper give so much attention to one news event. Before I finish reading all of it, I receive a collect call from Bob, who is well aware of the commotion stirred up by *The Post*. He pumps me for more news.

"The news organizations that bought the exclusive syndication rights are so angry they're considering releasing your book early," I tell him. "They might even refuse to pay the contract price."

"Tom told me about that," Bob says.

"You should see the *Los Angeles Times* this morning. It's filled with stuff about the book. I'll bring it up with me when I visit."

"That'll be great. This whole thing's a nightmare. In many ways, I'm glad that I'm stuck in prison. At least the press can't get to me."

◆

Two days later, it's our twenty-ninth wedding anniversary, and I'm on my way to visit Bob. It's pouring rain, and large puddles fill the camp's parking lot. The dripping eucalyptus trees give off a wet, pungent smell. Tucking the *Los Angeles Times* into the picnic hamper, I put on my raincoat and slosh across the road to the Visitors Center. The line is long, but people are amazingly patient.

"Happy Anniversary," Bob says, giving me a light kiss. "Glad to see that you survived in one piece after all the hullabaloo over the book these past few days. Tom says it's been crazy."

Bypassing the mail, Bob pulls the *Times* out of the hamper and starts to read. He's so absorbed, he hardly reacts when the man behind us lights a cigarette. While I wait for Bob to finish, my mind drifts, and I absentmindedly focus on a small rip in the cushion of his chair. Each time he shifts positions, more of the white stuffing bulges out. The longer I sit here, the more incongruous this scene seems. *I hate this noisy room with its cheap chairs and cigarette smoke. What are we doing here, anyway?*

"The president, Henry, and Chuck sure aren't going to be very happy with this," Bob says from behind the paper. "I've got to write them and clarify things. Tom's furious at *The Washington Post*, and he's frantically trying to salvage the publishing contracts." Bob shifts positions, and some of the stuffing drops onto the floor. "On the other hand, Tom figures that the leak and the negative publicity are good for book sales."

"At least that's one plus," I say, setting two plates on the floor and dishing up the taco salad.

Bob leans down to pick up his plate. "Not a great way to spend an anniversary is it?" he asks.

"I used to think that picnics were romantic," I reply, wiping up two dabs of spilled Russian dressing.

"When I get out of jail, you've got a date to go dancing," Bob says. "*L'Escoffier* at the Beverly Hilton has a band, and I promise we'll go dancing on every anniversary."

When it comes time to leave, my raincoat is still damp and feels clammy when I put it on. The heavy rain doesn't let up on my drive back to Los Angeles, and our house is cold and dreary. But none of this matters. All I can think about is Bob's promise, and I head for the family room. Searching through a stack of old 78 records, I place three of them on the turntable and push the start lever. Grabbing one of Bob's sweaters, I place one sleeve on my left shoulder and hold the other in my extended right hand. Twirling and dipping in time to the beat of the romantic strains of "Symphony," "Why Do I Love You?," and "A Pretty

Girl is Like a Melody," I dance with Bob. The blue plaid couch and pine coffee table fade away as the two of us glide around the room. When the music stops, I clutch the sweater and stand motionless for a long time.

♦

ON FEBRUARY 27, *THE Ends of Power* hits the bookstores. Its red, white, and blue cover with its altered presidential seal is crisp and patriotic. Joe DiMona's writing style is easy to read, and Bob's book rapidly climbs to the top of *The New York Times* Best Sellers List. The Book of the Month Club chooses it as an alternate selection, and there are plans to print it in several foreign languages. Bob receives many requests from friends and strangers alike to autograph their copies. Having no way to do this, he asks me to order preprinted cards for him to sign. These can be inserted in the books when I mail them back to the individuals.

Newsweek carries sixteen pages of excerpts from *The Ends of Power,* and the magazine's red cover is electrifying. "Haldeman Talks" is in harsh yellow print above a picture of Nixon and Bob facing each other, nose-to-nose. The review is not complimentary.

> Haldeman's dark-side-up portrayal of Nixon enmeshed in Watergate is a devastating one. Haldeman's book, of course, is the work of a convicted principal in the Watergate conspiracy, and is likely to be read and judged accordingly. His allegations against Nixon and Colson in particular rest heavily on circumstantial rather than eyewitness evidence.

Henry Kissinger disputes the book's conjectures in an appearance on the *Today* show; Chuck Colson denies them in a public statement; and Nixon releases a statement saying that *his* memoirs will be published in May. John Dean sends a sarcastic letter to Bob, telling him that the use of the presidential seal on the jacket is illegal.

Bob is determined to counter the book's misconceptions, and in March, he's given the opportunity by Dell Publishing Company, who buys the rights for the paperback edition. Bob is encouraged to write an afterword, where he can address the book's speculations and inaccuracies.

April 1978

BY THE END OF April, Bob has served ten months of his sentence and is entitled to monthly town passes, as well as one overnight furlough every three months. On Friday, April 28, I pick him up at 7:00 a.m. for his first town pass. He has to be back by 7:00 p.m., and we can go as far as the Danish town of Solvang, which is twenty-one miles away.

The morning air is cool, and the sky is cloudless when I arrive in Lompoc. Bob checks out, and we leave for Hans Christian Andersen State Park, a small park on the outskirts of Solvang. Although the sign says, "*Velkommen*," it's too early in the day for visitors, and we are the only ones here. Clutching two Styrofoam cups of coffee and a bag of Danish pastries, we stake out a weathered wood picnic table. Joking about the irony of leaving one picnic table for another, Bob straddles the bench and helps himself to a cinnamon roll. Not far from us, a couple of blue jays are squabbling over some acorns under a large, sprawling oak tree.

Bob tells me that the parole board is scheduled to meet at the camp next week. Although Judge Sirica has reduced his sentence to one to four years, it's up to the board to determine his actual release date. Their decision will be based in part on letters they receive on his behalf, as well as an interview with both Bob and me. We have a lot riding on this, and I express some concern about my part.

"You'll do fine, Jo," Bob says, tossing a raisin to the blue jays.

John Ehrlichman was released yesterday, after serving eighteen months. He was found guilty in two trials, which causes me to be hopeful that Bob won't have to serve as long. A car enters the park, and two mothers get out with their young children.

Watching them walk over to the playground, Bob tells me that before he's released, he plans to finish reading Will and Ariel Durant's eleven-volume set of *History of Civilization*. He asks me to send him the *Age of Faith* and *Renaissance* volumes.

"Deputy Dog's our new warden," Bob says. "It's ridiculous. He spends all of his time driving around in his station wagon, spying on us. He's even making us clean up our rooms, and we have to turn in our extra mattresses."

"You have more than one?" I ask.

"Yeah. Prison mattresses are like thin sheets of cardboard. You need at least three to get a decent night's sleep."

At noon, we leave the park and drive into Solvang for lunch. The town is bustling with tourists, and occasionally someone recognizes Bob and gives him a smile. On Copenhagen Drive, we window shop and buy ice-cream cones at 31 Flavors.

Standing outside a bookstore, Bob talks about what he plans to write in the afterword of his book. He's convinced that President Nixon had no previous knowledge of the Watergate break-in, but he wants to say that Nixon's request for more information *could have been* the underlying *cause* for it. He also wants to make it clear that the president was involved in the *containment* of Watergate from Day One, but that he and Bob were not aware of any *cover-up* until March of 1973, when everything started to unravel. He emphasizes the difference between *cover-up, containment,* and *obstruction of justice.*

Licking his Jamoca Almond Fudge ice-cream cone, Bob says, "The White House should have pursued Watergate to its source *immediately* and cut it out whatever the cost. But…we didn't. And we paid a terrible price. Look where I am now."

By the time I get home after our twelve-hour visit, I'm exhausted both physically and emotionally. Although it's late, I'm still mulling over Bob's concerns about the book and his regrets about the way Watergate was handled.

When Henry Kissinger calls the next morning to tell me that he's writing the parole board on Bob's behalf, it gives me a lift.

"How's the book doing?" he asks.

"Bob's frustrated," I say. "He feels that he's taken a step backward."

Henry gives a raspy chuckle. "Tell him to consider it a step sideways, Jo."

"I will," I say. "Thanks, Henry. I needed that."

Six More Months

May 1978

AT 7:30 A.M. ON Friday, May 5, I leave home. In a few hours, Bob and I will meet with the parole board, and each of us will make a statement. We have been told that the board will give a lot of weight to what we say, and I'm nervous. I want to do everything I can to get Bob's sentence reduced to a year.

Feeling the need to collect my thoughts before arriving at the camp, I pull into a rest stop at the Gaviota Pass. A strong wind is blowing, and there's an unseasonable chill in the air. Slipping on a heavy, cable-knit sweater, I spend an hour reading the Christian Science Bible Lesson. The references give me confidence and strengthen my resolve.

After I check in at the Visitors Center, a guard escorts me across the field to meet up with Bob in "B" Barracks. Stopping at a room at the end of a long hall, the guard tries to open the door. It's stuck, and a call for help comes from inside. I recognize Bob's voice.

"What's going on?" the guard calls out, rattling the doorknob.

"I'm locked in," Bob shouts back. "The wind blew the door closed."

Subduing a laugh, I watch as the mortified guard rushes off to get help. The situation is eventually rectified by two guards who appear with the key. Once inside the room, I join Bob at a long wooden table, where we wait to be called for the interview. When we're informed that the parole board is running late and our meeting will be delayed for an hour, I tell Bob that I'm glad. I can use the extra time to review what I plan to say. I read my statement to him, and he listens intently. When I am done, his advice is reassuring; his compliments, genuine.

There are two men on the parole board, and the interview is taped. I'm up first. As I make my statement and answer their questions, I'm unruffled and articulate. Describing our close-knit family, I explain that I work full-time in real estate to cover our ongoing financial needs. I talk about Bob's positive attitude and lack of bitterness. Although I stress his integrity and honesty, one of the men refers to the severity of Bob's crime and says that a sentence of twelve to sixteen months could be considered very light.

When it's Bob's turn to talk, he states that his family needs him, both as a father and a wage-earner. He plans to find a job and become active in the community after he's released. He admits that the years following his resignation from the White House have been filled with doubt and uncertainty.

"This past year in prison, however, has been both a beginning and an end for me," he concludes. "I believe the time has finally come to move on."

On the whole, the men appear to be sympathetic, raising my hopes that Bob might even be released next month, after serving a year.

"We probably won't hear the results of the interview for a couple of weeks," Bob says as we walk back to the Visitors Center. "All we can do at this point is sit back and wait."

A sudden gust of wind kicks up the dust in front of us, and something blows into my eye. As I struggle to get it out, Bob reaches into his pocket and offers me his handkerchief. We both smile. I realize that he, too, is remembering the time on *Air Force One* when he gave me his handkerchief so begrudgingly.

Bob has changed since those days in the White House. I wonder if he realizes just how much.

◆

Susan continues to be deeply frustrated by her father's incarceration, and she writes him a letter. Later, she shows me his reply, where Bob writes in part:

> *Dear Sus,*
>
> *There is certainly no argument from me to your point that the whole thing isn't fair or right and that it is a terrible waste.... But we have to consider it in the overall and long-term*

*context.... From the long range viewpoint, it is possible to see
the potential for good that can eventually ensue.*

*All the lessons of history tell us not to concern ourselves solely
with the immediate present. And all the life stories of people who
have made a contribution show periods of interruption and
frustration. So much so that these things have become clichés.*

*...The worst part of all of this for me—and for many others in
here—is not my own concerns but my concerns about all of
you. If I knew you were all happily going ahead with your lives,
I would have no trouble handling my own.*

I'm grateful for Bob's calm acceptance of and positive perspective on this
experience. I often wish that I could find the same peace of mind.

June 1978

HEAVY FOG MOVES INTO the Los Angeles basin on the first of June. With the
arrival of "June gloom," the US Parole Commission rules that Bob must serve
eighteen months—not the year I thought, and hoped, might be a possibility.
He won't be released until December 20, six months from now.

Not only are Bob's release date and the weather discouraging, but this
whole month continues to be dismal. June 17 is the sixth anniversary of the
break-in, and once again, the media has a field day rehashing Watergate. June
20 marks the one-year anniversary of Bob's incarceration. And last, but not
least, I have my own run-in with the law. In the course of making the drive to
Lompoc six times this month, I receive *two* tickets for speeding.

Daylight saving time is back, which is both an advantage and disadvantage
for me. On the one hand, I can stay late at the camp and have both lunch and
dinner with Bob; on the other, I don't get home until almost midnight. The
late-night return drive is particularly long and boring, and I find ways to stay
awake, some traditional, others more innovative. I roll down the windows,
turn up the radio, and wear dark glasses. I make a stop for food, drive barefoot,
and use my left foot on the accelerator. I even resort to propping up our small,
portable TV on the floor of the passenger seat to watch a mini-series called
"Rich Man, Poor Man."

On Friday night, June 22, I'm desperately struggling to stay alert and pull into the parking lot of a Denny's in the San Fernando Valley. Following a cup of coffee and a slice of banana cream pie, I'm still drowsy, so I curl up on the Grenada's front seat and fall asleep. Before long, the car begins to shake, and when I spring up to see what's going on, I startle a young man and woman who are leaning against the hood, passionately embracing. As soon as they see me looming up in front of them, they scream and take off at a run. *What am I doing sleeping in my car? This is crazy.* I start the ignition and get back on the freeway.

To satisfy our parents' concerns about my safety, I have recently engaged the services of Westinghouse Alarm Company, which adds another dimension to my drive home. Now I have to stop at a public phone booth to alert the security patrol that I am almost home. It's a hassle, but it's reassuring to Mom, Dad, and Non. Tonight, it's almost midnight when I pull into a Burger King in Hollywood to make the call. When I reach home, a patrol car with its headlights on high beam follows me into the driveway. Blinded by the bright light, I struggle to get all of my picnic supplies from the car to the house. With two security men watching my every move, I eventually get the back door unlocked. Once I'm inside, they drive away. I drop the picnic hamper on the floor, greet the dogs, and vow to cancel the service as soon as I can.

Despite the difficulties that I experience this month, the awesome beauty of Lompoc's fields of flowers sends my spirits soaring. Blooming late this year due to the heavy winter rainfall, the acres of sweet peas are particularly profuse. I'm overcome by their rich colors and heady fragrance. The sight of them is breathtaking, and I will always hold these enchanting flowers close to my heart.

July 1978

RATHER THAN TAKING A block of time off this summer, I remain in Los Angeles. I continue to be busy at Coldwell Banker and spend one day a week visiting Bob. On the few occasions that I get down to Bay Island, it seems as if everywhere I turn, I face another memory of Bob. The hardest times are when the whole family is together and Bob is the only one missing. When Susan invites me to visit her in Minnesota, I jump at the chance to go someplace unfamiliar. I'm totally diverted as the two of us paddle a canoe down the St. Croix River and attend a Garrison Keillor concert in the park.

On Wednesday, July 19, it's hot in Lompoc, and there's not much shade on the patio at the Visitors Center. Bob and I finish our lunch of cold gazpacho, apples, and cheese, then drop our unwashed plastic dishes into the hamper. While playing Scrabble, he informs me that *The Washington Post's* early release of the syndication of his book has cut into the profits. I, in turn, tell him that through her expertise and drive, Lucy continues to be number one in residential sales nationally at Coldwell Banker, and that I'm pleased to report that my earnings are up.

Later, Bob mentions that he received a copy of the letter that Jim Neal, the chief prosecutor of the Watergate trial, wrote on his behalf to the parole board.

"I was thinking about writing Jim back," Bob says. "Enough time has passed since the trial, and I'd like to ask him to review the case from my viewpoint."

"Will he do that?" I ask, wondering if Mr. Neal would take the time to read a letter that attempts to disprove the government's case.

"Jim may be tough, but he's also fair," Bob replies. "If he's willing to look over what I have to say, he might find me innocent. The only way to convince him is to lay out, fact-by-fact, the details of my knowledge and perception during the cover-up."

"You're going to rehash the whole trial?"

"You bet I am. What's more, I've got to do it now, while my memory's still fresh." Bob pauses. "Look at it this way, Jo…as long as I'm in jail, I've got nothing better to do. What's more, I have nothing to lose."

When Bob puts it that way, I can't object.

Heat

WHEN FALL COMES, REAL estate picks up. Working irregular hours, I leave for Coldwell Banker early in the morning and get home late at night. I grab lunch on the run and overlap with Lucy in the office, as well as in the field. Our client list grows, listings are secured, houses are sold, and escrows are closed. My little black car with its shiny hubcaps and Lucy's mile-long limo are seen everywhere in Hancock Park. We are two very busy women.

I am thrilled when Hank and Heather announce their engagement. They plan to get married next June, and I only wish Bob could be here to share in the excitement. Instead, he writes Heath a long letter from the camp, welcoming her into the family.

At our picnic today, Bob talks about what his job options might be in the future. This is the first time that he has mentioned this, and I'm fascinated. Explaining that he wants to take his time and doesn't plan to make any decisions for at least six months after his release, he ticks off a list of possibilities. Radio talk show host, guest lecturer, or manager of a bed and breakfast. Possibly a joint business venture in either China or Russia. Writing a book about the Nixon presidency or teaching. Some of these come as a complete surprise; others do not. I think he would make a great lecturer or teacher, and I assume he ultimately will write the book he's always wanted to on Nixon's achievements. I'm surprised and concerned when he tells me that making money isn't a priority for him.

◆

A<small>NTICIPATING</small> B<small>OB'S</small> <small>FIRST</small> <small>OVERNIGHT</small> furlough, I feel giddy. It's as if we were going on a second honeymoon. The camp's regulations stipulate that Los Angeles is too far, so we decide on Santa Barbara. When a friend of the family offers us his studio apartment in Montecito, we accept. It's within walking distance of the ocean and sounds ideal.

I pack two overnight bags. One for Bob, and one for me. Following a brief check-out procedure at the camp, the two of us are on the road. I drive, and Bob sits in the passenger seat. In Santa Barbara, the weather is clear and unusually hot, and the beaches are crowded. The ocean is like glass. We stop at a market for breakfast supplies and at McConnell's for a pint of peach ice cream for Bob.

At last, we arrive at Bonnymede, where we will be staying. The attractive Spanish-style apartment complex is nestled among picturesque Monterey cypress trees across the street from the Biltmore Hotel. In addition to the beach, there's a pool and a tennis court.

The sun beats down on Bob and me as we unload the car. Collecting our overnight bags and the groceries, we climb the outside stairs to a second-story bachelor unit. Bob unlocks the door, and as soon as we step inside, I'm in his arms. The only thing I'm aware of is his holding me. I'm not sure who closes the door, and I don't know how the ice cream gets into the freezer. Nothing seems to matter. Outside, Santa Barbara is experiencing a heat wave, and the thermometer soars to 105 degrees. Thick rays of sunshine filter through the half-opened plantation shutters. Our bags sit by the door, where Bob and I left them.

In the late afternoon, we put on shorts and take a walk along the beach. The sun is a huge red ball, shining through an eerie rosy haze. Waves of heat rise up from the sand, and the ocean is still. It just sits there, not moving. The two of us stroll along the edge of the water, weaving among the throngs of people and masses of brightly colored umbrellas. Many families are wading in the water to keep cool. Men roll up their trousers, women lift their skirts, and children are in their underwear.

Pulling a long strand of seaweed, a dark-skinned little boy runs past us. Accidentally flicking sand on us, he apologizes, "*Lo siento.*" Behind us, Bob and I leave a meandering trail of deep footprints in the wet sand. The scene is surreal.

The following afternoon as I drive Bob back to Lompoc, he relaxes in the passenger seat and takes in the scenery. I brace myself for our return to the camp. When we arrive, I linger in the parking lot to watch Bob as he walks over to the Administration Building. Wearing blue chinos and a white Oxford shirt, he carries in his left hand a paper bag with his toilet kit. As I drive away, all I can remember of the weekend is the oppressive heat and living in each moment as it happened, with no thoughts of the past or the future.

October 1978

IN LESS THAN THREE months, Bob will be home for good, and I start marking off the days on my calendar. On Wednesday, December 20, I write in heavy black letters, "FINAL VISIT...LOMPOC...RELEASE." I get goose bumps thinking about the date and how different our lives will soon be. Although Bob will have to report to a probation officer periodically and won't be able to vote, he'll be his own person and hopes to travel to the Holy Land sometime in the near future.

I'm excited, but I'm also apprehensive. *Will people treat us differently when Bob comes home? How long will it take for him to get a job? How long will I continue to work with Lucy?*

On October 10, Non's brother, Uncle Al, calls and, in an animated voice reports that Bob has only seventy-one more days at the camp. To Lucy, that's the equivalent of five closings; to me, it's eight visits and two town passes. Bob says, "Stop counting, Jo. I just want you to appear at prison one day and take me home."

November 1978

ANOTHER MONTH SLIPS BY, and tomorrow Bob will celebrate his second Thanksgiving at the camp. In order to arrive early, I spend the night at Andersen's Best Western Motel in Solvang. I don't check in until 10:45 p.m., and Room 150 smells of stale cigarette smoke. The décor is depressing, and the combination of loud neighbors and pouring rain keeps me awake most of the night.

The next morning, the storm has moved on, and the air is crisp and clear. Being a holiday, the camp is crowded, and I join a long line of cars entering the parking lot. At the Visitors Center, Guard Martinez forms us into two lines, "A" and "B." Bob's number is 1489-163B, which puts me in the "B" line, where I'm number six on the list for town passes. Looking authoritative in his uniform, Martinez straightens his black tie. I grimace when I see that his tie-tack is a pair of tiny, silver interlocking handcuffs.

After checking out, Bob and I take off for the Parkers' home. Their front porch is decorated with bunches of dried corn stalks and a large pumpkin. The door opens, and two Golden Retrievers bound out to greet us. Wearing an apron over her jeans, Gay follows, with Mom and Dad right behind. The aroma of roast turkey comes from the kitchen, where David is under the sink, trying to fix a jammed disposal.

Everyone talks at once as we help my sister put the finishing touches on dinner. Joe, Davy, Chris, and Amy are in and out; David mashes the potatoes; Mom makes gravy; and someone grabs a camera to take a picture of Bob and me. Seated at the dinner table, the ten of us bow our heads for a moment of silence. I am so grateful.

"This is the day the Lord hath made. Let us rejoice, give thanks, and be glad in it."

Truly Whole

December 1978

ON MONDAY, DECEMBER 10, I make my final visit to the camp, and it's hard to believe that in ten days I won't ever be doing this again. No more white line, chain-link fence, guards, or loudspeaker blasting out, "Haldeman, you have a visit." No more three-hour drives up and down the coast. Best of all, there will be no more picnics. When I tell Lucy that I plan to burn the picnic hamper and dispose of the pea green dishes after this last visit, she asks if she can come to the wake.

Bob and I are in high spirits as we enthusiastically discuss the plans for his homecoming. Invitations are in the mail for our open house on Saturday, December 23. After that we have much to look forward to: Christmas Eve with the Haldemans, Christmas morning with my parents, a week at Smoke Tree Ranch, and in February, an engagement party for Hank and Heather. There's a lot happening, and from now on, Bob will be a part of it. He talks about sleeping in a *real* bed, having unlimited use of the phone, driving a car, playing his guitar, and taking walks with Rufus.

Setting up the backgammon board, Bob hands me fifteen white checkers. As we take turns rolling the dice and moving our playing pieces, he gives me an update on his book. The paperback edition will be out this month, and Dell wants him to make a commercial promoting it. The publisher thinks that it would generate a lot of publicity if it is filmed while he is still at the camp. We both agree that is not a good idea.

Shade starts to creep across the patio, and there's a chill in the air. Bob reaches for his windbreaker, and as he puts it on, I study him. Over the past year and a half, his demeanor has mellowed. Except for an occasional flicker of the Haldeman look, his eyes no longer turn cold and steely. Without his crew cut and dismissive manner of speaking, the White House image of "Von Haldeman" has disappeared. Instead, I see a tan, handsome, fifty-two-year-old man with slightly hunched shoulders sitting opposite me. His meticulously coiffed, dark brown hair is starting to thin slightly in front. He smiles often, showing lots of white teeth. He is both patient and considerate.

◆

EARLY TOMORROW MORNING, WEDNESDAY, December 20, Bob will be released. I've waited a long time for this moment, and now the hours drag. First, I wash the car, and then I pack a few essentials for my overnight at the Parkers. The last thing I do is check on Bob's office upstairs. Standing in the middle of the room, I look around. This is his space, totally and completely. I picture him sitting in the overstuffed blue chair with his feet up on the ottoman. A stack of yellow pads and a container of blue felt tip pens are on the side table, and his Martin guitar is in its black case in the corner. A patch of afternoon sunlight is beating in on the gray carpet, where I visualize Rufus curled up in a tight ball. The president's inaugural quote hangs on the wall above the antique, pine desk.

"Until he has been part of a cause larger than himself, no man is truly whole."

It seems as if we've been living with these words forever. Bob has said that his cause was neither the presidency as an institution, nor the man, Richard Nixon. It was the unique combination of the two: President Nixon. To be a part of this cause, Bob left the private sector and became a public servant. He gave up priority time with his family, a good job as a high level executive, and a commitment to his local community. He brought with him a sharp intellect and strong managerial skills, as well as his undivided loyalty and dedication.

In the White House, Bob was given opportunities that only a handful of people ever get a chance to experience. He spent untold hours in the Oval Office, slept in the White House bomb shelter, was toasted by the president in the State Dining Room, and represented the Nixon administration at the opening of Disney World. When Neil Armstrong took his first step on the moon, Bob watched it in the Oval Office, and he was on the USS *Hornet* when the *Apollo 11* lunar module splashed down in the Pacific. Not only did Bob go on the historic trip to China, but its logistics were described as a "Haldeman masterpiece." As chief of staff, he ran the White House with "ruthless efficiency." He could be impatient and unbending, but he was consistently confident and in control.

Watergate was Bob's nadir. His resignation, the hearings, the trial, the appeal, and his incarceration tested him in ways that he had never been tried before. Strengthened by his faith and the support of his family and friends, he met each challenge head-on. I don't know if he has any regrets. I don't know if he ever questions the "what if's." I *do* know that his rough edges were softened, and he emerged as a changed person.

"Until he has been part of a cause larger than himself, no man is truly whole."

As I reread the quote, I wonder if what made Bob truly whole was in fact a combination of *both* the presidency of Richard Nixon *and* Watergate.

♦

THE NEXT MORNING, I'M up well before dawn. It's cold in the Parkers' family room, where I spent the night on a converted couch. Gay pokes her head into the room and asks if I want coffee and toast. I tell her that I'm too excited to eat much.

As I drive to Lompoc, a heavy morning mist hangs over the valley. The fog clears just as I turn into the camp parking lot. Across the road, a group of shivering reporters and photographers stand in an area that has been roped off for the press. I feel their eyes on me as I climb out of the car. Without any games, mail, or picnic hamper, I have nothing to carry, and I stuff my hands into the pockets of my jacket. It's too early for visitors. I am here alone.

At 6:50 a.m., a guard opens the main door of the two-story Administration Building, and Bob steps out into the yellowish glow of a weak December sunrise. Flashbulbs go off, and reporters shout questions from behind the line. An inmate calls out from a window, "Goodbye, Mr. America," and Bob waves.

Bob is smiling. No, he's beaming. There are little crinkles in the corners of his eyes. Taking my hand, he guides me over to the press area. Joyously happy, I'm briefly diverted by minutiae. A wayward tuft of chest hair is protruding from the open collar of Bob's shirt. Somehow, it reassures me that the scene is real. Handing me a brown paper bag with his belongings, Bob moves up to a battery of microphones.

"This is generally considered a special time of the year to rejoice. It certainly is for me." After thanking his supporters, Bob concludes with a simple statement. "Now I'm on my way home to rejoin my family, and I wish you all a very merry Christmas."

A reporter shouts, "Mrs. Haldeman, how does it feel to have your husband home?"

"Great!" I call back.

Bob wraps his arm around my shoulder, and we walk across the road to the parking lot. The warmth of his body next to mine assures me that everything is going to be fine. My earlier fears and concerns about the future vanish, and I know that the two of us together can, and will, make things work.

At the car, Bob opens the passenger door for me, and I climb in. For the first time in a year and a half, I look over to my left and see Bob. He is in the driver's seat, and we are going home.

THE END

Jo Haldeman sailing her Sabot at Newport Beach, 1994.

Epilogue

Summer 1994

I HAVE A SMALL sailboat. It's a Sabot, and there's just enough room in it for one person. My legs are cramped as I grab the tiller and push away from the dock. It's summer, and I'm back at Bay Island, where nothing ever seems to change. And yet, this year everything is different. Eight months ago, Bob passed away.

The wind causes my little boat to heel as I cross the channel. I'm alone with my thoughts, and my mind goes back in time. This is where it all began twenty-six years ago. It was a journey that took Bob and me to unbelievable heights, as well as to the deepest depths.

Then it gave us a second chance. After being released from prison, Bob took a year off to find the right job. Impressed with David Murdock, Bob became president and CEO of the hotel operation of Murdock Development Company. During this time, Bob and I went on a Bible tour of the Holy Land.

When he retired seven years later, we left Los Angeles and moved to Santa Barbara. Using our guest house as an office, Bob mentored small start-up businesses. He gave talks in the community, grew fantastic roses, rode his horse, Sam, on the beach, and took walks with Rufus. He was an enthusiastic Sunday School teacher, as well as the chapter advisor at the Beta House at the University of California at Santa Barbara. He doted on his grandchildren. And, true to his word, Bob took me dancing every year on our anniversary.

Bob had a remarkable lack of animosity and an exceptional ability to accept his destiny. He stayed in touch with President Nixon through infrequent phone calls and occasional visits. Bob did write a forty-six-page letter to Jim Neal, the chief prosecutor. In it, he described the various elements of the cover-up from his perspective and showed how each could be viewed in a radically different light than it was portrayed during the trial. Writing the letter had such a cathartic effect for him, he never felt the need to send it.

Bob's twenty-seven hours of movies were edited and narrated to be packaged as a television special on the Nixon White House. While he was working with G. P. Putnam's Sons and Sony Corporation to publish his daily journals in book form, along with a concurrent CD-ROM, Bob became ill.

Bob passed away at home on November 12, 1993, at the age of sixty-seven. He never wavered in his reliance on Christian Science, and with full confidence in what lay ahead, he did just what he had always done—held to the positive and moved forward.

As soon as I enter the main channel, a blast of wind fills the sail. If Bob were here, he'd be in the windiest part of the bay, heeling and going as fast as possible. Without thinking, I find myself looking for him in his Sunfish.

I miss him with all my heart.

Afterword

OB'S DAILY JOURNALS WERE published posthumously in May 1994. Titled *The Haldeman Diaries: Inside the Nixon White House*, the book spent seven weeks on *The New York Times* Bestsellers List. Bob's movies package was never produced, and the movies were donated to the Nixon Foundation.

Non passed away not long after we moved to Santa Barbara. #11 Bay Island had to be sold when my parents passed away. The Ehrlichmans were divorced, and both John and Jeanne remarried. The eight seashells that I collected with Jeanne on the beach at Key Biscayne are on my dressing table. For a number of years, Bertha, our beloved housekeeper in Washington, called to speak to Ann on her birthday. I never burned the picnic hamper, and Nixon's portrait is still stored in the attic. A yellowing White House phone sits on a little table in the grandchildren's playhouse.

President Nixon's inaugural quote hangs on the wall of the family room. Every time I pass it, I am reminded of Bob and our years together in Washington.

"Until he has been part of a cause larger than himself, no man is truly whole."

Acknowledgments

THANK YOU, DEAR BOB, for taking me along on your unique ten-year journey. I never would have written this book without your insistence that I had a story to tell. I tried to present that story honestly, and in portraying both the highs and the lows, I came to realize that even in the depths of my experience, the heights were always there.

Although Non predeceased Bob, her unabashed pride in our country and devotion to her son were a constant inspiration as I wrote. In turn, my mother's enthusiastic reaction to each new chapter bolstered my confidence that I did indeed have a story to tell.

A special expression of appreciation is due to Dorothea Parfit, who was my mentor in my early years of writing. From my very first vignettes of life in Washington, she never doubted that I would eventually complete my story and find "revelation and resolution." Later, Dorothea's son Mike, an author and producer of documentaries, had enough faith in my book to encourage me to pursue publishing it.

Through the years, as I wrote, I came to value deeply the words of support, poignant silences, and heartfelt tears of Joan Kurze and Harriet Green. Sitting by the fire and reading to them every night during our annual visits to Yosemite Mountain Ranch, I gradually grew to better understand myself through their insights and comments.

My thanks to Kay Perrin and Margaret Foster, who opened their lovely homes in Montecito for me to share my writing with others. The Jo Haldeman Monthly Book Readings both entertained an interested group of friends and provided me with valuable feedback.

In reading my book, Jeanne Ehrlichman Bleuchel, Kathleen Bell, and Nancy Ziegler relived their experiences in the Nixon White House and confirmed my memory of various events.

I am indebted to Susan Kybett and Fred Hunter, who read the book with an author's eye and tried to convince me that I, too, was a writer. I greatly appreciate the professional advice and expertise of Oscie and Evan Thomas, who spent an afternoon on Bay Island discussing the Nixon years and then followed up with suggested edits. Thanks to Dee and Larry Higby for their helpful ideas, and special thanks to Dwight Chapin for both his critique of the book and his dedicated help in the publishing process.

I thank Tom Haldeman, Bill Horton, April Aubrey, and Kathy Bloomer (with her yellow Post-its) for their editing suggestions. I appreciate the perceptive professional advice of Larry Habegger, Bernadette Murphy, Jo and Willard Thompson, Hannah Carlson, and Joe Evanisko.

Thanks to the residents of Alta Vista who listened to me read my first drafts, plus Sally Smith, Janet Crisler, Helen Wilson, and Laurel Smith. Thank you, Marcia de Garmo, Jan Evans, John Murnane, Paul Klingenstein, Bill Bonham, Diana Cohen Robinson, Johan Wassenaar, Mike Ross, and Richard Berti for your helpful ideas.

The family of Ollie Atkins graciously provided the cover photo for the book. Lisa Jobe went above and beyond to search the Library of Congress for a specific newspaper headline. Ann's "Marlborough Mafia," Susan's moms' group, and the San Francisco reading group offered valuable feedback and advice.

I value the friendship of my neighbor, Caroline Willsie, who contributed to the edits and patiently listened to me vent my frustrations on our daily walks.

In developing my story, I worked side-by-side with my daughter-in-law, Heather Haldeman, who was writing her own memoir. I am deeply grateful for her help and for her steadfast advice to use my voice. I also appreciate my son Hank Haldeman's solid backing in this endeavor.

My strongest supporters and sharpest critics were my two daughters, Susan Haldeman and Ann Coppe, who were determined to see me produce the best book I possibly could. Without their unswerving dedication, long-suffering patience, and hands-on editing, I never would be where I am today. Thank you both for believing in me.

This book is the result of a widespread collaborative effort, and for all of you who have contributed suggestions and support, you have my heartfelt gratitude and appreciation.